Lecture Notes in Artificial Intelligence   8732

Subseries of Lecture Notes in Computer Science

LNAI Series Editors

Randy Goebel
University of Alberta, Edmonton, Canada
Yuzuru Tanaka
Hokkaido University, Sapporo, Japan
Wolfgang Wahlster
DFKI and Saarland University, Saarbrücken, Germany

LNAI Founding Series Editor

Joerg Siekmann
DFKI and Saarland University, Saarbrücken, Germany

T0212627

Jörg P. Müller   Michael Weyrich
Ana L.C. Bazzan (Eds.)

Multiagent System Technologies

12th German Conference, MATES 2014
Stuttgart, Germany, September 23-25, 2014
Proceedings

 Springer

Volume Editors

Jörg P. Müller
Technische Universität Clausthal
Institut für Informatik
Julius-Albert-Str. 4, 38678 Clausthal-Zellerfeld, Germany
E-mail: joerg.mueller@tu-clausthal.de

Michael Weyrich
Universität Stuttgart
Institut für Automatisierungs- und Softwaretechnik
Pfaffenwaldring 47, 70550 Stuttgart, Germany
E-mail: michael.weyrich@ias.uni-stuttgart.de

Ana L.C. Bazzan
Universidade Federal do Rio Grande do Sul (UFRGS)
Instituto de Informática
Caixa Postal 15064, 91501-970 Porto Alegre, Rio Grande do Sul, Brazil
E-mail: bazzan@inf.ufrgs.br

ISSN 0302-9743   e-ISSN 1611-3349
ISBN 978-3-319-11583-2   e-ISBN 978-3-319-11584-9
DOI 10.1007/978-3-319-11584-9
Springer Cham Heidelberg New York Dordrecht London

Library of Congress Control Number: 2014948672

LNCS Sublibrary: SL 7 – Artificial Intelligence

Typesetting: Camera-ready by author, data conversion by Scientific Publishing Services, Chennai, India

Printed on acid-free paper

Springer is part of Springer Science+Business Media (www.springer.com)

Preface

This book contains the proceedings of the 12th German conference on Multi-agent System Technologies (MATES 2014) which was held during September 23–25, 2014, in Stuttgart, Germany. The MATES conference series aims at the promotion of and the cross-fertilization between theory and application of intelligent agents and multiagent systems. It provides an interdisciplinary forum for researchers and members of business and industry to present and discuss latest advances in agent-based computing with prototyped or fielded systems in various application domains.

The MATES 2014 conference was organized in cooperation with the Distributed Artificial Intelligence chapter of the German Society for Informatics (GI), and sponsored by the GI. Moreover, it was co-located with the 37th German Conference on Artificial Intelligence and the 44th Symposium of the German Society for Informatics (INFORMATIK 2014). It also contained a joint session on "Electric Mobility, Agents, and Smart Grids" in cooperation with the GI Special Interest Group on energy information systems.

The set of regular MATES 2014 conference talks covered a broad area of topics of interest including market mechanisms, negotiation, game theory, agent-oriented planning, learning and control, multiagent systems engineering, as well as agent-based modeling and simulation. In keeping with its tradition, MATES 2014 also offered three excellent invited keynotes by well-known, reputed scientists in the domain, covering relevant topics of the broad area of intelligent agent technology: Ulle Endriss from Universiteit van Amsterdam addressed the role of computational social choice theory for multiagent systems; Peter Göhner from Unversität Stuttgart spoke about multiagent systems in applications of industrial automation; and Wolfram Burgard gave an overview of probabilistic techniques for mobile robot navigation (the latter keynote was shared with the KI 2014 conference).

Furthermore, the MATES doctoral mentoring program, chaired by Sebastian Lehnhoff, supported PhD students in their research and application of multiagent system technologies by providing the opportunity to present and intensively discuss their work with other students and experts of the field.

MATES 2014 received 31 submissions. Each paper was peer-reviewed by at least three members of an international Program Committee. Nine papers were accepted for long presentation, and seven papers were accepted for short presentation. They are included in this volume. In addition, the book contains two invited papers from our keynote speakers. It is our hope that the balanced set of theoretical and application-oriented contributions contained in this volume will stimulate further research in multiagent systems and technologies.

As co-chairs and in the name of the MATES Steering Committee, we are very thankful to the authors and invited speakers for contributing to this conference,

Sebastian Lehnhoff for chairing the Doctoral Consortium, the Program Committee members and additional reviewers for their timely and helpful reviews of the submissions, as well as the local organization team at the University of Stuttgart, especially Fernando Cimander, who did an excellent job maintaining the MATES conference homepage, and Stefan Wagner, who was our main liaison to the INFORMATIK 2014 conference. They all contributed in making MATES 2014 a success. We are also indebted to Alfred Hofmann and the whole Springer LNAI team for their very kind and excellent assistance in publishing these proceedings and for their continuing support for the MATES conference over the past twelve editions.

Finally, we hope you enjoyed MATES 2014 and drew some useful inspiration and insights from attending it.

September 2014   Jörg P. Müller
                                                Michael Weyrich
                                                Ana L.C. Bazzan

Organization

The MATES 2014 conference was organized in colocation with the 37th German Conference on Artificial Intelligence and the 44th Symposium of the German Society for Informatics (INFORMATIK 2014), and in cooperation with KI 2014 and with the GI Special Interest Group on Energy Information Systems.

MATES 2014 Chairs

Jörg P. Müller   TU Clausthal, Germany
Michael Weyrich   Universität Stuttgart, Germany
Ana L.C. Bazzan   UFRGS, Brazil

Doctoral Consortium Chair

Sebastian Lehnhoff   Universität Oldenburg, Germany

Program Committee

Thomas Ågotnes   Gal Kaminka
Luis Antunes   Wolfgang Ketter
Ana Bazzan   Franziska Klügl
Vicent Botti   Matthias Klusch
Lars Braubach   Andrew Koster
Nils Bulling   Winfried Lamersdorf
Massimo Cossentino   Paulo Leitao
Célia Da Costa Pereira   Beatriz López
Mehdi Dastani   Felipe Meneguzzi
Paul Davidsson   Emma Norling
Yves Demazeau   Ingrid Nunes
Jörg Denzinger   Andrea Omicini
Frank Dignum   Sascha Ossowski
Jürgen Dix   Marcin Paprzycki
Barbara Dunin-Keplicz   Mathias Petsch
Torsten Eymann   Paolo Petta
Maria Ganzha   Alexander Pokahr
Marie-Pierre Gleizes   Alessandro Ricci
Vladimir Gorodetsky   Jörg Rothe
Daniel Hennes   Jordi Sabater Mir
Koen Hindriks   René Schumann

Onn Shehory
David Sislak
Michael Sonnenschein
Matthias Thimm
Ingo J. Timm
Adelinde Uhrmacher

Rainer Unland
Wiebe Van Der Hoek
László Zsolt Varga
Matteo Vasirani
Gerhard Weiss
Franco Zambonelli

Auxiliary Reviewers

Tobias Ahlbrecht
John Collins
Maksims Fiosins
Yixin Lu
Marin Lujak
Marcin Paprzycki

Weronika Radziszewska
Patrizia Ribino
Luca Sabatucci
Federico Schlesinger
Valeria Seidita

Doctoral Consortium PC Members/Mentors

Massimo Cossentino
Maria Ganzha
Matthias Klusch
Felipe Meneguzzi

Jörg P. Müller
Alexander Pokahr
Jan-Philipp Steghöfer
Matthias Thimm

MATES Steering Committee

Matthias Klusch
Winfried Lamersdorf
Jörg P. Müller
Paolo Petta
Ingo Timm
Rainer Unland

DFKI GmbH, Germany
Universität Hamburg, Germany
TU Clausthal, Germany
University of Vienna, Austria
Universität Trier, Germany
Universität Duisburg-Essen, Germany

Table of Contents

Multiagent Systems Engineering, Modeling and Simulation

Social Choice Theory as a Foundation for Multiagent Systems

Ulle Endriss

Institute for Logic, Language and Computation (ILLC)
University of Amsterdam, The Netherlands

Abstract. Social choice theory is the study of mechanisms for collective decision making. While originally concerned with modelling and analysing political decision making in groups of people, its basic principles, arguably, are equally relevant to modelling and analysing the kinds of interaction taking place in a multiagent system. In support of this position, I review examples from three strands of research in social choice theory: fair division, voting, and judgment aggregation.

1 Introduction

Multiagent systems are systems composed of several autonomous agents, e.g., computer programs or robots, that interact with each other in a variety of ways, including coordination, cooperation, and competition. There are clear parallels to the ways in which individual people interact with each other as members of our society. It therefore is not surprising that formalisms and methods developed in the social and economic sciences, originally intended for the purposes of modelling and analysing humans and human society, have found rich applications also in the field of autonomous agents and multiagent systems.

A relatively recent example for this phenomenon is *social choice theory*, the study of mechanisms for collective decision making [1]. In this short paper I want to review some of the basic ideas developed in social choice theory and argue for their relevance to multiagent systems.

Social choice theory is usually considered part of economic theory, although besides economists also political scientists, philosophers, and mathematicians have contributed significantly to its development as a discipline. More recently, social choice theory, and specifically *computational social choice* [4,2], has also become a hot topic in computer science and artificial intelligence, with many new conceptual and technical contributions coming from this community.

To sketch the scope of social choice theory, particularly in view of possible applications in multiagent systems, it is useful to consider it side by side with two neighbouring disciplines, namely *decision theory* and *game theory*. Decision theory provides us with tools to model and analyse the decision-making capabilities of a single intelligent agent. For an agent to make a decision it needs to understand how its actions will impact on the state of the world around it and it needs to realise its own preferences over these possible alternative states of the

J.P. Müller, M. Weyrich, and A.L.C. Bazzan (Eds.): MATES 2014, LNAI 8732, pp. 1–6, 2014.

world, so as to be able to choose the best action. That is, decision theory is the right framework when we want to model a single agent *vis à vis* nature. Once we zoom in on nature and want to specifically model the fact that part of nature consists of other agents taking their own decisions, we enter the realms of game theory. This is the right framework to work in when, still taking the perspective on an individual agent, we want to model that agent's strategic behaviour *vis à vis* other agents. That is, while decision theory considers one agent at a time, game theory is concerned with such an agent's interactions with other agents. Social choice theory, finally, goes one step further in that direction and is concerned with such a group of interacting agents as a whole. In social choice theory we ask questions such as *"what is good for this group?"*, while we ask *"what is good for this agent?"* in decision theory and *"how can this agent do well, given that others try too?"* in game theory.

In the remainder of this paper I will briefly review three technical frameworks for social choice theory that model different aspects of collective decision making: deciding on a fair allocation of resources to agents, making a choice affecting all agents in view of their individual preferences, and aggregating the judgments of different agents regarding a number of logically related statements to come to a consistent view that appropriately reflects the position taken by the group as a whole. In other words, I will review the frameworks of *fair division* (Section 2), *voting* (Section 3), and *judgment aggregation* (Section 4).

2   Fair Allocation of Resources

Resource allocation plays a central role in multiagent systems research. For one, the problems people try to address by designing a multiagent system often just *are* problems of resource allocation (e.g., applications in electronic commerce). But also for other types of applications we often have to solve a resource allocation problem (e.g., allocating computing resources to different agents) along the way before our agents are in a position to solve the problem they have been designed to address.

Many resource allocation problems can be modelled as follows. We have a set of *agents* $N = \{1, \ldots, n\}$ and a set of (indivisible) *goods* $G = \{g_1, \ldots, g_m\}$. Each agent $i \in N$ is equipped with a *utility function* $u_i : 2^G \to \mathbb{R}$, mapping sets of goods to real numbers indicating the value the agent assigns to the set in question. An *allocation* is a function $A : N \to 2^G$, mapping each agent to a set of goods, that respects $A(i) \cap A(j) = \emptyset$ for all $i \neq j \in N$, i.e., no item may be assigned to more than one agent.

The question then arises: what is a *good* allocation? The answer most frequently given in the context of multiagent systems is that it should be an allocation that maximises the sum of individual utilities. That is, it should be an allocation A that maximises $\sum_{i \in N} u_i(A(i))$, the *utilitarian social welfare* of A. This certainly will be the right objective function to optimise in certain contexts. For example, if the utility experienced by each agent represents monetary revenue generated by that agent and as system designers we collect this revenue from all our agents, then what we are interested in is indeed the sum of individual utilities. But if the agents represent individual clients that make use of a multiagent platform we provide, then we may have rather different objectives. We may, for instance, wish to guarantee that individual agents are treated in a fair manner, so as to improve the user experience of our clients. Social choice theory offers a number of useful definitions for how to make the vague notion of *fairness* precise in the context of resource allocation [14]:

- We could look for an allocation A that maximises the *egalitarian social welfare* $\min\{u_i(A(i)) \mid i \in N\}$, i.e., the utility of the agent that is worst off.
- Alternatively, we could maximise the *Nash social welfare* $\prod_{i \in N} u_i(A(i))$, which may be considered a compromise between the utilitarian and the egalitarian point of view, as it sanctions both increases in total efficiency and reallocations from rich to poor agents.
- Or we could look for an allocation A that is *envy-free*, i.e., where $u_i(A(i)) \geqslant u_i(A(j))$ for all $i, j \in N$, meaning that every agent i values the set $A(i)$ of goods assigned to it no less than the set $A(j)$ assigned to any other agent j.

Elsewhere, my coauthors and I have argued for a systematic exploitation of the rich variety of fairness criteria developed in the classical literature on social choice theory as design objectives for multiagent systems [3].

An important class of fairness criteria that is not yet widely used in multiagent systems are *inequality indices*, quantifying the degree of economic inequality in a group of agents (see [6] for an introduction aimed at computer scientists).

3   Voting

Voting is a framework for choosing a best alternative from a given set of available alternatives, given the preferences of a group of voters over these alternatives. The classical example is that of political elections, where the alternatives are the candidates standing for election and voters express their preferences on the ballot sheet. But voting rules can also be used in many other contexts, including multiagent systems. For example, the alternatives may be different plans available to a group of agents to execute together, and each agent may have their own preferences over alternative plans, determined by the information and reasoning capabilities available to them.

Social choice theory provides a simple mathematical framework for modelling the process of voting. Its ingredients are a set of *agents* $N = \{1, \ldots, n\}$ (the voters), a set of alternatives $X = \{x_1, \ldots, x_\ell\}$, and one *preference order* $\succ_i$ for each agent $i \in N$. Every such preference order $\succ_i$ is taken to be a strict linear order on X (i.e., a binary relation that is irreflexive, transitive, and complete). We write $\mathcal{L}(X)$ for the set of all such linear orders. A *voting rule* is a function $F : \mathcal{L}(X)^n \to 2^X \setminus \{\emptyset\}$, mapping any given *profile* of preference orders (one for each agent) to a nonempty set of winning alternatives (due to the possibility of ties we cannot be sure to always obtain a single winner).

Voting theory provides many different such rules [16]. To exemplify the range, let us define two of them here:

- Under the *Borda rule*, every alternative obtains $\ell - k$ points whenever a voter ranks that alternative in position k in her preference ordering. Thus, if there are 10 alternatives, then your most preferred alternative receive 9 points from you, your second most preferred alternative receives 8 points, and so forth. The alternative with the most points wins.
- Under the *Copeland rule*, we elect the alternative that wins the largest number of pairwise majority contests against other alternatives (with half a point awarded for a draw).

Observe that the so-called *plurality rule*, under which every voter can nominate one alternative and the alternative with the most nominations wins the election, also fits into this framework. The reason is that we can think of it as the rule under which the alternative ranked on top most often wins. The plurality rule is the rule used in most political elections, but it does in fact have many undesirable properties. For example, in the scenario below, z wins under the plurality rule, yet every alternative other than z is preferred to z by a strict majority:

2 agents: $x \succ y \succ z$
2 agents: $y \succ x \succ z$
3 agents: $z \succ x \succ y$

Observe that both the Borda rule and the Copeland rule will instead elect the intuitively "right" winner, namely x.

When designing a decision making mechanism for a multiagent system, it is important to refer back to the classical literature on voting theory, which has examined many of the questions of relevance here in depth. Having said this, multiagent systems will often give rise to requirements that are somewhat different from those arising in the context of elections amongst humans. For example, due to the bounded rationality of autonomous software agents (and due to the fact that we can model such bonded rationality much more precisely in such cases than for a human agent), we may wish to drop or alter some of the classical assumptions regarding preferences. Specifically, the assumption of completeness, i.e., an agent's ability to rank any two alternatives, will not always be appropriate. This insight has led to work in the artificial intelligence literature on *voting with nonstandard preferences* [15,8]. In a similar vain, the alternatives that we need to choose between in the context of multiagent systems may not always be just simple "atomic" options, but they may come with some rich internal structure. This has lead to the research direction of *voting in combinatorial domains* in computational social choice [11,5].

Observe that, in principle, we could use voting rules also in the context of resource allocation. If we think of the set of all possible allocations of resources to agents as the set of alternatives, then each agent's utility function defines its preference relation over these alternatives.

4   Judgment Aggregation

Preferences are not the only types of structures we may wish to aggregate in a multiagent system. Other examples include in particular individual judgments regarding the truth or falsehood of certain statements. Such questions have been investigated in the literature on *belief merging* [10] and *judgment aggregation* [13], as well as the closely related *binary aggregation* [9].

Let us briefly review the basic framework of judgment aggregation here. An *agenda* is a finite set of formulas of propositional logic that is of the form $\Phi = \Phi^{+} \cup \{\neg\varphi \mid \varphi \in \Phi^{+}\}$, with Φ^{+} only including non-negated formulas. Now consider a set of *agents* $N = \{1, \ldots, n\}$ such that each agent $i \in N$ picks a *judgment set* $J_i \subseteq \Phi$ that is logically consistent and that includes either φ or $\neg\varphi$ for every $\varphi \in \Phi^{+}$. Let $\mathcal{J}(\Phi)$ be the set of all such consistent and complete judgment sets for the agenda φ. An *aggregator* is a function $F : \mathcal{J}(\Phi)^n \to 2^{\Phi}$, mapping profiles of such judgment sets (one for each agent) to subsets of the agenda (i.e., to judgment sets that may or may not also be consistent and complete).

An example is the *majority rule*, under which we accept all those formulas that are accepted by a majority of the agents. Unfortunately, this simple rule is often not satisfactory, as it can lead to paradoxical outcomes. For example, suppose that $\Phi^{+} = \{p, q, p \wedge q\}$. The table below show a profile with three agents (we assume that an agent accepts $\neg\varphi$ if and only if it does not accept φ):

	p	q	$p \wedge q$
Agent 1:	Yes	Yes	Yes
Agent 2:	Yes	No	No
Agent 3:	No	Yes	No
Majority:	Yes	Yes	No

Thus, even though each individual agent declares a consistent judgment set (e.g., agent 2 claims p is true and q is false, i.e., $p \wedge q$ is also false), the majority judgment set we obtain is inconsistent: you cannot accept both p and q but also reject $p \wedge q$. There are several proposals for alternative methods of aggregation that avoid this kind of problem, albeit often at the price of significantly increased complexity [12]. This includes, for instance, distance-based methods where we choose as outcome a consistent judgment set that minimises, in some sense, the distance to the input profile. Another approach amounts to choosing from amongst the agents one that may be considered a good representative of the group, to then implement that agent's advice [7].

In the same way as resource allocation problems can, in principle, be studied as voting problems, voting can, in principle, be embedded into judgment aggregation. The basic idea is to work with propositional variables of the form $p_{x \succ y}$, acceptance of which would then signal that an agent prefers x to y.

5   Conclusion

We have reviewed three frameworks for collective decision making and discussed their relevance to multiagent systems. Judgment aggregation and the closely related binary aggregation are the most general amongst them: they, in principle, allow us to aggregate any kind of information. The other two frameworks, voting and fair division, deal with one specific type of information to be aggregated, namely information on the preferences of the agents. Fair division, again, is more specific than voting, as it imposes specific constraints on the types of preferences held by agents over alternative outcomes. Despite this relative narrowness of scope, or maybe because of it, of the ideas discussed here, those pertaining to resource allocation are clearly the most widely used in multiagent systems research today. But also the others have clear potential for multiagent systems.

References

1. Arrow, K.J., Sen, A.K., Suzumura, K. (eds.): Handbook of Social Choice and Welfare. North-Holland (2002)
2. Brandt, F., Conitzer, V., Endriss, U.: Computational social choice. In: Weiss, G. (ed.) Multiagent Systems, pp. 213–283. MIT Press (2013)
3. Chevaleyre, Y., Endriss, U., Estivie, S., Maudet, N.: Welfare engineering in practice: On the variety of multiagent resource allocation problems. In: Gleizes, M.-P., Omicini, A., Zambonelli, F. (eds.) ESAW 2004. LNCS (LNAI), vol. 3451, pp. 335–347. Springer, Heidelberg (2005)
4. Chevaleyre, Y., Endriss, U., Lang, J., Maudet, N.: A short introduction to computational social choice. In: van Leeuwen, J., Italiano, G.F., van der Hoek, W., Meinel, C., Sack, H., Plášil, F. (eds.) SOFSEM 2007. LNCS, vol. 4362, pp. 51–69. Springer, Heidelberg (2007)
5. Chevaleyre, Y., Endriss, U., Lang, J., Maudet, N.: Preference handling in combinatorial domains: From AI to social choice. AI Magazine 29(4), 37–46 (2008)
6. Endriss, U.: Reduction of economic inequality in combinatorial domains. In: Proc. 12th International Conference on Autonomous Agents and Multiagent Systems, AAMAS (2013)
7. Endriss, U., Grandi, U.: Binary aggregation by selection of the most representative voter. In: Proc. 28th AAAI Conference on Artificial Intelligence (2014)
8. Endriss, U., Pini, M.S., Rossi, F., Venable, K.B.: Preference aggregation over restricted ballot languages: Sincerity and strategy-proofness. In: Proc. 21st International Joint Conference on Artificial Intelligence, IJCAI (2009)
9. Grandi, U., Endriss, U.: Binary aggregation with integrity constraints. In: Proc. 22nd International Joint Conference on Artificial Intelligence, IJCAI (2011)
10. Konieczny, S., Pino Pérez, R.: Merging information under constraints: A logical framework. Journal of Logic and Computation 12(5), 773–808 (2002)
11. Lang, J.: Logical preference representation and combinatorial vote. Annals of Mathematics and Artificial Intelligence 42(1-3), 37–71 (2004)
12. Lang, J., Slavkovik, M.: How hard is it to compute majority-preserving judgment aggregation rules? In: Proc. 21st European Conference on Artificial Intelligence, ECAI (2014)
13. List, C., Puppe, C.: Judgment aggregation: A survey. In: Anand, P., Pattanaik, P., Puppe, C. (eds.) Handbook of Rational and Social Choice. Oxford University Press (2009)
14. Moulin, H.: Axioms of Cooperative Decision Making. Cambridge University Press (1988)
15. Pini, M.S., Rossi, F., Venable, K.B., Walsh, T.: Aggregating partially ordered preferences. Journal of Logic and Computation 19(3), 475–502 (2008)
16. Taylor, A.D.: Social Choice and the Mathematics of Manipulation. Cambridge University Press (2005)

A Boolean Game Based Modeling
of Socio-Technical Systems

Nils Bulling

Department of Informatics
Clausthal University of Technology, Germany
bulling@in.tu-clausthal.de

Abstract. In this paper we introduce a formal model of socio-technical systems, in which communication and cooperation is limited, using (constrained) Boolean games. We study properties, in particular related to stability, of the emerging behavior of a socio-technical system.

1 Introduction

Socio-technical systems theory is concerned with the interplay between technical and social systems and their joint optimization [21]. The technical part of a *socio-technical system* (STS) represents, e.g., the physical infrastructure, available resources, and other non-social aspects. The social system includes agents, their social relations, their goals etc. Similar to *multi-agent systems* [22] (MASs), agents in STSs are often autonomous and partially self-interested, for example employees *work* for a company but they are not their weak-willed slaves without own interests. Hence, STSs are highly dynamic, even if the technical system is fixed, the social system is subject to frequent changes (e.g. employees leave or join a company, social norms change etc.). An STS can often be considered as a system of subsystems; we call them—in this paper—*organization units*. These units are somehow independent: information exchange, cooperation and communication between them can be limited and they have their own organization (sub)objectives. There can be various reasons for that, for example an insufficient IT-infrastructure, time and cost constraints, competition and conflicting interests. This is a major obstacle for the design of an STS as its overall behavior emerges from the behaviors of its organization units; e.g. the behavior of a large globally operating company emerges from the behavior of its various sites. As a consequence, decisions and actions taken in these independent units are interrelated and need to be coordinated to obtain a desired global system behavior [20,8,4,18]. This shows that to design effective, cost-efficient, stable, robust, adaptive STSs is an extremely challenging task. The research question addressed in this paper is as follows: how to formally model and to analyse STSs in which communication and cooperation is limited and/or information is restrained by involved agents (e.g. due to competing interests), in order to design good, stable STSs? Our model of an STS draws inspiration from Boolean games. Boolean games [10,11,3,14] represent a compact, computational model

J.P. Müller, M. Weyrich, and A.L.C. Bazzan (Eds.): MATES 2014, LNAI 8732, pp. 7–25, 2014.

of cooperation among autonomous agents. Agents control some propositional variables—they decide on their truth values—and try to satisfy their individual goals which are given as propositional formulae. Agents can usually not satisfy their goals on their own: they often depend on the actions of other self-interested agents. This requires cooperation and strategic reasoning. We use Boolean games to model organization units in STSs. Each organization unit has an organization objective which may not be publicly known to other organization units. Consequently, to achieve a good global behavior parts of these objectives must be disclosed to other units—as much as is needed to obtain a good behavior, but not too much to preserve confidentiality—in order to facilitate cooperation and coordination. We introduce confidentiality constraints in order to check whether the public information does not reveal confidential information. We also investigate the existence of incentive schemes to stabilize an STS. In summary, the contributions of this paper are as follows. A formal model of STSs which makes use of techniques from MASs. We propose to "distribute" Boolean games to stabilize the system behavior, and to use propositional formulae as means for coordinating between these games. We show how incentive engineering [23] can be applied to the STS domain. We also give some characterization results for stabilizing STSs.

The *paper is structured* as follows. First, we recall Boolean games and propositional logic. Then, we propose constrained Boolean games, a minor extension of Boolean games, define the concept of Nash equilibrium, and recall incentive schemes. In Section 3 we present our formal modeling framework—the key contribution of this paper. In Section 4 we analyse the existence of stable/good STSs and give some characterization results. In Section 5 and 6 we discuss related work and conclude, respectively.

2   Preliminaries and Constrained Boolean Games

In this section we review Boolean games and introduce constrained Boolean games, a variant of which will later be used to model organization units.

2.1   Preliminaries: Propositional Logic and Boolean Games

Propositional Logic. Let Π be a set of (propositional) variables and $X \subseteq \Pi$ a non-empty subset. We use $\mathsf{PL}(X)$ to refer to the set of propositional formulae using propositional variables from X. We assume the standard logical connectives $\neg, \wedge, \vee$ and $\rightarrow$. An X-*assignment* is a function $\xi : X \rightarrow \mathbb{B}$, where $\mathbb{B} = \{\mathsf{t}, \mathsf{f}\}$ is the set of Boolean truth values, assigning a truth value to each variable in X. $\xi|_Y$ refers to the assignment which equals ξ but the domain of which is restricted to Y. We write $\xi \models \varphi$ if X-assignment ξ satisfies $\varphi \in \mathsf{PL}(Y)$ where $\emptyset \neq Y \subseteq X$. A formula φ over X is *satisfiable* (resp. *valid*) if there is an X-assignment which satisfies φ (resp. if all X-assignments satisfy φ). If clear from context we will omit mentioning the sets X and Y and assume that an assignment is always defined on the variables contained in a formula. The set of all X-assignments is denoted by Ass_X. Given two assignments $\xi \in \mathsf{Ass}_X$ and $\xi' \in \mathsf{Ass}_{X'}$ with $X \cap X' = \emptyset$, the $X \cup X'$-assignment $\xi \circ \xi'$ is defined as: $(\xi \circ \xi')|_X = \xi$ and $(\xi \circ \xi')|_{X'} = \xi'$. Finally, for $\varphi \in \mathsf{PL}(Y)$ and an X-assignment ξ, we denote by $\varphi[\xi]$ the formula that equals φ but each variable $p \in X$ occurring in φ is replaced by $\top$ (resp. $\bot$) if $\xi(p) = \mathsf{t}$ (resp. $\xi(p) = \mathsf{f}$).

Boolean Games. Apart from minor modifications, we follow the definition of Boolean games of [11]. A *Boolean game* (BG) is a tuple $\mathsf{G} = (\mathsf{N}, \Pi, c, (\gamma_i)_{i \in \mathsf{N}}, (\Pi_i)_{i \in \mathsf{N}})$ where $\mathsf{N} \subseteq \mathbb{N}$ is a non-empty, finite set of players, Π is a finite, non-empty set of (propositional) variables, $\Pi_i \subseteq \Pi$ is the set of variables controlled by $i \in \mathsf{N}$. We require that $(\Pi_i)_{i \in \mathsf{N}}$ forms a partition of a *subset* of Π (as in [13] we do not require that all variables are controlled by some player). $c : \Pi \times \mathbb{B} \to \mathbb{R}_+$ is a cost function and $\gamma_i \in \mathsf{PL}(\Pi)$ an *objective* or *goal* of player i. For example, $c(p, \mathsf{t}) = 4$ models that setting variable p true incurs costs of four. We write $\mathsf{Ctrl}(A) = \bigcup_{i \in A} \Pi_i$ for the set of variables controlled by $A \subseteq \mathsf{N}$, $\Pi_0 = \Pi \backslash \mathsf{Ctrl}(\mathsf{N})$ for the set of *environmental variables*, and $\widehat{\Pi} = \mathsf{Ctrl}(\mathsf{N}) = \Pi \backslash \Pi_0$ to refer to the set of variables controlled by the players in N.

Example 1 (Boolean game)

(a) Let $\mathsf{G}_1 = (\mathsf{N}, \Pi, c, (\gamma_i)_{i \in \mathsf{N}}, (\Pi_i)_{i \in \mathsf{N}})$ where $\mathsf{N} = \{1, 2, 3\}$, $\Pi = \{p_1, \ldots, p_5\}$, $\gamma_1 = (p_1 \wedge p_2) \vee (\neg p_1 \wedge \neg p_2)$, $\gamma_2 = (\neg p_1 \wedge p_2) \vee (\neg p_2 \wedge p_1)$, $\gamma_3 = p_1 \wedge p_3$. The variables are controlled as follows: $\Pi_1 = \{p_1\}$, $\Pi_2 = \{p_2, p_5\}$, and $\Pi_3 = \{p_3, p_4\}$. Note that the game has no environmental variables. We define the cost function: $c(p, \mathsf{t}) = 1$ and $c(p, \mathsf{f}) = 0$ for all $p \in \Pi \backslash \{p_4, p_5\}$ and $c(p_4, \mathsf{t}) = c(p_4, \mathsf{f}) = c(p_5, \mathsf{t}) = c(p_5, \mathsf{f}) = 1$. G_1 is a BG.
(b) Let $\mathsf{G}_{\{2,3\}}$ be the BG obtained from G_1 with player 1 being removed, that is $\mathsf{G}_{\{2,3\}} = (\{2, 3\}, \Pi, c, (\gamma_2, \gamma_3), (\Pi_2, \Pi_3))$. Then, variable p_1 is an environmental variable (i.e. controlled by no player). Analogously, let $\mathsf{G}_{\{1\}}$ be the BG obtained from G_1 with players 2 and 3 being removed. The environmental variables in $\mathsf{G}_{\{1\}}$ are $\Pi \backslash \{p_1\}$.

2.2 Constrained Boolean Games and Information

We extend Boolean games with a *global constraint* φ on action profiles of the players. Such a constraint is a propositional formula which restricts the choices of players. Only those action profiles of players are "permitted" which satisfy φ. We note that the enforcement of a constraint often requires communication or other means to coordinate players' actions, as players need to take into consideration the actions of other players to obtain an assignment satisfying φ. This is the same as with Nash equilibria: the solution concept says nothing about how players should coordinate their actions in order to agree on an equilibrium.

Definition 1 (Constrained Boolean game, consistent assignment). *A constrained Boolean game is given by* $\mathsf{G} = (\mathsf{N}, \Pi, c, (\gamma_i)_{i \in \mathsf{N}}, (\Pi_i)_{i \in \mathsf{N}}, \varphi)$ *where* $\mathsf{G}' = (\mathsf{N}, \Pi, c, (\gamma_i)_{i \in \mathsf{N}}, (\Pi_i)_{i \in \mathsf{N}})$ *is a BG and* $\varphi \in \mathsf{PL}(\Pi)$ *a (global) constraint. We also write* $\mathsf{G} = (\mathsf{G}', \varphi)$. *An assignment* ξ *is said to be* φ-consistent *iff* $\xi \models \varphi$.

For obvious reasons, we will identify a Boolean game $\widehat{\mathsf{G}}$ with the constrained Boolean game $(\widehat{\mathsf{G}}, \top)$ and vice versa ($\top$ imposes no constraints on assignments).

A global constraint can impose restrictions on the truth values of variables of the players as well of the environment. In this paper, we are mainly interested in constrained Boolean games where φ is built over environmental variables only. Such a constraint can be interpreted as information given to the players about the truth values of the environmental variables. One could see that as the players' beliefs (based on the given information carried by the constraint) about the behavior of the environment. This is similar to [13] where each player has a belief about the environmental variables. In the STS setting the motivation is that φ provides information about other organization units of the STS. We assume that the information carried by φ is known to all players, e.g. by being publicly announced to the players by the system principal. Finally, we note that information can be vague; for this reason, we use propositional formulae, as also discussed in [13], rather than (partial) truth assignments. For example, players may be informed that $x \vee y$, but they have no specific information about x nor about y. For future work, it would also be interested to consider the case in which players have individual information about other variables, as in [13].

Definition 2 (Boolean game with information). *A constrained Boolean game $(\mathsf{N}, \Pi, c, (\gamma_i)_{i \in \mathsf{N}}, (\Pi_i)_{i \in \mathsf{N}}, \varphi)$ is a BG with information if $\varphi \in \mathsf{PL}(\Pi_0)$.*

Example 2 (Boolean game with information). The Boolean game $\mathsf{G}_{\{2,3\}}$ from Example 1 in combination with $\varphi = p_1$ is a Boolean game with information. It models that players 2 and 3 have the information that p_1 is true.

2.3   Payoff and Nash Equilibrium

In the following we assume that $\mathsf{G} = (\mathsf{N}, \Pi, c, (\gamma_i)_{i \in \mathsf{N}}, (\Pi_i)_{i \in \mathsf{N}}, \varphi)$ is a constrained Boolean Game. Let us define max_G as $\sum_{p \in \Pi}[c(p, \mathsf{t}) + c(p, \mathsf{f})] + 1$; the number is greater than the maximum cost of any course of action in G. We lift the cost function c of a constrained Boolean game to assignments. We define $c(\xi) = \sum_{p \in X} c(p, \xi(p))$ for an X-assignment ξ. Then, the *utility* of a Π-assignment ξ for player i is defined as follows (cf. [11]) where γ_i is the goal of player i: $\widehat{\mu}_i^\mathsf{G}(\xi) = \mathsf{max}_\mathsf{G} - c(\xi|_{\Pi_i})$ if $\xi \models \gamma_i$; and $\widehat{\mu}_i^\mathsf{G}(\xi) = -c(\xi|_{\Pi_i})$ otherwise. The utility function $\widehat{\mu}_i^\mathsf{G}$ computes the utility independently of whether ξ is φ-consistent. It is an auxiliary function and models, due to the term max_G, that a player always prefers an assignment which satisfies its goal over one that does not. Ultimately, we are interested in the *worst case utility* which is defined next. For a $\widehat{\Pi}$-assignment ξ the *worst case utility of player i*—note that ξ is not defined on environmental variables—is defined by

$$\mu_i^\mathsf{G}(\xi) = \begin{cases} \min\{\widehat{\mu}_i^\mathsf{G}(\xi') \mid \xi' \in \mathsf{Ass}_\Pi, \xi'|_{\widehat{\Pi}} = \xi, \xi' \models \varphi\} & \text{if } \varphi[\xi] \text{ is satisfiable} \\ -c(\xi|_{\Pi_i}) & \text{otherwise.} \end{cases}$$

The worst case utility models the worst case assignment of the environmental variables for player i, but it is assumed that the environmental variables respect the constraint φ. In this sense, φ is a global constraint which requires some kind of enforcement/communication mechanism. We can now define standard solution concepts. We assume that the set of players is given by $N = \{1, \ldots, k\}$. A *Nash equilibrium* is a $\widehat{\Pi}$-assignment $\xi = \xi_1 \circ \cdots \circ \xi_k$ where $\xi_i \in \mathsf{Ass}_{\Pi_i}$ such that for all $j = 1, \ldots, k$ and all $\xi'_j \in \mathsf{Ass}_{\Pi_j}$ we have that $\mu^G_j(\xi) \geq \mu^G_j(\xi_1 \circ \cdots \circ \xi_{j-1} \circ \xi'_j \circ \xi_{j+1} \circ \cdots \circ \xi_k)$. The set of Nash equilibria of a constrained Boolean game G is defined as $\mathcal{NE}(G)$. Similarly, one can define other standard solution concepts known from game theory, like Pareto optimality or dominant strategies. We leave a study of them for future work.

Example 3 (Nash equilibria)

(a) Firstly, let us consider the Boolean game G_1 from Example 1. The game does not have any Nash equilibria. The goals of players 1 and 2 do not allow any stable point: we observe that for any truth value of p_1 and p_2 either player 1's or player 2's goal is true (but never both). Moreover, if player i's goal is true, $i \in \{1, 2\}$, player $3 - i$ can (by flipping the truth value of p_i) ensure that its goal becomes true and player i's goal false.

(b) The BG $G_{\{2,3\}}$ from Example 1 has the unique Nash equilibrium $\xi \in \mathsf{Ass}_{\Pi_2 \cup \Pi_3}$ with $\xi(p) = f$ for all $p \in \Pi_2 \cup \Pi_3$. This is easy to see: no player can guarantee to achieve its goal, because for any $\Pi_2 \cup \Pi_3$-assignment there is a value of p_1 which makes γ_2 and γ_3 false (possibly not at the same time). Hence, the best/cheapest actions for players 2 and 3 are those that make all their variables false.

(c) The Boolean game with information $(G_{\{2,3\}}, p_1)$ has the four Nash equilibria $\mathcal{NE}((G_{\{2,3\}}, p_1)) = \{(f, t, f, f), (f, t, t, f), (f, t, f, t), (f, t, t, t)\}$ where each tuple represents a truth assignment of p_2, p_3, p_4 and p_5 (in this order).

(d) The Boolean game with information $(G_{\{1\}}, p_2)$ has a unique Nash equilibrium: $\mathcal{NE}((G_{\{1\}}, p_2)) = \{\xi \in \mathsf{Ass}_{\Pi_1} \mid \xi(p_1) = t\}$. We will use both notations, this one and the one of (c), to represent assignments.

2.4 Incentive Schemes

Nash equilibria may not exist or there may be several of them; often, both is undesirable [23]. One way to change the behavior of players is to use taxes or incentives. The technique of *incentive engineering* in Boolean games has been studied in [23]. Here we consider incentives as payoffs given to the players rather than taxes imposed on them. Formally, an *incentive scheme* for a constrained Boolean game (G, φ) over Π is a function $\iota : \widehat{\Pi} \times \mathbb{B} \to \mathbb{R}$. The interpretation of $\iota(p, t) = 5$ is that setting variable p to t is incentivized by five (units of payoff). We denote by $G \oplus \iota$ the game that equals G but which has as cost function c' with $c'(p, v) = c(p, v) - \iota(p, v)$ for all $p \in \widehat{\Pi}$ and $c'(p, v) \equiv c(p, v)$ for all $p \in \Pi_0$ where c is the cost function of G. Similarly, we write $(G, \varphi) \oplus \iota$ for $(G \oplus \iota, \varphi)$.

3   Formal Modeling of Socio-Technical Systems

A *socio-technical system* (STS) is composed of two (sub)systems: a technical and a social one. The technical system provides, e.g., the technology, resources, and the physical infrastructure. The social system represents the agents, their abilities, goals, and models the interrelation between agents, as well as social and organizational constraints which are imposed on the agents to ensure the successful functioning of the STS. In the following we assume, as before, that Π is a non-empty, finite set of (propositional) variables.

3.1   Formal System Model

A technical system $\mathcal{T}$ consists of a set of available objects/artifacts (e.g. resources and machines), which are modeled by propositional variables $\Pi_{\mathcal{T}} \subseteq \Pi$, and a set of *technical constraints* that affect the size and structure of an STS. A technical constraint is modeled by a vector $T = (t_1, \ldots, t_j)$ of positive integers. The length of T represents the number of *technical units* (e.g. offices). The above technical constraint T has j technical units. The number t_i, $1 \leq i \leq j$, specifies the number of agents which can be located in the ith technical unit. A technical system defines the static structure of an STS; for example, a technical constraint T can represent the available offices in a building or (more or less independent) distributed parts of a company, and their capacity. We assume that communication and cooperation across different technical units is limited.

Definition 3 (Technical system). *A technical system (over Π) is given by a tuple $\mathcal{T} = (\Pi_{\mathcal{T}}, \{T_i\}_{i \in I}, \mathsf{tcost}_{\mathcal{T}})$ where $I \subseteq \mathbb{N}$ is a non-empty, finite index set; $\Pi_{\mathcal{T}} \subseteq \Pi$ is a non-empty, finite set of variables; each $T_i = (t_1, \ldots, t_{j_i})$ is a finite, non-empty sequence of positive integers, one for each $i \in I$; and $\mathsf{tcost}_{\mathcal{T}} : I \to \mathbb{R}_+$ is a cost function. The value $\mathsf{tcost}_{\mathcal{T}}(i)$ defines the costs needed to realize T_i. A vector T_i is called technical constraint. The lth element of the technical constraint T_i, t_l, defines the capacity (or size) of the lth technical unit. Technical units are implicitly defined by the length of T_i (i.e. there are technical units $1, \ldots, |T_i|$).*

Example 4 (Technical system). Consider the technical system $\mathcal{T}_1 = (\{p_1, \ldots, p_5\}, \{T_1, T_2\}, \mathsf{tcost}_{\mathcal{T}})$ with $T_1 = (5)$ and $T_2 = (1, 3)$, $\mathsf{tcost}_{\mathcal{T}}(1) = 1$ and $\mathsf{tcost}_{\mathcal{T}}(2) = 3$. The system models two possible infrastructures: the first consists of a single technical unit of size 5 and costs 1, where the second models two technical units of sizes 1 and 3, respectively, and cost 3.

Next, we introduce an *agent society* from which an STS draws its members. It models the available agents, their capabilities and individual goals.

Definition 4 (Agent society). *An agent society (over Π) is a set $\mathcal{A} = \{(\Pi_1, \gamma_1, \mathsf{c}_1), (\Pi_2, \gamma_2, \mathsf{c}_2), \ldots\}$ where each $\gamma_i \in \mathsf{PL}(\Pi)$, each $\Pi_i \subseteq \Pi$ is a finite, non-empty set of variables, and $\mathsf{c}_i : \Pi_i \times \mathbb{B} \to \mathbb{R}_+$. We call elements of $\mathcal{A}$ agents[1] and identify $(\Pi_i, \gamma_i, \mathsf{c}_i)$ with a_i.*

Intuitively, $a_i = (\Pi_i, \gamma_i, \mathsf{c}_i)$ represents an agent that is capable of controlling variables in Π_i, which has γ_i as individual goal and c_i as cost function. A social

---

[1] We use the notion *agent* to refer to actors in STSs, and *player* to refer to the actors in a (contrained) Boolean game.

system consists of a subset of agents—drawn from an agent society—and defines their relations and powers. Our relational model between agents is rather simplistic. It prescribes how agents are divided into *organization units*. We assume that each organization unit S has a private *organization objective* δ which is known only to the agents in the unit, but, *per se* not to members of other units. In order to obtain an efficient overall behavior across organization units, an STS has to provide communication and cooperation mechanisms. For this purpose, each organization unit publicly and truthfully[2] announces parts of its private objective, we call it the *public organization objective* δ^I, to inform other units. There are plenty of reasons why organization units belonging to the same STS may not want to reveal their complete objectives; for example, they may be in competition. This is similar to the idea of Boolean secrecy games [6] where players try to hide their true goals. Finally, agents from the same agent society are able to control specific variables. The intuition is that the agents have, e.g., the power to operate a machine or the knowledge to work with a piece of software. There can be several agents with overlapping capabilities. In our modeling, we make the assumption (of rather technical nature) that control in an STS is exclusive, in the sense that only one agent is permitted to exercise its power over a specific variable. Thus, an STS has to define which agents have the rights to exercise their powers. This is modeled by a function pow. For example, a company can prevent an employee to access specific data by taking aways the necessary permissions.

Definition 5 (Social system). *A* social system *over an agent society* $\mathcal{A}$ *(over* Π*) is given by* $\mathcal{S} = (\mathsf{Agt}, \mathsf{pow}, (S_1, \delta_1, \delta_1^I), \ldots, (S_s, \delta_s, \delta_s^I), \iota)$ *where*

- $\mathsf{Agt} \subseteq \mathcal{A}$ *is a finite, non-empty set of agents.*
- $\mathsf{pow} : \mathsf{Agt} \to 2^\Pi$ *such that for each* $a_i = (\Pi_i, \gamma_i, \mathsf{c}_i) \in \mathsf{Agt}$ *we have that* $\mathsf{pow}(a_i) \subseteq \Pi_i$ *and* $\mathsf{pow}(a_i) \cap \mathsf{pow}(a_j) = \emptyset$ *whenever* $i \neq j$. *For a set* $A \subseteq \mathsf{Agt}$ *we write* $\mathsf{pow}(A)$ *for* $\bigcup_{a \in A} \mathsf{pow}(a)$. *(The function is called* power function *and describes which capabilities an agent is allowed to exercise in a social system. The first constraint expresses that an agent must be able to control the variables assigned to it; and the second, that no two agents are allowed to exercise their power over the same variable.)*
- *The tuple* $(S_i, \delta_i, \delta_i^I)$ *is called* organization specification, S_i organization unit, δ_i *(private)* organization objective *and* δ_i^I public organization objective. *We require that the organization units* $(S_1, \ldots, S_s)$ *form a partition of* Agt *and that each* $S_i \neq \emptyset$ *for* $i = 1, \ldots, s$.
- *We have that* $\delta_i, \delta_i^I \in \mathsf{PL}(\mathsf{pow}(S_i))$ *such that* $\delta_i \wedge \delta_i^I$ *is satisfiable for* $i = 1, \ldots, s$; *that is,* δ_i *and* δ_i^I *are propositional formulae over* $\mathsf{pow}(S_i)$.
- $\iota : \mathsf{pow}(\mathsf{Agt}) \times \mathbb{B} \to \mathbb{R}$ *is an incentive scheme.*

Note that we assume that the organization objectives δ_i and δ_i^I are built only over variables of the very organization unit S_i. If it included also variables of other units, then this would create new inter-dependencies. The assumption that

---

[2] The study of non-truthful announcements is left for future research.

$\delta_i \wedge \delta_i^I$ is satisfiable models that the organization units do not lie about their objectives—though, the assumption is not crucial in this work. The relaxation of both assumptions would be interesting directions for future research. The latter relates to mechanism design and truthful mechanisms.

Example 5 (Social system). Let $\mathcal{S}_1 = (\mathsf{Agt}, \mathsf{pow}, (S, \delta, \delta^I), \iota)$ be the social system consisting of $\mathsf{Agt} = \{a_1, a_2, a_3\}$ representing the three players of the Boolean game G_1 of Example 1(a). That is, $a_i = (\Pi_i, \gamma_i, \mathsf{c}_i)$ where $\mathsf{c}_i \equiv \mathsf{c}|_{\Pi_i}$ for $i = 1, 2, 3$ and each agent has the same power as the corresponding player in G_1, i.e. $\mathsf{pow}(a_i) = \Pi_i$ for $i = 1, 2, 3$. The social system consists of the organization specification (S, δ, δ^I) with $S = \mathsf{Agt}$, $\delta = p_5 \wedge p_1 \wedge ((p_2 \wedge p_3) \vee p_4)$ and $\delta^I = \top$. Moreover, $\mathcal{S}_1$ provides the incentive scheme $\iota \equiv 0$. The organization unit has the private organization objective δ but announces only $\delta^I = \top$. Here, the public objective is irrelevant as there is only a single organization unit.

We define another social system $\mathcal{S}_2$ that equals $\mathcal{S}_1$ but consists of the two organization specifications $(\{a_1\}, p_1, p_1)$ and $(\{a_2, a_3\}, p_5 \wedge ((p_2 \wedge p_3) \vee p_4), p_2)$. In this STS, $\mathcal{S}_1$ discloses that it has the objective p_1, where $\mathcal{S}_2$ discloses that it has p_2 has objective.

A social system has to be embedded in a technical one. It is hardly possible, e.g., to find an office building which can host thousands of workers. Formally, this is captured by the following definition:

Definition 6 ($\mathcal{T}$-consistency). *Given a technical system $\mathcal{T} = (\Pi_\mathcal{T}, \{T_i\}_{i \in I},$ tcost) and a social system $\mathcal{S} = (\mathsf{Agt}, \mathsf{pow}, (S_1, \delta_1, \delta_1^I,), \ldots, (S_s, \delta_s, \delta_s^I), \iota)$ over the same set of variables, we say that $\mathcal{S}$ is consistent with $T_j = (t_1^j, \ldots, t_g^j)$ in $\mathcal{T}$ if there is an injective mapping $f : \{1, \ldots, s\} \to \{1, \ldots, g\}$ such that $|S_i| \le t_{f(i)}^j$ for $i = 1, \ldots, s$. We say that $\mathcal{S}$ is consistent with $\mathcal{T}$, $\mathcal{T}$-consistent in short, if there is an element T_j in $\mathcal{T}$ such that $\mathcal{S}$ is T_j-consistent.*

The mapping f ensures that all agents in the organization unit S_i can be embedded into the $f(i)$th technical unit of $T = (t_1, \ldots, t_g)$. This requires that the capacity of this technical unit, which is $t_{f(i)}$, is greater or equal to $|S_i|$. Finally, an STS is essentially given by a technical system and a consistent social system, both over the same set of variables. Note that we implicitly assume that each agent has a "size" of one. We are ready to formally define an STS.

Definition 7 (Socio-technical system). *An STS over Π is given by a tuple $\mathfrak{ST} = (\Pi, \mathcal{T}, T, \mathcal{S})$ where $\mathcal{T}$ is a technical system (over Π), T is a technical constraint included in $\mathcal{T}$ and $\mathcal{S}$ is a T-consistent social system over Π.*

Example 6 (Socio-technical system). The social systems $\mathcal{S}_1$ and $\mathcal{S}_2$ from Example 5 are both $\mathcal{T}_1$-consistent where $\mathcal{T}_1$ is the technical system from Example 4. $\mathfrak{ST}_1 = (\Pi, \mathcal{T}_1, T_1, \mathcal{S}_1)$ and $\mathfrak{ST}_2 = (\Pi, \mathcal{T}_1, T_2, \mathcal{S}_2)$ are both STSs. The former consists of a single organization unit grounded in the technical constraint T_1, and the latter of two organization units grounded in the technical constraint T_2.

3.2   Organizational Behavior and Equilibria in STSs

Agents in an STS can be autonomous and self-interested; they do not necessarily care about the organization objective at first place. So, a crucial question is how to model and to influence the agents' behaviors. We follow a game theoretical approach to model the agents' decision-making. For the remainder of this section, let us assume that we are given the STS $\mathfrak{ST} = (\Pi, \mathcal{T}, T, \mathcal{S})$ with $\mathcal{T} = (\Pi_{\mathcal{T}}, \{T_i\}_{i \in I}, \mathsf{tcost}_{\mathcal{T}})$ and $\mathcal{S} = (\mathsf{Agt}, \mathsf{pow}, (S_1, \delta_1, \delta_1^I), \ldots, (S_s, \delta_s, \delta_s^I), \iota)$. Each S_i consists of elements $a_j^i = (\Pi_j^i, \gamma_j^i, \mathsf{c}_j^i)$ for $i = 1, \ldots, s$ and j ranging over some appropriate set. We associate with each organization unit S_i a Boolean game with information[3]. The players in the game are the agents in S_i with their capabilities defined as in the STS. An agent's behavior does not only depend on the other agents in S_i but also on those belonging to organization units other than S_i; how exactly those agents behave, however, is not known to the members in S_i. Thus, we assume that the members of S_i believe that the other agents act in line with the public organization objective of their organization unit. This gives rise to the following definition:

Definition 8 (Induced Boolean game with information). *The Boolean game with information associated with the STS $\mathfrak{ST}$ and S_i, $i \in \{1, \ldots, s\}$, is defined as $G_{\mathfrak{ST}}(i) = (\mathsf{N}_i, \Pi, c, (\gamma_j^i)_{j \in \mathsf{N}_i}, (\mathsf{pow}(a_j))_{j \in \mathsf{N}_i}, \Delta_i)$ where $\mathsf{N}_i = \{j \mid a_j \in S_i\}$, $\Delta_i = \bigwedge_{j \in \{1, \ldots, s\} \setminus \{i\}} \delta_j^I$ and $c(p, v) = c_j^i(p, v) - \iota(p, v)$ for $p \in \mathsf{pow}(a_j)$ for some $a_j \in S_i$ and $c(p, v) = 0$ otherwise, for all $p \in \Pi$.*

We note that an agent $a_j \in S_i$ corresponds to a player $j \in \mathsf{N}_i$ in the induced Boolean game; there is a bijection between players and agents. Formula Δ_i models the information the players in N_i have about the possible behaviors of other organization units.

Example 7 (Induced Boolean games). We consider the STSs $\mathfrak{ST}_1$ and $\mathfrak{ST}_2$ from Example 6.

(a) $\mathfrak{ST}_1$ induces the Boolean game (with information) $(\mathsf{G}_1, \top)$ from Exp. 1(a).
(b) $\mathfrak{ST}_2$ induces the two Boolean games with information $G_{\mathfrak{ST}_2}(1) = (\mathsf{G}_{\{1\}}, p_2)$ and $G_{\mathfrak{ST}_2}(2) = (\mathsf{G}_{\{2,3\}}, p_1)$ presented in Example 1(b).

Note that both games are only equivalent to those introduced previously because the incentive schemes of the social systems are given by the constant function 0.

The *behavior* of an STS is the result of all combinations of all equilibria of the induced Boolean games with information. The idea is that the players in $G_{\mathfrak{ST}}(i)$ assume that the other players choose their actions consistently with Δ_i and that they try to maximize their utilities accordingly. It is important to note that players of some induced Boolean game—corresponding to agents of the same organization unit—usually have no *specific* information about the other players'

---

[3] In future work, we plan to use constrained Boolean games. Additionally, they allow to put constraints on the agents within an organization unit.

actions outside $G_{\mathfrak{ST}}(i)$; i.e., *how exactly* those players try to satisfy Δ_i. Thus, the system has multiple possible behaviors of which some can be desirable and others undesirable. In order to remove the undesirable ones, however, communication, cooperation, and appropriate control mechanisms are necessary. One such mechanism is incentive engineering discussed in Section 4.

Definition 9 (Behavior of an STS). *The $\mathcal{NE}$-behavior of $\mathfrak{ST}$, $\mathcal{B}_{\mathcal{NE}}(\mathfrak{ST})$, consists of all assignments $\xi : \Pi \to \mathbb{B}$ such that there are assignments $\xi^i \in \mathcal{NE}(G_{\mathfrak{ST}}(i))$ with $\xi|_{\mathsf{pow}(S_i)} = \xi^i$ for $i = 1, \ldots, s$.*

The organization cost of a specific assignment consists of two parts: the cost of the realization of the technical system and the incentives that have to be paid to the agents. The cost of the $\mathcal{NE}$-behavior of a STS is given by the cost of the most expensive $\mathcal{NE}$-behavior.

Definition 10 (Cost). *The organization cost of an assignment ξ in $\mathfrak{ST} = (\Pi, \mathcal{T}, T, \mathcal{S})$ is defined as $\mathsf{ocost}_{\mathfrak{ST}}(\xi) = \mathsf{tcost}(T) + \sum_{p \in \Pi} \iota(p, \xi(p))$. The $\mathcal{NE}$-behavioral cost of $\mathfrak{ST}$ is defined as $\mathsf{ocost}_{\mathfrak{ST}}^{\mathcal{NE}} = \max_{\xi \in \mathcal{B}_{\mathcal{NE}}(\mathfrak{ST})} \{\mathsf{ocost}_{\mathfrak{ST}}(\xi), \mathsf{tcost}(T)\}$.*

Example 8 (Nash behavior of an STS). The Nash behaviors of the STSs $\mathfrak{ST}_1$ and $\mathfrak{ST}_2$ can easily be computed using Example 3:

(a) $\mathfrak{ST}_1$ is constructed from a single organization unit. As a consequence, the behavior of the STS agrees with the Nash equilibria of its induced Boolean game with information. We have that $\mathcal{B}_{\mathcal{NE}}(\mathfrak{ST}_1) = \mathcal{NE}((G_1, \top)) = \emptyset$. This indicates that the STS $\mathfrak{ST}_1$ is *unstable*.

(b) The behavior of $\mathfrak{ST}_2$ is more complex. The STS consists of two organization units and their induced Boolean games with information $(G_{\{1\}}, p_2)$ and $(G_{\{2,3\}}, p_1)$, respectively. The behavior of the STS is the combination of the Nash equilibria of both games, which were determined in Example 3. We have that $\mathcal{B}_{\mathcal{NE}}(\mathfrak{ST}_2) = \{(\mathsf{t}, \mathsf{f}, \mathsf{t}, x, y) \mid x, y \in \{\mathsf{t}, \mathsf{f}\}\}$ where each tuple specifies the truth value of $(p_1, \ldots, p_5)$ and thus corresponds to a truth assignment of Ass_{Π}.

The behavior emerges from the behavior of the agents in an STS. What can be said about the behavior apart from stability? Of course, it would be desirable if the behavior satisfied the objectives of all organization units.

Definition 11 (Organizational effectivity). *We say that $\mathfrak{ST}$ is weakly (resp. strongly) organizationally $\mathcal{NE}$-effective iff we have that $\xi \models \delta_i$ for some $\xi \in \mathcal{B}_{\mathcal{NE}}(\mathfrak{ST})$ (resp. for all $\xi \in \mathcal{B}_{\mathcal{NE}}(\mathfrak{ST})$ and $\mathcal{B}_{\mathcal{NE}}(\mathfrak{ST}) \neq \emptyset$) and all $i = 1, \ldots, s$.*

The following result shows that organizational effectivity is a local property of the organization units.

Proposition 1. *$\mathfrak{ST}$ is weakly (resp. strongly) organizationally $\mathcal{NE}$-effective iff we have $\xi \models \delta_i$ for some $\xi \in \mathcal{NE}(G_{\mathfrak{ST}}(i))$ (resp. for all $\xi \in \mathcal{NE}(G_{\mathfrak{ST}}(i))$ and $\mathcal{NE}(G_{\mathfrak{ST}}(i) \neq \emptyset$) and for all $i = 1, \ldots, s$.*

3.3 Objectives and Confidentiality Constraints in STSs

In the previous section we introduced the behavior of an STS as the behavior emerging from the behaviors of the organization units. Which properties does the behavior satisfy and thus an STS enjoy? In the following we consider two different kinds of properties: (i) a *system objective* and (ii) a *confidentiality constraint*. The former specifies how an STS should (ideally) behave; it can represent the task/purpose of a system. The confidentiality constraint models which information is allowed to be passed within a system. For example, the designer may want to keep the (sub)objective ψ of an organization unit confidential. In this case the public organization objectives must not imply ψ.

Definition 12 (System specification). *A system objective Υ^o and a confidentiality constraint Υ^c over Π are propositional formulae over Π. The tuple (Υ^o, Υ^c) is called* system specification.

The system objective crucially depends on the agents' behaviors where the confidentiality constraint is mainly related to the public organization objectives. We distinguish two types of confidentiality constraints: *weak confidentiality* is provided by an STS if the public organization objectives do not imply the confidentiality constraint (i.e. there must be some assignments satisfying the public organization objectives and $\neg \Upsilon^c$); *strong confidentiality* takes into consideration the $\mathcal{NE}$-behaviors of an STS only. Similarly, we distinguish between *weak* and *strong implementation* of a system objective. In the weak setting, we require that there is *some* system behavior which satisfies the objective; its stronger variant requires this for *all* behaviors. Clearly, in the former case additional communication and/or coordination mechanisms are needed to ensure that a "good" behavior will actually emerge.

Definition 13. *Let $\mathfrak{ST} = (\Pi, \mathcal{T}, T, \mathcal{S})$ be an STS and (Υ^o, Υ^c) be a system specification. We say that:*

(a) *$\mathfrak{ST}$ ensures* weak confidentiality[4] *of Υ^c if $\bigwedge_{j \in \{1,\dots,s\}} \delta_j^I \wedge \neg \Upsilon^c$ is satisfiable.*

(b) *$\mathfrak{ST}$ ensures* strong confidentiality *of Υ^c if there is an assignment $\xi \in \mathcal{B}_{\mathcal{NE}}(\mathfrak{ST})$ with $\xi \models \bigwedge_{j \in \{1,\dots,s\}} \delta_j^I \wedge \neg \Upsilon^c$.*

(c) *$\mathfrak{ST}$ weakly implements Υ^o if there is an assignment $\xi \in \mathcal{B}_{\mathcal{NE}}(\mathfrak{ST})$ which satisfies Υ^o.*

(d) *$\mathfrak{ST}$ stronlgy implements Υ^o if all assignments $\xi \in \mathcal{B}_{\mathcal{NE}}(\mathfrak{ST})$ satisfy Υ^o and $\mathcal{B}_{\mathcal{NE}}(\mathfrak{ST}) \neq \emptyset$.*

Finally, we say that $\mathfrak{ST}$ ensures (Υ^o, Υ^c) if $\mathfrak{ST}$ ensures strong confidentiality of Υ^c and strongly implements Υ^o.

---

[4] We only consider the public part of the organization objective; alternatively, one could assume that all agents in an organization unit are aware of their actual (private) organization objective and of the public objectives of the other organization units. In this case, weak confidentiality would refer to the condition: for all $i = 1, \dots, s$ we have that $\delta_i \wedge \bigwedge_{j \in \{1,\dots,s\} \setminus \{i\}} \delta_j^I \wedge \neg \Upsilon^c$ is satisfiable.

Proposition 2. *If an STS ensures strong confidentiality of a confidentiality constraint then it also ensures weak confidentiality of the constraint. If an STS strongly implements a system specification then it also weakly implements the system specification.*

Example 9 (Confidentiality and implementation in STS). Let the system specification $\Upsilon^o = p_5 \wedge p_1 \wedge ((p_2 \wedge p_3) \vee p_4)$ and the confidentiality constraint $\Upsilon^c = p_1 \wedge p_2$ be given. We consider the STSs $\mathfrak{ST}_1$ and $\mathfrak{ST}_2$ of Example 6.

(a) $\mathfrak{ST}_1$ neither weakly nor strongly implements Υ^o. The STS ensures weak confidentiality of Υ^c because $\top \wedge \neg(p_1 \wedge p_2)$ is satisfiable. Strong confidentiality is not ensured because $\mathcal{B}_{\mathcal{NE}}(\mathfrak{ST}_1) = \emptyset$.

(b) $\mathfrak{ST}_2$ weakly implements Υ^o, which is witnessed by the behavior $(\mathsf{t}, \mathsf{f}, \mathsf{t}, \mathsf{t}, \mathsf{t}) \in \mathcal{B}_{\mathcal{NE}}(\mathfrak{ST}_2)$ but not strongly, which is e.g. witnessed by $(\mathsf{t}, \mathsf{f}, \mathsf{t}, \mathsf{f}, \mathsf{f}) \not\models \Upsilon^o$ and $(\mathsf{t}, \mathsf{f}, \mathsf{t}, \mathsf{f}, \mathsf{f}) \in \mathcal{B}_{\mathcal{NE}}(\mathfrak{ST}_2)$. $\mathfrak{ST}_2$ does neither ensure weak nor strong confidentiality of Υ^c because $p_1 \wedge p_2 \wedge \neg(p_1 \wedge p_2)$ is not satisfiable.

4   Designing Good STSs: Incentive Engineering

The formal framework allows to pose interesting questions, for example: Is there an STS that weakly/strongly implements a system objective and ensures weak/strong confidentiality of a confidentiality constraint? Is there a social system which is consistent with a given technical system such that the resulting STS weakly/strongly implements a system objective and ensures weak/strong confidentiality of a confidentiality constraint? Is there a technical system for a given social system such that the previous properties are satisfied? Given an STS and a system specification, how to incentivize agents such that the system specification is ensured?

In Example 9 we have seen that the STS $\mathfrak{ST}_2$ neither strongly implements system specification Υ^o nor does it ensure weak confidentiality of Υ^c. Thus, if the STS were designed to ensure the system specification (Υ^o, Υ^c) it would miss its aim. Is there a better STS? Firstly, we observe that the public organization objectives $\delta_1^I = p_1$ and $\delta_2^I = p_2$ of organization units S_1 and S_2, respectively, never ensure the confidentiality constraint $\Upsilon^c = p_1 \wedge p_2$ (we are still considering Example 9). However, these public objectives are needed to coordinate the two organization units S_1 and S_2 to achieve stability. Suppose that the public organization objective of S_2 was $\delta_2^I = \top$ instead. Then weak confidentiality of Υ^c would be ensured in the resulting STS as $p_1 \wedge \top \wedge \neg(p_1 \wedge p_2)$ is satisfiable. This change, however, affects the behavior of the agents in organization unit S_1 as they no longer have specific information about organization unit S_2. The unique Nash equilibrium in the induced Boolean game with information, which is now $(\mathsf{G}_{\{1\}}, \top)$, is given by (f): player 1 cannot satisfy its goal—as both truth values of p_2 must be considered possible—and the cost of setting p_1 to false is smaller than for setting p_1 to true. As a consequence, the modified STS does not anymore weakly implement the system objective Υ^o. In order to achieve both—implementation of the system objective and the ensuring of the confidentiality constraint—the STS can provide an incentive to player 1 to set p_1 to true. This is called *incentive engineering* and has been studied in [23]. Note that here, we consider incentives as payoffs given to the players rather than taxes imposed on them. The next example illustrates incentive engineering in the context of STSs.

Example 10 (Incentive egineering). Firstly, in line with the previous discussion we modify the social system $\mathcal{S}_2$ from Example 5 as follows:

$$\mathcal{S}_3 = (\mathsf{Agt}, \mathsf{pow}, (\{a_1\}, p_1, p_1), (\{a_2, a_3\}, p_5 \wedge ((p_2 \wedge p_3) \vee p_4), \top), \iota')$$

where the incentive scheme ι' is defined by $\iota'(p_1, \mathsf{t}) = \iota'(p_4, \mathsf{t}) = \iota'(p_5, \mathsf{t}) = 2$, and $\iota'(p, \mathsf{t}) = \iota'(p, \mathsf{f}) = 0$ on all other inputs. Let $\mathfrak{ST}_3$ denote the STS $(\Pi, \mathcal{T}_1, \mathcal{T}_2, \mathcal{S}_3)$. We have that $\mathcal{NE}(\mathsf{G}_{\mathfrak{ST}_3}(1)) = \{(\mathsf{t})\}$. To see this, we first observe that player 1 cannot guarantee its objective (as discussed above), with neither assignment of p_1 given the public objective $\delta_2^I = \top$. Consequently, player 1 chooses its cheapest action which is now setting p_1 to true, as $c(p_1, \mathsf{t}) = 1 - 2 = -1 < 0 = 0 - 0 = c(p_1, \mathsf{f})$ due to the new incentive scheme ι'.

Similarly, we have $\mathcal{NE}(\mathsf{G}_{\mathfrak{ST}_3}(2)) = \{(\mathsf{f}, \mathsf{t}, \mathsf{t}, \mathsf{t})\}$. Players 2 and 3 have the information $\delta_1^I = p_1$, i.e. player 1 will make p_1 true. Player 2 will make p_2 false to satisfy its objective γ_2, and player 3 will make p_3 true. Both players believe that player 1 makes p_1 true, as $\delta_1^I = p_1$. Variables p_4 and p_5 do not affect the truth of the players' objectives. Hence, players 2 and 3 will choose the cheaper action which means to set p_4 and p_5 true, given the incentive scheme ι'. Combining the Nash equilibria of both induced Boolean games yields a unique Nash behavior of $\mathfrak{ST}_3$ which is: $\mathcal{B}_{\mathcal{NE}}(\mathfrak{ST}_3) = \{(\mathsf{t}, \mathsf{f}, \mathsf{t}, \mathsf{t}, \mathsf{t})\}$.

We observe that the STS $\mathfrak{ST}_3$ ensures strong confidentiality of $\Upsilon^c = p_1 \wedge p_2$, because $(\mathsf{t}, \mathsf{f}, \mathsf{t}, \mathsf{t}, \mathsf{t}) \models p_1 \wedge \top \wedge \neg(p_1 \wedge p_2)$ and strongly implements $\Upsilon^o = p_5 \wedge p_1 \wedge ((p_2 \wedge p_3) \vee p_4)$. However, this positive result has its price: the *cost* of $\mathfrak{ST}_3$ is $\mathsf{ocost}_{\mathfrak{ST}_3}^{\mathcal{NE}} = 3 + 6 = 9$ (costs of the technical system plus the costs of the paid incentives). In comparison, the cost of $\mathfrak{ST}_2$ is only 3 as $\iota \equiv 0$.

A key problem in STSs is the joint optimization of the social and technical system. Incentives provide just one way to optimize an STS. Also, they cannot be used to implement all system objectives; this follows from [23, Proposition 8]. A reorganization of the organization units, however, *can stabilize* an STS, even if this cannot be achieved by the standard use of incentives as illustrated next.

Example 11 (Stabilizing an STS). By [23, Proposition 8] the STS $\mathfrak{ST}_1$ from Example 8(a) cannot be stabilized: the conjunction of the goals of both players $\gamma_1 \wedge \gamma_2 = ((p_1 \wedge p_2) \vee (\neg p_1 \wedge \neg p_2)) \wedge ((\neg p_1 \wedge p_2) \vee (\neg p_2 \wedge p_1))$ is not satisfiable, and for all assignments one of the players can deviate to achieve its goal. Thus, the Boolean game $\mathsf{G}_1 \oplus \iota$ does not have Nash equilibria for any incentive scheme ι; the behavior of $\mathfrak{ST}_1$ is empty. However, if we modify the technical system and use $\mathfrak{ST}_2$ instead of $\mathfrak{ST}_1$ we can guarantee a $\mathcal{NE}$-behavior, as shown in Exp. 9(b).

Some Characterization Results. A natural question to pose is whether the incentive scheme of an STS can be modified in such a way that it implements a system objective, ensures confidentiality and organizational efficiency. Therefore, given an STS $\mathfrak{ST}$ and an incentive scheme ι we denote by $\mathfrak{ST} \oplus \iota$ the STS which equals $\mathfrak{ST}$ but the incentive scheme of which is replaced by ι. In the following we characterize a sufficient and necessary condition for the existence of an appropriate incentive scheme. We make use of quantified Boolean formulae. A quantified Boolean formula (QBF) [17] allows to quantify (existentially and universally) over truth values of propositional variables. For example, the QBF $\exists x \forall y (x \rightarrow y)$ expresses that there is a truth value $t_x \in \mathbb{B}$ of x such that for all truth values $t_y \in \mathbb{B}$ of y, "t_x implies t_y". The formula $\exists x \varphi$ is a compact representation of $\varphi[x = \top] \vee \varphi[x = \bot]$ where $\varphi[x = v]$ equals φ but each free occurrence of x is replaced by $v \in \{\top, \bot\}$; and analogously for $\forall x \varphi$.

Remark 1 (Quantified Boolean formulae). Let $X = \{x_1, \ldots, x_n\}$ be a set of variables. We write $QX\varphi$ for $Qx_1 \ldots Qx_n\varphi$ where $Q \in \{\forall, \exists\}$. Then, a formula $\exists X\varphi$ is QBF-satisfiable if there is a truth assignment ξ of the variables in X such that $\varphi[\xi]$ is satisfiable, where $\varphi[\xi]$ is the QBF equivalent to φ but each free occurrence of a variable $x \in X$ in φ is replaced by $\bot$ (resp. $\top$) if $\xi(x) = \mathsf{f}$ (resp. $\xi(x) = \mathsf{t}$); and analogously for more complex QBF. We note that $\varphi[\xi]$ can still contain variables. The QBF-satisfiability and QBF-validity problems are **PSPACE**-complete; for more details on QBF we refer e.g. to [17].

The authors of [23] have analysed when a Boolean game can be stabilized by incentive/taxation schemes (stabilization problem). Lemma 1 represents an analogous result for constraint Boolean games. In contrast to (standard) Boolean games we have to take into consideration the global constraint φ and the fact that not all variables are necessarily controlled by players, i.e. whenever $\Pi_0 \neq \emptyset$. Before we state our lemma we consider the QBF

$$\Theta_i^Y = (\exists \Pi_i (\exists Y(\varphi) \wedge \forall Y(\varphi \rightarrow \gamma_i))) \rightarrow (\exists Y(\varphi) \wedge \forall Y(\varphi \rightarrow \gamma_i))$$

where $i \in \mathsf{N}$, $Y \subseteq \Pi$, and Π_i is the set of variables controlled by player i. (In the following, recall the notation from Section 2.1.) For now, we are interested in instantiations of the form $\Theta_i^{\Pi_0}$. We observe that the variables in Π_i occur potentially unbound (i.e. free) in φ as well as in γ_i on the right-hand side of the implication. We consider the formula $\bigwedge_{i \in \mathsf{N}} \Theta_i^{\Pi_0}$ and assume that ξ is a satisfying Π-assignment (observe that $\xi|_{\Pi_0}$ can be seen as irrelevant as no variables from Π_0 occur free). Then, ξ defines an "action" $\xi|_{\Pi_i}$ for each player i. Each conjunct $\Theta_i^{\Pi_0}$ encodes that $\xi|_{\Pi_i}$ is a best response to the other players' actions defined by ξ, i.e. player i has no incentive to unilaterally deviate from $\xi|_{\Pi_i}$. Following the definition of worst case utility given in Section 2.3, the premise of $\Theta_i^{\Pi_0}$, $\exists \Pi_i (\exists \Pi_0(\varphi) \wedge \forall \Pi_0(\varphi \rightarrow \gamma_i)))$, expresses that player i can deviate from $\xi|_{\Pi_i}$ to $\xi_i \in \mathsf{Ass}_{\Pi_i}$ (existential quantification over Π_i) such that $\varphi[\xi|_{\widehat{\Pi} \setminus \Pi_i} \circ \xi_i]$ is satisfiable (subformula $\exists \Pi_0(\varphi)$), and all assignments $\xi_0 \in \mathsf{Ass}_{\Pi_0}$ of the environmental variables that yield, together with the players' actions, a φ-consistent assignment $\xi|_{\widehat{\Pi} \setminus \Pi_i} \circ \xi_i \circ \xi_0$ satisfy i's goal (subformula $\forall \Pi_0(\varphi \rightarrow \gamma_i)$). The conclusion of $\Theta_i^{\Pi_0}$ expresses that $\xi|_{\widehat{\Pi}}$ allows for a φ-consistent assignment (the part $\exists \Pi_0(\varphi)$) and ensures that i's goal will be satisfied for all φ-consistent assignments extending

$\xi|_{\widehat{\Pi}}$. As this reasoning holds for every player, ξ is a Nash equilibrium. This is formally stated in the following Lemma, which can be proved similarly to [23].

Lemma 1. *Let* $\mathsf{G} = (\mathsf{N}, \Pi, (\gamma_j)_{j \in \mathsf{N}}, (\Pi_j)_{j \in \mathsf{N}}, \varphi)$ *be a constrained Boolean game. Then,* $\Gamma = \bigwedge_{i \in \mathsf{N}} \Theta_i^{\Pi_0}$ *is QBF-satisfiable iff there is an incentive scheme* ι *such that* $\mathcal{NE}(\mathsf{G} \oplus \iota) \neq \emptyset$.

Proof (Sketch). First, we observe that the formula Γ is true iff there is a $\xi \in \mathsf{Ass}_{\Pi}$ such that for each player $i \in \mathsf{N} = \{1, \ldots, k\}$, if there is a $\xi_i \in \mathsf{Ass}_{\Pi_i}$ such that $\varphi[\xi|_{\widehat{\Pi} \backslash \Pi_i} \circ \xi_i]$ is satisfiable and for all $\xi_0 \in \mathsf{Ass}_{\Pi_0}$ we have that $\xi|_{\widehat{\Pi} \backslash \Pi_i} \circ \xi_i \circ \xi_0 \models \varphi \to \gamma_i$, then $\varphi[\xi|_{\widehat{\Pi}}]$ is satisfiable and for all $\xi_0 \in \mathsf{Ass}_{\Pi_0}$, $\xi|_{\widehat{\Pi}} \circ \xi_0 \models \varphi \to \gamma_i$. We sketch the proof of the lemma. "$\Rightarrow$": Let ξ be a satisfying truth assignment of Γ. Following the argumentation above no agent i can deviate from $\xi|_{\Pi_i}$ to enforce its goal if not already satisfied by ξ (modulo the subtleties of φ-consistent assignments). Thus, one can define an incentive scheme ι such that each player i chooses the action/assignment $\xi|_{\Pi_i}$. Then, no agent i would deviate from $\xi|_{\Pi_i}$ and $\xi|_{\Pi_1} \circ \cdots \circ \xi|_{\Pi_k} \in \mathcal{NE}(\mathsf{G} \oplus \iota)$. "$\Leftarrow$": Suppose $\xi \in \mathcal{NE}(\mathsf{G} \oplus \iota)$. Then, no player can deviate to obtain a better outcome; in particular, no player with an unsatisfied objective can choose different actions to satisfy it (again, modulo the subtleties of φ-consistent assignments). It follows that the QBF is true under the assignment $\xi \circ \xi_0$ for an arbitrary $\xi_0 \in \mathsf{Ass}_{\Pi_0}$. $\square$

Next we apply the result of Lemma 1 to the STS setting. $\mathcal{NE}$-effectivity requires that each Nash equilibrium satisfies the objectives of the organisation units. The analog for Boolean games, the *weak implementation problem*, is investigated in [23]. It is the case that the formula $\bigwedge_{i \in \mathsf{N}} \Theta_i^{\Pi_0} \wedge \psi$ is QBF-satisfiable iff there is a Nash equilibrium ξ which satisfies ψ. Hence, for a given organization unit S_i with organization objective δ_i and $Y_i = \Pi \backslash \mathsf{pow}(S_i)$, the formula $\bigwedge_{a_j \in S_i} \Theta_j^{Y_i} \wedge \delta_i$ expresses that the induced Boolean game with information $G_{\mathfrak{ST}}(i)$ has a Nash equilibrium which satisfies δ_i. With this observation we can characterize whether an STS can be stabilized in such a way that there is a behavior which is organizationally $\mathcal{NE}$-effective.

Proposition 3. *There is an incentive scheme* ι *such that* $\mathfrak{ST} \oplus \iota$ *with organization units* $S_1, \ldots, S_s$ *is organizationally* $\mathcal{NE}$-*effective iff* $\bigwedge_{i=1,\ldots,s} (\bigwedge_{a_j \in S_i} \Theta_j^{Y_i} \wedge \delta_i)$ *is QBF-satisfiable where* δ_i *is the objective of organization unit* S_i *and* $Y_i = \Pi \backslash \mathsf{pow}(S_i)$ *for* $i = 1, \ldots, s$.

Proof (Sketch). By Proposition 1 the satisfaction of an organization constraint δ_i only depends on the variables $\mathsf{pow}(S_i)$. Hence, the satisfaction of δ_i is independent of the other organization objectives. The same holds for $\Theta_j^{Y_i}$. Applying the same reasoning as in Lemma 1, we have that for each satisfying assignment ξ_i of $\bigwedge_{a_j \in S_i} \Theta_j^{Y_i} \wedge \delta_i$, it holds that $\xi_i \in \mathcal{NE}(\mathsf{G}_{\mathfrak{ST}}(i) \oplus \iota)$ and $\xi_i \models \delta_i$. The opposite direction holds analogously. Then, the claim follows from Proposition 1. $\square$

Finally, we can use the previous results to obtain a characterization of the existence of an incentive scheme that allows a Nash behavior which is weakly organizationally $\mathcal{NE}$-effective, weakly implements a system specification, and ensures weak confidentiality.

Theorem 1. *Let (Υ^o, Υ^c) be a system specification and $\mathfrak{ST}$ an STS with organization units $S_1, \ldots, S_s$. There is an incentive scheme ι for $\mathfrak{ST}$ such that $\mathfrak{ST} \oplus \iota$ is weakly organizationally $\mathcal{NE}$-effective, weakly implements Υ^o and ensures weak confidentiality of Υ^c, each of these properties wrt. the same assignment $\xi \in \mathcal{B}_{\mathcal{NE}}(\mathfrak{ST} \oplus \iota)$, iff $\exists \Pi \left(\bigwedge_{j \in \{1, \ldots, s\}} \delta_j^I \wedge \neg \Upsilon^c \right) \wedge \Upsilon^o \wedge \left(\bigwedge_{i=1, \ldots, s} (\bigwedge_{a_j \in S_i} \Theta_j^{Y_i} \wedge \delta_i) \right)$ is QBF-satisfiable.*

Proof (Sketch). Let $\mathsf{N} = \{1, \ldots, k\}$. "$\Leftarrow$": Let $\xi = \xi|_{\Pi_1} \circ \cdots \circ \xi|_{\Pi_k}$ be a satisfying truth assignment. By Proposition 3 and by defining an incentive scheme ι analogously to Lemma 1, $\mathfrak{ST}$ is organizationally $\mathcal{NE}$-effective. Then, by Definition 9, $\xi \in \mathcal{B}_{\mathcal{NE}}(\mathfrak{ST} \oplus \iota)$. Straightforwardly, weak implementability of Υ^o follows. Weak confidentiality holds as there is some truth assignments which satisfies $\bigwedge_{j \in \{1, \ldots, s\}} \delta_j^I \wedge \neg \Upsilon^c$. "$\Rightarrow$": Follows analogously to the reasoning of Lemma 1.   □

5   Related Work

The authors of [18] model STSs as multi-agent systems. They use an ontology to address agent interoperability. The focus is on knowledge representation and how agents' knowledge can be merged. Our work focusses on the strategic behavior of the agents and on analysing stability of the emerging behavior of STSs. In [15,2,12] the design of STSs is considered from a software engineering perspective. The authors of [9] argue that a system perspective and an agent perspective should be used alongside; our formal model somehow includes both perspectives (the optimization of the technical system and the equilibrium analysis wrt. the social system). [8] proposes an architecture of STSs that allows the system to adapt to changing situations. Norms to govern STSs were proposed in [20]; in particular, the author considers an STS as multi-stakeholder system consisting of autonomous entities which are not necessarily controlled by a single organization. Formal tools for specifying and verifying STSs are investigated in [7]; a strategic dimension and stable points are not considered in that work. The authors of [19] analyze causality, complexity and the modeling of STSs on a rather informal level. In our approach some of these ideas are formally modeled by Boolean games, in particular the strategic dimension and the decomposition into smaller parts (organization units). We try to find good configurations of STSs that satisfy a system specification. This is related to [4] where a planning-based process is used to explore different configurations of STSs, in particular it is considered how objectives can be delegated to agents. The authors also briefly discuss system stability from a game theoretical point of view, which is related to the work we propose here. Our model, however, is more abstract and focusses on steady states of strategic interactions. In recent years, much work has been directed towards Boolean games [10,11,3,14], some of which underlies our modeling. A key question is whether a game has a *stable solution*, for example whether the core is non-empty or whether the game has a stable set [10].

In [11] taxation schemes are proposed to incentivize or disincentives agents to execute specific actions in order to change the set of equilibria. Communication of truth values [13] and verifiability of equilibria [1] are further proposals to stabilize Boolean games. Here, we use three different techniques to stabilize STSs: firstly, incentive schemes as proposed in [23]; secondly, public organization objectives which influence the behavior of agents, this is related to [13]; and thirdly, different technical systems are used to impose constraints on the cooperation and communication capabilities of agents[5]. This is motivated by the observation that "to a large extent, the underlying organization model is responsible for how efficiently and effectively organizations carry out their tasks" [16, page 2]. Note, that the former two approaches do not restrict the agents' autonomy where the third one affects autonomy by constraining the physical infrastructure.

6   Conclusions

In this paper we proposed a formal modeling of socio-technical systems (STSs). The technical part of an STS defines, e.g., the physical infrastructure and the technical units. The social part frames the organization units, agents, and their social relationships. The behavior of an STS emerges from the behaviors of the organization units which are modeled as Boolean games with information—an extension of the Boolean game model. Private and public organization objectives, which are announced by each organization unit, are used to coordinate the behavior of the otherwise independent parts of the system. Furthermore, we introduced system objectives and confidentiality constraints to specify properties that an STS should ensure and information that should not be disclosed to the public, respectively. We used different mechanisms to ensure them and to stabilize the behavior of the system: incentive schemes to influence the behavior within an organization unit; public organization objectives to coordinate the behavior on the inter-organization level, and technical constraints to foster and to suppress cooperation among agents. Finally, we presented some first characterization results about the existence of appropriate incentive schemes in order to stabilize an STS and to ensure a given system specification.

Future Work. The focus of this paper was to propose a formal modeling of STSs. We also gave first characterization results. In our future work we plan to elaborate on these characterization results and to analyze the computational complexity. Also, there are many open question wrt. implementability and optimality, some of which were already stated in Section 4. In particular, the effect of changes in the underlying technical system wrt. the system behavior is left for future work. Furthermore, apart from non-cooperative solution concepts we would like to investigate cooperative solution concepts; thus, assuming that members of the same organization unit are cooperative. One could also constrain the behavior of players by constrained Boolean games to achieve stability.

---

[5] This also relates to a discussion at [5]: It was discussed to extend cooperative games with normative constraints restricting the coalitions that are allowed to deviate from a given action profile wrt. the CORE solution concept.

A computational complexity analysis is left for future work as well. Also the connection to mechanism design and non-truthful information disclosure seems to be promising avenue for future work.

References

1. Ågotnes, T., Harrenstein, P., Van Der Hoek, W., Wooldridge, M.: Verifiable equilibria in boolean games. In: Proceedings of the Twenty-Third International Joint Conference on Artificial Intelligence, pp. 689–695. AAAI Press (2013)
2. Baxter, G., Sommerville, I.: Socio-technical systems: From design methods to systems engineering. Interacting with Computers 23(1), 4–17 (2011)
3. Bonzon, E., Lagasquie-Schiex, M.-C., Lang, J., Zanuttini, B.: Boolean games revisited. In: ECAI, pp. 265–269 (2006)
4. Bryl, V., Giorgini, P., Mylopoulos, J.: Designing socio-technical systems: from stakeholder goals to social networks. Requirements Engineering 14(1), 47–70 (2009)
5. Bulling, N., Dastani, M., Grossi, D., Harrenstein, P., Knobbout, M., Tamminga, A., van der Hoek, W., Zaluski, W.: NorMAS Workshop, Working Group "Norms and Game Theory", Leiden, NL (August 2013), http://www.lorentzcenter.nl/lc/web/2013/585/extra.pdf
6. Bulling, N., Ghosh, S., Verbrugge, R.: Reaching your goals without spilling the beans: Boolean secrecy games. In: Boella, G., Elkind, E., Savarimuthu, B.T.R., Dignum, F., Purvis, M.K. (eds.) PRIMA 2013. LNCS, vol. 8291, pp. 37–53. Springer, Heidelberg (2013)
7. Coronato, A., De Florio, V., Bakhouya, M.: Formal modeling of socio-technical collective adaptive systems. In: 2012 IEEE Sixth International Conference on Self-Adaptive and Self-Organizing Systems Workshops (SASOW), pp. 187–192. IEEE (2012)
8. Dalpiaz, F., Giorgini, P., Mylopoulos, J.: Adaptive socio-technical systems: a requirements-based approach. Requirements Engineering 18(1), 1–24 (2013)
9. De Bruijn, H., Herder, P.M.: System and actor perspectives on sociotechnical systems. IEEE Transactions on Systems, Man and Cybernetics, Part A: Systems and Humans 39(5), 981–992 (2009)
10. Dunne, van der Hoek, P.E., Kraus, W.S., Wooldridge, M.: Cooperative boolean games. In: Padgham, L., Parkes, D.C., Müller, J.P., Parsons, S. (eds.) AAMAS, vol. (2), pp. 1015–1022. IFAAMAS (2008)
11. Endriss, U., Kraus, S., Lang, J., Wooldridge, M.: Designing incentives for boolean games. In: Sonenberg, L., Stone, P., Tumer, K., Yolum, P. (eds.) AAMAS, pp. 79–86. IFAAMAS (2011)
12. Fischer, G., Herrmann, T.: Socio-technical systems: a meta-design perspective. International Journal of Sociotechnology and Knowledge Development (IJSKD) 3(1), 1–33 (2011)
13. Grant, J., Kraus, S., Wooldridge, M., Zuckerman, I.: Manipulating games by sharing information. Studia Logica 102(2), 267–295 (2014)
14. Harrenstein, P., van der Hoek, W., Meyer, J.-J., Witteveen, C.: Boolean games. In: Proceedings of the 8th Conference on Theoretical Aspects of Rationality and Knowledge, pp. 287–298. Morgan Kaufmann Publishers Inc. (2001)
15. Jones, A.J., Artikis, A., PittThe, J.: design of intelligent socio-technical systems. Artificial Intelligence Review 39(1), 5–20 (2013)

16. Jonker, C.M., Sharpanskykh, A., Treur, J., Yolum, P.: A framework for formal modeling and analysis of organizations. Applied Intelligence 27(1), 49–66 (2007)
17. Papadimitriou, C.H.: Computational Complexity. Addison-Wesley, Reading (1994)
18. Porello, D., Setti, F., Ferrario, R., Cristani, M.: Multiagent socio-technical systems. An ontological approach
19. Rouse, W.B., Serban, N.: Understanding change in complex socio-technical systems. Information, Knowledge, Systems Management 10(1), 25–49 (2011)
20. Singh, M.P.: Norms as a basis for governing sociotechnical systems. ACM Transactions on Intelligent Systems and Technology (TIST), 1–21 (2013)
21. Trist, E.L., Bamforth, K.W.: Some social and psychological consequences of the longwall method. Human Relations 4, 3–38 (1951)
22. Wooldridge, M.: An Introduction to Multi Agent Systems. John Wiley & Sons (2002)
23. Wooldridge, M., Endriss, U., Kraus, S., Lang, J.: Incentive engineering for boolean games. Artificial Intelligence 195, 418–439 (2013)

Evaluating Strategies for Penny Auctions Using Multi-Agent Systems

Fabian Lorig, Matthias Gräf, Steffen Walter, and Ingo J. Timm

University of Trier, Business Informatics 1, 54296 Trier, Germany
{lorigf,s4magrae,s4stwalt,itimm}@uni-trier.de
http://wi1.uni-trier.de

Abstract. During the last years, all-pay auctions have been established as a new type of online auctions. They differ from common auctions like eBay, as making a fee-based tender will increase the remaining auction time slightly and the item's price by only a single cent. These so called penny auctions end when the auction time expires resulting in the majority of the bidders losing their stake.

However, various countries considered this trend to be dangerous due to its uncertain outcome, hence, providing penny auctions has been prohibited. Furthermore, the question whether all-pay auctions must be assumed being gambling games has been discussed by scientists as well. For matching different argumentations concerning empirical evidence and statistics we propose an approach of using multi-agent systems for evaluating penny auctions. By using software agents for the representation of competing bidders pursuing different strategies, the simulation of distinct scenarios for identifying potentially dominant strategies is provided.

1 Introduction

Entertainment shopping has gained popularity during the last years. It comprises different ways of selling goods and simultaneously provides amusement to the interacting customers. All-pay auctions, especially penny auctions, are associated to this trend. In contrast to conventional auction platforms like eBay[1] the goods being sold by all-pay auctions are offered by the platform provider itself. Hence, the entire income earned will remain in the providing company. The incentive for participating in this type of online auctions is the customer's possibility to purchase the goods offered far below market price.

Especially penny auctions grew in popularity as each bid increases the buying price by only one cent. Hereby, certainly electrical goods can be purchased for very low prices. Auctions selling tablet computers or smart phones with market values above 600\$ are frequently being sold for less than 30\$. This is possible, as the participant has to pay bidding-fees each time he/she makes a tender or purchase bids prior to bidding. Additionally, the remaining auction time will be increased by a small amount of time, mostly between five to ten seconds, when

---

[1] http://www.ebay.com/

J.P. Müller, M. Weyrich, and A.L.C. Bazzan (Eds.): MATES 2014, LNAI 8732, pp. 26–40, 2014.

a tender is made. The highest bidder, who makes the last bid before the auction time runs out, receives the good for the price he bid.

Penny auctions provide the possibility of huge discounts compared to the product's market price. However, on the other hand the risk of loss increases as well, because the fees paid for unsuccessful bids will not be refunded. This leads to the situation, that the highest bidder receives a considerable discount whereas the other participants sustain a loss. Furthermore, due to the bidding-fees mentioned, a selling price of less than 90% of the good's market price will still result in a profit margin for the vendor.[9]

Therefore, penny auctions have become a controversial issue and countries like Switzerland have already forbidden this type of online auctions.[2] As statement of grounds, this sales strategy has been declared as illegal gambling. Also scientific studies support this notion confirming that the outcome of a penny auction is unpredictable.[5] Apart from that other studies conclude the existence of bidding strategies increasing the probability of success.[10] The findings considering profits, selling prices and strategies of the listed studies were mainly based on empirical observations of real online auction platforms. Because of that, the researchers were not able to influence the parameters, e.g. the number of participants or the strategies chosen. Thus, a profound consideration regarding a variety of scenarios was not possible.[7,13]

According to the *Treaty on Gambling Industry in Germany*^{2}[4] gambling games are defined by the following basic conditions:

- The chance of winning must be acquired by purchase
- The winning decision must (mainly) depend on luck or the uncertain occurrence or outcome of future events
- Betting for money on the occurrence or outcome of future events

Consequently, for being able to judge if penny auctions meet the requirements for illegal gambling, a method for evaluating whether luck mainly influences the result of these auctions needs to be outlined.

The use of simulation for evaluating bidding strategies and optimizing sellers revenues in online auctions is an established approach.[1,3] Also, different algorithmic bidding strategies for high-valued items in penny auctions have been designed. However, this has been done using descriptive statistics not considering the bidder himself.[10] The suitableness of intelligent agents for evaluating bidding strategies in penny auctions has been regarded by Storch, using machine learning techniques for end-of-auction prediction.[11] Furthermore, different approaches applying agent-based simulation for reconstructing online auctions have been published as well.[6,8]

Yet, a differentiated agent-based consideration of bidding strategies and scenarios, especially in the context of penny auctions, was not provided. For that reason, we propose the use of multi-agent systems for the conception and implementation of an artificial penny auction platform. By providing the possibility to apply individual strategies and to let participants, represented by software

---

^{2} Staatsvertrag zum Glücksspielwesen in Deutschland (GlüStV).

agents, compete against each other, a variety of scenarios can be evaluated. Furthermore, a variety of strategies can be examined in different artificial environments in order to identify dominant strategies.

This paper is structured as follows: First, the concept of the system being developed will be described. Afterwards, different bidding strategies being considered within this work are explained. How the system has been implemented is described in chapter 4 and followed by the presentation of the simulation's results. In a final step the results will be discussed and prospects will be shown.

2   Concept

The penny auction platform is designed as a multi-agent system, where every participant will be represented by a single software-agent. This approach facilitates the implementation of autonomous bidders using certain strategies regardless of their opponents. In order to coordinate the simulated auctions, a master agent is in charge of the entire system's communication.

There are six different product groups being offered, each of them containing four distinct goods. An extract of the product overview is listed in table 1. The product groups have been chosen in regard to different price categories, starting with cheap movie DVDs and ending with expensive tablet computers. As this paper focuses the evaluation of bidding strategies, the way these products are used is not considered any further. The market prices stated have been determined using common prices being offered by online stores.[3]

Within each product group a matrix represents the similarity of the items being offered. Thus, heterogenous groups of bidders being interested in certain goods can be created, as most of the offered goods are very likely. Furthermore, the same item can be auctioned a predefined number of times. This enables the participants to adjust their *Independent Private Value (IPV)*, the individual amout of money a bidder is willed to spend on a certain good, as the availability of an item decreases. The system prohibits the auction sale of two items of the same product group at the same time, precisely as the original system does. Finally, each of the bidding agents maintains a list of items, which have not been auctioned yet, similar to the preview of the upcoming offers.

The bidding agents make bids while the sum of their invested bidding costs and cost for the next bid does not exceed their IPV for the current product. A participant's IPV is calculated by using a random distribution including an expected value of approximately 80% of the product's market value. We assume that people attending penny auctions are unwilling to pay the market price and therefore have a lower IPV compared to the regular price. The IPVs of the same product group's remaining items are set by using the product matrix and the IPV of the participant's favored item. This entails that each agent desires one product of every product group, but also makes bids on similar products up to a comparatively lower monetary value.

---

[3] The prices were determined during October 2012.

Table 1. Extract of the item list separated by product categories

Product Group	Item	Market Price
Tablet Computers	Apple IPad 3	579
	Sony Xperia Tablet	499
	Samsung Galaxy Tab	419
	Microsoft Surface	679
Video Game Consoles	Play Station 3	249
	Xbox 360	219
	Nintendo Wii U	299
	Nintendo Wii	99
Smartphones	Samsung Galaxy S3	437
	HTC One XL	495
	Apple iPhone 5	699
	Samsung Galaxy Nexus	299
Movies (Blu Ray)	The Dark Knight Rises	15
	The Dark Knight	12
	Ted	15
	The Intouchables	13

In case an agent purchased his favored item, he wont bid on items of the same product group any longer. We assume the desire for buying two identical or similar items does not exist. In addition, the probability of an agent not participating in an auction for a single item of a product group during the complete simulation run can be set as well. Moreover, every agent uses a particular strategy, which is set at the beginning of a simulation run. The different strategies will be explained in chapter 3.

On real auction platforms the bidding-fees vary between 50 and 75 cents. Every bid increases the final buying price by one cent and the remaining auction time is extended by up to 15 seconds. Due to performance issues the total length of auctions is restricted within the simulation system. Additionally, the bidding-fee is set to 75 cents increasing the product's value by 10 cents and the auction time is extended by up to five seconds. This adjustment is made for increasing the system's performance by reaching the participant's IPVs faster. Besides, the budget of the bidding agents is unlimited by default. The settings and assumptions were determined in respect of the issues which shall be addressed by the simulation platform. The factors for evaluating strategical bidding behaviors were focused.

Moreover, the design of the system enables human bidders to actively participate in the auctions using a graphical user interface. The human actor is represented by an additional agent inside the system, which processes the given input. This feature is just used for monitoring purposes within the scope of this work.

Furthermore, the master agent is responsible for the documentation of the auction process. Every auction's data are stored for evaluation purposes including a list of all bidders who made a proper bid, an overview of all IPVs and every registered agent's amount of invested money. In addition, for every simulation run the results of all single agents are saved. This includes important key values like bidding costs, invested amount, return on investment (ROI), amount of auctioned items, value of goods and profit.

3   Strategies

The goal of the simulation is to examine different strategies in penny auctions in terms of their probability of success. The eight strategies examined in this paper can be divided into three sub-groups which will be discussed in the following chapter. In order to compare those strategies two random-based strategies are used as reference strategies.

3.1   Random-Based Strategies

Agents following random-based strategies place their bids randomly in several auctions. After doing so they go to sleep mode for random time intervals. In this paper, two different variations of random-based strategies are used: on the one hand the *Singe-Bid* (RS) and on the other hand *Bid-O-Matic* (RBMS). Single-Bid means that one single bid is placed, while between three and ten bids will be made in a row when using the Bid-O-Matic strategy. The term *Bid-O-Matic* refers to a feature offered by QuiBids[4]. Users can use a bot that automatically rebids as soon as another user has placed a higher bid.[10].

3.2   Continuous Bidding Strategies

The pool of continuous bidding strategies contains strategies that make agents bid steadily from the beginning of the auction until the highest bid reaches their IPVs. The first strategy, which is called *Perpetual-Bid-O-Matic strategy* (PBMS), is the simplest strategy. Bidders using this strategy start bidding regardless of the remaining auction time, right after an auction has started. They rebid immediately after they are being outbid by another participant. The second strategy is called the *Continuous-Time strategy* (CTS). This strategy makes an agent only place bids within the last second of an auction. Once the agent is outbid this behavior will be repeated. Equivalent to the random-based strategies, Bid-O-Matic variations (CTBMS) of the Continuous-Time strategy exist as well. The only difference between CTS and CTBMS agents is that CTBMS agents place a row of bids instead of single bids. Within such a row of bids, the remaining auction time will not be considered.

---

[4] http://www.quibids.com

The main disadvantage of the continuous bidding strategies is the risk of high bidding costs. The longer an auction lasts, the higher the bidding costs get. However, if an auction ends at an early stage, a continuously bidding agent has the chance to win this auction paying a price far below its IPV due to the strategy used.

3.3 Calculating Strategies

The set of calculating strategies contains a Single-Bid (EPS) and a Bid-O-Matic variation (EPBM) of the so-called *Ending-Pattern strategy*. At the beginning of an auction, the Ending-Pattern strategy is identical to the Continuous-Time strategy. However, after a certain number of bids, agents using the Ending-Pattern strategy compute the probability of other agents placing the next bid based on the number of distinct bidders participating. According to this, agents pursuing these strategies place bids or rows of bids considering counter probabilities. The Ending-Pattern strategy is based on the assumption that an auction is in its final stage while there are only a few participants placing bids. In this case, it is assumed that there is a lower probability of getting outbid again.

The main advantage of the calculating strategies is that the bidding costs for long-lasting auctions can be reduced. However, since the agent's calculation can be inappropriate, the risk of losing an auction increases as well.

3.4 Case-Based Strategies

Agents following a case-based strategy try to determine the optimal point of time to enter an auction by comparing the active auction to similar auctions which have already been finished by then. Before bidding, the mean value and standard deviation of all previous auctions will be calculated. Overall, there are three different strategies in this group (CBPBMS, CBS and CBBMS) which are similar to the three continuous bidding strategies. The only difference is that agents using case-based strategies only participate in an auction as long as a certain item price is not reached.

The advantage of case-based strategies is that no bidding costs arise in the early stage of an auction. However, if an auction ends before the expected price is reached, the auction cannot be won with a case-based strategy.

4 Implementation

In order to run simulation experiments the system has been implemented using the open source framework JADE[5]. The simulation system mainly consists of the two classes *MasterAgent* and *ClientAgent*. The entire communication within the system is taking place between the master agent and the clients via a direct connection. Furthermore a *HumanClientAgent* can join the auction and interact

---

[5] Java Agent Development Framework (`http://jade.tilab.com`)

with the system using a GUI. The specific strategies described in chapter 3 can be accessed by a software agent via an interface, which simplifies the implementation of further strategies.

In order to make a bid the client is forced to register at the master agent in advance. After registering successfully, a reference will be stored in the *Master-AgentGui* and can then be observed by the person running the simulation. In addition, the *MasterAgentGui* provides the GUI for creating any desired number of bot agents (even during runtime), to set the parameters of the auction and to start the auction process.

During a simulation experiment the communication between the master agent and the bidders takes place using a strict protocol, which is shown by the sequence diagram in figure 1. After a successful announcement is made the bidding agents will be informed about the start of an auction. Hereafter, the agents are able to make a bid. If the bid reaches the master agent in time, before the auction time is up, the master agent will accept the bid, update the highest bidder, increase the bid price and the auction time remaining. As a further step the master agent sends the new information to all bidding agents known. This information is used by the participants to considers whether a bid has been successful or an opponent made its bid earlier.

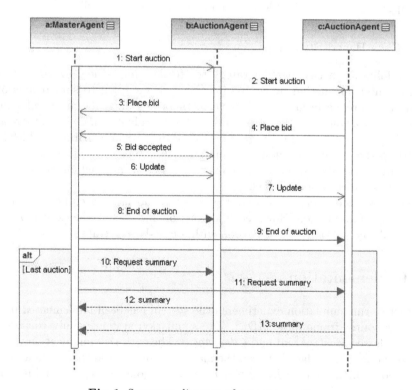

Fig. 1. Sequence diagram of a penny auction

The bidding process described will be repeated until none of the registered agents places any further bids and the remaining auction time runs up. In this case the master agent informs every bidding agent, including the winner, that the auction has ended and announces the final price. If the last item of the item list has been auctioned the master agent requests an individual summary from all participants of the auction, which includes bidding fees and total expenses, as well as the total value of the won goods for evaluation purposes. Finally, all participants will be discarded by the master agent and further auctions will be initiated the same way.

5   Simulation Experiments

The simulation experiments were run on six dual core computers with a cumulative simulation time of about 93 days. 28 different scenarios were simulated with 43 625 items receiving 49 178 205 bids being auctioned. Each scenario consisted of several rounds (between 25 and 40), where each round within a scenario was attended by the same agents. In each round, a newly generated item list was auctioned. Moreover, the IPVs of every agent were regenerated for every new round.

The first five scenarios contained the same number of participants of all agent types. The results of these scenarios will be discussed in 5.1. In further experiments, the eight strategies were tested individually in distinct scenarios against 50 of the two randomly acting agent types. According to this, groups of 25 agents following each strategy were analyzed separately against 40 RS agents and 40 RBMS agents. Additionally, every strategy was examined in a scenario against groups of ten agents applying each of the nine remaining strategies.

The results regarding the agents bidding continuous are discussed in section 5.2, while section 5.3 contains the evaluation of the calculating and the case-based strategies.

5.1   Performance of the Strategies Using Standard Deviation

Each of the five preliminary scenarios examined the behavior of all strategies in case of a steady number of strategically acting types of agents. In the first case one single agent using each of the eight strategies is opposing 40 agents of each random strategy. After 30 iterations, the strategy of the CBS agent was measured to be most successful. On average this agent generates a profit of 276,10 Euros with a standard deviation of 154,15 and median of 300,30 Euros.

The CTS agent achieves similar results with an average profit of 270,05 Euros (standard deviation 133,91; median 283,85). With a profit margin of 24,02 Euros (standard deviation 123,31) per round the EPS agent achieves the lowest positive result. But the median of −9,75 Euros clarifies that the EPS agents most likely produce negative results.

As shown in figure 2a the Bid-O-Matic variations of the three most successful strategies obtain much better results compared to the random agents. Even

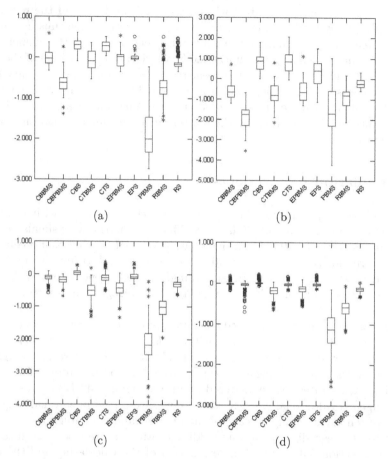

Fig. 2. The profit earned by an identical number of agents using a certain strategy. (a) 40 RB and RBMS agents competing against one agent of each other group, (b) one of each agent type (c) 10 of each agent type (d) 25 of each agent type.

though it is not possible to gain a positive result with the Bid-O-Matic strategies under these circumstances in the longterm. Obviously, the PBMS agent achieved the worst results due to negative outcome in every round, despite the highest variance.

Changing the scenario in the way that just one of each random agents participates, the same three types of agents are profitable (fig. 2b). Distinctly, the highest outcome with a remarkable increase of the profit is provided by the CBS agent (mean 716,91 Euros, median 880,50 Euros and standard deviation 451,92) as well as by the CTS agent (mean 716,91 Euros, median 880,50 and standard deviation 451,92). Also, the EPS agent is able to raise his profit to 277,69 Euros (standard deviation 729,32). Whereas for the remaining agents the loss rises.

Therefore, the auctioneer gains a profit of 112 773,40 Euros after 26 rounds, despite the small number of participants. In the long term, the Bid-O-Matic

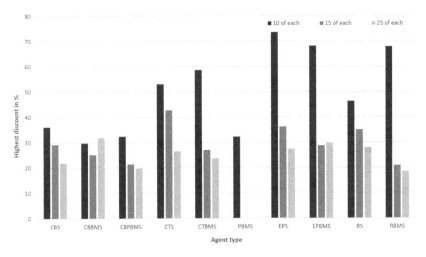

Fig. 3. Highest discounts achieved for different number of participants

strategy turns out to be a bad choice as in average it attains more loss than the random RS agent despite occasionally high profits.

In case the number of all types of agents is raised to 10, 15 or 25 only CBS agents make profit in average (fig. 2c and 2d). However, the larger the number of agents, the lower the average profit. This could be explained the way, that more agents using the same strategy are lowering the probability of success of every singly agent. Nevertheless, it can be noted that the Single-Bid-variation of the case-based strategies in uniform-distributed scenarios is the most successful and the only one making profit.

As well, the issue that an increasing number of bidders results in the CBBMS and CBPBMS agents improving their profit the most, regarding the average profit in relation to the other strategies, is noticeable. This could be explained by the fact, that a larger number of strategically acting agents causes more steady prices and additionally a lower diversification. Thus, the probability to obtain large discounts decreases, which causes a significant disadvantage of the continuous bidding strategies.

Concurrently, the advantage of the continuous bidding strategies disappears, by which the performance loss of the CTS agents towards the other agents could be explained. Figure 3 illustrates this issue and shows how the biggest discounts decrease for the particular types of strategy for one auction item with increasing number of participants. At the same time it becomes obvious that for the case-based agents this decrease has the lowest effect.

Moreover, the well performance of the case-based Bid-O-Matic strategies within scenarios containing an increasing number of participants could primarily be explained by the omission of the high discounts of the other strategies. This is highlighted by the number of won auctions per type of strategy as well. As seen in figure 4, the relation of won auctions between the different types of strategies does not change significantly. Most of the auctions are won by the three strategic

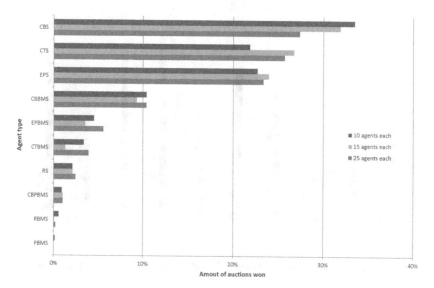

Fig. 4. Auctions won by each strategy type and number of agents

Single-Bid variations and even the ratio of the CBBMS- and CBPBMS-agents remains approximately constant.

Furthermore, the simulated scenarios show that the profit of the auctioneer raises, if the number of agents increases, whereas the relative increase of the profit drops. In case of 100 participants the profit of the auctioneer is 1 458 274,80 Euros and it increases by approximately 12.1% when simulating 150 participants. When the number of participants reaches 250 the profit increases by additional 11.1%. This results from the issue, that the participants bid not exceeding a certain percentage of the item's market value. This results in a positive side effect for participants of the auction. In case of a loss they have less deficits, because the number of bids is distributed to multiple bidders. At the same time the probability of winning decreases as well.

5.2   Performance of Continuous-Bidding Strategies

First we take a look at the PBM strategy. The agents using this strategy generated almost the worst results in all simulation runs regarding profit resp. loss per round. These results were foreseeable, because in return to a high bid a counterbid is made immediately. Due to the bad results, this strategy will not be considered any further.

Within the group of agents bidding continuous the Continuous-Time strategy without Bid-O-Matic achieved the best results. When testing one single strategy versus 100 random strategies the agent with this strategy shows the best performance towards the others with an average profit of 313,63 Euros per round (RS: -567,58; RBMS: -113,54; tab. 2a). This scenario has been repeated 30 times and only caused a loss for the agent one single time. This result is the consequence of

Table 2. Continuous strategies versus random-based strategies

		CTS	RBMS	RS
(a)	Quantity	1	50	50
	Mean	313,63	-567,86	-113,54
	SD	175,14	270,78	87,41
	Median	274,2	-591,85	-133
	Min	-12,2	−1 263,5	-285,6
	Max	729,8	427,5	582

		CTBMS	RBMS	RS
(b)	Quantity	1	50	50
	Mean	84,36	-629,78	-111,76
	SD	258,45	230,99	92,85
	Median	83,95	-653,25	-135,3
	Min	-485,8	−1 291,5	-257,6
	Max	883,2	402,3	539,6

		CTS	RBMS	RS
(c)	Quantity	25	80	80
	Mean	-43,26	-935,38	-308,95
	SD	112,91	272,28	116,80
	Median	-44,25	-938,7	-305,2
	Min	-444,5	−1 815,8	-739,9
	Max	371,6	-77,7	495,1

		CTBMS	RBMS	RS
(d)	Quantity	25	80	80
	Mean	-149,28	-918,75	-213,31
	SD	175,70	267,47	81,87
	Median	-135,85	-931,7	-219,75
	Min	-924	−1 694,7	-450,8
	Max	447	140,4	200,6

the fact, that the CT strategy bids continuously at a certain point of time and thus it places its bids just before the end of auction. This procedure causes a large number of cheap buys for the CTS agent in certain setting. The success of CTS agents in this scenario indicates the results of the study of Jeffrey Stix [10], which attests the best probability of success to the Continuous-Time strategy.

The Bid-O-Matic variation of the CT strategy (CTBMS) is successful as well as a single agent competing versus solely random-based participants and gains a profit of 84,36 Euros per round in average (tab. 2b). However, the profit is not higher than the CTS agent's, because the use of series of bids is counterproductive. The bidding costs increase and the agent's IPV will be reached more quickly. This results in the agent winning less items but investing more money.

In the experiment running 25 CTS resp. CTBMS agents against 80 random agents the CT strategy can not be proved successful. Many equal agents bid before the countdown ends and thus bump up the auction price (table 2c and 2d). This negative effect is intensified by the use of series of bids in case of the CTBMS variation. While the standard variation has an average loss of -43.26 Euros, -149.28 Euros were registered for the Bid-O-Matic variation.

For every type of strategy, table 3 shows: The accumulated bidding-fees per round (k_g), the value of the auctioned goods (roi), the average profit (g) and the number of auctioned items (#i). The average profit is calculated from the difference between the market value of the auctioned goods and the total costs, which are derived from the bidding costs and the price of the won items. Considering the profit (27.23 Euros) the CTS agent gets the second place, behind the case-based agents (31.81 Euros). It is noticeable that the CTS agent receives the

Table 3. Continuous strategies versus all strategies

	k_g	roi	g	#i
CBS	79,47	395,21	31,81	1,568
CTS	185,44	599,20	27,23	1,92
EPS	138,23	357,96	-26,72	1,48
CBBMS	167,31	81,68	-144,40	0,416
RS	298,52	43,92	-282,98	0,248
EPBMS	480,89	103,78	-434,67	0,444
CTBMS	529,74	71,56	-492,27	0,336
RBMS	1066,19	20,82	-1053,86	0,08
PBMS	2265,91	2,00	-2264,39	0,004
CBPBMS	257,61	0,90	-257,40	0,024

most items (1.92 per round) and gains by far the highest value of goods (599.20 Euros; second is CBS with 395.21 Euros).

5.3   Performance of Calculating and Case-Based Strategies

The calculating strategies appeared to perform better than the random-based strategies. However, the results showed as well that the Ending-Pattern strategies tended to gained loss in an environment of random-based agents. The Bid-O-Matic variation performed better (14,22 Euro, standard deviation 178,15) but the distribution of the reults was increased as well (from 216,20 Euro loss to 607,30 Euro profit). The fact that the Ending-Pattern strategies attained worse results in this scenarios can be explained by the fact that the estimation of the auctions end is more difficult against agents bidding random-based.

When competing alone, case-based strategies operated very successful against random-based agents. Though, the CBPBMS agent, just as the PBMS agent, gains the highest loss in all scenarios. This is why these strategies will not be considered any further within this paper. The CBS agent's profit was 280,97 Euro per round in average (standard deviation 159,18). Furthermore it shows a median of 287,65 Euro and a maximum loss of only -1,60 Euro. In fact CBBMS agents gained profit as well (104,19 Euro) but the standard deviation (203,39) is higher, too.

Making 25 CBS agents compete against 80 random-based agents will not result in profits gained but compared to the random-based agents the results are slightly better. The negative results generated by the CBS agents in this scenario can be explained by the advance in knowledge which is available to all 25 agents, thus, the benefit cannot be utilized.

A CBS agent bidding against agents using all nine other strategies will result in the highest profit. Moreover, it is the only strategy gaining profit in this scenario at all. It needs to be generally remarked that the Single-Bid variation of the case-based strategies is the one being successful in most of the experiments.

6 Conclusion

Among bargain hunters platforms selling goods using penny auctions have gained popularity. Participants have to pay for each bid made, however, the bidding-fee is higher than the actual increase of the auction price. This results in a lower product price being perceived by the customer. In fact, the total price paid for the good is hidden as it consists of both, the bidding fees and the final price.

Various countries have forbidden penny auctions, as they are considered to be gambling games. Therefore, this paper aimed on proposing a framework for evaluating, whether dominant strategies are existing in the context of penny auctions. In case these strategies are not existent, the result of penny auctions would only rely on fortune and comply with the definition of gambling games.

For a differentiated consideration of distinct user strategies under variable circumstances, we proposed the use of multi-agent systems for generating artificial auction platforms. By using intelligent agents for the representation of users trying to purchase goods by auction, a set of strategies can be implemented as the agent's goals. This enables us to reproduce the processes taking place on auction platforms by simulating them. Additionally, it provides the possibility for comprehensive examination of simulation platforms and validation of hypotheses considering the existing mechanisms.

After simulating a variety of scenarios and strategies we can conclude, that participants of penny auctions cannot earn profit in the long term. Even though strategies providing a higher success rate then random strategies were identified, no dominant strategy could be found. By and large, agents using the case-based Single-Bid strategy performed the best, although the loss sustained by these agents tended to be average.

The Continuous-Time strategy, identified by Jeffrey Stix [10] to be the most promising bidding strategy, performed the best in single tests against 40 of each of the random-based agent types regarding the profit earned. However, increasing the amount of agents using bidding strategies will worsen the results attained by agents using the Continuous-Time strategy. Nevertheless, the fact that CTS-agents perform the best against agents acting randomly can be seen as a confirmation of the results formulated by Stix. As most of the users participating in penny auctions are unexperienced and bid randomly the scenario simulated is most consistent with the real world.[12]

Furthermore the simulation experiments performed in the context of this paper showed that none of the analyzed strategies can realize profit under all circumstances. In the best case participants making use of these strategies were rather able to earn small profits, but most of the strategies lead to high losses. In fact, the experiments showed that the auctioneer was the only person to benefit from penny auctions.

The proposed approach and the first results presented within this paper are meant to be seen as a first consideration of using multi-agent systems for

evaluating auction mechanisms. By providing a GUI enabling humans to participate in the artificial auction platform, mixed environments can be facilitated for
further consideration. As part of future work, additional scenarios and factors
influencing penny auctions and coordination mechanisms in general shall be considered as well. Especially individual perceptions, regarding the calculation of
the personal IPV, need to be taken into account. In general the irrational "human
factor" seems to be a central aspect which necessarily needs to be incorporated
into a model when simulating human behavior.

References

1. Bapna, R., Goes, P., Gupta, A.: Simulating online yankee auctions to optimize
   sellers revenue. In: Proceedings of the 34th Annual Hawaii International Conference
   on System Sciences, p. 10. IEEE (2001)
2. Camenzind, B.: Betreiber von Online-Auktionen verurteilt (2012),
   https://www.ktipp.ch/artikel/d/
   betreiber-von-online-auktionen-verurteilt
3. Chen, B., Sadaoui, S.: Simulation and verification of a dynamic online auction. De-
   partamento deficiencias de la computación. Universidad de Regina, Canadá (2003)
4. GlüÄndStV: Staatsvertrag zum Glücksspielwesen in Deutschland (Glücksspiel-
   staatsvertrag) (2012), http://www.regierung.oberbayern.bayern.de
5. Hinnosaar, T.: Penny auctions are unpredictable (2010)
6. Mizuta, H., Steiglitz, K.: Agent-based simulation of dynamic online auctions. In:
   Proceedings of the Winter. Simulation Conference, vol. 2, pp. 1772–1777. IEEE
   (2000)
7. Nanney, J.: Entertainment shopping (2010), http://www.eecs.harvard.edu
8. Rabuzin, K., Bakoš, N.: Agent-based simulation model of online auctions in Net-
   Logo. In: CECIIS 2010 (2010)
9. Stix, E.: An empirical study of online penny auctions (2012),
   http://cs.brown.edu/research/pubs/theses/ugrad
10. Stix, J.: Designing a bidding algorithm for online penny auctions (2012),
    http://cs.brown.edu/research/pubs/theses/ugrad
11. Storch, D.: Towards an Intelligent Bidding Agent in QuiBids Penny Auctions
    (2013), http://cs.brown.edu/research/pubs/theses/ugrad/2013/storch.pdf
12. Wang, Z., Xu, M.: Learning and strategic sophistication in games (2012),
    http://www.economics.neu.edu/zwang
13. Wolf, A.: Strategieentwicklung für Entertainment Shopping Auctions am Beispiel
    Swoopo. Masterarbeit, Goethe Universität, Frankfurt am Main (2011)

Robustness Analysis of Negotiation Strategies through Multiagent Learning in Repeated Negotiation Games

Jianye Hao[1], Siqi Chen[2], Gerhard Weiss[2], Ho-fung Leung[3], and Karl Tuyls[4]

[1] Massachusetts Institute of Technology
jianye@mit.edu
[2] Maastricht University
{siqi.chen,gerhard.weiss}@maastrichtuniversity.nl
[3] The Chinese University of Hong Kong
lhf@cuhk.edu.hk
[4] University of Liverpool
k.tuyls@liverpool.ac.uk

Abstract. Automated negotiation techniques play an important role in facilitating human in reaching better negotiation outcomes, and until now lots of research efforts have been devoted to designing effective negotiation strategies. To evaluate the performance of different strategies, one important evaluation criterion is *robustness*, which is to investigate which negotiating strategies the agents are going to adopt finally if they are given the opportunity to repeatedly negotiate and allowed to change their choices. However the current way of evaluating the robustness suffers from several drawbacks. First, it is assumed that all agents can have access to the global payoff information, which may not be available beforehand in practice. Second, it is based on the single-agent best deviation principle, however, in practice, each agent may change their strategies simultaneously and in any possible rational way. To this end, we firstly propose the *repeated negotiation game* learning framework to evaluate the robustness of different negotiation strategies, in which each agent can adopt any rational learning approach to make decisions without knowing the global payoff information beforehand. In this way, we are able to provide more realistic and fine-grained robustness analysis and more insights in terms of the relative robustness of different negotiating strategies can be revealed from our analytical results.

1 Introduction

Automated negotiation techniques can, to a large extent, alleviate the efforts of human, and also facilitate human in reaching better negotiation outcomes in complex negotiations. To this end, until now lots of state-of-the-art negotiation strategies [8,6,15,7,5,12] have been proposed to maximize agents' individual benefits from negotiation by exploiting their opponents as much as possible. In recent years, the international competition - *automated negotiating agents competition (ANAC)* [2,1] held by researchers from automated negotiation area has

J.P. Müller, M. Weyrich, and A.L.C. Bazzan (Eds.): MATES 2014, LNAI 8732, pp. 41–56, 2014.
© Springer International Publishing Switzerland 2014

emerged accordingly. This competition provides a general negotiation platform and benchmarks, which enables different negotiation strategies to be evaluated within realistic negotiation environments.

In the current setting of ANAC, the performance of different negotiation strategies are evaluated based on the criterion of *efficiency*, i.e., each strategy's average payoff obtained against the rest of participants over different domains. Efficiency is indeed an important evaluation criterion to consider. However it only reflects the static aspect of negotiation, which assumes that each participant's strategy is fixed beforehand. In real life, it is common to encounter repeated negotiations between multiple parties in many scenarios such as e-commerce negotiation between different sellers and buyers [10]. This thus gives the agents (or people) the opportunity to choose different negotiation strategies against different opponents at different negotiation stages based on the past negotiation performance. Therefore in practice the current efficiency criterion may not be quite useful, since the most efficient strategy in one static negotiation setting may become the most inefficient one in another setting. The efficiency of a negotiation strategy makes sense only when the current negotiation setting is stable, however, it is unclear which strategy will be eventually adopted by each agent and which strategy profile will be the stable one eventually. To this end, an alternative evaluation criterion, *robustness*, was firstly proposed by Baarslag et al. [1] to evaluate the performance of different negotiation strategies from a new perspective based on empirical game-theoretic analysis. In general, the robustness analysis focuses on investigating whether an agent would have the incentive to switch to other negotiation strategies, and which strategy (combination of strategies) would be finally adopted by agents if strategy switching is allowed.

The current way [1] of analyzing the robustness of negotiation strategies suffers from several drawbacks. First, the analysis requires the global information (i.e., average payoff between all pairs of negotiating strategies) to be available beforehand. However, from an individual negotiator's perspective, this kind of information is usually not available beforehand until they have actually participated in the negotiations. Second, the robustness analysis is based on the principle of the *single-agent best deviation*, i.e., only one agent is allowed to change its negotiating strategy in each round. However, in practice, it is highly likely that in each round each agent may change its negotiating strategy simultaneously and in any possible rational way which may not necessarily follow the principle of best deviation. We believe that enabling all agents to choose their negotiating strategies simultaneously and autonomously without knowing the global information can provide more realistic analysis and predictions of the dynamic changes of the agents' negotiating strategies and their relative robustness. It is not clear a priori if the agents are able to converge to a stable strategy profile or which strategy will be mostly likely to be adopted by each agent in such a situation. Third, based on the current robustness analysis approach, it reveals nothing about the relative robustness of each negotiating strategy within the best reply cycle if such a cycle exists.

To tackle the above issues, we first introduce the concept of *repeated negotiation game* to model the n-agent repeated negotiation problem (based on the empirical game-theoretic approach) in which each agent is allowed to choose its negotiating strategy independently in each round. To obtain the set of negotiating strategies, we perform comprehensive simulations among all the state-of-the-art strategies entered into the final rounds of ANAC from 2010 to 2012, and choose the top six strategies as our candidate strategies. It is reasonable to assume that any rational agent would employ certain rational learning approach to decide which negotiating strategy to choose through repeated interactions [11]. In this work, we focus on three representative rational learning approaches from multiagent learning literature: Ficitious Play [4], Q-learning[14], and Win or Learn Fast - policy hill climbing (WoLF-PHC) learning [3]. From our analysis, we are able to gain more insights in terms of the relative robustness of different negotiating strategies compared with the previous robustness analysis based on single-agent best deviation [1].

The remainder of the paper is organized as follows. In Section 2, we review some backgrounds of evaluating the robustness of negotiating strategies and the limitation of previous approach. In Section 3, we describe the repeated negotiation game framework we propose to evaluate the robustness of negotiation strategies. In Section 4, we present the robustness evaluation results of different negotiation strategies under our framework and compare with previous approach. An overview of related work in automated negotiation area is given in Section 5. Lastly we conclude and point out some future work in Section 6.

2   Background and Problem Description

Recently some attention has been given to investigate the dynamic aspect of negotiating strategies by evaluating the *robustness* [1] of the current state-of-the-art negotiating strategies, based on the game-theoretic approach. Since there exist an infinite number of possible negotiation strategies that the agents may take, we cannot apply the standard game-theoretic approach to perform such an analysis by explicitly considering all possible strategies. Therefore, the tool of empirical game theoretic (EGT) analysis is adopted to achieve this goal instead, which is originally developed to analyze the Trading Agent Competition. EGT analysis is a game-theoretic analysis approach based on a set of empirical results. It handles the problem of the existence of infinite possible strategies by assuming that each agent only selects its strategy from a fixed set of strategies and the outcomes for each strategy profile can be determined through empirical simulations. This technique has been successfully applied in addressing questions about robustness of different strategies from various domains including continuous double auction [13], trading strategies in previous years' TAC competitions [9] and different negotiation strategies [1,15,5].

Given a set of negotiation strategies, different from the setting of ANAC, each agent is free to select any strategy from this set as its negotiation strategy. For each bilateral negotiation, the corresponding payoff received for each participating agent is determined as its average payoff against its opponent over all domains, which can be obtained through empirical simulations. Based on the bilateral negotiation outcomes, the average payoff of an agent in any given tournament can be determined by averaging its payoff obtained in all bilateral negotiations against all other agents in the tournament. Specifically, for a given tournament involving a set $\mathcal{P}$ of agents, the payoff $U_p(\mathcal{P})$ obtained by agent p can be calculated as follows,

$$U_p(\mathcal{P}) = \frac{\sum_{p' \in \mathcal{P}, p' \neq p} u_p(p, p')}{|\mathcal{P}| - 1} \tag{1}$$

where $u_p(p, p')$ represents the corresponding average payoff of agent p negotiating against another agent p' which is obtained from simulation results. Note that agent p and p' can use either the same or different strategies.

An agent has the incentive to deviate its current strategy to another one if and only if its payoff after deviation can be statistically improved, provided that all the other agents keep their strategies unchanged. There may exist multiple candidate strategies that an agent has the incentive to deviate to, usually we only consider the best deviation available to that agent in terms of maximizing its deviation benefit [1,15]. Given a strategy profile, if no agent has the incentive to unilaterally deviate from its current strategy, then this strategy profile is called an *empirical pure strategy Nash equilibrium*. In general, a game may have no empirical pure strategy Nash equilibrium. Another useful concept for analyzing the stability of the strategy profiles is *best reply cycle*, which is a subset of strategy profiles in which, for any strategy profile within this subset, there is no single-agent best deviation path leading to any profile outside the cycle. In other words, in a best reply cycle, all single-agent best deviation paths starting from any strategy profile within itself must lead to another strategy profile inside the same cycle.

Both *empirical pure strategy Nash equilibrium* and *best reply cycle* can be considered as two different interpretations of empirical stable sets to evaluate the *stability* of different strategy profiles. Based on these two concepts, the *robustness* of a strategy is evaluated using the concept of *basin of attraction* of a stable set [13]. The *basin of attraction* of a stable set is defined as the percentage of strategy profiles which can lead to this stable set through a series of single-agent best deviations. Accordingly, a negotiation strategy s is considered to be *robust* if it belongs to a stable set with a large *basin of attraction* [13,1]. However, as we previously mentioned, the current robustness analysis relies on a number of assumptions such that the analysis results may not be able to accurately reflect the relative robustness of different negotiation strategies in practical negotiation scenarios. Moreover, the current robustness analysis cannot provide a more fine-grained analysis in terms of the relative robustness of strategies within the same stable set when the stable set involves multiple negotiation strategies.

3   Robustness Analysis Framework

3.1   Repeated Negotiation Game

We propose analyzing the robustness of negotiation strategies within the framework of repeated negotiation games. We first define the single-shot *negotiation game* as follows. Given a set N of agents and a set S of negotiation strategies, the negotiation problem among n agents can be modeled as a single-shot normal-form game. Formally it can be represented as a tuple $\langle N, (S_i), (U_i) \rangle$ where

- $N = \{a_1, a_2, \ldots, a_n\}$ is the set of agents.
- S_i is the set of negotiating strategies available to agent a_i.
- U_i is the utility function of agent i as defined in Equation 1, and $U_i(\mathcal{P})$ corresponds to the average payoff agent a_i receives under the current negotiation tournament, where $\mathcal{P}$ is the strategy profile in the current round of negotiation.

Similar to the previous robustness analysis [1], in the *negotiation game* definition, we assume that each agent i may only select negotiating strategies from a set S_i of candidate strategies based on empirical game-theoretic analysis. In this way, we are able to handle the problem of the existence of infinite possible negotiating strategies, which would make the analysis infeasible. To select the set of strategies for our analysis, we first collect all the top 8 strategies that enter into the past 3-year ANAC competitions from 2010 to 2012 (24 strategies in total), and evaluate their relative rankings in terms of efficiency over a large number of negotiation domains through extensive simulations. We find that the top six strategies actually correspond to the top 3 strategies from ANAC 2011 and 2012, which indicates that the most recently developed negotiating strategies are more efficient and thus more likely to be adopted in practice. Therefore, we select the top six negotiating strategies as the set S of candidate strategies for our analysis, i.e., $S = \{\mathcal{G}, \mathcal{H}, \mathcal{I}, \mathcal{A}, \mathcal{C}, \mathcal{O}\}$.[1]

Since the negotiation game is defined based on empirical game theory, we can define the concept of *empirical pure strategy Nash equilibrium* in a similar way to the definition of pure strategy (mixed strategy) Nash equilibrium by using the finite strategy set S to replace the original infinite strategy set.

Definition 1. *An empirical pure strategy Nash equilibrium for an n-player negotiation game is a strategy profile* $(a_1^*, a_2^*, \ldots, a_n^*)$ *such that* $\forall i \in N$, *we have*

$$U_i(a_i^*, a_{-i}^*) \geq U_i(a_i, a_{-i}^*), \forall a_i \in S_i \qquad (2)$$

where S_i *($\forall i \in N$) is the finite set of strategies we choose to represent the original infinite set of strategies.*

---

[1] These bold letters are the abbreviations for the six negotiating strategies as follows: $\mathcal{G}$ – Gahboninho, $\mathcal{H}$ – HardHeaded, $\mathcal{I}$ – IAMhaggler2011, $\mathcal{A}$ – AgentLG, $\mathcal{C}$ –CUHKAgent, $\mathcal{O}$ – OMAC.

If the agents are allowed to use mixed strategy, then we can naturally define the concept of *empirical mixed strategy Nash equilibrium* similarly.

Definition 2. *An empirical mixed strategy Nash equilibrium for an n-player normal-form game is a strategy profile* $(\pi_1^*, \pi_2^*, \ldots, \pi_n^*)$ *such that* $\forall i \in N$, *we have*

$$\bar{U}_i(\pi_i^*, \pi_{-i}^*) \geq \bar{U}_i(\pi_i, \pi_{-i}^*), \forall \pi_i \in \Pi(S_i) \qquad (3)$$

where $\bar{U}_i(\pi_i^*, \pi_{-i}^*)$ *is player i's expected payoff under the strategy profile* (π_i^*, π_{-i}^*), *and* $\Pi(S_i)$ *is the set of probability distributions over player i's action space* S_i.

An *empirical mixed strategy Nash equilibrium* (π_1^*, π_2^*) is degenerated to an *empirical pure strategy Nash equilibrium* if both π_1^* and π_2^* are pure strategies.

We consider the general setting of the *repeated negotiation game* where each agent is free to choose its negotiating strategy simultaneously based on the feedback from the previous round. In each round, given the negotiation strategy profile of agents, the negotiation tournament starts and each agent i receives its own average payoff $U_i(\mathcal{P})$ from the current round. We assume that initially each agent has equal probability to select each of the negotiation strategy from its strategy space S_i. We evaluate the relative robustness of different negotiation strategies based on the corresponding probability that each strategy profile can be converged to. Given a particular negotiation strategy s, we define its *basin of attraction* as the accumulated frequency of all strategy profiles that the agents can learn to converge to and also involve strategy s. The robustness of a strategy s is then defined based on its basin of attraction. The higher the basin of attraction of a strategy s is, the more robust strategy s is. For example, consider two negotiation strategy s_1 and s_2, and the agents converge to (s_1, s_1) with probability of 0.8, and (s_2, s_2) with probability of 0.2. The basin of attraction of strategy s_1 and s_2 is 0.8 and 0.2 respectively, and thus we can say strategy s_1 is more robust then strategy s_2. The overall robustness analysis framework can be summarized as follows in Algorithm 1..

Algorithm 1. Overall Robustness Analysis Framework

1: Choose a learning strategy for each agent to determine its negotiation strategy each round
2: **repeat**
3:     Each agent choose its current-round negotiation strategy according to its learning strategy
4:     Each agent update its learning strategy based on the current round outcome.
5: **until** The negotiation game ends
6: Calcualte the basin of attraction of each negotiation strategy
7: Determine the relateive robustness of each negotiation strategy

---

3.2 Learning Strategies

A remaining question is how the agents should select their negotiating strategies each round. We assume that the agents are individually rational and thus each

---

Algorithm 2. Fictitious Play in Repeated Negotiation Games

1: Initialize the agent's belief about its opponents.
2: **repeat**
3:    Choose the negotiating strategy maximizing its average payoff (random choose one in case of a tie) based on its current belief.
4:    Update its belief based on the current round outcome.
5: **until** The negotiation game ends

---

agent is faced with the task of how to make decisions to increase its individual payoff as much as possible through negotiation given the uncertainty of the negotiating strategies chosen by others. We adopt three representative rational learning strategies from multiagent learning literature: fictitious play learning [4], Q-learning [14] and WoLF-PHC learning [3].[2] All the three learning strategies are rational in that they all aim at learning the policy of maximizing their individual payoffs based on the past feedbacks in different ways. Next we will describe how these three strategies can be applied to select negotiating strategies for agents in the context of repeated negotiation games respectively.

Fictitious Play Learning. Under fictitious play, an agent maintains the belief that its opponent makes decisions following a fixed mixed strategy and always chooses actions to maximize its average payoff regarding its current belief each round. In the context of n-player repeated negotiation game, the overall learning rule of fictitious play can be described as follows. Similar to the robustness analysis, fictitious play learning implicitly requires that each agent i should know its own utility over all strategy profiles in advance. Besides, it is well-known that a fictitious play learner may never learn its best strategy due to its erroneous belief of other players always playing fixed mixed strategies. To this end, we modify the original fictitious play by allowing each agent to make explorations occasionally, which thus gives the agents the opportunity to identify other possibly better strategies. Specifically, each fictitious play learner chooses action to maximize its expected payoff based on its current belief with probability $1 - \epsilon$, and make random selection with probability ϵ.

Q-Learning. Q-learning [14] is one representative reinforcement learning approach and has received much attention in multiagent learning literature. In the context of repeated negotiation game, each Q-learning agent i holds a Q-value $Q_i^t(s)$ for each negotiating strategy $s \in S_i$, and gradually updates its Q-value $Q_i^t(s)$ for each action s based its own payoff in each round. The Q-value update rule for each action s is as follows:

$$Q_i^{t+1}(s) = \begin{cases} Q_i^t(s) + \alpha_i(U_i^t(\mathcal{P}) - Q_i^t(s)) & \text{if } s \text{ is chosen} \\ Q_i^t(s) & \text{otherwise} \end{cases} \quad (4)$$

---

[2] It is worth noting that any other rational learning strategies could be used here.

where $U_i^t(\mathcal{P})$ is the payoff agent i obtains in round t under current outcome $\mathcal{P}$ by taking action s. Besides, α_i is the learning rate of agent i, which determines how much weight we give to the newly acquired payoff $U_i^t(\mathcal{P})$, as opposed to the old Q-value $Q_i^t(s)$.

In each round t, each agent i chooses its action based on the ϵ-greedy exploration mechanism as follows. With probability $1 - \epsilon$, it chooses the negotiating strategies with the highest Q-value from the set S of candidate strategies, and makes random selection from S with probability ϵ. The value of ϵ controls the exploration degree during learning. It initially starts at a high value and decreased gradually to zero as negotiation goes on.

WoLF-PHC Learning. WoLF-PHC learning [3] is a rational learning algorithm which incorporates the "win or learn fast" principle into the basic policy hill-climbing (PHC) algorithm [3]. In PHC algorithm, each round each agent maintains a Q-table for each negotiating strategy and updates it in a way similar to that in Q-learning algorithm, but it also explicitly keeps and updates its mixed strategy policy. Each round each agent's mixed strategy policy is updated in the direction of increasing the probability that the action with the highest Q-value with a fixed learning rate. WoLF-PHC learning algorithm extends the basic PHC algorithm by introducing two different learning rates to update its mixed strategy policy. The principle of WoLF update is that it selects the smaller learning rate to update its mixed strategy policy when it wins, and the larger one to update when it losses. A WoLF-PHC agent evaluates whether it wins or not by comparing its expected payoff by playing its current mixed strategy policy with that by playing the average mixed strategy policy over all previous rounds. If its expected payoff by adopting its current mixed strategy is higher, it means it wins, otherwise it losses. The overall description of the WoLF-PHC algorithm in the context of repeated negotiation game is shown in Algorithm 3..

Similar to Q-learning, one advantage of WoLF-PHC learning is that it also only requires the minimum amount of information for each agent, i.e., each agent only needs to know its payoff obtained from each round of negotiation. However, Q-learning only enables the agents to learn pure strategy policies, while WoLF-PHC enables the agents to learn mixed strategy policies.

4   Experimental Evaluation

4.1   Experimental Settings

The payoff matrix for each pair of negotiating strategies in $S \times S$ is obtained based on extensive simulations over all the possible negotiation domains shown in Table 1. For any negotiation game, given a negotiating strategy profile $\mathcal{P}$, the corresponding payoff $U_i(\mathcal{P})$ for each agent i can be easily calculated based on Equation 1 and the payoffs in Table 1.

We start with the simplest setting, bilateral repeated negotiation, in which only two agents repeatedly negotiate with each other. The second negotiation

---

Algorithm 3. WoLF-PHC Learning in Repeated Negotiation Games

1: Initialize $Q^0(s) = 0$, $\pi^0(s) = \frac{1}{|S|}$, $C = 0$, $\forall s \in S$.
2: Initialize two learning rates ρ_s, ρ_l.
3: **repeat**
4:    Choose a negotiating strategy s from S according to the current mixed strategy policy $\pi^t(s)$ with appropriate exploration.
5:    Update its Q-table based on the payoff obtained in the current round following Equation 4.
6:    Update its average mixed strategy policy as follows,
      $C = C + 1$, $\bar{\pi}^t(s) = \bar{\pi}^{t-1}(s) + \frac{\bar{\pi}^{t-1}(s) - \pi^t(s)}{C}$, $\forall s \in S$
7:    Determine the learning rate ρ^t to update its mixed strategy policy $\pi^t(s)$ as follows,

$$\rho^t = \begin{cases} \rho_s & \sum_{s \in S_i} \pi^t(s)Q^t(s) \geq \sum_{s \in S_i} \bar{\pi}^t(s)Q^t(s) \\ \rho_l & \text{otherwise} \end{cases} \tag{5}$$

8:    Update its mixed strategy policy w.r.t. the Q-table.

$$\pi^{t+1}(s) = \begin{cases} \pi^t(s) + \sum_{s' \neq s} \delta(s') & Q(s) \text{ is the highest} \\ \pi^t(s) - \delta(s) & \text{otherwise} \end{cases} \tag{6}$$

   where $\delta(s) = \min(\pi^t(s), \frac{\rho^t}{|S|-1})$
9: **until** The negotiation game ends

---

setting we consider is three-agent repeated negotiation, and the last setting is to consider six-agent repeated negotiation. For all settings, each agent is allowed to choose any negotiating strategy from the strategy set S. Since the negotiation game itself is symmetric, we only need to care about the number of agents choosing each negotiating strategy. Therefore, in the following analysis, we merge those strategy profiles with the same number of agents choosing each negotiation strategy and treat them as the same outcome to make the results clearer. For example, an outcome $(G : 1, A : 1)$ in a bilateral negotiation means one agent chooses strategy G and the other chooses A, and covers both the strategy profiles of (G, A) and (A, G). The parameter settings for each learning appraoch are listed in Table 2.

Table 1. Payoff matrix for the top six negotiation strategies average over all domains (For each strategy profile, only the row player's payoff is given since the game is symmetric.) The letters in bold are the abbreviations for each strategy.

Payoff	G	H	I	A	C	O
G	0.680	0.520	0.812	0.676	0.580	0.555
H	0.662	0.599	0.757	0.569	0.604	0.549
I	0.622	0.564	0.715	0.595	0.470	0.492
A	0.709	0.590	0.787	0.568	0.664	0.561
C	0.740	0.639	0.826	0.552	0.597	0.590
O	0.697	0.628	0.771	0.551	0.605	0.571

Table 2. Parameter Settings for Each Learning Approach

Payoff Matrix	exploration rate ϵ	Learning Rate α	Learning Rate ρ_s	Learning Rate ρ_l
Fictitious-Play	0.05	N/A	N/A	N/A
Q-learning	0.05	0.6	N/A	N/A
WoLF-PHC	0.05	0.6	0.2	0.5

4.2   Bilateral Repeated Negotiations

In this setting, we first give the robustness analysis results based on the previous robustness analysis approach [1]: there only exists a best reply cycle of $(G : 1, A : 1) \rightarrow (G : 1, C : 1) \rightarrow (C : 1, A : 1)$. In other words, for any initial state, the agents would always converge to and stick in this cycle, however, it says nothing about dynamic details within that cycle (e.g., the probability that each strategy profile would be finally adopted by the agents) and the relative robustness of the strategies within that cycle.

Figure 1(a) shows the dynamics of the average frequency the previous three outcomes can be achieved as a function of the number of rounds when both agents negotiates following fictitious play. This can be considered as the dynamic way of understanding how the three outcomes within the best reply cycle evolve from one to another. Whenever the probability of reaching one outcome is decreased, the probability of reaching its neighbor outcome is increased. We can also observe that the basin of attraction of $(G : 1, A : 1)$ and $(G : 1, C : 1)$ (i.e., the frequencies of reaching these two outcomes) is usually larger that that of the outcome $(C : 1, A : 1)$, which thus may indicate that strategy G is more robust than the other two strategies in practice.

Figure 1(b) and Figure 2(a) show the average probabilities that the previous three outcomes can be achieved as a function of rounds when the agents negotiate following Q-learning and WoLF-PHC respectively. Different from fictitious play, it turns out surprisingly that the basin of attraction of outcome (G: 1, A: 1) (i.e., the probability of reaching it) is much larger than the rest of outcomes in the best reply cycle. We hypothesize that it is because in fictitious play the agents are assumed to know their payoff information for each pair of negotiating strategies beforehand, while this is not allowed in both Q-learning and WoLF-PHC. This result may indicate that in practice it is most likely that any rational agent would choose strategy G to participate in a bilateral negotiation while its (rational) opponent chooses strategy A and vice versa. In other words, strategy C is not as robust as the other two strategies G and A even though all of them are within the best reply cycle. For both Q-learning and WoLF-PHC learning, we can easily calcualte the basin of attraction of these three strategies and thus obtain their relative robustness ranking as follows: $G > A > C$.

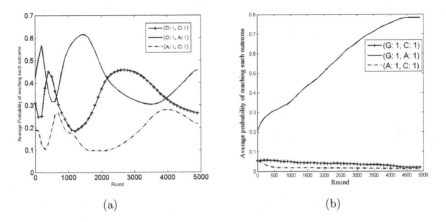

Fig. 1. Average probability of reaching each outcome for 2-agent case under a) fictitious play, b) Q-learning

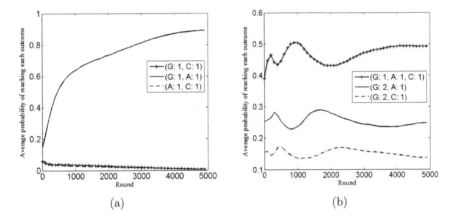

Fig. 2. (a) Average probability of reaching each outcome for 2-agent case WoLF-PHC learning, (b) Average probability of reaching each outcome for 3-agent case under fictitious play

4.3 Three-Agent Repeated Negotiation Tournaments over Six Strategies

Next we increase the number of agents in the negotiation and investigate the case of three-agent repeated negotiations where each agent is allowed to choose any negotiating strategy from S. We first give the analysis results based on the previous robustness analysis approach [1], which indicates that there only exists one best reply cycle: $(G : 2, C : 1) \rightarrow (G : 1, A : 1, C : 1) \rightarrow (G : 2, A : 1)$. This means that all these three strategies are more robust than the rest of strategies.

Figure 2(b) shows the average frequency of reaching the previous three outcomes as a function of rounds when all agents employ fictitious play. We can see that the frequencies of achieving these three outcomes are significantly different $((G : 1, A : 1, C : 1)$ ranks first, $(G : 2, A : 1)$ ranks second and $(G : 2, C : 1)$ ranks last) even though they are all within the best reply cycle. Based on this, we can also calculate the average frequency of each negotiating strategy can be adopted by the agents, and come to the conclusion of their robustness ranking as follows: $G > A > C$.

Figure 3(a) and 3(b) illustrate the average frequency the previous three outcomes can be reached as a function of the number of rounds when the agents employ Q-learning and WoLF-PHC respectively. The results for both cases are similar in that the probability of reaching outcome $(G : 2, A : 1)$ ($> 80\%$) is much higher than that of reaching the other two outcomes. This indicates that it is most likely that two agents would adopt strategy G while one agent adopt strategy A rather than always cycling around the three outcomes. Besides, this result also further confirms our previous conclusion that strategy C is not as robust as the other two strategies.

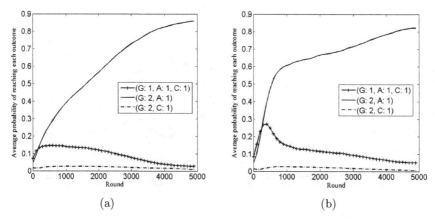

(a)   (b)

Fig. 3. Averag probability of reaching each outcome for 3-agent case under a) Q-learning, and b) WoLF-PHC learning

4.4   Six-Agent Repeated Negotiation Tournaments over Six Strategies

Finally we further increase the number of agents to be equal to the number of negotiating strategies. Based on the previous robustness analysis approach [1], we can know that there only exists one best reply cycle as follows: $(G : 4, A : 1, C : 1) \rightarrow (G : 4, C : 2) \rightarrow (G : 3, A : 1, C : 2) \rightarrow (G : 2, A : 2, C : 2) \rightarrow (G : 3, A : 2, C : 1) \rightarrow (G : 4, A : 2)$, which indicates that the agents will eventually reach this cycle and the three strategies G, A, and C are more robust than the rest of strategies. However, we cannot distinguish the relative robustness among these three negotiation strategies.

We present the dynamics of the frequency of reaching the previous six outcomes when all agents employ fictitious play in Figure 4(a). We can see that the frequencies of reaching each outcome vary dynamically, with $(G : 3, A : 2, C : 1)$ ranks first and $(G : 3, A : 1, C : 2)$ ranks second most of the time (the sum of the probabilities of reaching these two outcomes is about 70%). This means that it is most likely that the agents would frequently change their strategies between A and C during repeated negotiation, which thus indicates that strategy G is more robust than A and C, even though all of them are within the best reply cycle.

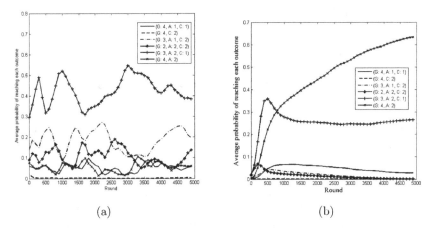

(a)   (b)

Fig. 4. Average probability of reaching each outcome for 6-agent case under a) fictitious play, b) Q-learning

Figure 4(b) and 5 illustrate the dynamics of the average frequency of reaching the previous six outcomes when the agents employ Q-learning and WoLF-PHC respectively. Both figures show similar results that the frequency of reaching outcomes $(G : 4, A : 2)$ and $(G : 3, A : 2, C : 1)$ dominates the rest of outcomes, i.e., the probability of reaching these two outcomes are much higher than the rest of them. Based on the average probabilities of reaching each outcomes within the best reply cycle, we can also approximately estimate the relative robustness of the three strategies G, A, and C, i.e., $G > A > C$, which is in consistent with the analytical results from previous two cases.

4.5   Discussion

From previous analysis results, we can see that our robustness analysis can provide more fine-grained analysis of the relative robustness of different negotiation strategies than the previous approach [1]. If there exists an empirical pure strategy Nash equilibrium, the corresponding interpretation under our analysis

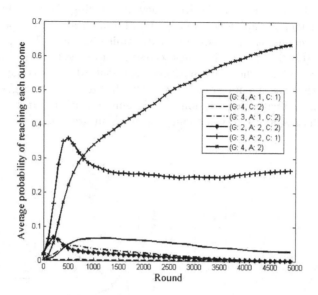

Fig. 5. Average probability of reaching each outcome for 6-agent case under WoLF-PHC learning

framework is that the negotiators learn to converge to that pure strategy equilibrium. If there exists a best reply cycle, for those learning strategies capable of learning a mixed strategy, one reasonable interpretation under our framework could be that the agents are actually learning to converge to the corresponding empirical mixed strategy Nash equilibrium.

From Section 4.2 to 4.4, only the results for one particular learning strategy are shown due to space limitation. However, it is worth noticing that for each tournament setting, the consistent analysis results are obtained for all three learning strategies. Intuitively, our analysis results reflect the relative robustness of different negotiation strategies when the negotiators are rational and have the freedom to choose their negotiation strategies based on their past experience. We believe that this kind of robustness analysis framework can better reflect the practical multi-agent negotiation scenarios (e.g., e-commerce area) which usually involves repeated negotiations [10], and thus provide more accurate predictions of which negotiation strategies are more likely to be adopted in practice.

5   Related Work

Baarslag et al. [1] firstly propose an alternative evaluation criterion, *robustness*, to evaluate the performance of different negotiation strategies from a different perspective based on empirical game-theoretic analysis. The authors investigate the relative robustness of the top 8 strategies participating in ANAC'11 competition in different tournament settings. Their analysis provides some interesting results. For the bilateral negotiation setting, it is found that the winning strategy in ANAC'11 is not the most robust strategy, and also no pair of agents adopting the same negotiating strategy is stable. For the setting of 8-player tournament with three strategies, it is surprisingly found that the Gahboninho strategy, which is not the winner strategy, seems to be the most robust strategy. For the last setting of 8-players tournament with 8-strategy, it is also found that the non-winner Gahboninho strategy is more robust than the winning strategy HardHeaded. All the previous robustness analysis can provide us with some useful insights about which strategies would be adopted by agents in practice. However, the robustness analysis is limited by the assumption of single-agent best-deviation and the requirement of global payoff information, which may not be realistic in practice. Last, when the agents end up with a best reply cycle, it provides us with little information about the relative robustness of the strategies.

Williams el al. [15] propose a novel concession negotiating strategy, which make concessions based on the observed concession of the opponent and other negotiation constraints under the elapsed real time. They evaluate the efficiency of their strategy against the state-of-the-art strategies under a number of benchmark domains taken from ANAC'10. The simulation results show that their strategy is more efficient in terms of the average payoff obtained over all opponents. The authors also evaluate the robustness of their strategy based on empirical game-theoretic analysis, and focus on the case of 5 players' tournament negotiation with the top 3 strategies. It is found that their strategy is the most robust one among all strategies considered and all agents have the incentive to switch to their strategy eventually. Their robustness analysis follows the work of Baarslag et al. [1], and thus suffers from the same limitations as theirs.

Chen and Weiss [5] propose a novel negotiating strategy, Dragon, which employs sparse pseudo-input Gaussian processes to support more accurate estimations of the opponent's behaviors. In their robustness analysis, they focus on the bilateral negotiation setting among eight strategies, and it is found that the only stable state is when one agent adopts the Dragon strategy while the other agent adopts the TheNegotiator Reloaded strategy from ANAC'12. The result indicates that Dragon strategy is robust compared with others in the bilateral negotiation setting. However, the robustness analysis also follows the work of Baarslag et al. [1], and thus the same limitations as theirs [1] apply here.

6   Conclusion and Future Work

We introduce the concept of repeated negotiation game and propose employing different rational learning strategies to provide more realistic and fine-grained analysis of the robustness of different negotiating strategies. We make extensive evaluation of the top 6 negotiation strategies participated in the past three-year negotiations under three different negotiation tournament settings. Through our analysis, we show that more insights in terms of the relative robustness of different negotiation strategies can be revealed, which are usually not available from the analysis using the previous approach [1]. As future work, we are going to further generalize the robustness evaluation process in a more formal and systematic way to make the robustness evaluation and analysis of different negotiating strategies more meaningful and efficient.

Acknowledgement. The work presented in this paper was partially supported by a CUHK Research Committee Funding (Direct Grants) (Reference no. EE13379).

References

1. Baarslag, T., Fujita, K., Gerding, E.H., Hindriks, K., Ito, T., Jennings, N.R., Jonker, C., Kraus, S., Lin, R., Robu, V., Williams, C.R.: Evaluating practical negotiating agents: Results and analysis of the 2011 international competition. Artificial Intelligence Journal 198, 73–103 (2013)
2. Baarslag, T., Hindriks, K., Jonker, C., Kraus, S., Lin, R.: The first automated negotiating agents competition (ANAC 2010). In: Ito, T., Zhang, M., Robu, V., Fatima, S., Matsuo, T. (eds.) New Trends in Agent-Based Complex Automated Negotiations. SCI, vol. 383, pp. 113–135. Springer, Heidelberg (2012)
3. Bowling, M.H., Veloso, M.M.: Multiagent learning using a variable learning rate. Artificial Intelligence 136, 215–250 (2003)
4. Brown, G.: Iterative solution of games by fictitious play. Activity analysis of production and allocation (1951)
5. Chen, S.Q., Ammar, H.B., Tuyls, K.I., Weiss, G.: Optimizing complex automated negotiation using sparse pseudo-input gaussian processes. In: AAMAS 2013, pp. 707–714 (2013)
6. Coehoorn, R.M., Jennings, N.R.: Learning an opponent's preferences to make effective multi-issue negotiation trade-offs. In: ICEC 2004, pp. 59–68 (2004)
7. Hao, J.Y., Leung, H.F.: Abines: An adaptive bilateral negotiating strategy over multiple items. In: WI-IAT 2012, pp. 95–102 (2012)
8. Hindriks, K., Tykhonov, D.: Opponent modeling in auomated multi-issue negotiation using bayesian learning. In: AAMAS 2008, pp. 331–338 (2008)
9. Estelle, J., Wellman, M.P., Singh, S., Vorbeychik, Y., Soni, V.: Strategic interactions in a supply chain game. Computational Intelligence 21(1), 1–26 (2005)
10. Saha, S., Biswas, A., Sen, S.: Modeling opponent decision in repeated one-shot negotiations. In: AAMAS 2005, pp. 397–403 (2005)
11. Sen, S., Airiau, S.: Emergence of norms through social learning. In: IJCAI 2007, pp. 1507–1512 (2007)
12. Song, J.Y.H.S.Z., Leung, H.F., Ming, Z.: An efficient and robust negotiating strategy in bilateral negotiations over multiple items. Engineering Applications of Artificial Intelligence 34, 45–57 (2014)
13. Vytelingum, P., Cliff, D., Jennings, N.R.: Strategic bidding in continuous double auctions. Artificial Intelligence 172(14), 1700–1729 (2008)
14. Watkins, C.J.C.H., Dayan, P.D.: Q-learning. Machine Learning 3, 279–292 (1992)
15. Williams, C.R., Robu, V., Gerding, E.H., Jennings, N.R.: Using gaussian processes to optimise concession in complex negotiations against unknown opponents. In: IJCAI 2012, pp. 432–438 (2012)

Using Multi-attribute Combinatorial Auctions for Resource Allocation

Ferran Torrent-Fontbona, Albert Pla, and Beatriz López

University of Girona, Girona 17071, Spain
{ferran.torrent,albert.pla,beatriz.lopez}@udg.edu
eia.udg.es/~ftorrent

Abstract. Social concerns about the environment and global warming suggest that industries must focus on reducing energy consumption, due to its social impact and changing laws. Furthermore, the smart grid will bring time-dependent tariffs that pose new challenges to the optimisation of resource allocation. In this paper we address the problem of optimising energy consumption in manufacturing processes by means of multi-attribute combinatorial auctions, so that resource price, delivery time, and energy consumed (and therefore environmental impact) are minimised. The proposed mechanism is tested with simulated data based on real examples, showing the impact of incorporating energy into task allocation problems. It is then compared with a sequential auction method.

Keywords: auctions, multi-attribute, smart grid, energy, resource allocation.

1 Introduction

In the coming years it will become crucial to incorporate energy into manufacturing process management due to environmental concerns, time-dependent electricity prices (see Figure 1) and new legislation (i.e. legislation based on energy related standards such as ISO:50001). Smart grids will use these variable prices to reduce overall energy requirements by, for example, filling valleys or cutting peaks in the energy load (see Figure 2), contributing to more sustainable use of energy. As a consequence, the problem of allocating resources to tasks needs to be revised from the energy point of view. In this regard, some previous works have claimed that the resource allocation problem is apt to be redesigned to take account of energy use [11], and some researchers have started to look for solutions in market-based frameworks, such as auctions [23]. However, in [23] the authors follow a single criteria optimisation formulation, considering energy consumption but not price. Including energy (not only energy costs but energy consumption and/or environmental footprint) in resource allocation alters the problem from a single criterion to a multi-criteria one, so all involved objectives should be handled at once. Moreover, when there are several tasks involved in the allocation problem, the problem itself becomes a combinatorial problem, not only due to the capacity limitations of the resource agents, but also due to variable energy prices, and modifications in time and energy consumption when an agent is responsible for more than one task.

Our research concerns production scheduling where the arrival of tasks is unknown in advance. Thus, in this paper we propose to allocate tasks under demand in such a way

J.P. Müller, M. Weyrich, and A.L.C. Bazzan (Eds.): MATES 2014, LNAI 8732, pp. 57–71, 2014.

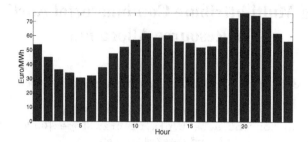

Fig. 1. Average day hourly energy price of the Spanish production market in December 2012 according to [20]. Electricity companies are expected to transfer these variable prices to customers to flatten their energy consumption curves.

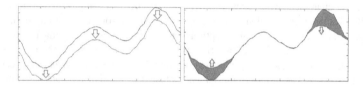

Fig. 2. On the left: illustration of energy efficiency where each curve correspond to a load shape. On the right: illustration of peak reduction and valley filling of an energy consumption curve.

that energy consumption, resource prices and delivery times are taken into account. To this end, our contribution is to solve this allocation problem using an auction mechanism with the following characteristics:

1. Multi-attribute, enabling the auction clearing by handling all the objectives involved: energy, price and delivery time.
2. Combinatorial, as several tasks can be allocated at once whilst bidders can send combinations of bids with different costs. Regarding energy, for example, a bidder could offer two OR bids, one with an energy consumption equals to 5 kWh for deploying task $T1$, and another one with a consumption of 7 kWh for deploying tasks $T1, T2$; however, it is not interested in performing $T2$ alone. This could be because task $T2$ consumes a lot of energy alone (i.e. it requires warming an engine), but its cost diminishes when performed after task $T1$.

Our starting point is the VMA2 auction framework [18], which enables us to deal with multi-attributes auctions, and the combinatorial auction approach with energy issues described in [23]. From these two previous work we define a new auction mechanism that we call a Multi-Attribute Combinatorial Auction (MACA). The main contribution of the paper is to put together these previous works, so as we extend the multi-attribute approach of VMA2 to handle bundles of tasks and introduce different attributes to the combinatorial approach of [23]. As a result, with MACA, we are able to allocate resources to tasks handling variable energy costs and other attributes. We also analyse the tool's performance in a real-world scenario.

This paper is organised as follows. In the following section we review some related work. In Section 3, we explain the auction approach. In section 4 we present the results obtained in experimental testing, and prove a discussion of them. In Section 5 we present our conclusions and propose some future work.

2 Related Work

Resource allocation and job scheduling problems are well-known problems which have been the focus of much research. For example, [1] formalizes the problem, considering multi-skill resources and proposing a Branch and Bound (B&B) algorithm to solve it, minimising the makespan; in [26] the problem is also formalized and the authors propose a heuristic method to solve the problem, optimising the task's execution cost and considering stochastic durations of the tasks. Furthermore, [3,4,18,21] propose solutions to the workflow scheduling problem using auctions due to the distributed nature of the context they consider. This is also the case in the present study; however these earlier studies do not consider combinatorial or multi-attribute auctions as we do.

Concerning multi-attribute auctions, a key work is [2], where the author describes different scenarios regarding the payment rule and demonstrates that to achieve incentive compatibility the payment should be derived by matching the evaluation of the payment and the provided attributes with the evaluation obtained by the second best bid. In a later work, [15] proposes an adaptation of the Vickrey-Clarke-Groves method [13] (VCG) for multi-attribute auctions under an iterative schema (bidders are allowed to modify their bids in response to the bids from other agents). In our work, we use a similar approach to determine the auction winner and its payment, however we do not allow iteration. In practice, bid iteration leads to a slower procedure due to the increase of communications and a possible loss of privacy for bidders, who may not want to reveal their offers to competitors. These drawbacks may be acceptable in cases where auctions appear only occasionally and where losing an auction might lead to a long period without workload for bidders. However, in our problem the allocation of resources to tasks is performed on a continuous basis on the arrival of new tasks; therefore we prefer to use Vickrey auctions, which provide equivalent results in a more straight forward mechanism [22]. Another interesting approach for multi-attribute auctions is VMA2 [18], which allows auctioning tasks and resources based on different kinds of attributes which can be defined by bidders and by attributes. However, VMA2 is intended for auctioning single and isolated tasks whilst we aim to auction bundles of tasks.

Public institutions are making great efforts to design and develop a future smart grid [5,6]. Moreover, many researchers are focusing on developing new household management systems that deal with time-dependent rates, [14], studying consumers' behaviour when faced with variable prices [7,10,14] and studying and designing a new negotiation system between electricity companies (distributors), producers and consumers [24]. Despite this great research, little work has been done relating to workflow management considering time dependent energy rates. In [9] Simonis and Hadzic developed some lower bounds based on cumulative constraints to use with the problem solving algorithm. In [11] the authors consider time-dependent energy rates in a workflow context and propose a solution to the scheduling problem by using reverse auctions, presenting a new formalization of the problem. In any of these previous approaches the consumption agreement is combined with the time-dependent rates, as we are doing here.

3   Methodology

In this paper we deal with job scheduling and resource allocation having in mind the new challenges posed by the smart grid and the environmental impact of the performance of tasks.

In particular, we are dealing with the problem of allocation of resources to tasks assuming a dynamic environment, such that tasks are unknown in advance of their arrival. In this scenario, an agent is in charge of handling task arrivals and assigning appropriate resources to carry out tasks. At a given moment of time, there are multiple tasks to be performed, each with different requirements. Resources that can deploy the tasks are handled by other agents. Resources are allocated to tasks following an auction protocol.

An auction is a method for buying and selling goods or items using a bid system in which the best bids obtain the sold items. In domains where the aim is to allocate or outsource tasks to third party companies it is common to follow a reverse auction schema: an auctioneer needs a task to be done and offers to pay an external provider for carrying it (becoming the buyer who aims to buy a service at the cheapest price) whilst bidders offer their working capacity at a given price (becoming the sellers who compete to offer the best working conditions at the cheapest price). This reverse auction schema is the one followed in this research.

The auction approach is of particular interest when we tackle allocation of energy consuming tasks under variable energy costs. In this case, auctions offer bidders the chance to handle energy costs for tasks, leaving the assignment process to the auctioneer: bidders provide offers to deploy tasks at a given time, at a given price and with the energy costs they would incur; thus, no alternatives other than those provided in the bid would be considered by the auctioneer.

However, the management of multiple attributes other than price (e.g. energy consumption and delivery times) requires a multi-criteria decision. Moreover, the dependencies between attributes and bidder's schedules (e.g. the time when a task is being performed conditions its costs due to variable energy prices) will push bidders to submit multiple bids with different attribute configurations. In consequence, we need to use a combinatorial multi-attribute auction mechanism. The mechanism is described below, according to the 4 main steps of the protocol: call for proposals, bidding, determining the winner, and payment. We consider companies as agents that act from self-interest in order to increase their own utility. They will aim to outsource tasks on the best possible terms (auctioneer agents) or they will aim to sell their resources in order to perform tasks at the highest prices for the lowest effort (bidder agents).

3.1   Call for Proposals

When an auctioneer needs to outsource a task it sends a call for proposals indicating the different tasks constraints and the required skills RQ_i to all the bidders $(a_1...a_n)$ inside the market. Each set of tasks is defined as a set of independent tasks $\mathbf{T} = \{T_1 \ldots T_{|\mathbf{T}|}\}$. Each task is defined as follows:

$$T_i = \langle \left[\underline{s_i}, \overline{s_i}\right], \left[\underline{et_i}, \overline{et_i}\right], \mathbf{RQ}_i \rangle \tag{1}$$

where $\underline{s_i}$ is the task earliest start time , and $\overline{s_i}$ the latest start time; $\underline{et_i}$ the earliest end time and $\overline{et_i}$ the latest end time; and $\mathbf{RQ}_i$ is a list with the resource skills required by the task. All of this parameters ($\left[\underline{s_i}, \overline{s_i}\right]$, $\left[\underline{et_i}, \overline{et_i}\right]$, $\mathbf{RQ}_i$) constitute the task constraints of our problem. Bidders aiming to perform a certain task need to have available resources with the required skills, otherwise they will be unable to perform the task. On the other hand, they should provide actual starting times for tasks and duration that agree with the task time windows $\left[\underline{s_i}, \overline{s_i}\right]$ and $\left[\underline{et_i}, \overline{et_i}\right]$.

3.2 Bidding

Once a bidder receives the auctioneer's proposal, if the bidder is interested in any of the auctioned tasks and is able to provide an offer according to the task's constraints, it offers a bundle of bids where each bid describes possible conditions (price, energy consumption and delivery time) under which the bidder can perform the task. It is worth noting that in doing so, each resource agent has its own energy constraints and resource capacity constraints, which are opaque to other agents, and which are summarised in the bids.

Every bidder can send several bids with different configurations for the same task, because (due to variable energy prices) the cost of performing a task may change depending on the time it is scheduled and on other tasks the bidder could be assigned to perform. This leads to combinatorial auctions, meaning that agents bid bundles of tasks at different prices and conditions. We followed the notation presented in [23] to express combinatorial bids where the kth bid proposed by the jth bidder to perform the ith task is defined as

$$B_{i,j,k} = \langle T_i @ s_{i,j,k} : (\mu_{i,j,k}, \epsilon_{i,j,k}, \delta_{i,j,k}), M_{i,j,k}, E_{i,j,k}, \Delta_{i,j,k} \rangle \tag{2}$$

where T_i is the ith task to which the bid is submitted, $s_{i,j,k}$ is the start time proposed by the bidder, $\mu_{i,j,k}$ is the price of the bid, $\epsilon_{i,j,k}$ is the energy consumption and $\delta_{i,j,k}$ is the duration; $M_{i,j,k}$, $E_{i,j,k}$ and $\Delta_{i,j,k}$ are $N \times 1$ vectors that indicate modifications on the price, energy consumption and duration (respectively) if the bid is accepted together with another bid of the same bidder. In this way $E_{i,j,k}(l)$ indicates a modification on the energy consumption of $B_{i,j,k}$ if the lth bid of bidder i is also accepted to perform its corresponding task.

In our work we consider three attributes: price, energy and duration. However, this can be generalised to apply more attributes according to the ethos suggested by [18].

3.3 Winner Determination Problem

Once bidding period is over, the auctioneer must decide which bids maximise its expected utility [19]. For that purpose it calculates the utility of each bid and seeks the optimal combination of bids with the highest utility. The utility of the auctioneer given a bid $B_{i,j,k}$ for having a task T_i made, is defined as follows:

$$u(T_i, B_{i,j,k}) = v(T_i) - f(B_{i,j,k}) \tag{3}$$

where $v(T_i)$ is the value considered by the auctioneer for having task T_i completed and $f(B_{i,j,k})$ is the cost of bid $B_{i,j,k}$ for the auctioneer considering all the dimensions involved in the allocation (economic cost, ending time and energy consumption). Note that, given T_i, maximising $u(T_i, B_{i,j,k})$ is equivalent to minimising $f(B_{i,j,k})$. Thus, the winner determination problem (WDP) is defined as:

$$argmin_{j,k} \sum_{i,j,k} x_{i,j,k} * f(B_{i,j,k}) \tag{4}$$

Subject to

- $x_{i,j,k} = 1$ if bid $B_{i,j,k}$ is selected; otherwise $x_{i,j,k} = 0$
- Each task is assigned to and executed by a single bidder/bid $\sum_{j,k} x_{i,j,k} = 1, \forall i$
- All tasks constraints are satisfied

However, this minimisation problem is not trivial due to the set-up times regarding $M_{i,j,k}$, $E_{i,j,k}$ and $\Delta_{i,j,k}$. One possible way to simplify the problem is to use auxiliary variables to express the final price $b_{i,j,k}$ of a bid, the final end time $t_{i,j,k}$, and the final energy consumption $e_{i,j,k}$:

$$b_{i,j,k} = \mu_{i,j,k} + \sum_{l=1}^{N_j} M_{i,j,k}(l) \cdot x_{i,j,l} \tag{5}$$

$$t_{i,j,k} = s_{i,j,k} + \delta_{i,j,k} + \sum_{l=1}^{N_j} \Delta_{i,j,k}(l) \cdot x_{i,j,l} \tag{6}$$

$$e_{i,j,k} = \epsilon_{i,j,k} + \sum_{l=1}^{N_j} E_{i,j,k}(l) \cdot x_{i,j,l} \tag{7}$$

where N_j is the number of bids sent by the jth bidder.

The winner determination problem can be then reformulated as follows:

$$argmin_{j,k} \sum_{i,j,k} x_{i,j,k} * f(b_{i,j,k}, t_{i,j,k}, e_{i,j,k}) \tag{8}$$

Subject to the same constraints as above. Note that the minimisation problem considers all tasks ($\forall i$).

Therefore the problem of the determination of the auction winner(s) can be solved by minimising f, which combines the different attributes of bids (price, time and energy), becoming by definition a key issue for the winner determination problem. For the mechanism to be feasible, we consider V (a particular case of f) as an aggregation function which must be a real-valued monotonic bijective function [17]. In particular, in this paper we use the weighted sum but other functions could be considered as well (see [17] for alternative evaluation functions):

$$V(b_{i,j,k}, t_{i,j,k}, e_{i,j,k}) = w_0 \cdot b_{i.j.k} + w_1 \cdot t_{i,j,k} + w_2 \cdot e_{i,j,k} \qquad (9)$$

$$\sum_k w_k = 1 \qquad (10)$$

The complexity of solving the problem is exponential [23,3], and complete methods cannot provide a solution in a realistic amount of time when the number of tasks and bids increases. Therefore, the use of meta-heuristic methods is a good alternative to obtain near optimal solutions. We decided to use Genetic Algorithm (GA) [12,8], because its use does not involve many mathematical assumptions about the problem (they can handle any kind of objective function and constraint). Also, it is a very effective tool for global search (there is no need for convexity in the objective function).

The GA used represents solutions as strings of bids (chromosomes) where each slot of the string corresponds to a particular task. To create new chromosomes it uses a selection operator, a crossover operator and a mutation operator. The selection operator is 3 tournament selection, [8], which consists in selecting 3 random chromosomes and choosing the best as the 1st parent. The process is repeated for choosing the 2nd parent. Once the parents are selected, it uses the 2 cross-point crossover operator, [8], to create 2 new chromosomes exchanging the genetic information of the parents. Finally, the new chromosomes mutate changing each bid (gene) for another randomly selected with a probability of 5%. To maintain the population, an elitism operator is used. It consists in removing all the chromosomes except the best. The algorithm is explained in Algorithm 1, where N_g is the number of generations and N_p is the size of the population.

Algorithm 1. Genetic Algorithm

Require: $N_g = 2000$, $N_p = 300$
1: Create N_p random chromosomes
2: **for** $g \leftarrow 1$ **to** N_g **do**
3:     **for** $i \leftarrow 1$ **to** $N_p/2$ **do**
4:         Select 2 parents using the 3 tournament selection
5:         Breed two new chromosomes using 2 cross-point crossover
6:         Apply mutation operator over the new chromosomes
7:         Compute fitness of the new chromosomes using V_0
8:     **end for**
9:     Elitism: remove all chromosomes except the N_p best
10: **end for**
11: select the best chromosome as solution

3.4 Payment

A payment rule is used to establish the economic amount that auctioneers must pay to the auction winner(s) for performing any task. Given the multi-dimensional nature of the allocation problem we are dealing with, payment is not only conditioned by the bidded economic amounts but also by other attributes. For instance, delivering a task later than agreed may involve receiving less money than the initial bid amount. Moreover, the auctioneer cannot assume that bidders will follow a truthful bidding strategy. In order to encourage bidders to bid truthfully regarding their economic costs the VCG payment mechanism can be used [25]. This payment considers that the payment $p_{i,j,k}$ for bidder j for performing task i according to bid $B_{i,j,k}$ will correspond to the difference of the welfare all bidders would have obtained if the winning bid had not been sent to the auction and the welfare they receive with the chosen allocation excluding the welfare for bid $B_{i,j,k}$. However, such a mechanism considers a single attribute, price, and does not guarantee that bidders deliver tasks to the terms agreed during the bidding process (i.e. due to estimation errors [18]). So we modify the VCG payment mechanism in order to reduce the auctioneer's utility loss when bidders do not deliver tasks to the agreed attributes.

The payment rule proposed is a two case method: on the one hand, when winning bidders are successful (delivering the task as agreed) they receive a payment $p_{i,j,k}$ according to a classical VCG auction schema. On the other hand, if the bidder delivers a task in worst conditions than the agreed (i.e. $t'_{i,j,k}, e'_{i,j,k}$ instead of $t_{i,j,k}, e_{i,j,k}$), it will receive a smaller payment in such a way that the valuation of the obtained payment $p_{i,j,k}$ and the delivered attributes matches the valuation of the initially presented bid, as follows:

$$V(p_{i,j,k}, t'_{i,j,k}, e'_{i,j,k}) = V(b_{i,j,k}, t_{i,j,k}, e_{i,j,k}) \tag{11}$$

where $t'i, j, k$ and $e'_{i,j,k}$ are the true delivery time and the final energy consumption. Therefore the payment is defined as follows:

$$p_{i,j,k} = \begin{cases} V^{-1}\left(\Phi_{i,j,k}, t'_{i,j,k}, e'_{i,j,k}\right) & \text{if } t'_{i,j,k} \prec t_{i,j,k}, e'_{i,j,k} \prec e_{i,j,k} \\ V^{-1}\left(V\left(b_{i,j,k}, t_{i,j,k}, e_{i,j,k}\right), t'_{i,j,k}, e'_{i,j,k}\right) & \text{otherwise} \end{cases} \tag{12}$$

where

$$\Phi_{i,j,k} = \sum_{(l,m,n) \in G_{-(i,j,k)}} V\left(b_{l,m,n}, t_{l,m,n}, e_{l,m,n}\right) - \\ \sum_{(x,y,z) \in G \backslash (x,y,z) \neq (i,j,k)} V\left(b_{x,y,z}, t_{x,y,z}, e_{x,y,z}\right) \tag{13}$$

where $\prec$ means *worse than*, G is the set of winning bids, $G_{-(i,j,k)}$ is the set of bids that would have won the auction if bid $B_{i,j,k}$ had not been sent, $G \backslash (x, y, z) \neq (i, j, k)$ indicates the set of winning bids different to $B_{i,j,k}$ and where

$$V^{-1}\left(\Phi_{i,j,k}, t'_{i,j,k}, e'_{i,j,k}\right)$$

is the reverse function of $V(b_{i,j,k}, t_{i,j,k}, e_{i,j,k}) = x$ which given $x, t_{i,j,k}, e_{i,j,k}$ returns $b_{i,j,k}$. Note that for achieving the set $G_{-(i,j,k)}$, we need to resolve the WDP but removing the bid $B_{i,j,k}$.

In this way bidders are encouraged to bid truthfully: on the one hand, if they underbid regarding any attribute, bidders do not increase their utility (and they could lose utility, because if they win they are forced to work under the bid conditions). On the other hand,

Table 1. Example of 3 bidders bidding for 3 different tasks. It shows the values of the attributes and the global value of the bids considering the weighted sum (with all weights equal to $\frac{1}{3}$ in Equation 9). Winning bids are in bold face. Numbers in brackets correspond to the bid values (considering set-up costs) if tasks T_1 and T_2 are assigned to bidder 2.

	T_1				T_2				T_3			
	b	e	t	V_0	b	e	t	V_0	b	e	t	V_0
Bidder 1	**20**	**5**	**5**	**10**	10	7	7	8	**6**	**5**	**3**	**5**
Bidder 2	20	10	6	12	**7 (5)**	**5 (4)**	**3 (3)**	**5 (4)**	10	7	7	8
Bidder 3	25	10	10	15	8	8	5	7	15	10	5	10

overbidding will reduce their chances of winning the auction. Finally, underdelivering confers a payment reduction which will reduce the bidder's utility (encouraging it to improve its attribute estimation) whilst avoiding a loss of utility from the auctioneer's side (for instance, paying less to the winning bidder will allow the auctioneer to hire better resources in future).

Example 1 (Payment rule example)
Consider the example of Table 1 where three different bidders have sent three bids each (for three tasks), and where the evaluation function V of the auctioneer is a weighted sum with all the weights set to $w = \frac{1}{3}$. According to the values of Table 1, bidder 1 is the winner for performing tasks T_1 and T_3, and bidder 2 is the winner for T_2.

When a task is delivered to the agreed conditions, the payment to the bidder for performing a task according to a particular bid is computed according to Equations (12) and (13). First, we compute the payment of bidder 1: $\Phi_{1,1,1}$ is the difference between the valuations of bids $B_{2,1,1}$, $B_{2,2,2}$ and $B_{3,1,3}$ (winning bids if bid $B_{1,1,1}$ had not been sent) and the valuations of bids $B_{2,2,2}$ and $B_{3,1,3}$ (winning bids except $B_{1,1,1}$). Thus, considering Table 1,

$$\Phi_{1,1,1} = (12 + 4 + 5) - (5 + 5) = 11 \tag{14}$$

Note that when we consider that bid $B_{1,1,1}$ is not sent, we have to consider set-up costs of bid $B_{2,2,2}$ because T_1 would have been assigned to bidder 2. Then, $b_{2,2,2} = 5$, $t_{2,2,2} = 3$, $e_{2,2,2} = 4$ and $V(5,3,4) = 4$.

Then, the payment $p_{1,1,1}$ corresponding to bidder 1 for doing task 1 according to $B_{1,1,1}$ is calculated according to Equation (12) as follows:

$$p_{1,1,1} = \frac{\Phi_{1,1,1}}{w} - \left(t'_{1,1,1} + e'_{1,1,1}\right) = \frac{11}{0.33} - (5 + 5) = 23 \tag{15}$$

Similarly, payments corresponding to bids $B_{2,2,2}$ and $B_{3,1,3}$ are 13 and 16 respectively if the tasks are delivered to the agreed conditions.

However, if we assume that bidder 2 does task T_2 with an energy consumption of $e'_{2,2} = 8$ instead of 5, the corresponding payment is calculated according the second branch of Equation (12). Thus,

$$p_{2,2,2} = \frac{V(b_{1,1,1}, t_{1,1,1}, e_{1,1,1})}{w} - \left(t'_{1,1,1} + e'_{1,1,1}\right) = \frac{5}{0.33} - (3 + 8) = 4 \tag{16}$$

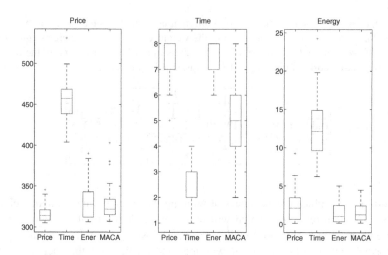

Fig. 3. Values of the attributes of the winning bids when we optimise a single attribute (monetary cost, time or energy) or the aggregation of all of them (horizontal axis). Y axis: (left) price, (center) time, (right) energy.

So, bidder 2 would receive a payment of 4 instead of 13 for not fulfilling the agreed energy consumption.

4   Experimentation

In this section we analyse the performance of the presented methodology using a multi-agent simulator based on real data [16]. First, we analyse the results when we perform uni-criteria allocations and when we perform a multi-criteria allocation. Second, we analyse the allocation results obtained with the multi-attribute combinatorial auction mechanism proposed in this paper and we compare them with the results obtained with VMA2, a multi-attribute (but) sequential auction (one task auctioned after the other). Finally we discuss the results achieved regarding our research objectives.

4.1   Experimentation Set-Up

The data over which we conducted experimentation is based on a real industry process[1]. Tasks are managed by an agent (auctioneer) that outsources some of its tasks to 7 other agents (bidders) with different skills. Each task requires a particular skill and conveys an economic cost, a particular execution time and an energy consumption. The tasks and attribute values are obtained from probability distribution functions which were modelled using data from real business processes[1]. Each bidder is assigned a particular energy tariff which conveys variable energy prices. Agents' behaviour is modelled as competitive and greedy.

---

[1] Data available at http://eia.udg.es/$~$apla/fac_data

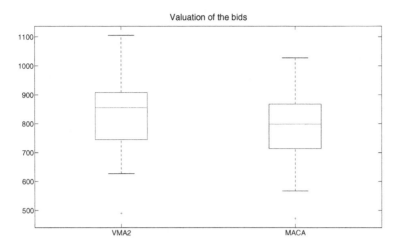

Fig. 4. Comparison of the average aggregated cost of the winning bids when using MACA or VMA2

4.2 Experiment 1: Uni-attribute versus Multi-attribute Combinatorial Auctions

The goal of the experiment is to point out the importance of aggregating all the objectives that an organisation needs to consider, especially, when they cannot be optimised simultaneously. Then the use of aggregation functions provides solutions with a trade-off between the objectives.

For that purpose, in this experiment we compare the allocation of the tasks of a single day considering uni-criteria (combinatorial auctions) and multi-criteria valuation functions (MACA). We computed the resulting task allocation using our auction mechanism considering a uni-attribute approach (considering only the price, or the delivery time, or the energy consumption of the bids in Equations (8) and (12)) and using a multi-criteria approach (determining the auction winner using aggregation function V). The experiment was conducted over 50 sets of tasks.

Figure 3 shows the box plot of the attributes of the winning bids when the auctioneer wants to optimise a single attribute (price, or time, or energy) or the aggregation of all of them. It points out that in this experiment, it is impossible to optimise all the attributes, i.e. the optimisation of time greatly increases the price and energy consumption. However, when we aggregate all attributes, the obtained allocation is a trade-off between the objectives. Such trade-off is determined by the aggregation function. For example, we see in Figure 3 that optimising the aggregation of all attributes, reports a solution in terms of price and energy very close to the optimal; and in terms of time the solution is between the optimal and the solutions obtained when we optimise only either price or energy (which are far worse than when we only optimise time).

ANOVA analysis over the values of price, time and energy of Figure 3 shows that the results obtained optimising different attributes can be considered that come from different distributions with p-values lower than 10^{-73}. Even the results from optimising either price, energy, or the aggregation (MACA) are different, with p-values lower

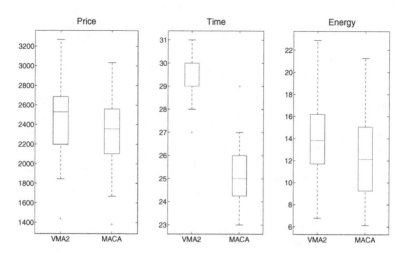

Fig. 5. Comparison of the values of the attributes of the the winner bids when using MACA or VMA2. The values for VMA2 consist of the aggregation of the results of auctioning one after the other the same tasks than in MACA.

than 10^{-2}. Even paired-response tests tell us that with a significance value of 0.05 we can consider that the values of either price or time or energy, obtained when we optimise the either price or time or energy respectively, are better than we optimise another objective.

4.3 Experiment 2: Multi-attribute Sequential versus Multi-attribute Combinatorial Auctions

Experiment 2 compared the performance of VMA2 and MACA. VMA2 [18] auctions one task at a time (sequential auction). Therefore, the order in which tasks are auctioned could affect the results. On the other hand, with the approach presented in this paper, MACA, all the tasks are auctioned at the same time (combinatorial). Although the benefits of combinatorial auctions as compared to sequential ones are very well known, in this paper we are considering multi-attribute auctions, both in VMA2 and MACA. In particular, experiment 2 is used to point to the cost differences when using each method.

For that purpose, we computed and compared the allocation for the tasks of a single day using a multi-attribute combinatorial auction approach (MACA) and a multi-attribute sequential auction approach (VMA2). Experiments were also repeated 50 times to obtain meaningful results. To compare VMA2 and MACA we auctioned the same tasks, but VMA2 auctioned them sequentially and MACA auctioned them concurrently. To compare the results we aggregated the results of VMA2. We calculated the makespan, for VMA2, as the difference between the ending of the last task and the auction time of the first time. MACA computes the makespan as the difference between the end time of the last task performed and the auction time.

Figures 4 and 5 show the results obtained in this scenario. As we expected, MACA outperforms VMA2 in terms of aggregated cost (price, time and energy) because it is able to consider bundles of tasks and is therefore, able to provide better allocation. We also tested the results with pair-response tests, which showed that we can assume that the aggregated cost of the winning bids when using MACA is lower than when using VMA2 at the significance level of 0.05. ANOVA analysis also discards that both collection of values come from a population with the same mean with a p-value of 0.0472.

Regarding the values of the attributes, pair-response tests also show that with a significance level of 0.05 we can assume that the values of the attributes using MACA and GA are better than VMA2. ANOVA analysis also discard that results of MACA and VMA2 regarding the values of the attributes come from populations with the same mean with p-values of 0.0417 (for price), $1.25 \cdot 10^{-35}$ (for makespan) and 0.012 (for energy consumption).

4.4 Discussion

Results obtained in the first experiments show that our auction mechanism, MACA, is able to deal with several objectives at a time, meaning that we are able to take account of energy issues when allocating resources to tasks. On the other hand, the second experiment corroborates the benefits of using MACA to deal with bundles of tasks, handling set-up constraints regarding different attributes (time, money, energy), which results in a better outcome than assigning tasks in a sequential way. Therefore, our new mechanism MACA improves upon previous mechanisms (such as VMA2), whilst meeting the multi-criteria requirements that enables it to deal with energy issues. Energy consumption is handled by the auctioneer, while the details of variable prices of energy usage are handled in private by the bidders. The auctioneer does not take into account energy usage constraints, it just seeks the best allocation of resources taking into account the attributes of the bids.

In future work it would be productive to include task precedence constraints within the auction model. To address this issue it is important to study how this precedence can be modeled within the call for proposals and the bidding steps, but also how delays might affect future tasks, how they might provoke bid withdrawals, and how these issues should be considered in the payment mechanism.

5 Conclusions

This paper has presented a multi-attribute combinatorial auction mechanism for allocating bundles of tasks under demand in environments where the production schedule is unknown in advance, and the cost of the performance is variable. In particular, we have applied the presented approach to allocate tasks based on economic cost, delivery time and energy consumption under variable energy prices.

To deal with the problem of allocating tasks based on more than one attribute we have used a multi-attribute auction mechanism which uses a multi-criteria function to establish the winner of the auction. The combinatorial dimension of the auction mechanism proposed enables bidders to handle variable costs for pairs of tasks, whilst the auctioneer focuses on selecting the best bids.

We tested the mechanism in a simulated environment based on real data, and the results show that the presented mechanism is suitable for allocating tasks and resources under demand while considering different attributes and taking advantage of combinatorial bids to reduce cost in terms of price, time and energy. Moreover, they show that the MACA mechanism outperforms VMA2.

The work remains open to further interesting lines of research, for instance, considering precedences between tasks and robustness issues in the winner determination problem and determining payment amounts.

References

1. Bellenguez-Morineau, O., Néron, E.: A branch-and-bound method for solving multi-skill project scheduling problem. RAIRO-Operations Research 41(2), 155–170 (2007)
2. Che, Y.: Design competition through multidimensional auctions. The RAND Journal of Economics (1993),
   http://works.bepress.com/cgi/
   viewcontent.cgi?article=1021&context=yeonkoo
3. Collins, J., Demir, G., Gini, M.: Bidtree ordering in IDA combinatorial auction winner-determination with side constraints. Agent-Mediated Electronic Commerce IV. Designing Mechanisms and Systems 2531, 17–33 (2002),
   http://dx.doi.org/10.1007/3-540-36378-5_2
4. Escudero, L.F., Landete, M., Marín, A.: A branch-and-cut algorithm for the Winner Determination Problem. Decision Support Systems 46(3), 649–659 (2009),
   http://www.sciencedirect.com/science/
   article/pii/S0167923608001838
5. European Co-Directorate for Research Co-operation Energy: European technology platform smartgrids - strategic research agenda for europe's electricity networks of the future (2007),
   http://www.smartgrids.eu/documents/sra/sra_finalversion.pdf
6. European Co-Directorate General for Research Sustainable Energy Systems: European smartgrids technology platform - vision and strategy for europe's electricity networks of the future (2006),
   ftp://ftp.cordis.europa.eu/pub/fp7/energy/docs/
   smartgrids_en.pdf
7. Gottwalt, S., Ketter, W., Block, C., Collins, J., Weinhardt, C.: Demand side management - A simulation of household behavior under variable prices. Energy Policy 39(12), 8163–8174 (2011)
8. Haupt, R., Haupt, S.: Practical genetic algorithms. John Wiley & Sons, Ltd. (2004),
   http://www.csbdu.in/pdf/Practical_Genetic_Algorithms.pdf
9. Simonis, H., Hadzic, T.: A resource cost aware cumulative. In: Larrosa, J., O'Sullivan, B. (eds.) CSCLP 2009. LNCS, vol. 6384, pp. 76–89. Springer, Heidelberg (2011),
   http://dx.doi.org/10.1007/978-3-642-19486-3_5
10. Jia, W., Kang, C., Chen, Q.: Analysis on demand-side interactive response capability for power system dispatch in a smart grid framework. Electric Power Systems Research 90, 11–17 (2012)
11. Lopez, B., Ghose, A., Savarimuthu, B.T.R., Nowostawski, M., Winikoff, M., Cranefield, S.: Energy-aware optimisation of business processes. In: Proceedings of the 3rd International Workshop on Agent Technologies for Energy Systems (ATES 2012), University of Otago, Valencia (December 2012),
   http://otago.ourarchive.ac.nz/handle/10523/2666

12. Luke, S.: Essentials of metaheuristics. Lecture notes, George Mason University (2013),
    http://cs.gmu.edu/~sean/book/metaheuristics/
13. MacKie-Mason, J.K., Varian, H.R.: Generalized Vickrey Auctions (July 1994),
    http://deepblue.lib.umich.edu/handle/2027.42/41250
14. Mohsenian-Rad, A.H., Wong, V.W.S., Jatskevich, J., Schober, R., Leon-Garcia, A.: Autonomous Demand-Side Management Based on Game-Theoretic Energy Consumption Scheduling for the Future Smart Grid. IEEE Transactions on Smart Grid 1(3), 320–331 (2010), http://ieeexplore.ieee.org/lpdocs/epic03/wrapper.htm?arnumber=5628271
15. Parkes, D.C., Kalagnanam, J.: Models for Iterative Multiattribute Procurement Auctions. Management Science 51(3), 435–451 (2005), http://pubsonline.informs.org/doi/abs/10.1287/mnsc.1040.0340
16. Pla, A., Gay, P., Meléndez, J., López, B.: Petri net-based process monitoring: a workflow management system for process modelling and monitoring. Journal of Intelligent Manufacturing, 1–16 (2012), http://dx.doi.org/10.1007/s10845-012-0704-z
17. Pla, A., Lopez, B., Murillo, J.: Multi criteria operators for multi-attribute auctions. Modeling Decisions for Artificial Intelligence (2012), http://link.springer.com/chapter/10.1007/978-3-642-34620-0_29
18. Pla, A., López, B., Murillo, J., Maudet, N.: Multi-attribute auctions with different types of attributes: Enacting properties in multi-attribute auctions. Expert Systems with Applications 41(10), 4829–4843 (2014), http://www.sciencedirect.com/science/article/pii/S0957417414000864
19. Ramchurn, S., Mezzetti, C.: Trust-based mechanisms for robust and efficient task allocation in the presence of execution uncertainty. Journal of Artificial Intelligence Research 135(1), 119 (2009), http://www.aaai.org/Papers/JAIR/Vol35/JAIR-3503.pdf
20. Red Eléctrica de España: Boletín mensual diciembre 2012. Tech. rep., Red Eléctrica de España (2013), http://www.ree.es/sistema_electrico/pdf/boletin_mensual/peninsular/dic2012.pdf
21. Sandholm, T., Suri, S., Gilpin, A., Levine, D.: CABOB: A fast optimal algorithm for winner determination in combinatorial auctions. Management Science 51(3), 374–390 (2005)
22. Sandholm, T.W.: Limitations of the vickrey auction in computational multiagent systems. In: Proceedings of the Second International Conference on Multiagent Systems (ICMAS 1996), pp. 299–306 (1996)
23. Torrent-Fontbona, F., López, B.: Comparison of workflow scheduling using constraint programming or auctions research report 13-01-rr. Tech. Rep. March, Institute of Informatics and Applications, University of Girona, Girona (2013), http://dugi-doc.udg.edu//handle/10256/7312
24. Vale, Z.A., Morais, H., Khodr, H.: Intelligent multi-player smart grid management considering distributed energy resources and demand response. In: Power and Energy Society General Meeting, pp. 1–7. IEEE (2010), http://ieeexplore.ieee.org/xpls/abs_all.jsp?arnumber=5590170&tag=1
25. Walsh, W., Wellman, M.: A market protocol for decentralized task allocation. In: Proceedings of the International Conference on Multi Agent Systems, pp. 325–332 (1998), http://ieeexplore.ieee.org/xpls/abs_all.jsp?arnumber=699077
26. Yu, Y., Pan, M., Li, X., Jiang, H.: Tabu search heuristics for workflow resource allocation simulation optimization. Concurrency and Computation: Practice and Experience 23(16), 2020–2033 (2011)

A Negotiation-Based Genetic Framework for Multi-Agent Credit Assignment

Kaveh Pashaei[1], Fattaneh Taghiyareh[1], and Kambiz Badie[2]

[1] Multi Agent Systems Lab, ECE Department,
University College of Engineering, University of Tehran, Tehran, Iran
[2] Knowledge Management and e-Organizations Group,
IT Research Faculty, Research Institute for ICT, Tehran, Iran

Abstract. Multi agent systems are a well-defined solution for implementing dynamic complex environments. One of the open issues of these systems is credit assignment problem. The main concern of credit assignment problem is to properly distributing feedback of overall performance, and brings about learning in each individual agent. In this paper a genetic framework for solving Multi-agent credit assignment problem is proposed. Our framework, Negotiation Based Credit Assignment, NBCA, applies negotiation for both enriching agents' knowledge as well as organizing populations by a mode analyzer. The proposed architecture includes a mentor agent which responsible for credit assignment without any context related information leading to a general solution. Furthermore, the mentor agent does not receive any information regarding correctness of a particular agent's behavior. Carry and non-Carry cases have been considered for evaluating this method. In addition, the effects of noise as a source of uncertainty on NBCA performance are examined. Our finding indicated that the proposed method is superior to previous credit assignment approaches. This is due to the argumentation and negotiation features of multi agent systems that are used to accomplish team learning and credit assignment respectively. The analysis of obtained results which are theoretically discussed, demonstrate that, in comparison with KEBCA (OR-type), our approach performs better than KEBCA after 5000 trials in 0% noisy environment. However, it performs worse than KEBCA in 10% and 30% noisy environment.

1 Introduction

In most problem solving activities in multi agent domains, a common and essential significant problem is how to train a collection of learning agents using only a global and team-level environment signal. More specifically, when a multi agent system is implemented to carry a specific task, usually the environment mentor cannot judge each agent's performance separately. Therefore, determining each individual agent's performance must be done within the learning system using a suitable strategy. This problem is called inter-agent credit assignment [1].

Inter-agent credit assignment, within this scope, multi agent credit assignment has particularly been proposed in several previous works [2–5]. The main problem in all these approaches is that, agents act independent of each other while

J.P. Müller, M. Weyrich, and A.L.C. Bazzan (Eds.): MATES 2014, LNAI 8732, pp. 72–89, 2014.

sharing a team reward. The mentioned gap means that, learning of agents in these works is performed on an individual level and knowledge sharing between agents is ignored. Furthermore, some of these approaches use initial knowledge for assigning credits to individual agents in multi-agent system.

Negotiation in multi-agent systems is a dominant aspect of agents' interactions that enable groups of agents to arrive at a mutual agreement regarding their beliefs, desires, and intentions. Particularly, because the agents are autonomous and cannot be assumed to be benevolent, agents must influence others to continue their acting in certain way. Thus, negotiation is vital for managing such inter-agent dependencies [6].

It appears as though a distributed environment with distributed characteristics, such as a negotiation environment, can achieve an effective control with regards to the performance of the agents in multi-agent decision making situation, when we consider appropriate credit assignment to these agents . With this type of environment, the behavior of main agents can be analyzed in order to find more suitable weight values for them at the next stages. On the other hand, genetic algorithms, GA, have been shown to be a particularly general computational procedure producing evolutionary behavior as a robust method of computational optimization [7]. Solving a problem using GAs, as powerful stochastic optimization methods based on concepts of natural selection and genetics, is an iterative approach. It involves intelligent trial and error, defining constraints and optimum criteria, coding the problem as a finite length string, choosing an initial population, defining a fitness function to evaluate a chromosome's performance and creating appropriate crossover and mutation operators. Many of the related studies [8, 9] assumed fixed genetic operators with no knowledge structure. An additional weakness with GA is that due to blindness in operation, such as cross over, the entire process of optimization may become time consuming. Therefore, thinking of GA in terms of outsourcing, as a system of interacting heterogeneous agents, allows us to extend the GA domain and approach demanding complications.

Taking the above points into account, a genetic algorithm framework can take the responsibility of optimizing credit patterns for main agents, so that a process of negotiation can be used instead of cross over operation to tune up the chromosomes of population in a meaningful manner. Additionally, negotiation processes in this framework can introduce valuable knowledge that can enable the GA framework to converge into optimal credit patterns in a shorter amount of time.

1.1   Goals and Assumption

In this paper, we propose a novel approach to multi-agent credit assignment problems using genetic framework, for which a negotiation environment functions as a cross-over operator. In this approach, we design a genetic framework with a MASC component, which is a complement of our multi-agent system. MASC module is based on genetic algorithms and promotes itself through intelligent agents' capabilities in order to assign correct credit to MAS module agents. In the MASC and MAS module, there are N agents corresponding to one another. These agents are responsible for credit assignment by means of argumentation and negotiation capabilities. The MASC is responsible for tuning the arrival chromosomes and updating the beliefs of corresponding agents in the MASC component. In addition, the MASC component has a Mentor agent, which is responsible for assigning the correct credits to agents via exploration and exploitation of state space. In this framework, every chromosome constructed based on the credits of agents is evaluated by a negotiation phase to split the chromosomes. In our system, we assumed that agents act independently of one another, while sharing their beliefs. Also, the Mentor agent receives team credit and carries propagation information in each trial. In order to test our method, we consider two simple cases to provide an easy understanding of our basic idea and show the feasibility of our proposed method. for evaluating our results, we present the results of [5], [2] and [10] that contain studies of AND-type and OR-type in a deterministic and noisy environment.

2   Related Works

Based on psychological attribution theory, [11] presents a preliminary computational approach to social credit assignment problem. Their works rely on commonsense heuristic of human inference and communication of causal representation of agents.

Hierarchical judgment composition for solving a structural credit assignment is presented in [12]. Specify domain knowledge in the form of prediction of future events and associate it with the immediate representation used by the mechanism for generating state abstractions. The induced method is used for assigning credit based on the association of explicit, predictive, and interpretable domain knowledge.

In [13], the authors show how Temporal and Structural forms of the credit assignment problem are equivalent. In this unified framework, a single-agent Markov decision process can be broken down into a single-time-step multi-agent process. Furthermore, they reveal that the Monte Carlo estimation or Q-learning is equivalent to different agent utility functions in a multi-agent system. This equivalence shows how an often neglected issue in multi-agent systems is equivalent to a well-known deficiency in multi-time step learning and sets the basis for solving time-extended multi-agent problems.

For learning effective stochastic policies in uncertain domains, such as a credit assignment method, first visit profile sharing, FVPS, is introduced in [14]. FVPS reinforces effective rules to make an agent acquire stochastic policies that cause it to behave very robustly within uncertain domains, without predefined knowledge or sub goals.

Solving MCA problem in general cases using a single technique is addressed in [10]. In their research, an approach that is based on agents' learning histories and knowledge is proposed to solve the MCA problem. They proposed knowledge evaluation based credit assignments with certainty, which is developed to judge agents action and to assign them proper credits. Two measures were recommended for evaluating their results. These measures are used in our research and introduced in later sections. Furthermore, KEBCA is tested in a noisy environment. It was observed that it has a noise filtering capability if the agents have the same, reliable, initial knowledge. The same theory is used in [15], where the authors proposed a solution for multi-agent credit assignment problem. In this work, the procedure attempted to keep track of the list of feedbacks until a single action difference appears in the list of feedbacks.

A general effective approach is used in [16]. This approach focuses on the advantages of profit sharing algorithm compared to Q-learning through the simulation of controlling cranes an area where conflicts among agents exist. This algorithm is promising for simulating the real world multi-agent systems because it makes agents robust against the uncertainty of state transition, perceptual aliasing, and also conflicts among agents.

In [17], the agent learned partially in simulation and from hard-coded reward, demonstrations, and human reward. Their algorithm uses reinforcement learning to improve over the initial sequences provided by the user, and it incorporates on-line feedback from the user during the learning process creating a novel dynamic reward shaping mechanism to converge faster to an optimal policy. Furthermore, in [18], the human trainer, an author of that study, followed a predetermined algorithm of giving positive reward for desired actions and negative reward otherwise. They explored how the Interactive Reinforcement Learning algorithm that enables a human trainer to provide both rewards and anticipatory guidance for the learner can be applied to a real-world robotic system.

In order to determine the application rates of different operators, [19] proposes a bandit-based AOS method, fitness-rate-rank-based multi-armed bandit (FR-RMAB). It uses a sliding window to record the recent fitness improvement rates achieved by the operators, while employing a decaying mechanism to increase the selection probability of the best operator. On the other hand, an important component of adaptive schemes is credit assignment, whereby operators are rewarded according to their observed performance. The notion of evolvability to adaptive operator selection, by proposing an autonomous search algorithm that rewards operators according to their potential for fitness rather than their immediate fitness improvement in presented in [20].

In [21], a robust learning credit assignment cerebellar model articulation controller based on a genetic algorithm is proposed. The cerebellar model articulation controller, CMAC, is a neurological model which has an advantage of learning speed. In this research, the obtained time is optimized by a genetic algorithm to increase its accuracy from their simulation results. It is evident that the proposed robust learning is effective and feasible for a learning scheme.

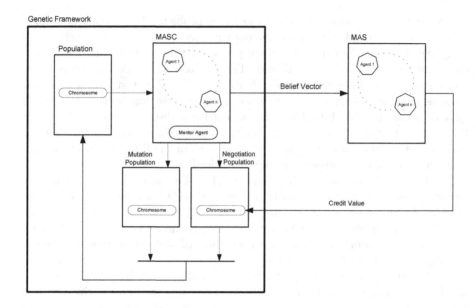

Fig. 1. Diagrammatic representation of the NBCA approach

3   The Proposed Approach

3.1   General Framework

In this method, we use historical information, which is stored in agents' beliefs, to answer the multi agent credit assignment problem. Our proposed algorithm uses agent negotiation features and mutation operators in the genetic algorithm in order to exploit and explore state space, respectively. This broad approach is called NBCA and is general enough to be applied in solving every problem regardless of its type. Figure 1 shows the overall diagrammatic view of the algorithm.

In the proposed approach, we design a genetic framework for solving MCA problem. The main component is MASC. This component, as the name implies, plays the role of a complement system for multi agent system component. In MASC, we define some agents corresponding to agents in MAS. Furthermore, we have a Mentor agent, which is responsible for making the final decision in assigning credit to each agent in MAS. The proposed algorithm is presented in Algorithm 1.

In the following we describe each step of the algorithm.

Negotiation. In order to tune the arrival chromosomes in MASC component, we use a strategic negotiation approach. In the negotiation model we assume that there are N agents: $Agents = \{A_1, A_2, ..., A_n\}$. In this model, the agents

Constitute a initial population which has m chromosomes and each chromosome has n gen;

while *convergence criteria is not reached* **do**

    while *there is a chromosome with no computed credit value* **do**

        Select chromosomes and Transfer it to the MASP component;

        Apply the negotiation operator on arrival chromosome (creates a new chromosome or keeps the the arrival chromosome);

        Send the chromosome to Mentor Agent;

        if *there is a agreement in negotiation phase* **then**

           | Transfer the chromosome to negotiation population;

        end

        if *the agreement is not reached (opt case)* **then**

           | Transfer the chromosome to mutation population;

        end

        MASC agents perform the argumentation to update their beliefs;

        Transfer updated belief vectors to MAS agents;

        Compute credit value of the chromosome by MAS component;

    end

    Combine the negotiation population and the mutation population to form new population;

end

Algorithm 1. NBCA Algorithm based on Negotiation and Argumentation

should agree upon the arrival chromosome. We suppose that agents negotiate during a pre-specified period of time: $\tau = \{0, 1, 2, ...\}$.

This period is specified and predetermined. In each period of time, t, from negotiation, if the negotiation is not complete in early stages, the agent whose turn it is at time t proposes an offer. In response to this offer, the other agents have three options: Yes, No and Opt. Each of the agents may accept an offer by choosing (Yes), reject an offer by choosing (No), or opt out of an offer by choosing (Opt).

Depending on the answers of agents, we have three situations: In situation one, if the offer accepted by the agents (all agents choose Yes option), then the negotiation is completed and this offer is transferred to the Mentor agent for final decision. After final verification, this offer is selected as a new chromosome and placed in a negotiation population.

Consider a second case where at least one of the agents abdicates from the negotiation (opt option). In this case, the negotiation is ignored and incompatibility is reported to the Mentor agent. The arrival chromosome is not manipulated and is transferred to a mutation population.

In a case where none of the agents choose the opt case and at least one of them chooses reject, the negotiation will continue in period $t + 1$ and agents will propose offers in a round-robin manner.

In this protocol, we assume that each agent which is responsible for answering the offer is not aware of the answer of other agents during the negotiation process. Furthermore, if an agreement is not reached after m rounds, the negotiation is stopped with a conflict deal and the arrival chromosome is placed in the mutation population.

In this approach, the result of negotiations in early steps may become an individual rational deal, but with an increase in steps , we will reach a Pareto optimum. Algorithm 2 demonstrate the pseudo code of negotiation process.

```
Agentsthread.agent[i];
Agents[i].start (chromosome);
Initialize t ∈ τ;
while t is lower than roundThreshold do
    agent[i] = generateRound(t);
    solution = agent[i].proposeOffer;
    for Agent[i] do
        opinion = verify(solution);
        agent[i] = receiveOptProb(c);
        if opinion = "Yes" then
            increase yOption;
        end
        if opinion = "No" then
            increase nOption;
        end
        if opinion = "Opt" then
            increase oOption;
        end
    end
    if yOption is equal to n as a number of agents then
        return [Solution, true];
    end
    else
        return [chromosome, false];
    end
end
return [chromosome, false];
```

Algorithm 2. Negotiation Process Pseudo Code

Mode Analysis. One of the most significant issues in forming new populations for solving MCA is that we are not able to perform randomly in separating mutation populations and negotiation populations. This means that the decision-splitting population is postponed and is done by MASC component. As mentioned, one of the main goals of MASC is to tune the arrival chromosome by updating belief of MAS agents and negotiation. The other aim of MASC is to decide how to separate the population. In other words, in the primary stages of the negotiation process which is carried out by MASC agents, the results of the negotiation process are considered to divide the population into a negotiation population and a mutation population.

This procedure is used so that if one of the agents in the negotiation process prefers the opt case, the chromosome is moved to a mutation population.

Furthermore, if the agents cannot reach an agreement during the negotiation process, the chromosome will relocate to the mutation population. If the negotiation process is successful, the tuned chromosome is transferred to negotiation population.

Argumentation. In order to share knowledge within the MASC agents, we use the argumentation approach. In this approach, agents use argumentation in order to exchange their beliefs and the process of argumentation is triggered after the agents agree on the criterion that is proposed in the negotiation phase. In the argumentation phase, the persuader[1] agents attempt to convince persuadee[2] agents to update their beliefs. This update also includes modifying agents' preferences. Using this approach ensures that with the transfer of persuader agents' beliefs to perssaudees, the convergence time is reduced. After the argumentation is completed, MASC agents update the corresponding agent in the MAS component. We should consider that the Mentor agent shares the knowledge of each agent with other agents and with an increase in trials, the negotiation and judgment time will be decreased. This is due to the learning in the argumentation phase and as a result, the convergence time will be reduced. The pseudo code of the argumentation approach is shown in Algorithm 3.

4   Testbed

The domain which is about to test the proposed algorithm is an add platform that has a group of five homogeneous agents with a parallel configuration and one step task is considered. Furthermore, it is assumed that Mentor agent assigns the credit due to the negotiation measure. Two 5-digit numbers are given to the MAS team to calculate their sum. Therefore, MAS and MASC components have 5 agents. These agents do not know the summation and should learn it via the Argumentation phase. In order to test, we consider two cases:

- Non-Carry Case: In this case, each digit is less than 5, so it will not produce any carry . Each agent has an action which falls between 0 and 8 (9 action) intervals.
- Carry Case: In this case, each digit can have an arbitrary value, so the summation may produce carry .Hence, each agent has an action which falls between 0 and 19 (20 action) interval.

The credit value is such that every correct action that is suggested by the agent is rewarded by +4 and every incorrect action is punished by 0. If the overall result is correct, in Non-carry case, the environment gives a credit value +20 and in the Carry case, the environment gives a credit value +24. The reward and punishment that are assigned to agents by Mentor agent is +10 and -10 respectively. In Carry case, there are some instances that can confuse Mentor agent. These instances are:

---

[1] Agents, who acts better in previous trials and get more credits than other agents.

[2] Agents, who get lower credits than the other agents.

- Mentor agent receives +24 from MAS, but all of the agents perform incorrect actions.
- Mentor agent receives +4 from MAS, but four of the agents perform correct actions.

To overcome this problem, we need to modify the MAS feedback. In the test platform where summation can have Carry, it is essential that the Mentor agent receives Carry propagation information in addition to credit value information. This means that the Carry propagation from each two digits to the next two digits should be determined. If not, agent learning and credit assignment would be impossible. Therefore, we added this feature as an attachment to credit value in Carry case and pass it to a Mentor agent. Figure 2 demonstrates the detail of attachment information as a Carry handling mechanism. We assumed that before the learning phase, none of the agents receive initial knowledge and the Mentor agent will be equipped by carry propagation information.

```
for Agent[i] do
    B = brf (B,P);
    D = options (B,I);
    I = filter (B,D,I);
    π= plan (B,I);
end
for Agent[i] do
    if succeed ( agent[i] ) then
        place agent[i] to expertClass;
    end
    else
        place agent[i] to nonExpertClass;
    end
    for agent[i] in nonExpertClass do
        while not [ reconsider (agent[i])] do
            get P;
            B = brf (B,P);
            Construct Preferred Extensions;
            while (there is no plan for I) do
                if ( reconsider (I,B) ) then
                    D = options (B,I);
                    I = filter (B,D,I);
                end
            end
        end
        if not (sound (π,I,B)) then
            π = plan (B,I);
        end
    end
end
```

Algorithm 3. Argumentation Process Pseudo Code

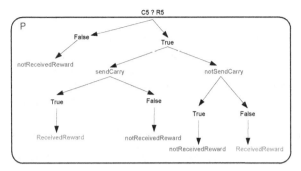

(a) The comparison of Reward and Carry in Stage 5 (first two digits)

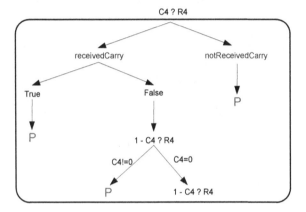

(b) The comparison of Reward and Carry in Stage 4 (second two digits)

Fig. 2. Carry Handling Mechanism

4.1 Uncertainty in Multi Agent Domain

As it is discussed in [22], uncertainty can occur in many ways. The use of uncertainty in multi-agent problems is due to the unpredictable and uncertain nature of environment. Such environment uncertainties are modeled here as noise. In order to study the effect of noise on credit assignment problem performance, we embedded simulated noise in credit value and evaluated the system behavior in these conditions. In other words, we attempted agent learning, skills, and ability to work together in the presence of teammates noisy actions. In the same way considered in [10], we assumed that, when there is 10% noise, the agent action changed to predecessor action with the probability of 5% and to the successor one in circular order with the same probability. In this study, we induce 10% and 30% noise in the environment and the results are reported and discussed.

4.2 Evaluation Indexes

For evaluating our proposed approach with different MCA approaches, we use correctness and performance evaluation indices that are introduced in [10]. Correctness is defined as the ratio of correct assignments to the number of agents. It measures how well the critic can guess suitable credits for the agents in each trial. An assignment is correct if the assigned credit does not have the reverse sign of agents real credit (what the agent should have received if it were judged individually). In other words, correctness at trial t is defined as equation 1.

$$C_t = \frac{|\{i|1 \leq i \leq N, Cr_i = RealCr_i \, or \, Cr_i = Undefined\}|}{N} \qquad (1)$$

Where N is the number of learning agents, Cr_i is the credit assigned to the agent, $RealCr_i$ is its real credit and Undefined denotes the cases when no credit is assigned. The MCA method (or the Mentor agent) is considered rational if its correctness is always one.

Performance shows the effect of MCA on group success. In other words, it is a scaled group performance index that denotes the ratio of a number of correct individual actions to the number of agents. This index is a function of the critic performance, the learning method, and its parameters. It qualifies the group in terms of its members, regardless of its task type. Performance is calculated as equation 2.

$$P = \frac{|\{agents | its \, action \, is \, correct\}|}{N} \qquad (2)$$

5   Experimental Results

In this section, the results of applying NBCA algorithm on the proposed test bed are discussed. We demonstrated performance and certainty of this algorithm in a noise-free and noisy environment. We compared and analyzed our results with results of the KEBCA [10] method. The reported results are achieved by averaging the records of over 30 separate simulations.

5.1 NBCA Correctness

Figure 3 shows the correctness of KEBCA, Carry, and non-Carry cases of NBCA in noise free environments. The correctness measure is used for evaluating the Mentor agent's ability to assign credits to agents. As illustrated in this figure the value of correctness for Case II (AND-type, OR-type) is 100%. This is because of utilization of the NP and NR strategy proposed in [10]. Comparing the results of NBCA correctness with KEBCA reveals that the number of correct credit assignments with the NBCA algorithm is 60% less than KEBCA in primary trials. The reason for this observation is that KEBCA uses primary knowledge. Consequently the correctness in early trials is 87%. In NBCA model, there is no initial knowledge about the number of agents that must be rewarded and therefore the correctness in primary trials is less than 30%.However, the capabilities of learning compensate for the lack of initial knowledge.

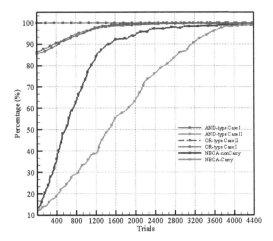

Fig. 3. Correctness of NBCA Algorithm

With an increase in the trial number and conduction of knowledge from per-suader agent to persuadee, the correctness is improved and reaches 100 percent. Thus, it is observable that by progression of learning, correctness is increased. When agents attain more knowledge, Mentor agent can assign correct credits to them. Furthermore, the progression of correctness in Carry case is less than non-Carry case and has 1600 more trials to convergence. The reason for this phenomenon is that complexity of Carry problem is high and needs more time and trials to convergence.

5.2   NBCA Performance

Figure 4 shows the performance of KEBCA and NBCA in a noise-free environment. Performance, P, is used for measuring the amount of agents' correct actions. The performance of non-Carry case of NBCA outperforms all other cases. This is because the knowledge of each sharing agent is five times greater than the knowledge of a single agent. The reason for this is, in proposed algorithms, due to the knowledge sharing within agents, the knowledge of each agent is five times greater than single agents. However, Performance of the Carry Case in initial growth is decreased in comparison with Case I of KEBCA. This is because, first, in Case I, we equipped critic agents with extra knowledge. Secondly, in the Carry case, there are 20 possible actions for agents, allowing for more complexity than non-Carry and KEBCA. In figure 5, performance of optimal Mentor agents and two intuitive strategies proposed in [10] NP and NR, are shown. A comparison of optimal performance curve with NBCA cases in Fig 4 denotes that, after 2000 trials, we are able to reach to the 98% of optimal case.. A relative assessment of the Carry case of NBCA curves with those of NP and NR demonstrate that our approach considerably outperforms other methods.

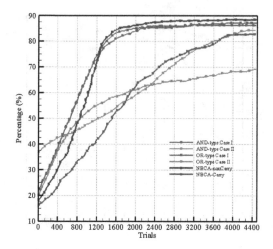

Fig. 4. Performance of NBCA Algorithm

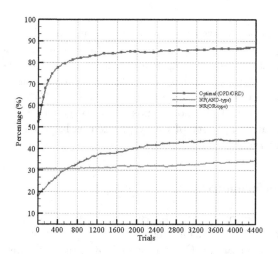

Fig. 5. Performance of optimal, NP and NR

5.3   NBCA in Noisy Environment

In figure 6a, performance of the proposed algorithm for non-Carry case in a noisy environment with 0, 10, and 30 percent noise are shown. In noisy environments, knowledge sharing between agents may increase convergence time or may cause divergence of the algorithm. Therefore, in these environments, we reduced the amount of belief sharing between agents. This reduction depends on the noisy environment.

In figure 6a, it can be seen that NBCA non-Carry reaches the noise free environment limit after 4000 trials. Furthermore, in the environment with 0% noise, our algorithm performs superiorly to KEBCA (AND-type) after 2300 trials (figure 6b). Even with 10% noise performance, our method is more acceptable than KEBCA after 6000 trials. However, with 30% noise, our algorithm has decreased performance compared to KEBCA (AND-type). This is due to the nature of our algorithm. In the proposed method, knowledge sharing is the major contributor and this capability may cause weaker results in high noise environments. Consequently, our algorithm is not optimal for environments with high noise levels.

In addition, we compare our nonCarry results that are shown in figure 6a with OR-type of KEBCA figure 6c. It is shown that our method outperforms the KEBCA (OR-type) in three noisy environments by 15%. The agents lose their gained knowledge after some trials. The reason for this observation is that learning rate is not small enough in KEBCA (OR-type).

Performance curves of Carry case of NBCA in 0, 10 and 30 percent noisy environment are depicted in figure 6d. A comparison of figure 6d with figure 6b illustrates that although KEBCA outperformed our method, the Carry case scenario favors our proposed method. This is due to the fact that the complexity of Carry case is high and considering this particular case in a noisy environment with knowledge sharing capability causes a lower performance.

Considering results of figure 6d in comparison with KEBCA (OR-type) demonstrates that our approach performs better than KEBCA after 5000 trials in 0% noisy environment. However, it performs worse than KEBCA in 10% and 30% noisy environment. As previously mentioned, figure 6d which shows the performance in 30% noise, does not differ noticeably from NR case. It is obvious that our approach acts better than NR in all cases.

6   Discussion

6.1   nonCarry Case Analysis

Experimental results of applying NBCA on nonCarry case demonstrate that, at the start of learning, agents can share their beliefs and knowledge to train themselves. Therefore, the collections of agents reach an acceptable level of performance in a noise-free environment. Furthermore, results show that the performance of the NBCA method outperforms all other cases. The role of the Mentor agent is one of the important contributors in the NBCA algorithm. This agent acts reasonably in separating populations to allow for a balance between exploration and exploitation. In other words, in the early stages of learning, due to the lack of effective information, Mentor agents attempt to explore the state space, but as the trials increase with increased performance, the exploitation plays the essential role. Analyzing the results of correctness implies that Mentor agents could not assign correct credits in the primary phase of learning due to the lack of initial knowledge. This is because Mentor agent does not have any reasonable idea in assigning credit to agents.

The experiments demonstrate that noisy environments highly affect NBCA performance. In a noisy environment, with an increase in uncertainty, we restrict

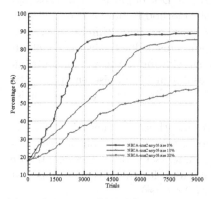

(a) Performance of NBCA in Noisy Environment nonCarry Case

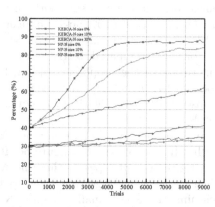

(b) KEBCA and NP performance in Noisy Environment AND-type

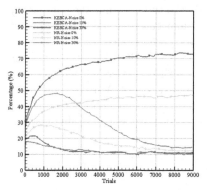

(c) KEBCA performance in Noisy Environment OR-type

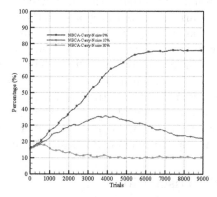

(d) NBCA performance in Noisy Environment Carry Case

Fig. 6. Simulation Results in Noisy Environment

knowledge sharing between agents. Agents need more trials to reach optimal performance. In these situations, because of existing noise, the reliability of agents beliefs decreases. When the noise in the environment is high, NBCA could not reach to optimal performance. Such results show the very important role of negotiation in the NBCA method. So, the NBCA algorithm is extremely sensitive to negotiation components, leading to lower performance in environments with high noise.

6.2   Carry Case Analysis

The presence of carry propagation influences both measure indices. The experimental results reveal that in a noise free environment, performance of the NBCA algorithm reaches near optimal performance. This implies that even though the complexity of Carry case problem may cause trouble, we are able to reach near-optimal conditions in this case. On the other hand, the learning phase, especially for Mentor agents, is a significant challenge that has not been addressed as of yet.

Furthermore, noisy environments highly affect the performance of NBCA algorithm in Carry case. When the environment has 10 percent noise, performance drops after a secular growth in early stages of learning trials. This negative aspect in the learning curves implies that the argumentation rate is high. Therefore, we should restrict belief sharing within agents to obtain reasonable results. This drawback is more noticeable in a 30 percent noisy environment. As a result, our NBCA method which is based on belief sharing capability of agents is not suitable for a highly noisy environment, particularly for sophisticated domains.

7   Conclusion and Future Works

In this paper, a negotiation based approach named NBCA was introduced to solve credit assignment problems. This approach uses a genetic algorithm framework that contains a MASC component for assigning proper credits to agents' actions. Results of implementing NBCA with correctness and performance evaluation measures were reported on Carry and non-Carry cases. Results revealed that the NBCA method improves speed and quality of learning when the experience of agents reaches optimal quality. Obtained results indicate that the proposed algorithm reach near-optimal performance, regardless of complexity of test bed, in noise-free environment. Therefore, this approach may be used as a general approach in different noise-free domains.

It was argued that the amount of initial knowledge generally affects learning scenarios. However, our proposed method reaches to optimal with an acceptable level of trials in the absence of any initial reliable knowledge; leading us to believe that our approach can act well for any type of case. It is generally believed that uncertain data or knowledge may decrease the learning and performance quality. When facing uncertain environments, NBCA was sensitive to the complexity of test bed. This is due to the belief sharing capability of agents during negotiation. Therefore, in noisy environments, it is necessary to consider some fine-tuning methods to decrease the effects of negotiation.

Currently, we are advancing into using two different validation methods which lack rigorous mathematical analysis. A substantial mathematical examination of NBCA, however, can add robustness to the algorithm to make it applicable on different heterogeneous test beds. Because our main objective in introducing NBCA is increasing learning capacity of each agent, detection of agents with incorrect knowledge and minimizing their effects on knowledge sharing can be considered as another direction for future research.

References

1. Alonso, E., D'inverno, M., Kudenko, D., Luck, M., Noble, J.: Learning in multi-agent systems. The Knowledge Engineering Review 16(3), 277–284 (2001)
2. Harati, A., Ahmadabadi, M.: Experimental analysis of knowledge based multiagent credit assignment. In: Rajapakse, J.C., Wang, L. (eds.) Neural Information Processing: Research and Development. STUDFUZZ, vol. 152, pp. 437–459. Springer, Heidelberg (2004)
3. Schneider, J.G., Wong, W.-K., Moore, A.W., Riedmiller, M.A.: Distributed value functions. In: Proceedings of the Sixteenth International Conference on Machine Learning, ICML, pp. 371–378. Morgan Kaufmann Publishers Inc., San Francisco (1999)
4. Holland, J.H.: Properties of the bucket brigade. In: Proceedings of the 1st International Conference on Genetic Algorithms, pp. 1–7. L. Erlbaum Associates Inc., Hillsdale (1985)
5. Harati, A., Ahmadabadi, M.: A new approach to credit assignment in a team of cooperative q-learning agents. In: 2002 IEEE International Conference on Systems, Man and Cybernetics, vol. 4, p. 6 (October 2002)
6. Beer, M., D'inverno, M., Luck, M., Jennings, N., Preist, C., Schroeder, M.: Negotiation in multi-agent systems. Knowl. Eng. Rev. 14(3), 285–289 (1999)
7. Goldberg, D.E.: Genetic Algorithms in Search, Optimization and Machine Learning, 1st edn. Addison-Wesley Longman Publishing Co., Inc., Boston (1989)
8. Srivastava, R.P., Goldberg, D.E.: Verification of the theory of genetic and evolutionary continuation (2001)
9. Cantú-Paz, E., Goldberg, D.: Are multiple runs of genetic algorithms better than one? In: Cantú-Paz, E., et al. (eds.) GECCO 2003. LNCS, vol. 2723, pp. 801–812. Springer, Heidelberg (2003)
10. Harati, A., Ahmadabadi, M., Araabi, B.: Knowledge-based multiagent credit assignment: A study on task type and critic information. IEEE Systems Journal 1(1), 55–67 (2007)
11. Mao, W., Gratch, J.: The social credit assignment problem. In: Rist, T., Aylett, R.S., Ballin, D., Rickel, J. (eds.) IVA 2003. LNCS (LNAI), vol. 2792, pp. 39–47. Springer, Heidelberg (2003)
12. Jones, J., Goel, A.: Hierarchical judgement composition: Revisiting the structural credit assignment problem. In: Proceedings of the AAAI Workshop on Challenges in Game AI, San Jose, CA, USA, pp. 67–71 (2004)
13. Agogino, A.K., Tumer, K.: Unifying temporal and structural credit assignment problems. In: Proceedings of the Third International Joint Conference on Autonomous Agents and Multiagent Systems, AAMAS 2004, vol. 2, pp. 980–987. IEEE Computer Society, Washington, DC (2004)
14. Arai, S., Sycara, K., Payne, T.R.: Experience-based reinforcement learning to acquire effective behavior in a multi-agent domain. In: Mizoguchi, R., Slaney, J.K. (eds.) PRICAI 2000. LNCS, vol. 1886, pp. 125–135. Springer, Heidelberg (2000)
15. Rahaie, Z., Beigy, H.: Toward a solution to multi-agent credit assignment problem. In: International Conference of Soft Computing and Pattern Recognition, SOCPAR 2009, pp. 563–568 (December 2009)
16. Arai, S., Miyazaki, K., Kobayashi, S.: Multi-agent reinforcement learning for crane control problem: designing rewards for conflict resolution. In: Proceedings of the The Fourth International Symposium on Autonomous Decentralized Systems. Integration of Heterogeneous Systems, pp. 310–317 (1999)

17. León, A., Morales, E.F., Altamirano, L., Ruiz, J.R.: Teaching a robot to perform task through imitation and on-line feedback. In: San Martin, C., Kim, S.-W. (eds.) CIARP 2011. LNCS, vol. 7042, pp. 549–556. Springer, Heidelberg (2011)
18. Knox, W.B., Stone, P., Breazeal, C.: Training a robot via human feedback: A case study. In: Herrmann, G., Pearson, M.J., Lenz, A., Bremner, P., Spiers, A., Leonards, U. (eds.) ICSR 2013. LNCS, vol. 8239, pp. 460–470. Springer, Heidelberg (2013)
19. Li, K., Fialho, A., Kwong, S., Zhang, Q.: Adaptive operator selection with bandits for a multiobjective evolutionary algorithm based on decomposition. IEEE Transactions on Evolutionary Computation 18(1), 114–130 (2014)
20. Soria Alcaraz, J.A., Ochoa, G., Carpio, M., Puga, H.: Evolvability metrics in adaptive operator selection. In: Proceedings of the 2014 Conference on Genetic and Evolutionary Computation, GECCO 2014, pp. 1327–1334. ACM, New York (2014)
21. A genetic algorithm based robust learning credit assignment cerebellar model articulation controller. Applied Soft Computing 4(4), 357–367 (2004)
22. Jin, Y., Branke, J.: Evolutionary optimization in uncertain environments-a survey. IEEE Transactions on Evolutionary Computation 9(3), 303–317 (2005)

Agent-Based Concepts for Manufacturing Automation

Peter Göhner and Michael Weyrich

University of Stuttgart, Institute for Industrial Automation and Software Engineering,
Pfaffenwaldring 47, 70550 Stuttgart, Germany
{peter.goehner,michael.weyrich}@ias.uni-stuttgart.de
http://www.ias.uni-stuttgart.de

Abstract. Manufacturing automation is an industrial field of application in which agent-based concepts are of a high relevance. Flexibility in engineering, quick and easy adaptation and evaluation of the systems are key issues in the domain and can significantly be improved using the paradigm of multi-agent systems. The approach of agent technology is very suitable to conceive assistant systems or control architectures which can be used throughout the engineering and the operation of automated manufacturing systems. This article presents an overview of the research undertaken the past years which has yielded workable concepts for typical use cases of the industry.

Keywords: manufacturing automation, multi-agent systems in automation, software agents, agent-based planning, agent-based engineering, decentralized systems, test and operation of manufacturing.

1   Introduction

Manufacturing automation has been a key driver to increasing productivity of factories for many years. So-called Smart Factories of the future might have capabilities to react to changes in products or product variants. These Smart factories can produce newly developed products quickly as they allow for an easy adjustment of the automated manufacturing equipment, which reduces time to market of new products.

Utilizing manufacturing automation provides high quality processes such as machining, assembly, packaging etc.

A key success factor of automated manufacturing systems is the capability to dynamically adjust to the requirements of production for new products or variants and production volumes. However manually adjusting the automation is time consuming if conducted by human operators and results in high costs.

New architectures of manufacturing automation systems are required to implement a Smart Factory. Though there is a wide variety of automation research, which can be deployed, there is a need for efficient automation architectures in engineering, commissioning and test processes.

One of the promising technologies is the multi-agent Technology which is becoming increasingly attractive for the software and hardware developments in manufacturing automation. Multi-agent systems promise to solve architectural problems that

J.P. Müller, M. Weyrich, and A.L.C. Bazzan (Eds.): MATES 2014, LNAI 8732, pp. 90–102, 2014.

are difficult or impossible for monolithic systems to cope with. Agents are an approach for intelligence and decentralized problem solving leading to superior system architectures. In comparison to the conventional control methods used in automation, the multi-agent technology can be more effective, flexible and easier to adjust.

The concept of multi-agent systems dates back to about four decades and many approaches have been made to deploy the technology in automation of manufacturing. First traces of the concept of agent systems were outlined in the Science fiction tales on Artificial Intelligence around the 1960s. A prime example is "A Space Odyssey" written by Arthur C. Clarke with concise visions of men-machine interaction, intelligence and sentience.

Research was conducted from the 1980s onwards, in the newly rising field of computer science and artificial intelligence where multi-agent systems were viewed as concepts for problem solving.

The past 20 years has seen agents and multi-agent systems in research yielding solutions which are deployed in industrial applications such as supply chain management, supervisory control of plants or manufacturing automation. Due to the broad nature of the agent concept, there are many interpretations of what exactly a multi-agent system is and what the core questions are.

Agent technology evolves from the relevant research conferences, technical committees of IEEE and VDI/VDE and multiple university textbooks that shape the domain.

1.1   The Concepts of Agent Technology

The agents act independently within their scope of actions to pursue prescribed goals. They can interact with each other and cooperate through negotiations in order to achieve these goals.

According to the VDI/VDE Guideline 2653 [12] the terminology is as following: "An agent is an encapsulated (hardware / software) entity with specified objectives. An agent endeavors to reach these objectives through its autonomous behavior, in interaction with its environment and with other agents. A multi-agent system is the interaction of a set of agents to fulfil one or more tasks. Runtime environments and platforms for technical agents are a possible basis for realizing multi-agent systems. However, they themselves are not multi-agent systems".

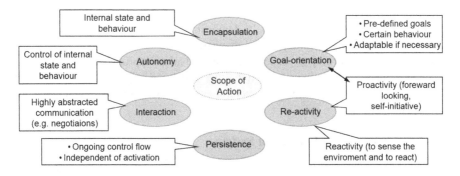

Fig. 1. Attributes of multi-agent systems

The behavior of a multi-agent system is determined at run-time by the dynamic co-operation of the individual agents [1]. The systems are often deploying different types of agents and those systems are referred to as multi-agent systems.

Fig. 1 presents the attributes of a multi-agent system which can be considered as an autonomous software entity.

According to the VDI/VDE Guideline 2653 [12] the properties of a multi-agent system are:

"**Scope of action:** The scope of action limits the application of the capabilities of an agent. Accordingly, the degree of flexibility of a technical agent is determined by a given scope of action.

Autonomy: Attribute of an agent which allows it to control its internal state and its behavior. Through autonomy, an agent acts and makes decisions based on its local knowledge and activities.

Encapsulation: Attribute of an agent which allows it to control the access to its individual constituents which are not visible externally. State, behavior, strategies and objective represent the individual constituents that are encapsulated within an agent.

Goal-orientation: Attribute of an agent which allows it to orientate its behavior to one or more objectives, which it attempts to accomplish.

Reactivity: The capability of an agent to sense the environment and to react accordingly.

Persistence: The capability of an agent to keep its internal state during its lifecycle.

Interaction: The capability of an agent to interact with other agents, in order to accomplish individual objectives or to manage dependencies among each other. The basis for the interactions among agents is a shared semantic, an underlying organizational context and a common terminology model, which are together referred to as ontology."

The basic concepts of agents are embossed by the autonomy of the agent and can encapsulate itself. Furthermore an agent retains its internal state during its lifecycle.

The communication schema of agents is sophisticated. They can for example negotiate with each other and are interactive.

In addition, agents are persistent as they have an ongoing control flow and are active and reactive. They can proactively demonstrate self-initiative, sense their environment and react to it in a goal oriented manner.

Agents can act according to predefined goals and adapt appropriately.

The systematic distribution of functionalities and knowledge in autonomous units controlled by agents, leads to a low structural coupling between system elements and multi-agent systems.

1.2   Architectures of Multi-Agent Systems

Agents require interaction and communication with other agents. Therefore they require knowledge about the existence of other agents in their neighborhood; they need a communication infrastructure, a messaging protocol and some sort of a dictionary of services provided by all agents.

There are different ways on how such a structure could be implemented in a multi-agent system for industrial automation. The commonly used structure is the FIPA reference model described in Fig. 2, a standard architecture of multi-agents systems.

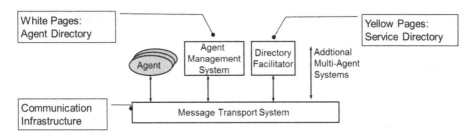

Fig. 2. Reference model of agent systems

This standard was conceived by the FIPA, the Foundation of Intelligent Physical Agents, Geneva, Switzerland in 1996 to 2002 (see www.fipa.org), this standard is heavily deployed in the community. An overview to the application impact and agent technologies in use can be found in [14].

According to that reference model, multi-agent systems have an interface to the message transport system to communicate with other agents. The communication infrastructure of the message transport system is standardized. With the help of an agent management system, agents are able to locate other agents to interact. For that purpose agents are listed in so-called "white pages" with their addresses. This administration is done by the agents themselves. They register or deregister themselves in the "white pages" depending on whether they are activated or deactivated.

The so-called directory facilitator provides information of services offered by the agents similar to the "yellow pages".

The communication infrastructure is standardized for the Message Transport System which aids agents in interacting among themselves.

The architecture of the multi-agent system can be based on the FIPA standard or any other concept as there is a lot of flexibility in the definition of the architecture due to the inherent flexibility of agent technology. However, the major weakness of the agent technology lies in the multiple task control. The runtime behavior is partially unpredictable due to the parallel nature of the executed tasks. This means that the behavior of a multi-agent system cannot be determined a priori as the decision making process is distributed and a result of the interaction of autonomous agents. In manufacturing automation this uncertainty is not acceptable for many industrial applications for reasons of safety and security. For such applications multi-agent systems are used in the engineering phase to conceive a control paradigm which is thereafter analyzed and implemented using conventional technologies.

2   Areas of Application in Manufacturing Automation

The sector of manufacturing automation is huge and entails a large number of application domains in various industries. This means agent technology is not limited to one field but has multiple means of usages.

Basically there are three identifiable areas:

• the engineering and planning of automated systems, focusing on the creation of the manufacturing systems;
• the manufacturing operations where an automation system produces goods;
• the phase of evaluation of systems in which the functions of an automated manufacturing system are tested.

These areas are elucidated below, highlighting the various cases of agent technology in manufacturing automation.

2.1   Engineering and Planning of Automated Systems Assisted by Agents

Manufacturing systems of today are exposed to volatile markets with changing requirements for the products produced. Automatic manufacturing systems need to be created quickly with limited effort or retrofitted based on existing installations.

The required flexibility is attainable with the help of modular design, adaptive automation and intelligent planning systems. Methodologies of engineering and planning are required to accommodate complexity and flexibility.

An approach to achieving flexible engineering and planning processes is a structured approach with processes which can be decoupled as much as possible and thereafter, executed concurrently.

The agent-based concept allows mechanisms to improve the planning process and provide tools to make it faster, more efficient and flexible due to the decentralized nature of the agent paradigm.

This paradigm is based on the concept of agents representing sub-systems or parts to support the planning of an automated system. Each agent has encapsulated engineering knowledge, follows planning goals and negotiates with the neighboring component agents, thereby automatically generating planning proposals.

In the following, some examples for agent-based engineering systems are given:

• Rauscher et al [2] uses a multi-agent system in the early design phase of a mechatronic design. Each model is represented by an agent holding specific knowledge about that model. So-called consistency rules are expressed in ontologies where attributes between the models during the design are monitored and violations alerted.
• Kratzer et al. [3] presents a similar approach to support the design of mechanic components by validating the current design against requirements and boundary conditions. Non-conformance designs are revealed and solutions are proposed to the designers.

- Tompkin [6] describes the deployment of multi-agent systems in a knowledge-based engineering process resulting in the reduction of the planning complexity.

The value of agent technology in engineering is to assist the expert by taking over the tedious and time consuming steps of the planning procedure as well as computer aided proposals of solutions or alternatives for decision making.

Example: Engineering Based on Sub-systems Supported by Agents

A concept of designing complex closed-loop control systems is shown in Figure 3. The independent design of decentralized open-loop control systems with multiple inputs and outputs and strong linkages between them is difficult to execute. This agent-based approach allows for the creation of simple controllers for the sub-processes. Each of these controllers is part of an agent with its own objectives and a set of actions. The agents interact with each other to get an optimal solution for the desired feedback-loop control problem [2].

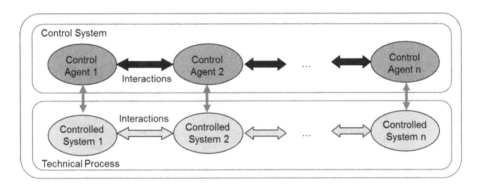

Fig. 3. Example of an agent-based design of a complex feedback control system

Consider a warehouse in which different parcels have to be stored. The manufacturing automation system has to take care of various system elements such as the parcels, conveyor belts, cages, separation devices, storage units, operator units etc.

A conventional logic control system would require a complex central program to control all the individual units. An approach based on agent technology would look into required services and define a "service agent" and "coordination agents". For instance a service agent would be defined for each of the major systems functions of a warehouse which are: initialization, store goods, retrieve goods, separate parts, check occupancy.

The resulting structure of the agent system is based on those services and decouples the overall control and reduces the complexity of the software.

Example of Agent Based Product Design Using Components

Consider a scenario where the engineering is based on a set of pre-engineered components or modules. Here the blue-print of the manufacturing automation system can be decomposed. Each of these components or modules can be represented by an agent in a computer aided planning system which administrate the design kit.

The agents can utilize their autonomy acting as virtual surrogates to form the networks of modules dynamically as well as the overall system. Once certain engineering or planning rules are implemented into the knowledge base of the system, the agents can take over the planning partially, by interacting between each other, selecting, configuring and connecting system components by proposing new alternatives and solutions.

Figure 4 illustrates an agent-based concept of an automated consistency check in a computer aided design process. Each part of the assembly which has to be designed is represented by one so-called "part agent". This agent acquires any changes made to the part by its designer and shares this information with other agents.

These "device agents" identify newly designed parts and their dependencies on each other. Thereafter the so-called "aspect agents" checks for consistency with regards to issues, such as costs, geometry or materials. If the consistency check is declined, potential alternatives will be investigated and presented to the designer.

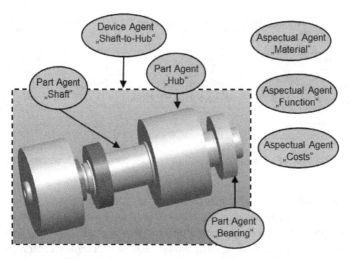

Fig. 4. Design support based on agent technology

The deployment of predefined rules and the modeling of resources allow a bottom-up planning based on dialog to form a design. See [3] for further reading.

More complex design tasks such as mechatronic systems consisting of mechanics, electronics and software need an automated consistency check. This is of particular interest in order to define changes, identify the impact of changes and automatically check the design.

2.2   Agents in Manufacturing Operation

During the operation phase, the automated manufacturing systems produce goods and materials. There are various use-cases which can typically benefit from the agent technology e.g. the process planning over the course of time can be optimized by agents making the system more efficient. This becomes even more relevant once unforeseen events such as failure of machine or shortage of supply materials occur and the plan needs to be updated on the fly during production.

Agents can also assist in retrofitting during production e.g. to manufacture a new slightly different product.

Example of Agent Based Scheduling

In Figure 5 the concept of an agent-based scheduling for manufacturing systems is displayed. In this example the overall system can be optimized using different types of agents. See also [8].

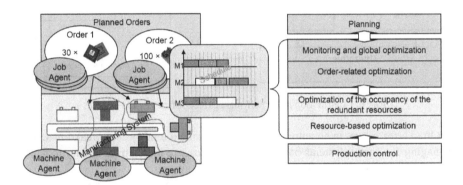

Fig. 5. Production optimization with multiple goal optimizations

For this purpose each order is represented by a "job agent". Job agents are appointed to orders and represent them. These agents try to optimize their order. They negotiate with "machine agents", which stand for an individual machine of the manufacturing system. The optimization target of a machine agent is to achieve the occupancy of redundant resources.

The decomposition of an order into machine jobs and the scheduling of the individual machines are done by means of the agents.

With the help of this concept, the schedule can be identified using a multilevel optimization structure taking the resource utilization and order constrains into conclusion. This approach is particularly flexible once unforeseen events occur, such as machine failures or supply shortage. The manufacturing system can automatically and dynamically adapt to a revised schedule.

Example of Agent for Self-management of Automation Systems

Manufacturing Automation systems become more flexible once they entail Self-X functionality. Self-healing, self-optimization or self-configuration provides functionality to reconfigure manufacturing during operation without modifications or retrofit. Agents implement the execution and coordination of such self-x functions.

Self-managing of automated systems consist of an operative automated system, a self-management interface and a self-management system as displayed in Fig. 6.

The self-management interface captures information out of the automated system.

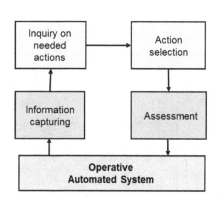
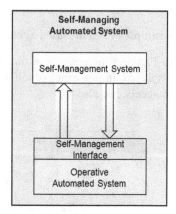

Fig. 6. Control loop in the self-management of automated systems

Often error occurs in an automated system causing a total system breakdown. Self-managing automated systems have the ability to react to these errors and try to handle them without losing the desired functionality of the system.

The self-management system uses the agent paradigm and ontologies to determine automatically if there are any actions necessary and which of them should be executed. These actions will be forwarded to the self-management Interface and then executed in the automated system.

The agent-based concept allows the autonomous execution of self-recovery and self-configuration processes in the automated system. The idea is to encapsulate the self-management functionality inside agents. Those agents are autonomous and can interact with the automation system and the operator to achieve a certain functional task.

These self-x functionalities will be provided through the agent-based self-management system where traceability and reproducibility are important requirements.

The self-management functionality depends strongly on the specific process of manufacturing automation. However, the roles of the agents can be generically defined.

A set of agents, the "self-management agents" takes charge of each individual function. Those agents are very specific to the details of the realization and focus on the individual process functionality which is to be self-managed. The agent captures the information, analyses it using a rule based approach and triggers a specific action. Both analysis as well as the decision for specific action can be supported by knowledge based processing approaches such as fuzzy logic. Additionally a "coordination agent" is deployed to synchronize the actions of the self-management agents.

Consider an elevator which has redundant sensors to detect the floor. The position at floor is detected with multiple sensors, say four sensors. If one of the sensors fails during operation the elevator would detect that issue using an internal model of the elevator. The self-management agent would identify the requirement to override the signal of the faulty sensor and take appropriate action to continue the operation as three out of four sensors are still operational. The self-management agent however would not directly interfere with the programmable logic controller (PLC), but would communicate with the coordination agent, which double-checks the self-healing case and launches the right reconfiguration program sequence in the PLC.

The advantage of the systems architecture of the multi-agent system is the structure of the control loop and the stepwise course of action. The system inquires the appropriated action after the capturing of information. Once the course of potential action is identified the system assess and decides for one course of action. Following this concept the self-management and self-healing follows a clear architecture conceived due to agent technology. See [13] for further reading.

2.3   Agents for Evaluation and Test of Automated Manufacturing Systems

One of the major parts of the creation process of an automation system is the evaluation or test phase. It is essential to prove the compliance of a manufacturing automation system with the quality requirements of the engineering and planning process.

The planning of the system evaluation, the specification, execution and test is usually a process which accompanies the whole development. System evaluation and testing are embedded in the system's lifecycle.

During its lifetime, a system is usually altered or retrofitted to adapt to new requirements and boundary conditions. Tests on the system have to be conducted regularly as any modification adds to the risk of introducing faults.

Malz et al. [4, 5] use a multi-agent system to support the evaluation and in particular the test management of software. The agents prioritize test cases by evaluating meta-information like change and fault histories of the tested software system. Those agents assign the available test resources to the test cases and trigger the execution.

The concept of an agent-based test management system is presented in Figure 7. System components of the automated manufacturing system especially altered software, has to be tested before it can be utilized.

All necessary test cases have to be specified before execution. However, the duration to run all those test cases taking all variants, input signal combinations, resources etc. into considering is typically short and not all cases can be applied in each test period. Hence, an optimization plan is necessary, as the test cases should be executed according to the relevance and importance keeping the timing to evaluate.

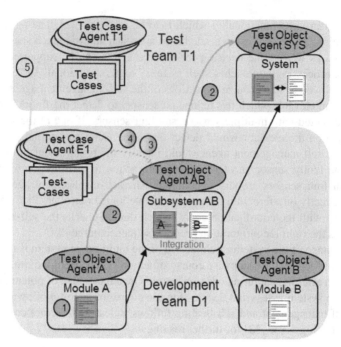

Fig. 7. Interaction of agents assigned to test objects associates to modules and sub-systems

A "test object agent" represents a single software module of the manufacturing automation system. This agent considers information like how many changes have been made in this module since last testing and how critical and relevant the module is to the overall system.

A "test case agent" represents a single test case: It coordinates the resources of this test case and cooperates with other agents to prioritize all test cases and to achieve an optimal test plan and usage of test resources. The result of the test management system is a prioritized list of all test cases with the calculated priority of each test case.

Test case selection techniques reduce the test suites by identifying only relevant test cases, for example based on changes of the source code. Prioritization techniques go one step further and order the test cases by their expected benefit for the test. Unlike test case selection, a test run that is executed based on prioritized test cases may be interrupted at any time but remaining the maximal benefit. Every test case prioritization technique can also be seen as a selection technique by skipping test cases, which have a lower priority and impact than a predefined threshold value. Test case prioritization techniques are described in [4].

3   Conclusion

Currently, the importance of agent-based approaches for developing, operating and evaluation / test of industrial systems are increasing. Agent technology has multiple advantages especially in areas of software development for automated manufacturing systems. For instance decentralized systems, which are distributed over a location, modular and exposed to changes of the system structure, are particularly relevant to the application of agent technology for two reasons:

Firstly, not all information of the future requirements is available and known at the time of engineering and planning of the automated manufacturing system.

Secondly, in order to be flexible and effective it has to support dynamic changes of the system to ad hoc network sub-systems for maximum optimization.

This paper demonstrates how agent technology can support the manufacturing automation in the fields of:

- Engineering and planning of manufacturing automation systems
- Operation of manufacturing systems and
- Evaluation and testing of system.

These application areas demonstrate the importance of agent technology and concepts providing continuous support during the whole lifecycle of the systems.

In the presented examples, agents demonstrated the ability to be autonomous software units, which are goal oriented, active, cooperative, flexible and adaptive.

This makes the agent paradigm a valuable tool for the analysis, engineering and implementation of complex manufacturing automation systems.

Over the past decades many achievements have been made to consolidate the various concepts of multi-agent systems. Despite the various research approaches, terminology and definitions are wide synchronized and specified. The multi-agent system design methodology has been extensively discussed in the community and set methods and tools are available which eases the use for non-research experts in the industrial field. Additionally various agent development platforms are in existence and criterions for the selection of individual solutions have been intensively discussed in the community.

A lot of research has been done to demonstrate and understand the usage of agent Technology use cases of industrial automation of production systems, energy management modular production plant design and logistics. Some of those cases could be reviewed in this paper. More examples are available in the literature which demonstrate the ability of the approach as for instance in [12] in which ten use cases are analyzed with the goal to demonstrate the potential of agent technology. However, considering the state-of-the-art and hard facts of industry implemented there is a very limited amount of multi-agent system implementation compared to conventional approaches for industrial control.

The authors believe that this paradigm will be a central concept for many future developments of flexible and decentralized networks based on autonomous and cooperation units in manufacturing automation. Many of the future cyber-physical system developments in manufacturing automation might not utilize the agent platforms of the community nor explicitly mention the agent technology but be inspired by the design concepts and methodology. This way the complexity of systems can be coped effectively making the architecture more flexibility and easier to handle.

References

1. Jennings, N.R.: On agent-based software engineering. Artificial Intelligence 117, 277–296 (2000)
2. Rauscher, M., Göhner, P.: Agent-based consistency check in early mechatronic design phase. In: DS 75-9: Proceedings of the 19th Intern. Conference on Engineering Design (ICED 2013), Design for Harmonies, Seoul, Korea. Design Methods and Tools, vol. 9, pp. 389–396 (2013)
3. Kratzer, M., Rauscher, M., Binz, H., Goehner, P.: An agent-based system for supporting design engineers in the embodiment design phase. In: Proceedings of the International Conference on Engineering Design, ICED (2011)
4. Malz, C., Jazdi, N.: Agent-based test management for software system test. In: IEEE International Conference on Automation, Quality and Testing, Robotics (AQTR), pp. 1–6 (2010)
5. Malz, C., Jazdi, N., Göhner, P.: Prioritization of Test Cases Using Software Agents and Fuzzy Logic. In: 2012 IEEE Fifth International Conference on Software Testing, Verification and Validation (ICST), pp. 483–486 (2012)
6. Tompkin, J.A., White, J.A., Bozer, Y.A., Frazelle, E.H., Tanchoco, J.M.A., Trevino, J.: Facilities Planning. Wiley, New York (1996)
7. Reichl, H., Wolf, J.: Things that think. TU-Berlin- Forschung aktuell, 1887–1898 (2001)
8. Pech, S.: Software Agents in Industrial Automation Systems. IEEE Software 30(3), 20–24 (2013)
9. Elbaum, S., Malishevsky, A., Rothermel, G.: Test case prioritization: a family of empirical studies. IEEE Transactions on Software Engineering 28(2), 159–182 (2002)
10. Li, Z., Harman, M., Hierons, R.M.: Search algorithms for regression test case prioritization. IEEE Transactions on Software Engineering 33(4), 225–237 (2007)
11. Rothermel, G., Untch, R., Chu, C., Harrold, M.: Prioritizing test cases for regression testing. IEEE Transactions on Software Engineering 27(10), 929–948 (2001)
12. VDI/VDE 2653 Sheet 1, 2 and 3: multi-agent systems in industrial automation: Fundamentals, Development and Application. Beuth Verlag, Berlin (2010)
13. Mubarak, H., Göhner, P.: An agent-oriented Approach for Self-Management of Industrial Automation Systems. In: INDIN 2010 (2010)
14. Müller, J., Fischer, K.: Application Impact of Multi-Agent Systems and Technologies: A Survey. In: Shehory, O., Sturm, A. (eds.) Agent-Oriented Software Engineering: Reflections on Architectures, Methodologies, Languages, and Frameworks, pp. 27–53 (2014)

Orchestrating the Sequential Execution of Tasks by a Heterogeneous Set of Asynchronous Mobile Agents

Shashi Shekhar Jha and Shivashankar B. Nair

Department of Computer Science and Engineering
Indian Institute of Technology Guwahati, Assam, India
{j.shashi,sbnair}@iitg.ernet.in

Abstract. Coordinated execution of a sequence of tasks by a group of heterogeneous agents possessing different capabilities is known to be a complex problem. Researchers have looked upon nature to capture the mechanisms embedded within the highly distributed swarms of insects to coordinate the execution of tasks by multiple entities. Stigmergy based interactions forms the key that regulates various processes within such swarms. This paper describes a technique by which a heterogeneous set of asynchronous mobile agents comprising a swarm commence the execution of their assigned tasks by coordinating amongst each-other using stigmergy. These mobile agents make use of stimulations from the environment to activate the execution of a sequence of tasks on a network of nodes in a near synchronous manner. A stigmergic cloning controller facilitates the cloning of on-demand agents to provide for parallel executions. The agents also inherently exhibit *self-healing*. The paper also describes results obtained from emulations performed over a LAN which proves the practical viability of the proposed approach.

Keywords: Synchronization, Swarm, Stigmergy, Mobile Agents, Stimulations, Population Control, Response Threshold.

1   Introduction

Synchronization of activities among the individuals of a swarm of living organisms is essential to manage the swarm in an efficient manner [3]. In nature, we witness various examples of synchronized activities among the individuals of a swarm which possess simple behaviours and perform minimalistic interactions that lead to the build-up of many a complex structure. Such activities are exhibited in the making of - termite mounds, wasp nests, ant hills, bee hives, etc. These architectural monuments are created using finely engineered techniques and can tolerate varying environmental conditions [4,8,29]. Researchers are still trying to unravel the physics behind the functioning of these highly distributed and decentralized insect colonies. Various theories and models have been proposed to aid in the understanding of techniques used by these social insects [6,21].

J.P. Müller, M. Weyrich, and A.L.C. Bazzan (Eds.): MATES 2014, LNAI 8732, pp. 103–120, 2014.
© Springer International Publishing Switzerland 2014

According to experimental evidences [1], it has been established that the individuals within a swarm perform actions which result in minor modifications to their environment. These modifications are then perceived by other individuals which in turn stimulate them to perform appropriate actions. Such an indirect form of communication which influences the collective coordination of activities amongst individuals has been termed as *Stigmergy* by Grassé [12]. These environmental changes lead to a chain-reaction resulting in orchestrating the various activities sequentially. The individuals respond to discrete stigmergy [19], based on the discrete set of stimuli with each stimulus triggering one category of individuals as in the construction of wasp nests and termite mounds [4].

Swarm intelligence based cooperation and coordination methods have been extensively applied in multi-robot and multi-agent communities [23,27]. Krieger *et al.* [20] have implemented dynamic task allocation based on the fixed response threshold model [2]. They assigned a team of robots to maintain a stock of energy at a nest. Whenever the nest energy level falls below the individual activation-threshold of a robot then it chooses the task of foraging thereby dynamically allocating the foraging task to individual robots. Jones and Mataric [17] have used simple rule-based approach to vary the number of foragers in a set of dynamically evolving concurrent tasks. Inspired by the Deneubourg's learning model [7] for foraging in ants, Labella *et al.* [22] have proposed an algorithm for division of labour in an object retrieval task where the ratio of the number of foragers to resters is altered adaptively. Liu *et al.* [24] use a similar mechanism for the foraging activity using three different types of cues viz. internal, environmental and social. Theraulaz and Bonabeau [30] have demonstrated a model using simulation that can exhibit the distributed nature of nest building in wasps. They postulated that the entire task of building a structure needs to be decomposed into a finite number of steps. Further, it is essential that the local configurations that are generated in a given state differ from those formed from an earlier or later step generating discrete stimulus. This prevents any possible disruption in the chain of events or tasks and thus prevents disorganization of the building activity. Werfel *et al.* [32] have shown how various complex structures can be created using robotic swarms. They assumed the environment to be caches of blocks and beacons which send out signals while the robots perceive them. This perception triggers specific rules as to where they should place the blocks. Weyns and Holvoet [33] have proposed an algorithm for regional synchronization of agents to perform simultaneous actions. Their algorithm combines the distributed two phase commit protocol with a logical clock and uses messages to communicate amongst the agents to form regional groups. Setting up of regional groups incurred communication overheads. They demonstrated their algorithm in a Packet-World simulation environment. The authors in [13] have designed a multi-agent based coordination and control model for manufacturing control systems using stigmergy. The authors argue that it is possible to generate and use short-term forecasts based on the intentions of the order agents in relatively simple systems. Parunak and Brueckner [31] have shown the self-organization in large multi-agent systems using the pheromone based model of an insect colony.

They have used concepts from thermodynamics to show the conditions under which coordination can emerge. Thus, the most crucial aspects to be looked into while devising a model that can mimic the stigmergic behaviour of the insects is the manner in which the entities comprising the swarm sense their environment. It also depends on the locality of discrete stimuli both temporally and spatially.

This paper extends our previous work [15] (using a fixed population of homogeneous mobile agents) and proposes a technique for near synchronous execution of tasks by a *heterogeneous* set of mobile agents. By heterogeneity, we mean that there are different types of mobile agents in the environment; each type capable of performing a distinct task. Each mobile agent perceives a stimulus from the environment and perform its assigned task. This technique also manages the change in population of these heterogeneous set of mobile agents so as to suit their current demand. The population of agents required to complete an activity is generated dynamically without any supervised control. Our central focus is to make heterogeneous mobile agents execute their assigned tasks T_1, T_2,....,T_m in a desired sequence. Hence an asynchronous agent needs to switch ON the execution of its assigned task only when the task previous in the sequence is executed at every relevant point in the environment. Thus the next task is never triggered anywhere in the environment till the previous task execution is completed. This synchronizes the execution of a specific task across all points in the environment. In succeeding sections we discuss the working of this technique coupled with stigmergy and supplement it with experimental results.

2   Mobile Agents

Mobile agents provide a fitting framework to realize population-based swarm algorithms. Their features such as autonomy, social ability and adaptability [5] along with the capability to migrate to other nodes of a network, carry their execution state and code and also clone provide for all the necessary characteristics of individuals in a swarm. In simple terms, these mobile agents can be considered as the nomadic information processing units that have the abilities to search for information and gather results, to reason and take decisions and to build plans over a network infrastructure [28]. Due to such features, mobile agents have a wide range of applications ranging from network management, electronic commerce, energy efficiency and metering, wireless sensors, grid computing, distributed data mining, human tracking, security, e-learning, etc. [28]

Several researchers have experimented the use of a mobile agent framework to try and realize bio-inspired paradigms. Kambayashi *et al.* [18] used mobile agents in a multi-robot environment for the design of an intelligent cart system using an evolutionary ant colony clustering algorithm. Godfrey and Nair [10] have emphasized the use of mobile agents to implement multi-mobile robot framework using algorithms derived from the biological immune system. In a recent work, Jha *et al.* [16] have used mobile agents to emulate the immune-network model of Artificial Immune Systems over a network of nodes to portray the emergence of the best antibodies for a given antigen. Holvoet and Valckenaers [14] have used mobile agents as lightweight agents coupled with stigmergy to exploit the environment as a design abstraction for managing complexity [34] using delegate Multi-Agent Systems approach. In this paper, we also exploits the concept of using the environment at the micro level to achieve a desired emergence of the overall behaviour of all the agents at the macro level.

Execution of a set of tasks in a synchronous manner can be achieved by employing either a centralized control wherein each node contacts a central server to get the next task in the sequence or by flooding the whole network (environment) with messages spreading the current state to other nodes. Both these methods incur a large consumption of valuable bandwidth. The challenge however is to synchronize the execution of a set of tasks sequentially in a decentralized manner with minimal overheads. In this paper we describe how a set of heterogeneous agents capable of performing distinct tasks communicate using stigmergy.

3   The Synchronization Model and Problem Description

The system under study comprises the following elements:-

- A set of m unique tasks $T = \{T_1, T_2, ..., T_m\}$.
- A network W of n nodes.
- A set of m different types of heterogeneous mobile agents $A = \{A_1^{T_1}, A_2^{T_2}, ... A_m^{T_m}\}$ with each $A_i^{T_i}$ capable of executing a unique task $T_i \in T$ and also cloning to form a population.

The set A forms the metaphor of the swarm or colony while its elements form the different types of individuals comprising the swarm. All the n nodes within the network W are passive entities i.e. they do not possess any information regarding the sequence of the tasks to be performed nor do they influence the order of their executions. Both the mobile agents and the nodes in the network are oblivious of the size of the network W and the population of each type of mobile agent $A_i^{T_i}$. Each type of mobile agent $A_i^{T_i}$ is assigned a distinct task T_i such that no two types of mobile agents have similar tasks i.e.

$$\forall A_i^{T_i}, A_j^{T_j} \in A, i \neq j, T_i \neq T_j$$

The mobile agents are capable of carrying programs (code) required to execute their assigned tasks. These agents can perceive various stimuli as and when they visit the nodes in the network W and deposit pieces of information onto the nodes as a consequence of completing the execution of their assigned tasks. A mobile agent A_i can migrate from one node to another using the *conscientious* migration strategy [26] if there exists a link connecting the nodes. Using this strategy, they try to avoid the nodes which they have recently visited in their endeavour to patrol the network. The population of this heterogeneous set of mobile agents varies as per the stigmergic population control mechanism proposed by Godfrey *et al.* [9,11] (discussed in the next section). A mobile agent $A_i^{T_i}$ commences the execution of its assigned task T_i when it has received stimulations greater than a threshold from the environment which in this case is the network of nodes. Thus, an agent $A_i^{T_i}$ satiates a node by executing a task T_i and hence changes the state of that node. In the present context, satiating or servicing a node means when the agent $A_i^{T_i}$ reaches the node, it supplies the code pertaining to its assigned task T_i and execution of the code at that node completes the associated task. This execution changes the state of the node so as to generate stimulations for the next task in the sequence to be executed within that node. The nodes form metaphors for the environment of the entities viz. the mobile agents comprising the swarm. Agents encounter nodes in various states as they migrate within the network. The ideal case to commence the execution of a new task in the network is when all the nodes are in a single state. If ρ is the number of distinct states that can be observed in the network at any moment of time then its value would be ideally expected to be unity. In practice, the actual value of ρ is always 2 since the state of a node changes as soon as an agent satiates it while there may be other nodes which are yet to be serviced for the same task. Therefore, if the value of $\rho = 2$ is maintained within the network, then it would essentially mean that only one type of agents are executing their respective tasks within the nodes in the network. However, a value of $\rho > 2$ essentially infers an out of sequence execution.

Hence, the main objective of this work is to synchronously execute all the tasks in the set T on all the nodes in the network W by ensuring that the value of $\rho \leq 2$ i.e.

$$\forall T_i \in T, \forall n \in W, \text{ Execute } T_i \text{ at } n$$

$$\text{such that } \rho \leq 2$$

By synchronous execution, we intend to imply that until all the nodes in the network W have finished their execution of a task T_i, the execution of the next task in the sequence of tasks i.e. T_{i+1}, should not commence. It may be noted that there ought to be no direct communication among the agents or the nodes lest this cause undesirable overheads as discussed earlier. A speed-up in the execution of a task T_i can be achieved if multiple agents capable of executing T_i exist in the network. This can be realized by cloning the agent. However, uncontrolled cloning has the obvious disadvantage of cluttering the entire network. In the next section we describe a stigmergy based cloning controller [9,11] to regulate the population of heterogeneous mobile agents. We then proceed to discuss the synchronization technique.

4   Population Control of Heterogeneous Mobile Agents

Godfrey *et al.* [9,11] have presented a model to control the population of a heterogeneous set of mobile agents in a network using stigmergy. They have used a novel concept termed *Cloning Resource* (S) to govern the dynamics of populations of different types of mobile agents within a network. According to their model, each node maintains a *Queue* which hosts all the mobile agents within a node. Each mobile agent carries within itself a record of its current

Lifetime (*L*) and *S* along with the set of services or tasks which it intends to deliver to the requesting nodes. Whenever a mobile agent provides its services to a node, it gains a *Reward* (R) in return. These *Rewards* alter *L* and *S* of that agent. The increase in the population of mobile agents occurs due to cloning (creating mobile agents of their own kind) while the decrease in population happens due to the termination of mobile agents which have exhausted their *lifetimes*. The *Queue* within each node is composed of four elements:

1. The *De-Queue Controller*: This takes care of handshaking with a neighbouring node to enable the transfer of a mobile agent out of the *Queue*.
2. The *En-Queue Controller*: Its task is complementary to the De-Queue Controller and caters to the request of migrating a mobile agent into the Queue.
3. *Lifetime Monitor & Queue Compactor* : This unit ensures that the lifetimes of each of the mobile agents within the *Queue* are decremented with each instant of time.
4. *Cloning Pressure Register*: This register keeps a record of the current *Cloning Pressure* which has been explained later.

This population control model works based on a reactive mechanism to maintain the population of mobile agents within the networked systems. This mechanism embedded within each mobile agent, senses the number of existing mobile agents in the *Queue* waiting for their turn to migrate to the next node. The number of agents within the *Queue* provides an estimation of the amount of free space for agents to populate within the *Queues* of the nodes in the network. Based on this, an agent decides whether or not to clone. The extent to which an agent can clone depends on the following parameters:

- The *Cloning Resource* available within the mobile agent,
- The *Rewards* gains by servicing the nodes and
- The *Cloning Pressure* which is proportional to the number of vacant slots in the *Queue*.

Cloning Resource, *S*, is charged partly by the rewards and partly by an inherent charging mechanism embedded within the mobile agent. Apart from *S*, the *Lifetime*, *L*, of the mobile agents also increases with the rewards they acquire. The decision as to whether or not a mobile agent, resident within the *Queue* of a node at time *t*, should clone is made based on the *Cloning Pressure*, $\theta_c(t)$ given by Equation 1 [9,11].

$$\theta_c(t) = \begin{cases} q_{th} - |q(t)| & for\ \theta_c > 0 \\ 0 & otherwise \end{cases} \quad (1)$$

where, q_{th} is the *Queue Threshold* and determines the maximum number of agents allowed within the *Queue*. $|q(t)|$ is the number of mobile agents present within the *Queue* at time *t* at a node.

The number of clones, $\eta(t)$, that a mobile agent A_i can generate at time *t* within the *Queue* of a node is determined by Equation 2 [9,11].

$$\eta(t) = \left\lfloor \theta_c(t) \frac{S_{av}(t)}{S_{max}} \right\rfloor \tag{2}$$

where, $S_{av}(t)$ is the available S within the agent A_i at time t and S_{max} is the maximum value of S that a mobile agent can possess.

A mobile agent A_i attempts to make clones if it has enough S to supply to the new clones as given by Equation 3 [9,11].

$$S_{av}(t+1) = S_{av}(t) - \eta(t)S_{min} \tag{3}$$

where, S_{min} is the minimum value of S that needs to be conferred to a clone.

The recharging of the S is governed by Equation 4 [9,11].

$$S_{av}(t+1) = \begin{cases} S_{av}(t) + \alpha_c e^{-1/S_{av}(t)} + \alpha_r R(t) & \text{for } S_{av}(t) \geq \gamma, \theta_c(t) \leq 1 \\ S_{av}(t) + \alpha_c + \alpha_r R(t) & \text{for } S_{av}(t) < \gamma, \theta_c(t) < 1 \\ S_{av}(t) + \alpha_c e^{(1-1/x)} + \alpha_r R(t) & \text{for } \theta_c(t) > \gamma \text{ where } x = \theta_c(t) \\ S_{max} & \text{if } S_{av}(t+1) > S_{max} \end{cases} \tag{4}$$

where $R(t)$ is taken to be 1 if the agent services a node; else as 0 at time t. α_c and α_r are constants and $\gamma = S_{min}$.

The increment in the *Lifetime*, L, of a mobile agent in the presence of a reward is given by Equation 5 [11,9].

$$L(t+1) = L(t) + \beta R(t) \tag{5}$$

where, β is a non-zero positive constant.

The authors in [9,11] have successfully portrayed the performance of their population control model for a heterogeneous set of mobile agents on static as well as dynamic networks. They have show-cased the selective rise and fall in the populations of different types of mobile agents based on the demand of their services in the network.

Since, the problem being tackled in this paper makes use of heterogeneous mobile agents to perform different tasks, such a population control framework is best suited. Further, such a framework alleviates the issue of finding the suitable number of agents of a kind to complete the service.

5 Synchronizing the Heterogeneous Set of Mobile Agents

In [15] a technique to synchronize the execution of a sequence of tasks using homogeneous mobile agents has been described. Homogeneity in their context, means that every agent is capable of executing all the tasks in the given sequence. The sequence in which the set of tasks are to be executed is also known a priori by all the agents. In this paper we go a step further to address the same problem of sequential execution of a set of distinct tasks in a sequence being performed at the nodes in a network, the synchronization of which is facilitated by a set of heterogeneous agents. By heterogeneity we mean that every agent is capable of

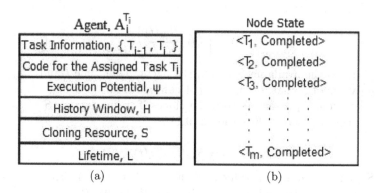

Fig. 1. (a) Structure of the mobile agent $A_i^{T_i}$ (b) Tuples deposited at a node in the network

carrying or servicing only one unique task in the given sequence. These agents are thus oblivious of the manner in which other tasks in the sequence are to be executed. Further, the fact that these asynchronous agents are oblivious of the sequence in which the set of tasks need to be executed as also the number of tasks in the sequence, unlike in [15], adds to the complexity of sequencing and synchronizing these executions. This paper describes a methodology to handle this extra complexity and further alleviates the agents to carry code and other information for multiple tasks.

As mentioned earlier, the main focus of this work is to stigmergically sense and trigger a task-switch uniformly and synchronously across all nodes constituting the network with no inter-agent communication or centralized control. Thus, if all the nodes in the network are in a state which requires the execution of task T_2 then the concerned mobile agents (including their clones) viz. $A_2^{T_2}$ should be providing the service to satiate them and migrating within the network so as to eventually complete the execution of this task at all nodes. Nodes that have been serviced for T_2 will transit to a state wherein they require the service of the next task viz. T_3. However, only when all the nodes transit to this new state should the agents assigned to service T_3 i.e. $A_3^{T_3}$, commence their executions at these nodes thereby achieving the required synchronization i.e. $\rho \leq 2$.

5.1 Task Distribution and Stimulations

In the proposed approach, the information about the sequence of tasks is partitioned among the different types of mobile agents. Each type of mobile agent possesses the knowledge of the task that it has been assigned to and the information about the task that occurs previous to its assigned task in the task sequence. Let $\{T_1 \rightarrow T_2 \rightarrow T_3\}$ in that order be the sequence of tasks assigned to agents $A_1^{T_1}$, $A_2^{T_2}$ and $A_3^{T_3}$ respectively. In this case, the mobile agents $A_1^{T_1}$, $A_2^{T_2}$ and $A_3^{T_3}$ would maintain the information $\{\phi, T_1\}$, $\{T_1, T_2\}$ and $\{T_2, T_3\}$ respectively. ϕ indicates that there is no task prior to the assigned one in the

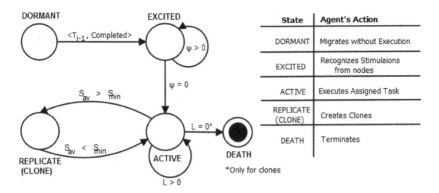

Fig. 2. State transition diagram of the mobile agent $A_i^{T_i}$ along with its behaviour in each state in the proposed technique

prescribed sequence. An agent carrying such an information would naturally be the first to be triggered. Whenever a mobile agent $A_i^{T_i}$ satiates a node for a task T_i, it deposits a tuple of the form $< T_i, Completed >$ on to that node. This stigmergic information flags the incoming agents that the task T_i has already been executed at this node. The deposition of such tuples refers to the change in the state of that node and hence provides the stimulations to the mobile agents to trigger the execution of the concerned task. For example, after the execution of task T_1 by the mobile agent $A_1^{T_1}$ on a node, the agent will deposit the tuple $< T_1, Completed >$ on that node. At a later stage, when the task T_2 is executed by the mobile agent $A_2^{T_2}$ on the same node, the latter adds the tuple $< T_2, Completed >$ so that the information available on that node becomes $[< T_1, Completed >, < T_2, Completed >]$. After the successful execution of all the tasks in the sequence of tasks T, the information on each of the nodes will be $< T_i, Completed > \forall i \in T$ as shown in Figure 1(b).

5.2 The Underlying Dynamics

In addition to the *Cloning Resource*, S, and *Lifetime*, L, as discussed in the previous section, each mobile agent also consists of another parameter called the *Execution Potential* (Ψ) which is analogous to the response threshold [2] required to switch ON the execution of the agent's assigned task. Figure 1(a) depicts all the parameters carried by a mobile agent. The *Execution Potential*, Ψ, of a mobile agent $A_i^{T_i}$ is responsible for the co-ordination of the synchronized executions of different tasks. Ψ for every agent is initialized to a non-zero positive value. Figure 2 depicts the various states of a mobile agent along with the associated transitions during the synchronization process. Initially, all types of mobile agents $A_i^{T_i}$ enter the system in the DORMANT state wherein they migrate without executing. An agent $A_i^{T_i}$ makes a transition to the EXCITED state as soon as it finds a node having the tuple $< T_{i-1}, Completed >$ which acts as a positive stimulation. These positive stimulations decrease the value of

Ψ of agent $A_i^{T_i}$. On the contrary if this agent (which has already transitioned to the EXCITED state) does not find the tuple $< T_{i-1}, Completed >$ (a negative stimulation) at a node then its value of Ψ increases. The equation governing the value of Ψ is given below.

$$\Psi(t+1) = \begin{cases} \Psi(t) - (1 - e^{-\sigma(t)})\Psi(t), \text{ for Positive Stimulation} \\ \Psi(t) + (1 - e^{-\sigma(t)})\Psi(t), \text{ for Negative Stimulation} \end{cases} \quad (6)$$

where the parameter $\sigma(t)$ is discussed later.

The mobile agent transits to the ACTIVE state as and when Ψ equals 0. In the ACTIVE state, the mobile agent $A_i^{T_i}$ starts the execution of its assigned task T_i whenever it migrates to a node that does not have the tuple $< T_i, Completed >$. Ψ is computed and used only when the agent is in the EXCITED state. It ceases to have any effect on the behaviour of the mobile agent beyond the EXCITED state.

Let $P_{T_i}^n \in \{True, False\}$ be a binary variable which takes the value $True$ $(False)$ if a tuple $< T_i, Completed >$ is present (absent) at a node n. The following logical statements describe the behaviour of a mobile agent $A_i^{T_i}$ at a node $n \in W$:

S1: $\neg P_{T_{i-1}}^n \wedge (\Psi > 0) \to$ Migration without Execution
S2: $P_{T_{i-1}}^n \wedge \neg P_{T_i}^n \wedge (\Psi > 0) \to$ Positive Stimulation (Equation 6)
S3: $\neg P_{T_{i-1}}^n \wedge (\Psi > 0) \wedge (STATE = EXCITED) \to$ Negative Stimulation (Equation 6)
S4: $\neg P_{T_i}^n \wedge (\Psi = 0) \to$ Execute Task T_i

The statement S1 describes the DORMANT state wherein the mobile agents migrate from one node to another in search of the positive stimulations required to switch to the next state. In statements S2 and S3, the agent perceives positive and negative stimulations respectively from the environment which changes the value of its Ψ (Equation 6). The agents following S2 and S3 are thus in the EXCITED state. When $\Psi = 0$ the agent transits to the ACTIVE state and behaves as per the statement S4 and starts to execute its assigned task. For illustration, consider the task sequence $T = \{T_1; T_2; T_3; T_4; T_5\}$ and set of agents $A = \{A_1^{T_1}, A_2^{T_2}, A_3^{T_3}, A_4^{T_4}, A_5^{T_5}\}$. Initially all the agents in A will be in DORMANT state within the network. Since the agent $A_1^{T_1}$ is assigned the first task in the task-sequence T, it will immediately switch to the EXCITED state due to the presence ϕ within its task information. While the agent $A_1^{T_1}$ is in the EXCITED state (statement S2 and S3) all other agents in A will continue to remain in the DORMANT state. Eventually the agent $A_1^{T_1}$ will transit to the ACTIVE state when its Ψ becomes 0 and start the execution of the task T_1 in the concerned nodes. Such executions would result in the deposition of the tuple $< T_1, Completed >$ on the concerned nodes in the network. Only on perceiving this tuple, will $A_2^{T_2}$ transit to the EXCITED state. The agent $A_2^{T_2}$ will continue to remain in the EXCITED state until its Ψ value becomes zero. As long as $A_2^{T_2}$ is in the EXCITED state, $A_3^{T_3}$, $A_4^{T_4}$ and $A_5^{T_5}$ will still remain in the DORMANT state. This chain of actions will continue until all the agents in A transit to the

Table 1. Change in the state of agents $A_1^{T_1}$ to $A_5^{T_5}$ within the network for the sequence $T = \{T_1; T_2; T_3; T_4; T_5\}$

Agent's State vs System Status	$A_1^{T_1}$	$A_2^{T_2}$	$A_3^{T_3}$	$A_4^{T_4}$	$A_5^{T_5}$
Initialization	DORMANT	DORMANT	DORMANT	DORMANT	DORMANT
Stimulation for Task T_1	**EXCITED**	DORMANT	DORMANT	DORMANT	DORMANT
Execution of Task T_1, Stimulation for task T_2	ACTIVE	**EXCITED**	DORMANT	DORMANT	DORMANT
Execution of Task T_2, Stimulation for task T_3	ACTIVE	ACTIVE	**EXCITED**	DORMANT	DORMANT
Execution of Task T_3, Stimulation for task T_4	ACTIVE	ACTIVE	ACTIVE	**EXCITED**	DORMANT
Execution of Task T_4, Stimulation for task T_5	ACTIVE	ACTIVE	ACTIVE	ACTIVE	**EXCITED**
Execution of Task T_5	ACTIVE	ACTIVE	ACTIVE	ACTIVE	ACTIVE

ACTIVE state as depicted in Table 1. As can be observed, the agents in the task sequence create stimulations for the succeeding agents. These stimulations are distributed temporally across the network making the agents execute their assigned tasks only when their turn comes up.

The parameter $\sigma(t)$ which regulates the amount of increment or decrement in Ψ is calculated in the following manner. Let $\xi(.)$ be a function that returns the time of an event at a node $n \in W$. We define a parameter Δ using $\xi(.)$ as,

$$\Delta := \xi(A_i^{T_i} \text{arriving at n}) - \xi(< T_{i-1}, Completed > \text{deposited at n}) \quad (7)$$

Hence, Δ is essentially the difference between the time when the status of a node was updated to $< T_{i-1}, Completed >$ by the agent $A_{i-1}^{T_{i-1}}$ and when the mobile agent $A_i^{T_i}$ arrived at that node. Every mobile agent maintains a record of its own task-specific Δ's in a *History Window* (H) of length ω ($\omega \geq 0$) within itself. Whenever, a mobile agent $A_i^{T_i}$ finds a node having $< T_{i-1}, Completed >$ (i.e. $P_{T_{i-1}}^n = True$), it finds the value of Δ using Equation 7 at that node. This new value of Δ is added to the H of $A_i^{T_i}$, if it is greater than the last recorded value i.e.

$$H_{new} \leftarrow H_{old} \cup \{\Delta^n\}, \text{ if } \Delta^n > \Delta_{\omega-1}$$

where Δ^n is the value of Δ at node n and $\Delta_{\omega-1}$ is the last recorded value of Δ in H of $A_i^{T_i}$.

Since the different types of mobile agents execute their assigned tasks in different time-slots (temporally distributed), the values of Δ within H are normalized between 0 and 1 using Equation 8.

$$Norm(\Delta_i) = \frac{\Delta_i - \Delta_0}{\Delta_{\omega-1} - \Delta_0}, \ \forall i \in [0, \omega - 1] \tag{8}$$

where Δ_i denotes the ith value in H.

The value of $\sigma(t)$ is calculated using Equation 9 as the standard deviation of $Norm(\Delta_i), \forall i \in H$. Thus, $\sigma(t)$ provides the extent of dispersion of the stimulations (requirement of a service in the network) that a mobile agent observes at time t.

$$\sigma(t) = \kappa \sqrt{\frac{\sum_{i=0}^{\omega-1} \{Norm(\Delta_i) - \mu\}^2}{\omega - 1}} \tag{9}$$

where,

$$\mu = \frac{\sum_{i=0}^{\omega-1} Norm(\Delta_i)}{\omega - 1} \tag{10}$$

κ is a non-zero positive constant and ω, as already mentioned, is the length of the *History Window, H*.

In the ACTIVE state, whenever a mobile agent $A_i^{T_i}$ executes its assigned task T_i on a node it receives a reward R in return. This reward recharges the *Cloning Resource, S* (as discussed in Section 4, Equation 4) of $A_i^{T_i}$. When the S of an agent $A_i^{T_i}$ crosses S_{min} so that it can confer enough Cloning Resource to the clone it transits to the REPLICATE state to create the clones as per Equation 3. The clone and the parent then transit back to the ACTIVE state as shown in Figure 2. Due to cloning the population of the mobile agent $A_i^{T_i}$ increases. Hence, the mobile agents whose assigned tasks are currently required to be executed on all the nodes in the network rise in population whereas the populations of the clones of the other type of agents decline due to their diminishing *Lifetimes* causing transitions from ACTIVE state to DEATH state. In the proposed technique, the system starts with a set of parent mobile agents assigned distinct tasks in T with infinite lifetimes. As the system progresses, the cloning controller ensures that the population of each type of mobile agent varies based on their demand within the network.

5.3   Self-healing

In real world scenarios, it may happen that a task completed by an agent at a node(s) may crash or breakdown due to some environmental effects. Consider the case of a task (T_i) of connecting two wires to make a bridge at a node. When the task is executed the change in environment within the node (i.e. $< T_i, Completed >$ is asserted at the node) allows for flow of information across the bridge. A failure could result at this node if for some reason this connection breaks (i.e. $< T_i, Completed >$ is deleted). Such problems could occur in an out-of-order manner across the network making ρ to be greater than 2. In such a case, the concerned agent(s) may need to re-execute the task(s) at the respective nodes while the other nodes are being serviced for a different task as per the sequence T. The proposed technique exhibits such a *Self-Healing* mechanism inherently.

As mentioned earlier in Subsection 5.1, the tuple deposited at a node after the completion of a task acts as the stigmergic information at that node which indicates the completion of that task within. When a task at a node fails then the concerned tuple is deleted from that node indicating the requirement of a the task to be re-executed. Such failures may be local to a node or may involve a set of nodes. This causes the agent assigned the concerned task to behave as per statement S4 (see Subsection 5.2) resulting in the re-execution of this task at the failed node. This agent thus receives a reward which in turn increases its cloning resource. These agents may thus transit to the REPLICATE state and clone. This quickens re-executions at the failed nodes ensuring faster recovery. Though such re-executions introduce asynchronization ($\rho > 2$), the *Self-Healing* mechanism enhances in the fault-tolerance capability and robustness of the system.

6 Emulating the Synchronized Task Execution

A discrete simulation is inherently synchronous and thus may underestimate the working and results of the proposed technique. In order to test the efficacy of the proposed technique it was thus imperative for us to emulate the environment comprising the nodes of a network and the mobile agents. In our experimentation, we have used Typhon [25], a mobile agent framework specifically suited for emulating mobile agents in real networks. Typhon is based on the Chimera Agent System that comes along with the LPA Prolog (www.lpa.co.uk). Typical features of a mobile agent within Typhon include mobility, code carrying ability, cloning, etc. A network of nodes can either be created within a local host by creating as many instantiations of Typhon within the physical system (localhost) or by starting similar instantiations on other systems connected as a physical network such as a LAN. We have used 10 different physical computer systems connected within a LAN out of which 9 were used to realize an emulated mesh overlay network while one of the computers (the non-participating node) was used to log the data generated during the experimentations, asynchronously.

7 Results and Discussions

The experiments were performed over two emulated mesh overlay networks having 50 and 100 nodes. Five conscientious mobile agents (parent mobile agents) each carrying a different task out of a sequence of five tasks were used in the experiments to test the efficacy of the technique. Following parameter values were used in the experiment: $\Psi(0) = 100, \kappa = 1, q_{th} = 4, S_{min} = 10, S_{max} = 100, \alpha_c = 0.1, \alpha_r = 15, \beta = 7, \omega = 5$.

All the parent mobile agents were given infinite lifetime while the initial lifetime conferred on a new clone was set to 10. Self-healing was emulated by forcing at set of 20 nodes chosen arbitrary at random in the network to crash the task T_2 while the service for the task T_4 was in progress. The mobile agents were initially placed in different nodes (chosen randomly) and were triggered to commence their patrolling within the network. Nodes and agents continuously sent information on the tasks being executed, the rewards, stimulations, Clonal Resource, etc., asynchronously to the non-participating node. It may be noted that the non-participating node was not a node in any of the networks used in the experiment nor did it influence the agents or participating nodes in any of their processes or actions.

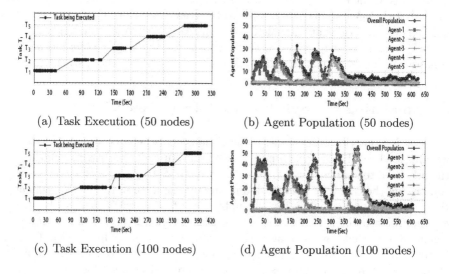

(a) Task Execution (50 nodes)   (b) Agent Population (50 nodes)

(c) Task Execution (100 nodes)   (d) Agent Population (100 nodes)

Fig. 3. Executions of Tasks- T_1 to T_5 in (a) for 50-node and (c) 100-node mesh networks along with the corresponding change in the populations of agents *Agent-1* through *Agent-5* in (b) and (d) respectively

The graphs in Figures 3(a) and (c) depict the execution of five different tasks by five different types of mobile agents in the network of 50 and 100 nodes respectively using the proposed synchronization technique. As can be observed from the graph, the execution of each type of task (T_1 through T_5) occurs almost without any overlaps (there is only one instance of overlap of execution of task T_2 with task T_3 in the 100-node network) with other tasks in the sequence. Further, the time for execution of each type of task (T_i) on all the nodes for both the networks varies in between 30 to 60 seconds. Some gaps can be noted in between the executions of consecutive tasks. These gaps, refereed as the *idle periods* are

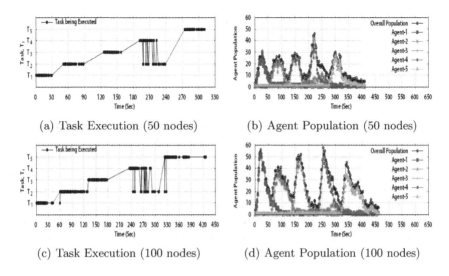

(a) Task Execution (50 nodes)   (b) Agent Population (50 nodes)

(c) Task Execution (100 nodes)   (d) Agent Population (100 nodes)

Fig. 4. Self-healing with failure of task T_2 at 20 nodes randomly selected in the network when the execution of task T_4 was in progress for the 50- and 100-node networks

generated as a result of the time taken by the mobile agents to acquire the level of stimulation to commence the execution of their assigned tasks.

The graphs in Figures 3(b) and (d) depict the change in the populations of different types of agents, *Agent-1* through *Agent-5* assigned with tasks T_1 through T_5, along with the change in the overall population of all the mobile agents in the network. One can easily observe the successive peaks in the graph which illustrates the rise in the population of agents which were currently servicing the nodes for their assigned tasks. This rise in agent population accounts for the parallel and concurrent executions of a task at different nodes in the network. It may be observed that the rise in population of agents is more in the 100-node network (around 60) than that of in the 50-node network (around 30) which shows the on-demand generation of agents.

The graphs in Figure 4 depict the order of execution of tasks and the change in population of agents during *self-healing*. As can be observed in Figures 4(a) and (c), when the mobile agent assigned to service task T_2, $A_2^{T_2}$, finds a node where the task T_2 has crashed, it automatically starts its service of the task T_2 and hence gain rewards which charges its S. This allows the mobile agent to clone and expand its search and service for the crashed task at other nodes in the network. A small rise in the population of *Agent-2* can be observed in Figures 4(b) and (d) at around 250th and 300th second respectively due to such cloning activities. Apparently, the crashed tasks does not affect the order of execution of tasks of other agents in the network.

Hence the results portray that the proposed technique is capable of streamlining the execution of different tasks for a heterogeneous set of mobile agents. Further the *self-healing* feature ensures that the failure of a task from the sequence T does not adversely affect the progression of executions. The equivalent range of *idle-times* in different networks shows the adaptiveness of the proposed technique in different environments.

8   Conclusions

Synchronized execution of a sequence of tasks is realizable using centralized control. However, in decentralized and distributed environments the only way to achieve this is to make the individual entities communicate with one another. This entails heavy overheads on the available networking infrastructure. Using stigmergy and discrete stimulations coupled with the concept of a cloning resource within each agent we have shown that it is possible to assess the situation of the environment and achieve synchronized execution. Results on networks of varying size have also shown similar performance. Stigmergic communication emerges when the agents sense the number of satiated and unsatiated nodes and orient themselves accordingly to serve for global synchronization.

The proposed technique also inherently exhibits *self-healing* making the overall system fault-tolerant. In future we intend to test the same technique in conjunction with dynamic and mobile networks and eventually realize a swarm of mobile robots coordinating and executing tasks in a specific sequence while at the same time performing *self-healing* as and when required.

Acknowledgements. The first author would like to acknowledge Tata Consultancy Services (TCS) for supporting him during the research reported in this paper.

References

1. Bonabeau, E., Dorigo, M., Theraulaz, G.: Swarm Intelligence: From natural to artificial systems, vol. (1). OUP USA (1999)
2. Bonabeau, E., Theraulaz, G., Deneubourg, J.L.: Fixed response thresholds and the regulation of division of labor in insect societies. Bulletin of Mathematical Biology 60(4), 753–807 (1998)
3. Bonabeau, E., Theraulaz, G., Deneubourg, J.L.: The synchronization of recruitment-based activities in ants. Biosystems 45(3), 195–211 (1998)
4. Camazine, S., Deneubourg, J., Franks, N., Sneyd, J., Theraulaz, G., Bonabeau, E.: Self-organisation in biological systems. Princeton University Press (2001)
5. Chess, D., Harrison, C., Kershenbaum, A.: Mobile agents: Are they a good idea? In: Tschudin, C.F., Vitek, J. (eds.) MOS 1996. LNCS, vol. 1222, pp. 25–45. Springer, Heidelberg (1997)
6. Deneubourg, J.: Application de l'ordre par fluctuations a la description de certaines étapes de la construction du nid chez les Termites. Insectes Sociaux 24, 117–130 (1977)
7. Deneubourg, J.L., Goss, S., Pasteels, J.M., Fresneau, D., Lachaud, J.P.: Self-organization mechanisms in ant societies (II): Learning in foraging and division of labor. From individual to collective behavior in social insects, p. 177 (1987)

8. Franks, N.R., Deneubourg, J.L., et al.: Self-organizing nest construction in ants: individual worker behaviour and the nest's dynamics. Animal Behaviour 54(4), 779–796 (1997)
9. Godfrey, W.W., Jha, S.S., Nair, S.B.: On Stigmergically Controlling a Population of Heterogeneous Mobile Agents Using Cloning Resource. In: Nguyen, N.-T. (ed.) Transactions on Computational Collective Intelligence XIV. LNCS, vol. 8615, 203 p. Springer, Heidelberg (2014)
10. Godfrey, W.W., Nair, S.B.: An immune system based multi-robot mobile agent network. In: Bentley, P.J., Lee, D., Jung, S. (eds.) ICARIS 2008. LNCS, vol. 5132, pp. 424–433. Springer, Heidelberg (2008)
11. Godfrey, W.W., Nair, S.B.: A Mobile Agent Cloning Controller for Servicing Networked Robots. In: Proceedings of 2011 International Conference on Future Information Technology, IPCSIT 2011, pp. 81–85. IACSIT Press (2011)
12. Grassé, P.: The automatic regulations of collective behavior of social insect and "stigmergy". Journal de Psychologie Normale et Pathologique 57, 1–10 (1959)
13. Hadeli, Valckenaers, P., Kollingbaum, M., Brussel, H.V.: Multi-agent coordination and control using stigmergy. Computers in Industry 53(1), 75–96 (2004)
14. Holvoet, T., Valckenaers, P.: Exploiting the Environment for Coordinating Agent Intentions. In: Weyns, D., Van Dyke Parunak, H., Michel, F. (eds.) E4MAS 2006. LNCS (LNAI), vol. 4389, pp. 51–66. Springer, Heidelberg (2007)
15. Jha, S.S., Godfrey, W.W., Nair, S.B.: Stigermgy-based Synchronization of a Sequence of Tasks in a Network of Asynchronous Nodes. Cybernetics and Systems 45(5), 373–406 (2014)
16. Jha, S.S., Shrivastava, K., Nair, S.B.: On Emulating Real-World Distributed Intelligence Using Mobile Agent Based Localized Idiotypic Networks. In: Prasath, R., Kathirvalavakumar, T. (eds.) MIKE 2013. LNCS, vol. 8284, pp. 487–498. Springer, Heidelberg (2013)
17. Jones, C., Mataric, M.J.: Adaptive division of labor in large-scale minimalist multi-robot systems. In: Proceedings of 2003 IEEE/RSJ International Conference on Intelligent Robots and Systems (IROS 2003), vol. 2, pp. 1969–1974. IEEE (2003)
18. Kambayashi, Y., Tsujimura, Y., Yamachi, H., Takimoto, M., Yamamoto, H.: Design of a Multi-Robot System Using Mobile Agents with Ant Colony Clustering. In: Proceedings of 42nd Hawaii International Conference on System Sciences, HICSS 2009, pp. 1–10 (January 2009)
19. Karsai, I., Pénzes, Z.: Comb Building in Social Wasps: Self-organization and Stigmergic Script. Journal of Theoretical Biology 161(4), 505–525 (1993), http://www.sciencedirect.com/science/article/pii/S0022519383710702
20. Krieger, M.J., Billeter, J.B., Keller, L.: Ant-like task allocation and recruitment in cooperative robots. Nature 406(6799), 992–995 (2000)
21. Kugler, P.N., Shaw, R.E., Vincente, K.J., Kinsella-Shaw, J.: Inquiry into intentional systems I: Issues in ecological physics. Psychological Research 52, 98–121 (1990)
22. Labella, T.H., Dorigo, M., Deneubourg, J.L.: Division of labor in a group of robots inspired by ants' foraging behavior. ACM Transactions on Autonomous and Adaptive Systems (TAAS) 1(1), 4–25 (2006)
23. Li, L., Martinoli, A., Abu-Mostafa, Y.: Emergent Specialization in Swarm Systems. In: Yin, H., Allinson, N.M., Freeman, R., Keane, J.A., Hubbard, S. (eds.) IDEAL 2002. LNCS, vol. 2412, pp. 261–266. Springer, Heidelberg (2002)
24. Liu, W., Winfield, A.F., Sa, J., Chen, J., Dou, L.: Towards energy optimization: Emergent task allocation in a swarm of foraging robots. Adaptive Behavior 15(3), 289–305 (2007)

25. Matani, J., Nair, S.B.: Typhon-A Mobile Agents Framework for Real World Emulation in Prolog. In: Sombattheera, C., Agarwal, A., Udgata, S.K., Lavangnananda, K. (eds.) MIWAI 2011. LNCS, vol. 7080, pp. 261–273. Springer, Heidelberg (2011)
26. Minar, N., Kramer, K.H., Maes, P.: Cooperating mobile agents for mapping networks. In: Proceedings of the First Hungarian National Conference on Agent Based Computing, pp. 34–41 (1998)
27. Murciano, A., del Millán, J.R., Zamora, J.: Specialization in multi-agent systems through learning. Biological Cybernetics 76(5), 375–382 (1997), http://dx.doi.org/10.1007/s004220050351
28. Outtagarts, A.: Mobile Agent-based Applications: A Survey. International Journal of Computer Science and Network Security 9, 331–339 (2009)
29. Resnick, M.: Turtles, termites, and traffic jams: Explorations in massively parallel microworlds. The MIT Press (1997)
30. Theraulaz, G., Bonabeau, E.: Modelling the collective building of complex architectures in social insects with lattice swarms. Journal of Theoretical Biology 177, 381–400 (1995)
31. Van Dyke Parunak, H., Brueckner, S.: Entropy and Self-organization in Multi-agent Systems. In: Proceedings of the Fifth International Conference on Autonomous Agents, AGENTS 2001, pp. 124–130. ACM, New York (2001)
32. Werfel, J., Bar-Yam, Y., Nagpal, R.: Building patterned structures with robot swarms. In: Proceedings of the 19th International Joint Conference on Artificial Intelligence, IJCAI 2005, pp. 1495–1502. Morgan Kaufmann Publishers Inc., San Francisco (2005)
33. Weyns, D., Holvoet, T.: Regional Synchronization for Simultaneous Actions in Situated Multi-agent Systems. In: Mařík, V., Müller, J.P., Pěchouček, M. (eds.) CEEMAS 2003. LNCS (LNAI), vol. 2691, pp. 497–510. Springer, Heidelberg (2003)
34. Weyns, D., Van Dyke Parunak, H., Michel, F., Holvoet, T., Ferber, J.: Environments for Multiagent Systems State-of-the-Art and Research Challenges. In: Weyns, D., Van Dyke Parunak, H., Michel, F. (eds.) E4MAS 2004. LNCS (LNAI), vol. 3374, pp. 1–47. Springer, Heidelberg (2005)

A Conceptual Framework of a Decision Support System for Operational Dispatching of Agricultural Bulk Goods – An Agent-Based Approach

Jens Mehmann[1] and Frank Teuteberg[2]

[1] Hochschule Osnabrück, Fakultät Wirtschafts- und Sozialwissenschaften,
Osnabrück, Germany
j.mehmann@hs-osnabrueck.de
[2] Universität Osnabrück, Fachgebiet Unternehmensrechnung und Wirtschaftsinformatik,
Osnabrück, Germany
frank.teuteberg@uni-osnabrueck.de

Abstract. Transportation planning may imply versatile and complex decision problems. The most distinctive feature of agricultural transportation planning is: a dynamic and rapid transaction of harvesting processes. During the harvesting process various actors such as farmers, contractors, agricultural traders, transportation companies and processing industries have to collaborate. This contribution presents a conceptual framework of a decision support approach for operational dispatching and its implementation based upon a multi-agent system (MAS). This agent-based approach enables users to conflate dispersed structure information, apply optimization techniques and provide a goal-oriented planning and transaction of transportation.

Keywords: Decision Support System, Multi-Agent System, Fourth Party Logistics (4PL), Agriculture.

1 Introduction and Motivation

Transportation volumes of the agricultural sector increase. This is a result of structural changes in the sector such as a steadily decreasing number of reception points and the emergence of major processing industries. In addition, an increasing commodity trading on the stock market as well as the current trend towards more energy supply through biomass indicate a change within the agricultural sector [1], [2]. As a result an increasing demand in transportation has to be met with available capacities, which are presently at their limits.

The transportation volume of the agricultural sector in Germany is at about 3.595.373.000t per year, of which 76% (2.734.098.000t) are commercial road traffic [3]. About 90% of this is inland traffic [3]. Other means of transportation are railroad cargo traffic, inland navigation and sea cargo handling, which serve as cross-boarder transport through import and export of agricultural goods. The value of the harvests of agricultural goods significantly impacts the transportation volumes and thus the dispatch of transports. The main influencing factors of dispatch are: people, management,

J.P. Müller, M. Weyrich, and A.L.C. Bazzan (Eds.): MATES 2014, LNAI 8732, pp. 121–137, 2014.
© Springer International Publishing Switzerland 2014

method, machines, material and the environment. For example, within the factor 'environment' weather determines the harvest period and for the harvest volumes stock markets determine price development and trading activities. At the same time legislation influences the dispatch of transportation depending on the use and processing of the goods with foodstuffs directives. Those directives impose quality criteria on the transportation means (Global Manufacturing Practice (GMP)) [4]. The quality of the harvested crop influences its utilization and thus the type of processing of the good (material) either for foodstuff or feeding stuff. Furthermore, the dispatch of transportation depends on the supply of cargo space and machinery. The latter is important because many harvested crops require specific means of transportation. Currently, people are the main factor for transportation dispatch. According to an online survey of 148 carriers in the sector, conducted in October and November 2012, transportation commissions are assigned based upon experience and individual preferences of the cargo loaders. The factor 'management' of this sector is characterized by little interconnectedness and few approaches of cooperation. In terms of the methodology, dispatching is accomplished mainly via phone and fax as well as sporadically via email. Presently, this may be characterized as 'ad hoc workflow' of transportation transaction. As a result transparency and oversight of transportation activities for the dispatch of agricultural bulk goods are slight. Figure 1 provides an overview of the main influencing factors [5].

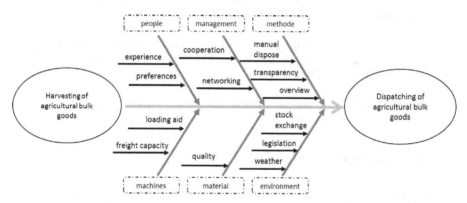

Fig. 1. Main influencing factors of dispatching agricultural bulk goods

In order to introduce market transparency as well as to pool the aforementioned key actors the authors examined the Fourth Party Logistic Provider (4PL) approach. With this approach requirements of a Transport Order Management System (TOMS) can be identified. The main challenge of a TOMS is to master the transition from the previous ad hoc workflow, in which each actor tries to optimize individual target criteria locally, to a global optimization of work flow with network-oriented target criteria and standardized information flow. The main part of a TOMS is the transaction of shipping orders.

The following paragraphs describe the conceptual framework as well as design considerations of a decision support system (DSS) for the transaction of shipping orders in the agricultural sector. This sector is characterized by loosely linked actors which create a transportation network of Germany. Furthermore, the transportation network is subject to dynamic alterations dependent upon varying harvest periods as they affect trading and transportation activities as well as the routes of transportation. From the point of view of a 4PL structural information is decentralized in the hands of the actors of the transportation network. For this reason a multi-agent architecture was selected, which represents actors as software agents integrated in a DSS. These actors may be endorsed with diverse manifestations and functions. In the first instance, a transportation planning agent (TPA) is developed. This agent is endowed with the capability to operatively dispatch agricultural bulk goods. The agent's activities are integrated in a conceptual framework of a TOMS.

These research activities are part of the third party funded research project KOMOBAR, which examines decision and communication strategies of cooperating mobile agricultural work machines. The following section provides terms and definitions. Section 3 sketches the state of the art of Transport Management Systems (TMS) and MAS. Section 4 elaborates on the functions of a TOMS based upon an implemented requirements analysis within the sector in combination with a validation of the MAS and taking into account practical values of the involved actors. The last section 5 discusses potential future research and benefits of the TOMS, for the 4PL approach and for the sector.

2   Background and Terminological Foundation

The 4PL approach introduces a neutral actor to a network who plans, implements and controls the requirements of customers. This actor is equipped with the capacity of the suppliers [6], [7]. The pooling of available information is supposed to create synergies among customers and suppliers. Practice-oriented approaches describe a successful implementation of 4PL in retailing [8] as well as automobile production [9]. These results encouraged the authors to review an adaption of the 4PL approach within the agricultural sector. Similar to the aforementioned branches, customers within the agricultural sector should be enabled to acquire traded goods safely and transparently. Moreover, transportation services suppliers may expect an efficient resource utilization. In order to implement the 4PL approach sufficiently a thorough analysis of the previous ad hoc workflow for the transaction of transportation including its applied methods, mechanisms and processes of the sector.

A typical ad hoc workflow is characterized by a non-standardized process, which can not always attain optimal results. Furthermore the ad hoc workflow is mainly determined by individual experience. However, an administratively supporting workflow follows well-defined procedures, apart from occasional exceptions [10]. Internal and cross-company business processes that are operated and controlled by IT support have key functions for the workflow management as well as the 4PL approach [11]. An increased process transparency, an improved integration of actors, an accelerated information flow and this way an improved efficiency result in an increased additional value of the workflow. A cross-company workflow is significant for a transportation management that controls the transportation of goods and includes all actors of the sector (traders, transportation providers, service providers, recipients and senders). This results from the timing process among the various actors. The literature [12] distinguishes central, decentral and hybrid transportation planning approaches that provide guidance for handling the complexity within those supply chains. This may also be relevant for the application in the agricultural sector.

Central transportation approaches plan and regulate the transportation network by help of a software instance. This includes the recognition of a transportation request message (TRM), transaction and controlling. The integration of various actor parameters which includes processing large data sets is a challenge. These data sets may alter permanently, but have to be processed instantly [13]. In addition, only local planning expertise is available for processing relevant information within a centralized planning system [14].

In case of a decentralized transportation planning approach network actors decide autonomously. Each of the actors may apply own specific target criteria, and individually decide either for acceptance, forwarding or rejection of a commission. In this case local knowledge is applied [14]. Yet, available local actor systems are linked due to software agents as well as predefined interfaces and protocols. This system landscape facilitates a data and information exchange beyond local scale.

Hybrid planning systems merge both centralized and decentralized planning approaches, whereby a centrally designed plan is being provided for autonomous units. In case of a deviation of the plan agents flag feedback, which may achieve control function on demand [13].

According to Wooldridge and Jennings [15] a software agent is a hardware or software-based computer system which operates without the direct intervention of humans or others. Software agents have some kind of control over their actions and internal state (autonomy). In addition, agents may have social capabilities in order to interact with other software agents or users. Moreover, agents are reactive and even proactive, and this way have the capability to interact with the environment (entities that are not agents nor users) [15]. Once single software agents are linked and start interacting, a multi-agent system (MAS) emerges. These MAS may generate and represent complex systems with various functions [16]. Agent-based approaches including MAS emerged from a number of scientific disciplines such as artificial intelligence, robotics or system science when object-oriented programming methods were applied and human interfaces have been examined [17]. The application of agent-based approaches is manifold and reaches from product developments to supply chain management (SCM) [18]. The following section discusses related agent-based approaches as well as previous knowledge and experience of the agricultural sector as well as the 4PL approach.

3   Related Research and Survey Results

In order to study possible applications of MAS within logistics the databases 'EBSCO', `Web of Science and Wiley Online Library were employed to browse for the keywords: MAS, agent, supply chain and logistic. This resulted in various descriptions of applications in the field of logistics in scientific journals and conference proceedings. For instance, Mishra et al [19] describe the MAS-based logistic management of a recycling process that supports the enterprise in the implementation of 'green' supply chains. Kaihara und Fujii [20] demonstrate an example of a gaming approach for the management of industrial collaboration with an MAS. Sheremetov und Rocha-Mier [21] demonstrate another example of a supply chain optimization with an MAS. The focus is here on dynamic structure and information alteration within a decision making process in a supply chain. Gerber and Klusch [22] describe the use of agents for mobile planning services in the agricultural sector for the harvesting process. The intended transport process takes place down-stream of the harvesting process. These examples examine possible applications of MAS upon various issues. However, the literature does not provide applied MAS in transportation planning with logistic service providers in the agricultural sector [23]. Effects of collaborative planning are discussed [24], however, only sporadic functions and issues suitable for the application of MAS are presented [25].

There are several approaches for agent endowment. For example, supply chain actors may be represented as software agents (e.g. Supplier Agent, Producer Agent, Distribution Agent, Warehouse, Purchasing) [21] [26], if the number of actors/agents is manageable, and the specific roles are different. Alternatively, agents may represent various planning functions [16], [27]. Lima [16] introduces an agent-based model that employs three different principle agents (client, order management and resource agent) for production planning and control. In contrast, Yee und Cheng-Wei [27] model a procurement process of a supply chain with a MAS. A number of practice-oriented approaches demonstrate partial solutions, where an MAS only contributes to a single problem, but cannot provide the entire solution [28]. For example, an MAS was employed to simulate an entire supply chain in order to calculate the lowest possible total logistic costs. This is achieved by an inventory management among agents [29].

Lee and Kim [18] demonstrate that especially those MAS should be employed which are capable of handling the dynamic and rational behavior for strategic commercial decisions. This is the case of applied transportation planning. On the one hand due to harvesting and trade activities agricultural transportation planning must be dynamic. On the other hand each of the involved actors behaves entrepreneurial with rational target criteria. For this reason transportation transaction must be implemented in a way that various sub processes can be clearly distinguished and represented by help of a MAS. Every agent is designed to control a sub process with the aim to keep the complexity low – especially for potential users. Decentralization is supposed to enable the integration of communication and information systems with the aim to minimize barriers at an early point of time within the process.

In the agricultural bulk sector different factors influence the dispatching. These are the temporal coordination (fast flow of information, flexibility), the sector specific factors (especially transportation requirements), low cooperation and competition of the actors. The quest for an appropriate method to implement a service provider (4PL) in the dispatching process resulted in an agent-based approach. This way each actor is represented within the dispatch of agricultural bulk transportation through the TOMS according to his access permissions and his specific requirements. Due to the competition among actors a transparent, neutral and anonymous dispatch is required. In addition, each actor wants to act anonymously. The added value of the 4PL is the coordination of transportation based upon the capabilities of the TOMS and the emerging cooperation of all involved actors. Through the TOMS each actor is expected to benefit from the added values. In addition to saving transaction costs the greatest potential are expected by the improved resources.The aforementioned requirements analysis [30], supported the idea to develop a TOMS which was integrated in a DSS for operative dispatch. Participants of this analysis requested order administration (acceptance, processing), a cross-network planning (a combination of freight orders, tour optimization and assessment, selection of service providers, choice of loading and unloading points, pricing, tracking and tracing) as well as transportation order controlling (parameters of the cost-benefit analysis and comparison of the planning and implementation parameter, documentation of the traceability).

Due to sector-specific impact factors derived from management of the sector as well as from the yet available methods how agricultural goods are dispatched, a test is required for the analysis to what extent a neutral 4PL employing an MAS-based and networked TOMS can contribute to an efficient dispatch of bulk goods in the agricultural sector.

Apart from modeling the entire TOMS the design of the agents for transportation planning was condensed, since synergies may be expected due to the application-oriented design of the agents. On the network scale the 4PL applies the travelling sales man problem (TSP) approach for the long-term planning over a period of one to six weeks. However once the transportation service provider is engaged the 4PL has to consider the Vehicle Routing Problem with the special case of the Pickup and Delivery Problem (PDP) on the short term. Hence, the design of a conceptual model including an implementation and validation of the transport planning agent are the first goals for this research.

4   A Conceptual Framework for an Agent-Based TOMS

TOMS are distinguished in the analysis of transport order demand, transport order planning, transport order transaction and transport order controlling [31]. The latter activity follows the transport order via the actors of a transportation chain. Various characteristics may be derived from the different sub ranges of transport order management (see table 1).

In order to describe the conceptual framework of a TOMS a description of the involved agricultural actors is required. Actors of a network who use such a system may resume several roles at the same time. For instance, a trader may also be a recipient as well as a transportation provider as long as he holds transportation capacity. However, a 4PL service provider can only play the role of a service provider. In addition the actors have specific properties and have to consider sector specific characteristics.

Table 1. Elicited characteristics of a TOMS

Analysis of transport order demand	Transport order controlling
<ul><li>Entry of transport order</li><li>Feedback to sender</li></ul>	<ul><li>Monitoring of business ratio</li><li>Provision of status reports</li><li>Controlling of deviations between target and performance</li></ul>
Transport order planning	**Transport order transaction**
<ul><li>Compilation of supply routes</li><li>Evaluation of routes</li><li>Selection of service providers</li><li>Identification of alternative means of transportation</li><li>Costs assessment</li><li>Order of services, compilation and sending of transport orders (nominal value)</li><li>Sending of transportation information to the involved actors</li></ul>	<ul><li>Provision of the goods by sender</li><li>provision means of transportation by transportation service provider</li><li>Informing the recipient</li><li>Track and trace of transportation activities</li><li>Invoicing of the transport order/service</li></ul>

Traders: the aim of a trader is to efficiently (in terms of transportation costs and emission volumes) transport goods from the sender to the recipient in a well defined time slot as economically as possible. This way commercial transactions generate transportation demand. Once generated the transportation demand order is endowed with criteria such as recipient's and sender's address, transport volume and the preferred transportation provider. In addition, the trader wants to monitor the transportation status. Furthermore the trader sells the goods including logistic costs and has to guarantee that the transportation provider is certified (GMP). This includes also a complete documentation of the origin and the quality of the goods.

Sender: the aim of a sender is to send goods in a well-defined time slot in order to finalize the commission with the trader accordingly. From a logistics point of view the sender wants to be informed in time about the transportation status, in order to consistently provide loading points with resources. Depending on the transport vehicle an appropriate equipment is to be provided. Transport vehicles can be a dump truck, tanker or walking floor. A dump truck or walking floor can be loaded by conveyor belts. The loading of a tanker is usually through a top opening. Based on the vehicle information and the information of the defined time slot preparations can be performed that minimize the downtime of the transportation provider.

Recipient: the aim of the recipient is to receive goods purchased from a trader in a well-defined time slot. From a logistics point of view the recipient requires precise information about the scheduled unload of the transportation provider, in order to provide the required resources. The use of the resources to discharge corresponds analogously to the restrictions of the loading. Furthermore, monitoring of the transportation status is desired.

Service provider: the aim of a services provider is to employ available resources in a network efficiently. The transportation planning is a complex planning task because of the agricultural factors (good, vehicle, equipment loading point, equipment unloading point, quality of goods, certification of the transportation provider). The TOMS supports the bundling of information flow as well as the conflation of various transportation demands for transport order planning. Considering the sector specific characteristic that all actors are loosely connected and decide by themselves which information to share. Based upon the transport order planning, transportation providers are selected, transportation costs requested and transmitted to the trader. Once confirmed, transport orders and loading information are sent to the transportation provider. Sender and recipient receive advise, and the transportation status is monitored by track and trace. Finally, the transport order controlling for routing the entire network and invoicing of transportation. One task of the service provider in the sector is the representation of the added value for all actors through a controlling.

Transportation provider: the aim of the transportation provider is to utilize the available resources (vehicle fleet). This can be accomplished by simulating transportation during the planning phase in order to minimize empty trips as well as CO_2 emission. In the agricultural sector the available resources are especially in the harvest very limited so that the shift of transports or orders is the only possibility. In addition the selection of the vehicle is influenced by the freight as well as the load and unload resources.

During previous interactions of the actors mainly direct trade of goods is applied. This enables all trading partners (sender, recipients and traders) to both employing their own vehicle fleets as well as engaging transportation providers. Because of the solitary character of transport orders and the segmented transportation control an agent-based transportation planning should be implemented by a single service provider.

Figure 2 depicts the conceptual framework of a TOMS including its actors and the respective agents.

The model architecture is partitioned in three different layers: 1) the presentation layer, 2) the logical layer and 3) the database connection. The presentation layer holds the interface agent who assigns permissions to various actors. The logical layer contains the TOMS which is partitioned in the transportation demand agent (TDA), the transportation planning agent (TPA), the transportation transaction agent (TTA) and the controlling agent (CA). Each of the agents has particular functions. The database is a mySQL relational database.

The TDA decides whether the TRM can be dispatched based upon his own parameters and specific properties of the TRM. Furthermore, an instant feedback indicates missing parameters of the TRM. In addition, an instant feedback informs the actor whether the service provider accepts the TRM or the usual ad hoc procedure should be applied.

The TPA performs an automated dispatch including an improved employment of resources. To this end the TRM is subdivided in TO. Moreover, various TRM are linked and a transportation providers are selected automatically. In contrast to an ad hoc process the TPA is capable of reducing the complexity of dispatch by bundling all TO.

The TTA provides a target-matching procedure, which is demand-oriented based upon the information from other agents in the system. To date target adjustment is only done selectively.

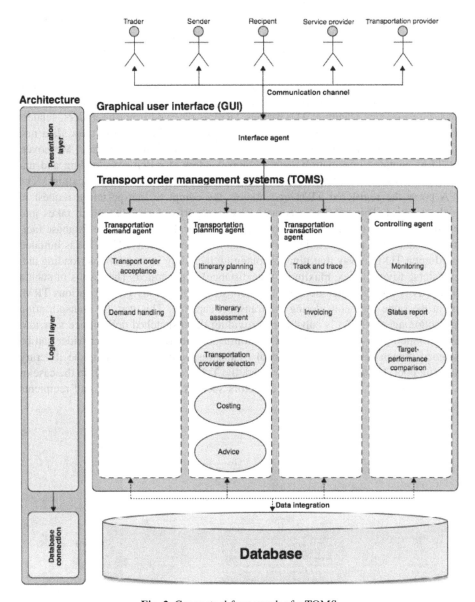

Fig. 2. Conceptual framework of a TOMS

The controlling agent collects all generated data for the stakeholders. The TOMS enables actors to benefit from the added value of the 4PL including a planning and cooperation. Apart from saving transaction costs the improved use of resources has the highest potential for economisation.

Based upon the demand for itinerary planning from the sector the TPA was developed as the first prototype. The agent was programmed in Java, and linked to the mySQL database. In addition to the existing itinerary planning a complete lookup procedure, a tabu search (TS) and a simulated annealing (SA) were implemented. The application of an array of algorithms and heuristics supported the examination of the most suitable procedures. The dependent parameters hereby were: TRM, computing time and cost savings. At the same time planning periods can be selected, and other parameters such as cruising speeds for transportation vehicles and computing time can be configured. Figure 3 depicts the graphical user interface (GUI) of a dispatching device for itinerary planning. The various TRM as received from the traders, senders and recipients is compiled by the TDA. The TPA is able to access these data and process them according to his functionality and additional information's. Moreover, the TRM contains information such as time window for delivery, loading and un-loading address and characteristics, tonnage, as well as vehicle specifications. The TPA pools the registered TRM and assigns the complete transportation request to single vehicles. This process generates new transport orders (TO) which takes into account a delivery tour for the transportation provider. Furthermore the database faci-litates a data set of transportation services and transport capacity. The TPA is initiated based upon TO in a way that itinerary planning including its restrictions (loading aid, time slots, driving times, maximum tour distance) is generated. The results of such a TPA activity are generated delivery tours consisting of various TO and various TRM, and at the same time considering the transport capacity. This way the transportation transaction agent (TTA) is capable of providing the dispatched deliverance tour to a transportation provider. Once the TO is confirmed the transportation provider can be assigned, which results in the removal of the respective TO's out of the itinerary planning pool. If the assignment is refused, the TO's remain in the pool. In the case of a successful assignment, the involved actors such as senders, traders and recipients are informed.

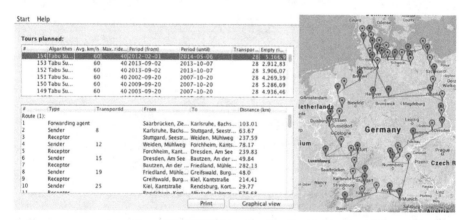

Fig. 3. GUI for route planning

In view of communication capacity and fault management the TTA is not yet en-tirely implemented. In the conceptual framework this agent receives those data in XML data format, and transmits status information to other agents. This way TO are registered, (the order starts: loading) and logged off (the order stops: unloading).

Furthermore, track and trace data of the transportation status, possible faults (downtime for loading and unloading, traffic jam, breakdown) should be communicated. All together, this should enable the agent to automatically react upon those signals. As soon as the transportation provider signals the accomplishment of the TO, invoicing as well as crediting of the transportation service will be disposed. During the entire order process the trader should be enabled to track the order status with his own GUI for the TPA. In addition, this agent compiles the TRM. The Sender and recipients have GUI for transport order tracking, where the notification function of the TPA provides an overview of incoming and outgoing transports.

The controlling agent is supposed to collect all generated data of the transport order process and compiles them for the use of the respective actors. This way relevant parameters are supplied for transportation providers, traders, senders and recipients.

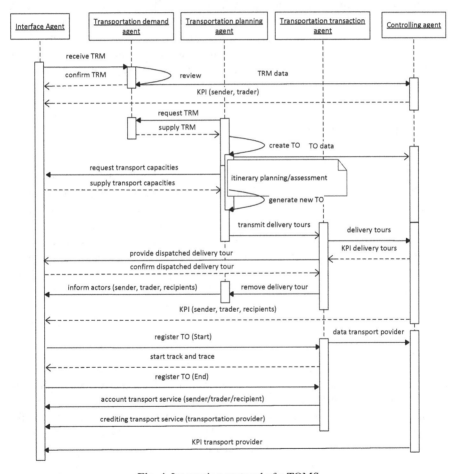

Fig. 4. Interaction protocol of a TOMS

Based upon those parameters a number of evaluation criteria are generated for guiding each of the involved actors and to demonstrate development perspectives of the TOMS and the involved actors.

On the basis of TOMS the information flow is accelerated in contrast to the previous adhoc process. Thereby time can be saved which allows a transportation planning for a more efficient use of resources. In addition, the TOMS enables a transparent flow of information between the actors.

Figure 4 describes the interaction protocol of the described agents. All current research activities focused on the implementation of the TPA. The reason to start with this agent is that especially the agricultural specific challenges and characteristics have to be considered in this agent. Furthermore the functions of the transportation demand agent is implemented so that the TPA can perform the functions. The delivery tours are currently available in XML format for the TTA.

In the following the experimental evaluation of the TPA is demonstrated, because of its strategic significance as first prototype. The TPA allows an improved transportation planning via Algorithms. Based on the Algorithms' more restrictions of the agricultural transport planning can be considered against to the manual adhoc process. In addition the dispatching based on the TPA allows a transportation planning in smaller time intervals.

5   Experimental Evaluation

In order to validate the transportation planning agent an experiment was conducted. About 150,000 TO transacted within a period of two to three years (2010-2012) and about 200 transportation providers including their geographical data serve as input variables. Those data were provided by a research partner who is himself a wholesale trader within the agricultural sector. These are real-world data from past activities, which have the capacity to represent real-world actors under sector-specific conditions. Each of the TO has a loading and unloading position as well as a time slot for transportation transactions. Other parameters such as quantities, price as well as loading and unloading times were neglected. For the itinerary planning the methods tabu search (TS) and simulated annealing (SA) were employed.

Key parameter of the Tabu Search is the length of the tabu list. A too short tabu list < 3 can result in cycles. Cycles should be avoided because these calculate same solutions. In the described experiment the authors apply a tabu list length of   32.

Key parameter for the Simulated Annealing are the temperature and the cooling down rate. The temperature represents the duration of the experimental runtime in seconds/1000. For example, an experiment with an 8h runtime complies with a temperature of   28800/1000. T and r were divided by 1000 in the experiment because the procedure needs small numbers to work with the probability of the Boltzmann's theorem. Usually these parameters are given and are not calculated. Based on the practical time-based approach the calculation was necessary.

The complete lookup procedure is only suitable for dispatching a maximum of 11 TO because more TO would result in unacceptably long runtimes. However, this method can be applied for tour optimization at a later model stage. For this reason a number of restrictions have been specified: a maximum of 40 weekly hours, the transportation provider has to return to his origin by the end of the week. The aim is minimization of empty trips. A computer with the following features has accomplished all calculations:

- Processor: Intel® Core ™ i5-3550CPU@3,30GHz;
- Memory: 8,00 GB;
- Windows 7 Enterprise-Service Pack 1,
- System:64 Bit OS.

The Computation times of one, two or eight hours determined termination conditions of the respective procedure, which is derived from real practice-oriented everyday work. A calculation time of one hour represents a rearrangement procedure in the case of failure. A calculation time of two hours describes the required dispatch during forenoon or afternoon of any working day. The dispatch of eight hours describes the available computation power during inactive work periods. The TO sample set also describes practice-oriented periods. Exactly 20 TO describe a dispatch effort of one hour and 100 TO describe the dispatch effort of half a day. Hence, 2000 TO correlate with the dispatch effort of two weeks. The reduction of empty trips in kilometer served as measurand, since this way efficiency enhancement can be delineated. In addition, possible costs savings can be derived.

Each experiment was carried out by selecting the number of the TO and the planning method and the runtime (1h, 2h, 8h). For the number of TO a randomly selected period was chosen from the data. Due to the graduation of the runtime we did 12 experiments with 1h, 12 experiments with 2h and 12 experiments with 8h. The empty kilometers calculated by the TPA were set in relation to the empty kilometers of the adhoc process. Table 2 presents the experimental results.

Table 2. Generated experimental results of the transportation planning agent

TO	Methods	Empty trip in km			Empty trip (adhoc) in km	Saving in km			Saving in %		
		1h	2h	8h	-	1h	2h	8h	1h	2h	8h
20	TS	3316	3316	3316	5404	2088	2088	2088	39	39	39
	SA	3288	3287	3287		2117	2117	2117	39	39	39
50	TS	11774	11453	11229	15695	3921	4242	4467	25	27	28
	SA	11585	11186	11055		4110	4510	4640	26	29	30
100	TS	19151	19151	18741	29591	10440	10440	10850	35	35	37
	SA	18965	18902	18387		10625	10689	11204	36	36	38
200	TS	34841	34829	33889	52944	18103	18116	19055	34	34	36
	SA	33968	30279	28504		18976	22665	24440	36	43	46
1000	TS	153406	150057	150051	224429	71022	74371	74377	32	33	33
	SA	147775	142080	141237		76653	82349	83192	34	37	37
2000	TS	311329	295081	285974	440493	129164	145412	154519	29	33	35
	SA	289829	287303	273750		150664	153190	164581	34	35	37
					Average saving tabu search				32	34	35
					Average saving simulated annealing				34	36	38

The experiment demonstrates that calculating with the TS method results in less empty trips than the SA method. Essentially, the application of a transportation planning agent can save 25 – 46% of empty trips due to route generation. Depending on the quantity of automatically dispatched TO the reduction of empty trips can vary between 2,000 and 164,000 km, which corresponds to a dispatch time frame of one to two weeks. In addition, there is more potential in terms of dispatch effort since every itinerary route has an average of 9 TO, which may entail a decreasing dispatch effort by a factor of 9.

The transportation planning agent selected service providers automatically based upon the vicinity of the provider to the loading point. If transportation providers receive specific request for particular routes, the TTA of a transportation provider is addressed.

6   Summary and Outlook

In summary, this effort describes the design and development of a DSS for operative dispatching of agricultural bulk goods by means of an MAS including a 4PL approach for this sector. The collected research results can be clustered in the decision for an MAS, in the decision for 4PL service provider and the findings for the agricultural supply chain

The decision for an MAS resulted from the complex and dynamic planning requirements of that sector. For this reason a requirements analysis of the sector was conducted in order to determine relevant functions. The conceptual framework of the TOMS integrates all relevant actors including their specific functions and characteristics of the sector. Due to the distinctive autonomy of the different actors the model is based upon autonomously acting agents. These agents are capable of handling the associated requirements of the real-world actors. On the one hand the individual autonomy of each actor/agent is preserved, on the other hand an optimal itinerary planning can only be achieved due to the network character of the overall model. Based on Lee and Kim [18] we presented a practice orientated approach where the transport planning has a very flexible time dimension in a network. To the best of our knowledge this is the first approach which combines MAS and the 4PL approach in the agricultural sector.

The 4PL service provider has the main responsibility for the planning procedure. He pools information, and receives this way a more comprehensive basis for planning in comparison to the other actors. In addition, due to concerted communication the number of interfaces can be minimized. The committed supply of status information for each of the involved actors minimizes queries and accelerates information flow since prompt decisions are yet possible. The planning activities of the 4PL service provider applying the transportation planning agent depends upon the number of incoming TRM as well as the supply of transportation provider capacity. Both parameters fluctuate depending on harvesting periods and general trade activities. The 4PL approach is described in a variety of branches but the authors are not aware of any approaches in the agricultural bulk logistics.

The agricultural bulk logistics has a high potential in terms of coordination the TO and cooperation of the actors considering the dynamic characteristics of the sector. Each actor can maintain his autonomous choice in the presented TOMS. Nevertheless, the existing adhoc process can be supported by the implemented agents. In the long term, the TOMS can replace the existing adhoc process completely. This would be a leap innovation for the sector. For this purpose more convince in the rather conservative-driven industry is required. A first contribution should make the evaluated experiment.

The evaluation experiments indicate that higher quantities of TO in the planning correlate with a higher reduction of empty mileage. Hence, there is an increased chance of financial savings. At one hour computation time the saving potential is about 32-34%. At an increased run time additional savings of merely 2-4% have been achieved. Thereby, SA excels the TS method. This may be due to the faster methodological approach: in contrary to TS, SA calculates multiple routes within the same time slot.

The experiment is limited by the initial parameters as well as the structure of the conceptual framework of the TOMS. Initial parameters in form of sector-specific information describe discrete relationships as well as recurrent transport volumes in a data set. Moreover, the experiment was calculated with a regular PC. Specialized data processing centers may compute different results because more calculations can be done per given time slot. However, employing a PC underlines the applicability in practice. Within the conceptual framework of the TOMS currently a maximum of 2,000 TO were calculated, which correlates with a TO influx of two weeks. The implementation of the TPA supports a minimization of the present ad hoc work flow and fosters the assignment of itinerary tours. For future developments the presented agents will be finalized. Those agents carry standardized information flows and interfaces. In addition, the overall systems performance and the user friendliness of the various agents will be improved with the help of the relevant real world actors. Moreover, criteria for the evaluation of actors by the controlling agent will be further specified. Finally, the TPA will be tested with additional heuristics including the implementation of forecasting data.

References

1. Bundesamt für Ernährung, Landwirtschaft und Verbraucherschutz,
   `http://www.bmelv.de/SharedDocs/Downloads/Broschueren/`
   `EckpunktepapierPreisvolatilitaet.pdf?__blob=publicationFile`
   (February 20, 2014)
2. Bundesamt für Naturschutz (2010),
   `http://www.bfn.de/fileadmin/MDB/documents/themen/`
   `erneuerbareenergien/`
   `bfn_position_bioenergie_naturschutz.pdf` (March 16, 2014)
3. Bundesministerium für Ernährung, Landwirtschaft und Verbraucherschutz: Transport landwirtschaftlicher Güter, Tabelle 354 (2011)

4. EudraLex: Volume 4 Good manufacturing practice (GMP) Guidelines, http://ec.europa.eu/health/documents/eudralex/vol-4/ (March 16, 2014)
5. Ishikawa, K.: What is total quality control? The Japanese way, Prentice Hall business classics. Prentice-Hall, Englewood Cliffs (1985)
6. Mukhopadhyay, S.K., Setaputra, R.: The role of 4PL as the reverse logistics integrator. International Journal of Physical Distribution & Logistics Management 36(9), 716–729 (2006)
7. Win, A.: The value a 4PL provider can contribute to an organization. International Journal of Physical Distribution & Logistics Management 38(9), 674–684 (2008)
8. Prümper, W., Butz, C.: Der Internal 4PL — Best Practice "Metro Group". In: Baumgarten, H., Darkow, I., Zadek, H. (Hrsg.) Supply Chain Steuerung und Services. Springer, Heidelberg (2004)
9. Schmitt, A.: 4PL-Providing^{TM} als strategische Option für Kontraktlogistikdienstleister. Eine konzeptionell-empirische Betrachtung, DUV (2006)
10. Xu, L.-D.: Information architecture for supply chain quality management. International Journal of Production Research 49(1), 183–198 (2011)
11. van der Aalst, W.: Loosely coupled interorganizational workflows: modeling and analyzing workflows crossing organizational boundaries. Information & Management 37(2), 67–75 (2000)
12. Langer, H., Schönberger, J., Kopfer, H., Timm, I.J.: Integration zentraler Prozess-Optimierung und lokaler Agenten-basierter Prozess-Anpassung für das Management von Transportprozessen in dynamischen Umgebungen. In: Koschke, R., Herzog, O., Rödiger, K.H., Ronthaler, M. (Hrsg.) INFORMATIK 2007 - Informatik Trifft Logistik. Band 1, pp. 429–432. Springer (2007)
13. Lai, I.K.W.: The strategic changes by adopting internet-based interorganizational systems. Management Research News 30(7), 495–509 (2007)
14. Gomber, P., Schmidt, C., Weinhordt, C.: Electronic markets for decentralized transportation planning. Wirtschaftsinformatik 39(2), 137–145 (1997)
15. Woolridge, M., Jennings, N.R.: Intelligent Agents – Theory and practice. Knowledge Engineering Review 20(2), 115–152 (1995)
16. Lima, R.M., Sousa, R.M., Martins, P.J.: Distributed production planning and control agent-based system. International Journal of Production Research 44(18/19), 3693–3709 (2006)
17. WanSup, U., Huitian, L., Hall, T.J.K.: A Study of Multi-Agent Based Supply Chain Modeling and Management. I-Business 2(4), 333–341 (2010)
18. Lee, J., Kim, C.: Multi-agent systems applications in manufacturing systems and supply chain management: a review paper. International Journal of Production Research 46(1), 233–265 (2008)
19. Mishra, N., Kumar, V., Chan, F.T.S.: A multi-agent architecture for reverse logistics in a green supply chain. International Journal of Production Research 50(9), 2396–2406 (2012)
20. Kaihara, T., Fujii, S.: Game theoretic enterprise management in industrial collaborative networks with multi-agent systems. International Journal of Production Research 46(5), 1297–1313 (2008)
21. Sheremetov, L., Rocha-Mier, L.: Supply chain network optimization based on collective intelligence and agent technologies. Human Systems Management 27(1), 31–47 (2008)
22. Gerber, A., Klusch, M.: AGRICOLA - Agents for mobile planning services in agriculture. Künstliche Intelligenz, KI 1/2004, 38–42 (2004)

23. Hellingrath, B., Böhle, C.: Integrierte agentenbasierte Produktions- und Logistikplanung in der Supply Chain. KI - Künstliche Intelligenz 24(2), 115–122 (2010)
24. Dudek, G.: Collaborative Planning in Supply Chains. A Negotiation-Based Approach. Springer, Heidelberg (2004)
25. Hellingrath, B., Böhle, C., Küppers, P., Könning, M.: Dezentrales Koordinationskonzept zur multilateralen kollaborativen Produktions-und Distributionsplanung. In: Tagungsband der Multikonferenz Wirtschaftsinformatik 2012, Braunschweig, pp. 187–197 (2012)
26. Garcia-Flores, R., Wang, X.Z.: A multi-agent system for chemical supply chain simulation and management support. OR Spectrum 24(3), 343–370 (2002)
27. Yee, M.-C., Cheng-Wei, W.: Multi-agent-oriented approach to supply chain planning and scheduling in make-to-order manufacturing. International Journal of Electronic Business 5(4), 427–454 (2007)
28. Mes, M., Heijden, M., Schuur, P.: Interaction between intelligent agent strategies for real-time transportation planning. Central European Journal of Operations Research 2(2), 337–358 (2013)
29. Liang, W., Huang, C.: Agent-based demand forecast in multi-echelon supply chain. Decision Support Systems 42(1), 390–407 (2006)
30. Mehmann, J., Teuteberg, F., Freye, D.: Requirements for a 4PL-Platform in After-Crop Logistics. In: Proceeding of the EFITA 2013 (EFITA, WCCA, CIGR VII), Turin (2013)
31. Flender, H.: Modellgestützte Analyse zur Optimierung von Transportnetzwerken. In: Kuhn, A. (Hrsg.) Unternehmenslogistik. Verlag Praxiswissen, Dortmund (2010)

Planning with Numeric Key Performance Indicators over Dynamic Organizations of Intelligent Agents

Florian Pantke, Stefan Edelkamp, and Otthein Herzog

Center for Computing and Communication Technologies (TZI),
University of Bremen, Am Fallturm 1, 28359 Bremen, Germany
{fpantke,edelkamp,herzog}@tzi.de

Abstract. In this paper we present a PDDL-based multi-agent planning system for reasoning about key performance indicators (KPIs) in an industrial production planning and control application scenario. On top of PDDL, numeric key figures and associated objectives are configured by the user at run-time and then processed automatically by the system in order to maximize overall goal satisfaction. The organizational structure of the system is a hierarchical multi-agent planning and simulation environment, with KPI objectives being propagated top-down and achievements being assessed bottom-up. KPIs can be automatically aggregated over dynamic groups of agents, with the ability of deliberately planning for reorganization. The planner supports continuous numeric action parameters, which it keeps lifted as sets of intervals before grounding them in delayed fashion with a mathematical optimizer. Plan generation and execution are interleaved. A case study with a simulated shop-floor demonstrates the basic practicability of the approach.

Keywords: Planning and Scheduling, Mathematical Optimization, Interval Arithmetic, Key Performance Indicators, Manufacturing Control.

1 Introduction

Many business processes and information systems in production planning and control are subject to organizational performance measurement by means of key performance indicators (KPIs), in which hierarchically decomposable quantitative key figures are assessed and aggregated at different organizational levels, with associated goals declared and communicated throughout the organization. In most applications, subsets of these goals mutually conflict. Economically suitable trade-offs are called for in these cases [19]. An intelligent agent prepared to deal with performance figures and their dynamics has to reason about the degree of goal achievement related to the level of autonomous control [38]. Such objective achievement can be ascertained through periodic comparison of the actually attained performance values with the desired target values.

In practice, the organizational structure over which the performance statistics are collected may unpredictably or deliberately change over time and mathematical optimization problems may remain at the action executing level. For instance,

J.P. Müller, M. Weyrich, and A.L.C. Bazzan (Eds.): MATES 2014, LNAI 8732, pp. 138–155, 2014.
© Springer International Publishing Switzerland 2014

a numerical multi-criteria optimization problem present at a production action of a shop-floor milling machine might require real-valued action parameters and finding suitable assignments for them that trade off between minimization of throughput times, production costs as well as tool abrasion and maximization of machine utilization, resulting workpiece quality, and adherence to delivery dates. Computation of statistics (e.g., median throughput time over the set of orders processed by a certain machine) requires automatic key figure aggregation over dynamic groups of objects. As it cannot emulate these notions efficiently in terms of Nebel's compilation schemes [30], the expressiveness of PDDL (e.g., [18]) up to its most recent variants (e.g., [27]) is insufficient for modeling such KPI-based control problems in a multi-agent environment.

In this paper we present a multi-agent planning system for reasoning about KPIs in an industrial production planning and control application scenario. For this purpose, we extend the PDDL feature set to support numeric KPIs and associated objectives, with the classic PDDL 2.1 numeric state variables (termed *fluents* in the respective literature) acting as atomic inputs into user-defined key figure aggregation rules. KPI objectives are processed by the agents during local planning and for global inter-agent coordination to maximize the overall goal satisfaction in the system. KPIs can be automatically aggregated over changing groups and hierarchies of agents, with the ability of deliberately planning for future reorganization. We also introduce continuous numeric action parameters for the modeling of mathematical optimization problems at the action level. Our planner follows a two-tier approach to handle such parameters. In a first combinatorial planning stage, it partially grounds the planning operators, keeping the numeric parameters lifted as sets of intervals over $\mathbb{R}$. They are grounded in a second planning step with a mathematical optimizer. In the agent system, plan generation and execution are interleaved to react to the dynamics in the application scenario and to recover from unsatisfied constraints in some plans.

The paper is structured as follows. First, we introduce the application scenario of multi-agent production planning and control on a simulated shop-floor, which consists of a pair of milling machines to which a sequence of incoming customer orders needs to be assigned for manufacturing. We then describe the architecture of our KPI framework and its general approach to KPI assessment and KPI-based control in multi-agent systems as well as the actual configuration of user-defined performance figures and objectives in our framework. Next, we take a closer look at the planner itself and the expressiveness of the introduced modeling devices using the shop-floor scenario as an example. Finally, we provide experimental results that, as a proof-of-concept, show the general functioning of the system and its approach to KPI-based planning for a given set of KPI objectives and we discuss some related work.

2   Multi-Agent Production Planning and Control

The KPI assessment and planning framework that will be described in the next section has been realized as a Java programming library and was integrated into

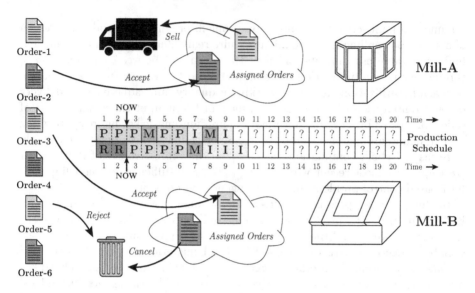

Fig. 1. The INTAPS multi-agent production planning and control scenario

the existing INTAPS multi-agent system for production planning and control on simulated shop-floors [28], which uses JADE [1] as its agent platform. A novel PDDL-based domain-specific planning component was implemented for it that supports reasoning about KPIs over dynamic organizational hierarchies, which is required in this application scenario.

The simulated shop-floor, which is visually exemplified in Fig. 1, consists of several production resources like machine tools with configurable properties (such as the kind of product parts they are able to produce, numeric cost- and maintenance-related attributes, etc.) to which subsets of constantly incoming customer orders need to be assigned during simulation runs. This main scheduling problem is approached in a distributed fashion by means of message-based Contract Net negotiation [17] between different types of agents. Each machine tool is represented and autonomously managed by a resource agent and each customer order by an order agent. An additional group agent collects user-configured global KPIs over the group of all resource agents and is able to derive and propagate target values for the local key figures of each machine tool from the global set of key figure goals via mathematical optimization.

Time is discretized, with a single simulation run consisting of a fixed number of time slots of equal length. At the beginning of each slot, a central simulation management agent randomly instantiates a certain number of order agents from a configurable list of templates with different properties such as product type, lot count, deadline given in remaining time slots, work volume (e.g., in cm^3 for milling machines), and contract price. The newly spawned order agents instantly send out calls for proposals to all resource agents in the system and wait for their response. Based on its local state and KPI objectives, each resource agent then has to decide which orders it would prefer to insert into its individual production queue at a certain position, which orders is should rather reject due to its current state and the given contract conditions, and which already enqueued orders it must cancel, e.g., because of deadline troubles. This happens by invocation of the domain-specific KPI planner, which always plans optimistically with respect to Contract Net bidding. Unsuccessful proposals are handled with plan repair, i.e., partial replanning.

After all communicative actions from the bidding process are completed at the beginning of the time slot, each machine can execute a single unit-time action fragment from its generated production plan, i.e., from the beginning of the durative action sequence of its most recent KPI planner output. This way, the execution of durative actions longer than a single time slot is split across multiple slots in the simulation. At the end of each time slot, all key figure values are updated and stored in a central database for later retrieval and statistical evaluation.

The main executive action of a resource agent in each time slot may either be producing a specific order, performing maintenance (to increase the health level of its machine tool), repair (for fixing its machine tool when it went out of order as a direct consequence of poor maintenance), or idling. On many machine tools, production can happen at different speeds within a permissible range (e.g., variable cutting speeds on a milling machine). The chosen speed may directly affect resulting workpiece quality, production duration, production cost, and tool wear. In our PDDL planning model, which will be presented in detail in Sect. 3.2, the production speed is represented as a continuous numeric parameter of the production action in the normalized range $[0, 1] \subset \mathbb{R}$. Workpiece quality is tracked with a key figure in the same range. Whenever the production quality falls below an order's minimum quality requirement, the order fails quality assurance testing. As a consequence, it cannot be delivered to the customer and is treated as canceled, with a monetary contract penalty being incurred. The same holds for the case that the order's delivery due date is missed. Consequently, the speed parameter of each production action as well as the exact sequence of production actions executed by each machine tool need to be carefully chosen in a way to achieve the best possible trade-off between different KPI objectives formulated with respect to monetary revenue, machine utilization, maintenance state, and possibly many other user-defined criteria. This constitutes a mixed combinatorial and numerical optimization problem at the operational level.

3 Methodology

3.1 Key Figure Assessment in Multi-Agent Systems

In the distributed key figure assessment framework, each agent measures time-stamped quantitative data from its local scope of visibility on a regular basis, e.g., via production data acquisition from its sensory input and executed actions. Based on these real-valued measurands, which act as atomic inputs into the KPI model (and are analogous to PDDL numeric fluents), the system user can define

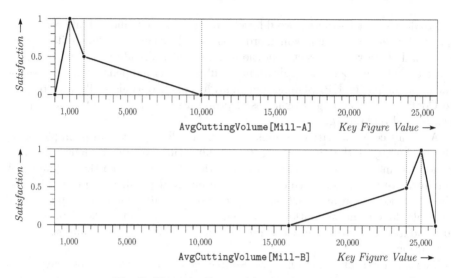

Fig. 2. Piecewise-linear objective functions

sets of composed key figures that aggregate the measurands and other composed key figures through sequences of basic arithmetic operations and statistic functions. Objectives for selected key figures are declared by means of user-configurable objective functions, which map the respective key figure value to a satisfaction level in the normalized range $[0, 1] \subset \mathbb{R}$. In the current implementation, the objective functions are specified as piecewise-linear functions (PWLFs), which allow for easy GUI-based modeling while simultaneously enforcing clamping to the permitted range in an intuitive way. Two example key figure objective PWLFs are shown in Fig. 2.

The entirety of all configured key figure objectives defines a multi-criteria optimization problem in form of a vector-valued function, for which a Pareto optimum is sought. Single points of the Pareto frontier can be determined by feeding a suitable scalarization of the component functions, e.g., their weighted average, into a general mathematical optimizer [15]. The KPI framework supports the computation of all first partial derivatives for this purpose by employing automatic differentiation [22] and is thereby able to precisely quantify the mutual key figure influences at arbitrary points. However, to support arbitrary non-linear functions that are not continuously differentiable at all points, our KPI planner makes use of the Differential Evolution [35] optimization algorithm, which does not rely on gradients. The resulting target values for the atomic measurands and composed key figures are used by the agents for inter-agent coordination to ensure that all agents jointly aim for the same global system state. The local planning component of the agents may either use these target values or directly utilize the scalarized objective function as its real-valued plan metric, like it is done in our experiments.

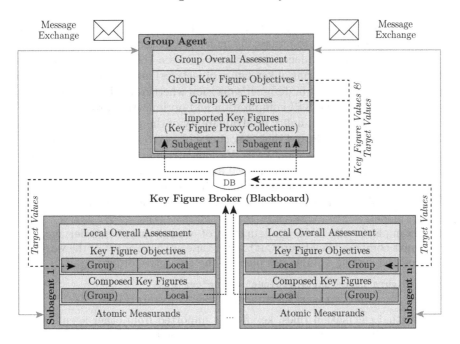

Fig. 3. Key figure assessment in a hierarchical agent organization (cycle-free organizational graph of depth 1)

To aggregate key figures over organizations of multiple agents, the latter can be arranged in hierarchies, which may change their structure over the course of time as a direct result of the agents' actions. In addition to its local measurands, each agent can import measurand and composed key figure values from agents further down the organizational graph. Logging and exchange of key figure values is facilitated by the key figure broker component of the KPI software framework, which manages distributed access to a central database for permanent data storage and retrieval. Domain-specific inter-agent communication related to key figures and their objectives, such as negotiation of joint target values, happens via message exchange. KPI objectives and target values are commonly propagated top-down, while current key figure values and objective achievements are assessed bottom-up within the hierarchy. This approach to global KPI assessment over groups of agents is depicted in Fig. 3 for a simple hierarchy of depth 1. In general, the shown subagents may have further subagents up to arbitrary depth.

As the global KPI model may get relatively large in real-world scenarios, its redundant computation and optimization as a whole by each individual agent may prove impractical. Therefore, the framework offers the possibility of treating the local agent KPI models as black boxes by hiding the computation rules of the composed key figures from other agents. In this approach, with respect to optimization, all key figures whose values are imported from other agents are locally treated as if they were atomic measurands. While this can significantly reduce the size of the local models and optimization problems, it may cause the optimization process to generate practically unachievable target values for imported key figures due to the hidden dependencies between them. As a result, global system performance (in terms of key figure objectives) may decrease. Hence, this approach requires the system designer's decision whether for the given use case a gained tractability of the KPI computation and optimization process is worth a possible loss of Pareto optimality or attainability of the generated target values.

For setting up the KPIs and their associated objectives, the system provides a configuration interface based on XML. Various attributes, such as a descriptive text, unit of measurement, or an interval discretization, can be assigned to each key figure. Our PDDL problem and domain files simply reference sets of external configuration files for initialization of the agents' key figure models within the planning model.

For example, in the XML configuration of a local customer order agent, we can define a composed key figure `CuttingVolume` as the product of the workpiece count and the cutting volume per piece of the respective order:

```
<KeyFigure name="CuttingVolume" unit="ccm"
           definition="Workpieces * cWorkVolumePerPiece" />
```

In the textual calculation rules, key figures imported from other agents can be accessed by following the respective key figure name by the name of the desired agent further down the hierarchy enclosed in square brackets. At each agent in the organization, named agent groups can be defined. For automatic aggregation of key figures over groups of agents, the respective group name is referenced with a preceding '$', e.g., for computing the average cutting volume over three different groups of orders handled by a local machine tool agent:

```
<KeyFigure name="AvgCuttingVolume" unit="ccm"
           definition="avg(CuttingVolume[$ORDERS],
                           CuttingVolume[$SOLD_ORDERS],
                           CuttingVolume[$CANCELED_ORDERS])" />
```

This example requires that all agents in the groups ORDERS, SOLD_ORDERS, and CANCELED_ORDERS have a key figure by the name of `CuttingVolume`. Figure 4 shows how the value of such an aggregated key figure is influenced by the dynamic group membership status, e.g., due to the organizational effects of a planned action. An objective for `AvgCuttingVolume` is declared by defining its objective PWLF via a set of control points. Figure 2 displays this function at the top:

```
<Objective target="AvgCuttingVolume">
  <ControlPoint value="0"      satisfaction="0" />
  <ControlPoint value="1000"   satisfaction="1" />
  <ControlPoint value="2000"   satisfaction="0.5" />
  <ControlPoint value="10000"  satisfaction="0" />
</Objective>
```

3.2   PDDL-Based Planning with KPIs

For planning with key performance indicators, we have extended the discrete-effect subset of PDDL 2.1 [18] with new key figure related features. Our extended

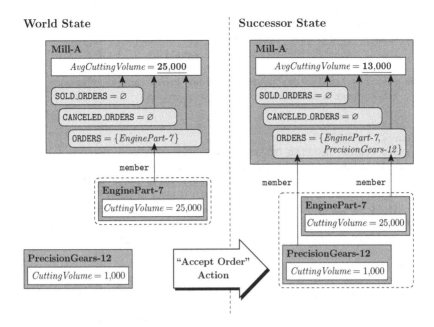

Fig. 4. Influence of organizational change on aggregated key figure values

language version supports numeric fluents, durative actions, and conditional effects. Continuous effects by way of a `#t` variable are not supported, as the key figure assessment in our framework always happens at defined discrete time points. The syntax extensions are enabled with the `:keyfigures` requirement that subsumes the also new requirements `:agent-typing`, `:agent-graph`, and `:numeric-parameters`. The first of the latter three makes the **agent** object type available, which is used for assigning sets of key figures and associated objectives to agent-type planning objects. As described above, this is done via external XML configuration files, which are specified within a newly introduced `:templates` clause. In this clause, also the available KPI aggregation groups at each agent are declared, and a call to an application-specific KPI collection constructor can be made for each user-defined subtype of **agent**. After this, numeric PDDL expressions can reference any of the key figures declared in the XML files just like common PDDL fluents. However, only the atomic measurands are writable by action effects. Composed key figures are read-only with respect to their value.

The `:agent-graph` requirement introduces the built-in predicates (`link` *parent child*) and (`member` *parent-agent group-name member-agent*) for managing the edges present in the organizational graph and the group membership status of the agents, respectively. Actions are only applicable in a given world state if they do not create cycles in the world state's organizational graph, which in turn could lead to cycles in the key figure aggregation rules.

```
(define (domain IntaPS)
(:requirements :keyfigures :durative-actions :conditional-effects
               :quantified-preconditions :equality)

(:types resource local-order peer peer-order group-manager - agent
        sched-order - local-order finalize - object)

(:templates
  (resource
    (groups ORDERS CANCELED_ORDERS SOLD_ORDERS CURRENT - local-order)
    (init da-intaps) (config "keyfigures-resource.xml"))
  (local-order (init op-intaps) (config "keyfigures-order.xml"))
  (peer (groups ORDERS CANCELED_ORDERS SOLD_ORDERS CURRENT - peer-order)
        (init da-intaps))
  (peer-order (init op-intaps))
  (group-manager (groups RESOURCES - (either resource peer))))

(:constants sell cancel - finalize)
(:predicates (RushOrder ?o - local-order) (Handled ?o - local-order))
(:functions (RepairCounter ?r - resource) (Active ?o - local-order))  [...]
```

Fig. 5. Key figure setup in the PDDL domain file (new features underlined)

Different to existing automated PDDL planners that are able to reason about propositions and numbers and to derive heuristics guiding the planning process, we support parameterized actions with continuous numeric arguments from subsets of $\mathbb{R}$. They are enabled with the :numeric-parameters requirement, which makes the number type available for use in action parameter declarations. The :keyfigures requirement makes all mathematical operations that are available in the KPI framework accessible to the numeric PDDL formulas, e.g., floor, ceil, avg, median, std, etc.

Figures 5 and 6 display parts of the PDDL domain file used in our experiments. The former shows the general domain and key figure setup; the latter the milling machines' production action. The duration of this action inverse-proportionally depends on the continuous ?speed parameter, which controls the metal removal rate in cm^3/min. In addition, the numeric effects use this parameter and the action duration in their measurand and PDDL fluent update formulas. Interpolation is applied for computation of the resulting workpiece quality, the incurred production cost, and tool wear, which in the simplified shop-floor scenario all linearly depend on the production speed. If the produced order does not meet both its production deadline and required quality level, it is canceled directly after production (cf. the conditional effects at the end of the PDDL operator and the conditions related to its parameter ?f).

The PDDL domain file is used unaltered by all resource agents throughout the entire simulation. However, different files can be assigned to different agents if desired. For the planning process performed in each time slot, each resource agent generates an individual problem file with all necessary logical propositions

[...]

```
(:durative-action Produce
 :parameters (?r - resource ?o - sched-order ?speed - number ?f - finalize)
 :duration (= ?duration (ceil (+ (RemainingSetupContent ?o)
    (/ (* (RemainingWorkpiecesContent ?o) (cWorkVolumePerPiece ?o))
       (+ (cMinProduceCapacity ?o) (* ?speed (ProduceCapacityDiff ?o)))))))
 :condition (and
  (at start (and (<= ?speed 1) (>= ?speed 0) (> (RemainingWork ?o) 0)
           (< (cMinProduceCapacity ?o) (cMaxProduceCapacity ?o))
           (<= (+ (Stock ?r) (Workpieces ?o)) (cMaxStock ?r))
           (forall (?c - sched-order) (or (= ?c ?o)
                (and (not (= ?c ?o)) (not (member ?r CURRENT ?c)))))
           (link ?r ?o) (member ?r ORDERS ?o)
           (not (or (member ?r SOLD_ORDERS ?o)
                    (member ?r CANCELED_ORDERS ?o)))))
  (at end (and (> (MaintenanceLevel ?r) 0)
           (or (= ?f cancel) (and (= ?f sell)
                   (>= (QualityAccumulator ?o) (cRequiredQuality ?o))
                   (>= (RemainingTimeToDeadline ?o) 0)
                   (<= ?speed (QualitySpeedLimit ?o)))))))
 :effect (and
  (at start (and (member ?r CURRENT ?o)
         (increase (QualityAccumulator ?o) (/ (* (cQualityFactor ?r)
           (RemainingWorkpiecesContent ?o) (+ (cSlowProduceQuality ?o)
             (* ?speed (ProduceQualityDiff ?o)))) (WorkpiecesContent ?o)))
         (decrease (MaintenanceLevel ?r) (/ (* (cWearoutFactor ?r)
           (RemainingWorkpiecesContent ?o) (+ (cSlowProduceWearout ?o)
             (* ?speed (ProduceWearoutDiff ?o)))) (WorkpiecesContent ?o)))
         (decrease (Money ?r) (/ (* (cProductionCostFactor ?r)
           (RemainingWorkpiecesContent ?o) (+ (cSlowProduceCosts ?o)
             (* ?speed (ProduceCostDiff ?o)))) (WorkpiecesContent ?o)))
         (forall (?o - sched-order) (and
           (increase (ElapsedThroughputTime ?o) (* (Active ?o) ?duration))
           (decrease (RemainingTimeToDeadline ?o) (* (Active ?o) ?duration))
         ))))
  (at end (and (not (member ?r CURRENT ?o)) (Handled ?o)
         (assign (RemainingLotCount ?o) 0)
         (assign (RemainingSetupTime ?o) 0)
         (assign (RemainingLotSize ?o) 0)
         (assign (RemainingTimeForPiece ?o) 0)
         (increase (PlannedProductionSlots ?r) ?duration)
         (increase (HistoryProductionSlots ?r) ?duration)
         (decrease (Money ?r) (* (CostsPerSlot ?r) ?duration))
         (when (= ?f sell) (and (member ?r SOLD_ORDERS ?o)
                            (increase (Money ?r) (Revenue ?o))))
         (when (not (= ?f sell)) (and (member ?r CANCELED_ORDERS ?o)
                            (decrease (Money ?r) (MaxPenalty ?o))))))))
)))
```

Fig. 6. Production action in the PDDL domain file (new features underlined)

as well as measurand and fluent assignments, based on its current state and beliefs about the objects in its current visibility scope. For the plan metric, an expression of the form (:metric maximize-agents *list-of-agents*) is added to the problem description. This maximizes the weighted average of the objective functions of all key figure goals defined for the specified agents. The order agents, on the other hand, do not perform any PDDL-based planning in our application scenario. Their rather simple behavior is completely rule-based and reactive.

3.3   The Planning Process

Allowing action parameters with continuous numeric values raises the question how the resulting infinite branching factor in the planning world states can be suitably handled by the planner. In such models, determining whether an action is applicable in a state corresponds to checking the system of equations and inequalities for feasibility, which is given by all numeric action conditions in the current plan and those of the tested action. Unfortunately, in the general non-linear case, this problem is undecidable. Perfect action applicability tests are therefore impossible. Since not all cases of unsatisfiability can be efficiently detected, defects in the constructed plans caused by temporarily inserting infeasible actions into the latter must be detected and repaired at a later time.

The planner approaches the planning problem in two phases. It first grounds the PDDL operators with respect to the logical expressions and discrete object parameters by applying the method described by Koehler and Hoffmann [26], but keeping the continuous parameters ungrounded as sets of intervals over the real line. It then starts enumerating potentially possible sequential plans using the partially grounded actions in a combinatorial forward-planning process, which considers INTAPS-specific control rules as a guide (e.g., for pruning). As some of the numeric expressions in the plan actions as well as in the world states' fluent assignments now refer to intervals instead of single real numbers, interval arithmetic [6,29] is used for testing the unsatisfiability of the numeric action conditions [33]. In general, this may lead to a certain number of false negatives, e.g., as a result of the dependency problem discussed in the interval arithmetic literature, but can prove as a usable heuristic in many practical cases. To determine the real-numbered values of the continuous parameters, plans from this phase are sorted by the right endpoint of the interval evaluation of their plan metric, with the best n plans then fed into the Differential Evolution optimizer after conversion of all numeric action conditions into constraint functions (usually with small values of n due to the incurred high computational cost). This constitutes the second planning stage, which finally selects the plan with the best real-numbered plan metric value, passes it to the agent for execution, and discards all plans for which it did not find any feasible points in reasonable time (i.e., the false negatives from the action infeasibility checks). However, if n is chosen too small, the process might not be able to find any feasible or optimal plan at all. If remaining plan defects or unexpected events that preclude action execution are detected by the agent during execution, replanning is triggered in the next time slot. The planning process in each slot is depicted in Fig. 7. An

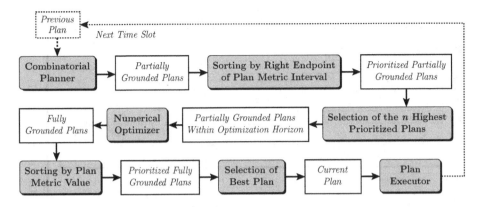

Fig. 7. The planning process in each discrete time slot of the simulation, based on the already partially executed plan from the previous slot

example illustrating how the constructed plans progress through the planning and execution stages and are ranked and filtered by the utility of their final state S_F is given in Fig. 8. Actions with violated conditions are shown crossed out.

Generated plans are time-stamped durative action sequences. For the intermediate partially grounded plans from the first combinatorial planning stage, the common PDDL plan syntax has been extended with an interval notation:

```
     0   : (Accept Mill-A EnginePart-8) [0]
     0   : (Reject Mill-A EnginePart-9) [0]
     0   : (Reject Mill-A PrecisionGears-4) [0]
     0   : (Reject Mill-A PrecisionGears-5) [0]
     0   : (Accept Mill-A PrecisionGears-6) [0]
     0   : (Reject Mill-A PrecisionGears-7) [0]
     0   : (Produce Mill-A EnginePart-8 [0, 0.8] sell) [[2, 7]]
 [2, 7] : (Produce Mill-A PrecisionGears-6 [0, 0.2] sell) [[2, 3]]
```

For the experiments in this paper, in which catastrophic interval widening did not occur, already small values $3 \leq n \leq 10$ showed as suitable. A detailed analysis of the possible problems concerning proper constraint satisfiability detection in the first planning stage and the influence of the optimization horizon n on the final plan quality and total planning time in this regard is presented in a different article [33], in which global KPI coordination is not employed and different order attribute values and optimal production speeds are used that were carefully chosen to maximize the occurrence of the problematic cases.

4   Experiments

To demonstrate the general usefulness of our KPI-related modeling devices and the viability of our planning approach, we have conducted two experiments with different KPI objectives, each comprising 50 randomized simulation runs over 20 time slots. In the evaluation setup, the shop-floor consists of two metal cutting

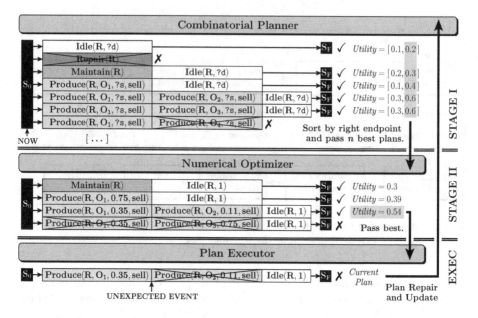

Fig. 8. Plan construction and processing by the agents' planning and execution stages

milling machines `Mill-A` and `Mill-B`, to which two classes of orders with equal probabilities of occurrence, `PrecisionGears` and `EnginePart`, need to be assigned. The necessary cutting volume is 1,000 cm^3 for the former and 25,000 cm^3 for the latter. At their respective optimal production speed, which the resource agents must determine, each order takes two time slots to produce and yields the same monetary profit at its successful sale. In each time slot, a total of six orders are instantiated to be scheduled for acceptance or rejection by each machine.

In the first experiment INDIFFERENT, only the maximization of the earned monetary value is set as a local KPI objective for each machine tool. This serves as the main production incentive and ensures that all monetary aspects of the planning operators are included in the plan metric. The second experiment SPLITTING introduces an additional objective on the `AvgCuttingVolume` key figure of each resource agent. Figure 2 shows the respective objective function assigned to `Mill-A` at the top and the one assigned to `Mill-B` at the bottom. This pair of PWLFs is supposed to cause `Mill-A` to accept mostly `PrecisionGears` and `Mill-B` mostly `EnginePart` instances.

Figure 9 reveals that this goal of the SPLITTING experiment was indeed achieved by the agents. It shows the statistical distribution of the final average cutting volumes attained by each machine at the end of each of the 50 simulation runs per experiment. It is clearly visible that in the INDIFFERENT experiment, both mills do not have a clear preference for a specific order class, which results in a median value close to the center of the possible range of `AvgCuttingVolume`. In contrast, SPLITTING shows a strong preference in the order acceptance behavior of both machines. `Mill-A` achieves a low average cutting volume of

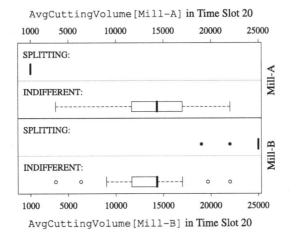

Fig. 9. Statistic of the achieved average cutting volume over 50 simulation runs

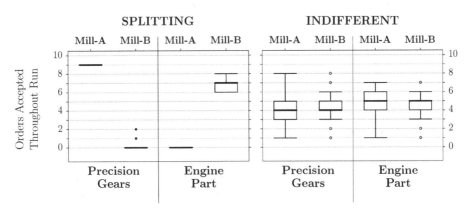

Fig. 10. Accepted order counts per simulation run

1,000 cm^3 by always choosing `PrecisionGears` for production in all runs, while `Mill-B` in most of the cases reaches a high average value of 25,000 cm^3 by picking `EnginePart` (with only a few outliers visible in the plot).

Figure 10 shows statistics on the total number of orders accepted on each machine per simulation run for both classes. The fact that `Mill-A` only accepts `PrecisionGears` in the SPLITTING experiment is visible in the left box-and-whisker diagram, in which the respective boxes collapse to simple bars. `Mill-B` achieves an only slightly weaker separation in this experiment. For the INDIFFERENT runs, the median order acceptance count is 4 for `PrecisionGears` and 5 for `EnginePart` on both machines.

In the majority of cases, the machines are able to identify the optimal production speeds, which are 0.1 for `PrecisionGears` and 0.75 for `EnginePart` in most cases. It appears that our planning system is able to appropriately adjust the agent behavior to the defined KPI objectives in this scenario. Java heap consumption of the agent system, including all agents and two planners running in parallel with a search space of up to 13,436,927 constructible and 942 actually generated interval plans per slot, peaks at $\sim$ 850 MB. Each simulation run takes between four and six minutes on a quad-core AMD Phenom II X4 940 CPU.

5   Related Work

Literature on logistical management and performance measurement [4,9] shows that while traditional systems focus on minimizing direct costs through low material costs, high capacity utilization, and high direct labor efficiency, however, modern manufacturing systems [7] and service operations also need clear measures on quality, lead times, flexibility, and other criteria. To make such systems adhere to and dynamically adjust to the organization's qualitative and quantitative business goals, key performance indicators have to be designed and properly operationalized [3,19]. While control and coordination frameworks for numeric key figures have been suggested [32], they usually lack the crucial planner component.

Besides production planning and control, industrial planning applications include modular high-speed printer control [36] and power balancing in electricity networks [34]. The integration of planning, plan execution, and simulation is fundamental to automated reasoning [21] and subject to many current research efforts [25,12], ranging from robotics [10] to knowledge engineering [14]. Multi-agent PDDL planning includes work on language definition [5], heuristics [37], and self-interested agents [31]. A multi-agent planning competition has been proposed by Kovacs [27].

With the modeling features described in this paper, we contribute to the areas of multi-agent, numeric, and *continuous planning*. Different to numeric effects over continuous time as in PDDL 2.1 and PDDL+ (an extension of PDDL 2.1 with processes and events), we are interested in action parameters with continuous, real-valued domains within a discrete-time model. Without rough discretization, current planning technology is hardly able to deal with this form of expressiveness. Especially in the presence of non-linear numeric expressions, individual action applicability in a given world state is, in general, undecidable for such models. To deal with possible defects in the generated plans that might arise due to this difficulty, our agent system relies on interleaved planning, plan execution, and subsequent plan repair. This also allows it to quickly react to unexpected events in the environment.

A similar but less general concept than continuous action parameters are action duration inequalities, which have been discussed by Fox and Long in their seminal paper on PDDL 2.1 [18]. However, this language extension has not been progressed much further. In planning tasks with duration inequalities, the execution time of actions can be constrained to certain subranges of the real line without being fixed a priori. Examples outside the ones mentioned in Sects. 5.2 and 5.3, ibid., include the DESERT-RAT domain [16]. In this scenario, several fuel tanks are available for a truck to enable it to eventually reach a certain crossing distance. Tanks can be loaded, unloaded, and used for refueling. Driving out or back changes the truck's distance from its base. As long as it neither runs out of fuel nor drives back past its base, the time driven by the truck can be freely chosen. The problem has been modeled in PDDL 2.1 and solved by discretization [13].

All these examples, in principle, induce infinite branching in their planning states. While a flexible validation tool for PDDL+ plans exists that supports continuous processes and events [24], planners for infinite domains are rare. Before numeric fluents were introduced in PDDL, the PRODIGY [8] planner modeled numeric conditions and effects with the aid of real- or integer-valued action parameter assignments. In following this approach, it already suffered from the instantiation problem that is inherent to parameters with infinite domains such as subsets of the real numbers and it was not able to satisfactorily solve this.

Significant steps towards a PDDL+ planner for continuous linear numeric change have been made [11]. Another modern planning system [2] shows a successful translation of selected PDDL+ domains to hybrid automata [23] and discusses subtle issues in the different semantics of the two. The converted problems are solved with a subsequent call to the SPACEEX [20] model checker.

In the different context of probabilistic planning for continuous state and action MDPs, Zamani et al. [39] use actions $a(y)$ that are parameterized with a real vector y. The continuous state may conditionally depend on y and, in turn, influence y. An example for such continuous action is moving a Mars rover, which receives rewards for taking pictures. The optimal value function is computed by a modified and exact value iteration algorithm that applies the rule $Q(a) = \max_y Q(a, y)$ as one additional step in the Q-learning function update. To compute this step analytically, the maximum is forwarded to each case of the partitioned value function. Efficient representations of Q are obtained by using extended algebraic decision diagrams, which are further pruned with LP solvers.

6   Conclusion

Current planners show good performance but are, at the same time, often not capable of meeting industrial requirements in terms of language expressiveness and system dynamics. In this paper, we have presented a novel framework for agent-based planning that supports the concept of *management by measurement* and is able to reason about and adjust to key performance indicators and associated goals such as frequently employed in contemporary business information systems and production processes. To this end, the planner extends PDDL modeling with automatic key figure aggregation over dynamic organizational hierarchies and continuous numeric action parameters for the representation of mathematical optimization problems at the operational level. For the future, we aim at further improving the performance of our domain-specific planning module and its numeric search heuristics to make it better suited for real-world problem sizes, which currently are still difficult to handle due to their large search space sizes.

References

1. Bellifemine, F., Caire, G., Poggi, A., Rimassa, G.: JADE: A software framework for developing multi-agent applications. Lessons learned. Inform. Software Tech. 50(1-2), 10–21 (2008)
2. Bogomolov, S., Magazzeni, D., Podelski, A., Wehrle, M.: Planning as model checking in hybrid domains. In: 28th Conference on Artificial Intelligence (AAAI) (2014)
3. Bourne, M., Mills, J., Wilcox, M., Neely, A., Platts, K.: Designing, implementing and updating performance measurement systems. Int. J. Oper. Prod. Man. 20(7), 754–771 (2000)
4. Bowersox, D.J., Closs, D.J.: Logistical Management: The Integrated Supply Chain Process. McGraw-Hill, New York (1996)
5. Brafman, R.I., Domshlak, C.: From one to many: Planning for loosely coupled multi-agent systems. In: 24th International Conference on Automated Planning and Scheduling (ICAPS), pp. 28–35 (2008)
6. Brönnimann, H., Melquiond, G., Pion, S.: The design of the Boost interval arithmetic library. Theor. Comput. Sci. 351(1), 111–118 (2006)
7. Bussmann, S., Jennings, N.R., Wooldridge, M.: Multiagent Systems for Manufacturing Control: A Design Methodology. Springer (2004)
8. Carbonell, J.G., Blythe, J., Etzioni, O., Gil, Y., Joseph, R., Kahn, D., Knoblock, C., Minton, S., Perez, A., Reilly, S., Veloso, M., Wang, X.: Prodigy 4.0: The manual and tutorial. Tech. Rep. CMU-CS-92-150, Carnegie Mellon University, Computer Science Department, Pittsburgh (1992)
9. Chow, G., Heaver, T.D., Henriksson, L.E.: Logistics performance: Definition and measurement. Int. J. Phys. Distrib. Logist. Manag. 1(24), 17–28 (1994)
10. Claßen, J., Röger, G., Lakemeyer, G., Nebel, B.: Platas—Integrating planning and the action language Golog. KI 26(1), 61–67 (2012)
11. Coles, A.J., Coles, A., Fox, M., Long, D.: COLIN: Planning with continuous linear numeric change. J. Artif. Intell. Res. (JAIR) 44, 1–96 (2012)
12. Dearden, R., Boutilier, C.: Integrating planning and execution in stochastic domains. CoRR abs/1302.6799 (2013), http://arxiv.org/abs/1302.6799
13. Edelkamp, S.: First solutions to PDDL+ planning problems. In: Workshop of the UK Planning and Scheduling Special Interest Group (PlanSig), pp. 75–88 (2001)
14. Edelkamp, S., Frank, J., Kellershoff, M.: Knowledge engineering through simulation. In: ICAPS-Workshop on the International Knowledge Engineering Competition (2007)
15. Ehrgott, M.: Multicriteria Optimization, 2nd edn. Springer (2005)
16. Fine, N.J.: The jeep problem. Amer. Math. Monthly 54(1), 24–31 (1947)
17. Foundation for Intelligent Physical Agents: FIPA Contract Net interaction protocol specification (2002), http://www.fipa.org/specs/fipa00029
18. Fox, M., Long, D.: PDDL2.1: An extension to PDDL for expressing temporal planning domains. J. Artif. Intell. Res. (JAIR) 20, 61–124 (2003)
19. Franceschini, F., Galetto, M., Maisano, D.: Management by Measurement: Designing Key Indicators and Performance Measurement Systems. Springer (2007)
20. Frehse, G., Le Guernic, C., Donzé, A., Cotton, S., Ray, R., Lebeltel, O., Ripado, R., Girard, A., Dang, T., Maler, O.: SpaceEx: Scalable verification of hybrid systems. In: Gopalakrishnan, G., Qadeer, S. (eds.) CAV 2011. LNCS, vol. 6806, pp. 379–395. Springer, Heidelberg (2011)
21. Ghallab, M., Nau, D.S., Traverso, P.: Automated Planning: Theory and Practice. Elsevier (2004)

22. Griewank, A.: On automatic differentiation. In: Iri, M., Tanabe, K. (eds.) Mathematical Programming: Recent Developments and Applications, pp. 83–108. Kluwer (1989)
23. Henzinger, T.A., Kopke, P.W., Puri, A., Varaiya, P.: What's decidable about hybrid automata? J. Comput. Syst. Sci. 57(1), 94–124 (1998)
24. Howey, R., Long, D., Fox, M.: VAL: Automatic plan validation, continuous effects and mixed initiative planning using PDDL. In: 16th IEEE International Conference on Tools with Artificial Intelligence (ICTAI), pp. 294–301 (2004)
25. Jiménez, S., Fernández, F., Borrajo, D.: Integrating planning, execution, and learning to improve plan execution. Computational Intelligence 29(1), 1–36 (2013)
26. Koehler, J., Hoffmann, J.: On the instantiation of ADL operators involving arbitrary first-order formulas. In: 14th Workshop on New Results in Planning, Scheduling and Design (PUK), Berlin, pp. 74–82 (2000)
27. Kovacs, D.L.: A multi-agent extension of PDDL3.1. In: ICAPS-Workshop on the International Planning Competition, pp. 19–27 (2012)
28. Lorenzen, L., Scholz, T., Timm, I.J., Rudzio, H., Woelk, P., Denkena, B., Herzog, O.: Integrated process planning and production control. In: Kirn, S., Herzog, O., Lockemann, P., Spaniol, O. (eds.) Multiagent Engineering: Theory and Application in Enterprises, pp. 91–114. Springer (2006)
29. Moore, R.E., Kearfott, R.B., Cloud, M.J.: Introduction to Interval Analysis. SIAM, Philadelphia (2009)
30. Nebel, B.: Compilation schemes: A theoretical tool for assessing the expressive power of planning formalisms. In: Burgard, W., Christaller, T., Cremers, A.B. (eds.) KI 1999. LNCS (LNAI), vol. 1701, pp. 183–194. Springer, Heidelberg (1999)
31. Nissim, R., Brafman, R.I.: Cost-optimal planning by self-interested agents. In: 27th Conference on Artificial Intelligence (AAAI), pp. 732–738 (2013)
32. Pantke, F.: Intelligent agent control and coordination with user-configurable key performance indicators. In: Kreowski, H.J., Scholz-Reiter, B., Thoben, K.D. (eds.) Dynamics in Logistics, pp. 145–159. Springer (2011)
33. Pantke, F., Edelkamp, S., Herzog, O.: Combinatorial planning with numerical parameter optimization for local control in multi-agent systems. In: 2nd International Conference on System-Integrated Intelligence: Challenges for Product and Production Engineering (SysInt). Procedia Technology. Elsevier (2014)
34. Piacentini, C., Alimisis, V., Fox, M., Long, D.: Combining a temporal planner with an external solver for the power balancing problem in an electricity network. In: 23rd International Conference on Automated Planning and Scheduling (ICAPS), pp. 398–406 (2013)
35. Price, K.V., Storn, R.M., Lampinen, J.A.: Differential Evolution: A Practical Approach to Global Optimization. Springer (2005)
36. Ruml, W., Do, M.B., Zhou, R., Fromherz, M.P.J.: On-line planning and scheduling: An application to controlling modular printers. J. Artif. Intell. Res. (JAIR) 40, 415–468 (2011)
37. Stolba, M., Komenda, A.: Relaxation heuristics for multiagent planning. In: 24th International Conference on Automated Planning and Scheduling (ICAPS), pp. 298–306 (2014)
38. Windt, K., Becker, T., Jeken, O., Gelessus, A.: A classification pattern for autonomous control methods in logistics. Logistics Research 2(2), 109–120 (2010)
39. Zamani, Z., Sanner, S., Fang, C.: Symbolic dynamic programming for continuous state and action MDPs. In: 26th Conference on Artificial Intelligence (AAAI), pp. 1839–1845 (2012)

Employing Automatic Temporal Abstractions to Accelerate Utile Suffix Memory Algorithm

Erkin Çilden and Faruk Polat

Department of Computer Engineering,
Middle East Technical University,
Ankara, Turkey
{ecilden,polat}@ceng.metu.edu.tr

Abstract. The main objective of the memory based reinforcement learning algorithms for hidden state problems is to overcome the state aliasing issue using a form of short term memory during learning. Extended sequence tree method, on the other hand, is a sequence based automated temporal abstraction mechanism that can be appended to a reinforcement learning algorithm. Assuming a fully observable problem setting, it tries to find useful sub-policies in solution space that can be reused as timed actions, providing significant savings in terms of learning time. This paper presents a way to expand a well known memory based model-free reinforcement learning algorithm, namely Utile Suffix Memory, by using a modified version of extended sequence tree method. By this way, learning speed of the algorithm is increased under certain conditions. Enhancement is shown empirically via experimentation on some benchmark problems.

Keywords: Reinforcement Learning, Utile Suffix Memory, Partially Observable Markov Decision Process, Extended Sequence Tree.

1 Introduction

Reinforcement Learning (RL) is a family of machine learning methods [12], usually based on Markov Decision Process (MDP) model. RL concept defines a way of adaptation by means of learning by exploration through time via interaction with the environment.

Implicitly, MDP model assumes equally distant time slices of action triggers. Recent studies focused on relaxation of this assumption so that timed-actions (actions taking more than one time step) can also be invoked, which are usually called *temporal abstractions*. This relaxation makes it possible to extend the action set with sub-policy invocation macros, and comes with some advantages like saving learning time and being able to transfer sub-policy packages.

There are a number of different approaches for invoking temporal abstractions within a RL algorithm. While it is quite possible to provide the abstraction information to the agent before learning, automated ways to derive abstractions has recently gained significant attention. State-action-reward sub-sequence analysis and unification of common parts of useful sub-sequences is an effective way

J.P. Müller, M. Weyrich, and A.L.C. Bazzan (Eds.): MATES 2014, LNAI 8732, pp. 156–169, 2014.
© Springer International Publishing Switzerland 2014

to derive abstractions automatically during RL, which is called *sequence based automatic temporal abstraction* [4] [9].

Partially Observable MDP (POMDP) is a generalization of MDP where states and state transition dynamics are no longer available to the agent. POMDP defines a more realistic, but difficult problem category for RL algorithms, since the agent is provided with limited *observations* instead of complete state information, i.e. the state information is *hidden* from the agent.

To overcome the adversities of learning under partial observability, some methods assume that the underlying state transition model is known by the agent in advance (*model-based* methods), while others assume that the agent should learn using the observation semantics only (*model-free* methods). An effective model-free solution is incorporating a form of memory to derive internal state estimations to discriminate ambiguous observations, which is an extensively studied area of in research [1] [6] [8] [11].

Application of temporal abstractions to RL algorithms under partial observability is a new area of research. Automatic temporal abstraction in model-free setting is even less studied, with a very few attempts for methods that search for a memoryless solution [2] [14]. Memory based model-free setting is still relatively unexplored.

This paper proposes a way to augment one of the important memory free RL algorithms for hidden state problems, namely Utile Suffix Memory (USM) algorithm [8], with an existing sequence based automatic temporal abstraction method, namely *extended sequence tree* (EST) [4]. We append USM with a modified version of EST, called EST_{MSR} [2], which is originally designed to speed up RL with hidden state to find optimal memoryless policies. We show how EST_{MSR} can make use of the additional information provided by USM, and improves USM performance.

2   Background

2.1   Reinforcement Learning with Hidden State

Most RL methods basically estimate a *value function* (i.e. function giving the value of being in a state on the way to goal) incrementally, to solve an MDP.

It is possible to invoke a RL algorithm for a problem with hidden state (i.e. POMDP without implicit access to the underlying states) simply by replacing "states" with "observations". However, when observations are the only sources of information about the environment, a challenging problem called *perceptual aliasing* arises. Perceptual aliasing is the situation where the same observation is obtained by the agent in two distinct states (for which optimal actions are probably different) [1]. In fact, perceptual aliasing makes the problem non-Markovian, violating a precondition for convergence guarantee of classical RL methods.

Theoretically, a memory keeping all previous observations and actions provides sufficient statistics to satisfy the Markov property. Unfortunately, this solution is not practically feasible. Instead, there are methods that try to estimate the this information under various assumptions of limited memory [1] [6] [8].

2.2   Utile Suffix Memory Algorithm

Utile Suffix Memory (USM) algorithm [8] is one of the fundamental memory based reinforcement learning algorithms for partially observable problems. Using a history database of observations, actions and rewards, the agent eventually learns to estimate states based on statistical differences among same observations with different history, effectively overcoming the perceptual aliasing problem by time.

At the core of USM lies a suffix tree, representing short term history of raw experiences, called *instances*. There is no limit on the depth of the tree. Depth is dynamically increased throughout learning process as necessary to resolve necessary perceptually aliased states via observation-action histories.

USM suffix tree is a clustered form of agent's observations and actions back in time, with a clustering schema in which deeper layers of the tree add distinctions based alternately on previous observations and actions. There are three types of nodes in terms of distinctive meaning: *Internal nodes* are old leaf nodes and currently have no significance other than identification of a path from root to a leaf. *Official leaf nodes* constitute the current Q table, each holding a Q value for a pair of distinctive state and action. *Fringe nodes* are potential future official leaf nodes and are continually applied statistical tests (Kolmogorov-Smirnov, or K-S test, in our setting) for identifying new distinctions.

A history instance represented by USM at time step t is a transition $I_t = \langle I_{t-1}, a_{t-1}, o_t, r_t \rangle$, and is deposited in the leaf node whose suffix, σ, matches some suffix of the actions and observations of the transition instances that precede I_t in time. In other words, a transition I_t belongs to the leaf with a label that is some suffix of $[...o_{t-3}a_{t-3}o_{t-2}a_{t-2}o_{t-1}]$. The set of instances associated with the leaf labelled σ is written $I_t(\sigma)$. The suffix tree leaf which instance I_t belongs to is written $L(I_t)$.

2.3   Automatic Temporal Abstractions

Temporal abstractions can be introduced to a RL algorithm as a design clue, or can be extracted automatically by the agent during learning. One of the automatic discovery methods is based on identification of sub-goals and tries to achieve a useful partitioning scheme [5] [10]. The other track makes use of common sub-sequence analysis of multiple successful histories, without identification of sub-goals [4] [9]. We name the latter approach as *sequence based* way of learning abstractions, which is a relatively less explored area, and is based on the *options framework* [13].

2.4   Extended Sequence Tree Method

Extended sequence tree (EST) method [4] is a sequence based automatic temporal abstraction procedure, transforming useful histories into a tree data structure, in order to make it possible to incorporate conditional branching in action selection, and make use of available abstractions in a compact and effective way.

Algorithm 1. REINFORCEMENT-LEARNING-WITH-EST

1: initialize T to an empty EST
2: initialize policy π ▷ set initial policy arbitrarily
3: **repeat**
4:      observe state s and append it to empty history e
5:      **repeat**
6:          $a \leftarrow$ SELECT-ACTION(s, T) ▷ handle both EST and underlying
         reinforcement learning algorithm
7:          perform a, observe s' and r ▷ r is the immediate reward
8:          $\pi \leftarrow$ RL-UPDATE(s, s', a, r)
9:          append a, r and s to e
10:        $s \leftarrow s'$
11:      **until** s is terminal
12:      $T \leftarrow$ UPDATE-SEQUENCE-TREE(T, e)
13: **until** some convergence criterion is met

EST method is a structural and procedural extension on top of a RL algorithm (a simplified pseudo-code is given by Algorithm 1). There are three basic components of EST. The first one is the EST data structure, which is an n-ary tree as a repository of successful sub-policies. The second one is the update mechanism invoked regularly upon episode terminations (Algorithm 2, called at line 12 of Algorithm 1). The third one is the action selection procedure of RL (called at line 6 of Algorithm 1) which shall be modified in such a way that it can switch the control flow among action selection of underlying RL and the EST method, by comparing the expected value of the current situation calculated by RL and the expected value of the experiences accumulated at the first level of the EST data structure. The resulting annotated RL algorithm discovers and utilizes useful temporal abstractions in the form of options, by generating an EST data structure and using it as a meta-action guide.

The tree is used for memorization of successful sub-policies, derived from recorded histories (Algorithm 2). All promising probable sub-histories are extracted from a full-length successful history by means of state equivalences. All derived sub-histories are then transformed into the tree data structure representing the sequences in a compact manner, where each path from the root to a leaf represents a successful sub-policy. As the underlying RL continues to operate, if the agent reaches a state that might be the initiation condition of an option represented within the EST, the modified action selection mechanism may decide to follow the corresponding option.

Since the underlying RL algorithm stays intact, provided that the action selection mechanism allows sufficient exploration, this extended learning algorithm preserves many of the theoretical properties –such as convergence to an optimal value function or policy– of the underlying RL method. The reported test results demonstrate the advantages of EST over the other approaches in the literature [4].

Algorithm 2. UPDATE-SEQUENCE-TREE(T, e)

Require: T is an EST
Require: e is a history of the form $s_1 a_1 r_2 ... s_{t-1} a_{t-1} r_t s_t$ observed by the agent during a specific period of time.
Ensure: T updated
1: $H \leftarrow$ GENERATE-PROBABLE-HISTORIES(e)
2: **for all** h of H **do**
3:     ADD-HISTORY(h, T)
4: **end for**
5: UPDATE-NODE(root node of T)   ▷ recursively traverse and update tree for maintenance
6: **return** T

2.5 Automatic Temporal Abstractions for Reinforcement Learning with Hidden State

Studies on automatic temporal abstraction for model-free RL algorithms are limited. [14] attempts to derive simple abstractions automatically for a hidden state problem, but the method suffers from irrelevant macro generation since it does not have mechanisms to explicitly handle perceptual aliasing. [2] attacks the same problem by trying to get rid of adverse effects of perceptual aliasing. By design, this method lacks identification of intermediate useful abstractions.

To our knowledge, our study is the first attempt to invoke an automatic temporal abstraction to a memory based model-free RL algorithm. Our method is based on the work done in [2], which will be briefly explained in the next section.

2.6 EST Abstraction with Misleading Sub-policy Removal

Originally, the definition of EST method assumes a fully observable problem setting. For partially observable problems, since the state information is hidden from the learning agent, an obvious way to invoke EST abstraction is to apply EST directly over observations, instead of states. Unfortunately, this method simply does not work. Perceptual aliasing causes undesirable ambiguities while trying to build successful history candidates through observation equalities. Then the error is transferred to the EST data structure which generally tends to mislead the agent during an option exploitation.

[2] attacks this problem by modifying EST data structure and regularly pruning it to get rid of misleading paths, in order to reduce the adverse effects of perceptual aliasing. The method, named EST with Misleading Sub-policy Removal (EST_{MSR}), is shown to improve learning performance of SARSA(λ) as the underlying RL method. SARSA(λ) is highly cited for its relatively better performance on finding memoryless optimal policies for problems with hidden state.

For EST_{MSR}, the original EST data structure is augmented with extra information and redefined as follows:

Definition 1. *A history aware extended sequence tree data structure (HA-EST) is a tuple $\langle N, E \rangle$, where N is the set of nodes, and E is the set of edges.*

- *Each node represents a unique action sequence that is used to reach that node. The root node, denoted by $\emptyset$, represents the empty action set.*
- *If the action sequence of node q can be obtained by appending action a to the action sequence represented by node p, then p is connected to q by an edge with label $\langle a, \psi \rangle$. This connection is denoted by the tuple $\langle p, q, \langle a, \psi \rangle \rangle$. ψ is the eligibility value of the edge to indicate how frequently the action sequence of q is executed.*
- *q holds a list $\langle \langle o_1, \Pi_1^p \rangle, \xi_{\langle o_1, \Pi_1^p \rangle}, R_{\langle o_1, \Pi_1^p \rangle} \rangle, ..., \langle \langle o_k, \Pi_k^p \rangle, \xi_{\langle o_k, \Pi_k^p \rangle}, R_{\langle o_k, \Pi_k^p \rangle} \rangle$ stating that action a can be chosen at node p if current observation and previous continuation set element makes a pair that is in $\{\langle o_1, \Pi_1^p \rangle, ..., \langle o_k, \Pi_k^p \rangle\}$ which is called the continuation set (CS) of node q, denoted $cont_q$.*
- *Π_i^p denotes the element of $cont_p$ that is the immediate ancestor of current CS element, meaning that Π_i^p was the previous CS element chosen in the previous option exploitation step.*
- *A CS element is indexed by the pair $\langle o_i, \Pi_i^p \rangle$.*
- *$R_{\langle o_i, \Pi_i^p \rangle}$ is the expected total cumulative reward that the agent can collect by selecting action a upon gathering a pair $\langle o_i, \Pi_i^p \rangle$ after having executed the sequence of actions represented by node p.*
- *$\xi_{\langle o_i, \Pi_i^p \rangle}$ is the eligibility value of pair $\langle o_i, \Pi_i^p \rangle$ at node q and indicates how frequently action a is actually selected at some state yielding the pair $\langle o_i, \Pi_i^p \rangle$.*

HA-EST makes it possible to differentiate discovered options that are "derived" through observation equalities from the ones that are "actually experienced". Additionally, unlike in EST, every CS element in a node is now a step on a unique path from root node to a leaf node, which makes the HA-EST data structure suitable for a pruning mechanism

Broadly speaking, EST_{MSR} method replaces all states (s) with observations (o), and EST variables with HA-EST variables in Algorithms 1 and 2, as well as in GENERATE-PROBABLE-HISTORIES procedure. It also alters the UPDATE-NODE procedure, replacing all state variables (s_i) with the tuple $\langle o_i, \Pi_i^p \rangle$.

Every history represented by HA-EST is potentially ambiguous. In other words, any path from the root node to a leaf node through CS elements may involve observations that are aliases of some distinct states. These paths should be removed from the tree, so that eventually only unambiguous sub-policies remain. Even when the number of perceptually aliased states are high for a problem, just a few "discriminating" observations (i.e. observations corresponding to states that do not suffer from perceptual aliasing) may lead as the initiation points for unambiguous successful histories.

This pruning mechanism is handled in two phases. The first phase is the ADD-HISTORY procedure, whose updated version is given in Algorithm 3. A *Forbidden Sub-policy Repository* (FSR) is defined to store histories in the form of observation-action sequences. The aim of FSR is to keep track of sub-sequences

Algorithm 3. ADD-HISTORY(h, T)

Require: h is a history of the form $o_1 a_1 r_2 ... o_{t-1} a_{t-1} r_t o_t$

Require: T is a HA-EST

1:    $h' \leftarrow o_1 a_1 ... o_{t-1} a_{t-1} o_t$ ▷ rewards removed

2:    **if** any path in FSR is a prefix of h' **then**   ▷ history has ambiguities

3:       exit   ▷ do not add history to HA-EST

4:    **end if**

5:    $\Pi \leftarrow NULL$ ▷ parent CS element link

6:    $R[t] \leftarrow r_t$ ▷ time indexed array of discounted cumulative rewards

7:    **for** $i \leftarrow t - 1$ to 1 **do**

8:       $R[i] \leftarrow r_i + \gamma R[i+1]$

9:    **end for**

10: $n_{current} \leftarrow$ root node of T

11: **for** $i \leftarrow 1..t - 1$ **do**

12:      **if** $\exists$ a node n such that $n_{current}$ is connected to n by an edge with label $\langle a_i, \psi \rangle$ **then**

13:         Increment ψ.

14:         **if** n contains a CS element indexed by $\langle o_i, \Pi \rangle$ **then** ▷ update values in CS element found

15:            Increment $\xi_{\langle o_i, \Pi \rangle}$

16:            $R_{\langle o_i, \Pi \rangle} \leftarrow R_{\langle o_i, \Pi \rangle} + \alpha(R[i] - R_{\langle o_i, \Pi \rangle})$

17:         **else**   ▷ create new CS element in n

18:            Add a new tuple $\langle \langle o_i, \Pi \rangle, 1, R[i] \rangle$ to node n.

19:         **end if**

20:       **else**

21:         Create a new node n containing the tuple $\langle \langle o_i, \Pi \rangle, 1, R[i] \rangle$.

22:         Connect $n_{current}$ node to n by an edge with label $\langle a_i, 1 \rangle$.

23:       **end if**

24:      $\Pi \leftarrow$ link to CS element that contains $\langle o_i, \Pi \rangle$ in n ▷ prepare parent link for next iteration

25:      $n_{current} \leftarrow n$

26: **end for**

---

that have previously been proven to be misleading. Using FSR, ADD-HISTORY prevents insertion of sub-sequences that were added into FSR before, and constructs the CS element links as defined in Definition 1.

The second phase of pruning takes place in the modified action selection mechanism that links the underlying RL algorithm with the EST method. Under the assumption that the problem domain is deterministic and stationary, if an option execution through HA-EST fails, it means the tree path that has been followed was misleading the agent. In this case, the exploited path is immediately removed from the tree, starting with the last visited CS element up to the root node.

[2] empirically shows that, for problems with deterministic nature, EST_{MSR} can effectively speed up SARSA(λ) as the underlying RL method, generating optimal memoryless policies faster, if one exists.

Algorithm 4. GENERATE-PROBABLE-HISTORIES(h)

Require: h is a history of the form $o_1a_1r_2...o_{t-1}a_{t-1}r_to_t$
1: $best[L_{t-1}] \leftarrow L_{t-1}a_{t-1}r_tL_t$ ▷ $best$ holds current most promising history candidates
2: $R[L_{t-1}] \leftarrow r_t$ ▷ $R[L_t]$ holds the total cumulative reward for $best[L_t]$
3: **for** $i \leftarrow t - 2$ down to 1 **do**
4: ▷ from rear to front
5:   **if** $R[L_i]$ is not set or $r_{i_1} + \gamma R[L_{i+1}] > R[L_i]$ **then**
6:    ▷ if L_i is either not encountered before or has a lower return estimate
7:     $best[L_i] \leftarrow L_ia_ir_{i+1} \circ best[L_{i+1}]$ ▷ create or update the candidate history
   corresponding to state L_i.
8:     $R[L_i] \leftarrow r_{i+1} + \gamma R[L_{i+1}]$ ▷ update maximum reward.
9:   **end if**
10: **end for**
11: let $best_o$ be a multimap ▷ reduce all history entries to single observations
12: **for** every element of $best$ indexed by l **do**
13:   $h_o \leftarrow$ apply ω to state entries of all transitions in $best[l]$
14:   $best_o[\omega(l)] \leftarrow h_o$
15: **end for**
16: **return** $best_o$

---

3   Accelerating USM Algorithm Using EST_{MSR}

In this paper, we unite EST_{MSR} with USM in order to speed up USM learning. We present a way to integrate USM data structure into EST_{MSR}, so that the resulting method can remember and make use of some intermediate abstractions that EST_{MSR} would typically prune immediately. We will call the new method $EST_{MSR/USM}$ to emphasize the mutual dependency of MSR pruning mechanism and USM tree data structure on the way to success.

The original EST mechanism makes use of state equivalences during the construction of useful history portions, based on experiences. For this equivalence test, EST_{MSR} directly uses observations instead of states, and prunes the paths that are experienced to be misleading later on. One of the most important limitations of EST_{MSR} is that, although it generates some intermediate abstractions (i.e. sub-policies that are free of perceptual aliasing problem, but do not lead to a goal state) at the early steps of learning, it prunes them later due to its all-or-nothing nature.

USM data structure, on the other hand, is capable of differentiating observation instances, dynamically updated throughout learning. Most of the time, USM method can discriminate some observations at the early stages of learning. With the USM data structure, the state equivalence test of EST can be carried on using USM states for the given history instances. By this way, beginning at the very early stages, history generation can be done more effectively using *suffixes*, or equivalently by using the leaf nodes of USM.

For this purpose, we modify GENERATE-PROBABLE-HISTORIES function of EST_{MSR} to make the state equivalence test through USM leaf nodes instead of sole observations, as given in Algorithm 4. L_i stands for $L(I_i^h)$ where I_i^h is the instance of the history h at time i. $\omega(L)$ gives the observation of the instance represented by L.

Note that, a resulting CS elements of HA-EST data structure will still involve single observations, not suffixes or observation-action sequences. This will let $EST_{MSR/USM}$ mechanism be invoked more frequently, especially at the beginning of learning, compared to a hypothetical USM instance based design. All of the other mechanisms of EST_{MSR} remain unchanged.

With $EST_{MSR/USM}$, much deeper HA-EST trees are generated and used for option exploitation. Probability of catching and making use of repeating observation sequences in the domain that are useful on the path to goal increases, which is not possible for EST or EST_{MSR} for partially observable problems. On the average, since the number of option paths will increase in the long term (i.e. pruning mechanism will be less eager, since more HA-EST paths will succeed to reach the goal), we can expect $EST_{MSR/USM}$ to grasp some useful intermediate abstractions and improve USM as the underlying reinforcement learning algorithm.

In a sense, $EST_{MSR/USM}$ is a generalization of EST, since it reduces to ordinary EST mechanism if the problem is fully observable, deterministic and stationary, and USM fringe depth parameter is set to zero.

4   Experiments

We experimented the performance of USM with $EST_{MSR/USM}$ compared to USM alone, using four grid navigation based benchmark problems.

4.1   Problems and Settings

One of the benchmark problems is *tiny navigation environment (Mini-hall)* [7]. Agent's facing direction (one of the four compass directions) together with the walls around its current location determines its observation semantics. It can execute actions "rotate-left", "rotate-right" to change its facing direction, and "go-forward" to move one cell forward (Figure 1(a)).

Virtual office [3] problem is another grid navigation problem, where the agent has no facing direction and it can move in the four neighbouring cells. The agent is initially in any one of the cells in the left room. The problem has two bottleneck states and two goal states that can be reached through each bottleneck state separately. This clearly defines a hierarchical structure in solution policy (Figure 1(b)).

Another problem is *McCallum's maze* [8]. Observation and action semantics are the same as in *Virtual office* problem. The agent is initially in one of the four corner cells of the grid. Figure 1(c) is an illustration of the domain together with observation identifiers corresponding to states.

Finally, we propose an extension of *McCallum's maze*, as illustrated in Figure 1(d). It is identical with the original problem, except that it has additional hallways. While observations identified by 2 and 8 are uniquely disambiguates

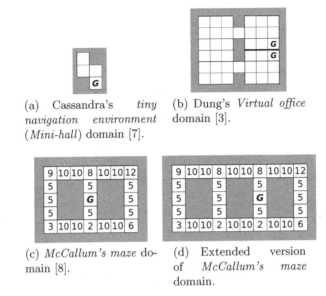

(a) Cassandra's *tiny navigation environment* (*Mini-hall*) domain [7].

(b) Dung's *Virtual office* domain [3].

(c) *McCallum's maze* domain [8].

(d) Extended version of *McCallum's maze* domain.

Fig. 1. Grid navigation problems selected for experimentation

their corresponding states in the original maze, there are two of them both in this domain. So, ambiguity of the observations are spread to all of the states except the starting states (i.e. the four corners). In other words, there are no distinguishable abstraction packages near the goal state, thus an abstraction procedure should make use of intermediate abstractions to achieve a speed-up.

Table 1 summarizes the experimented problem domains, providing the sizes of problems in terms of state, action and observation spaces ($|S|$, $|A|$ and $|\Omega|$, respectively), and the reference publication for the domain.

Learning settings used for experimentation are given in Table 2. For every problem domain, 100 experiments are executed and the results are averaged over the episodes of each run. ϵ-Greedy is used as the action selection strategy for all problems, with a constant ϵ value. "Reward-per-step" is the performance criterion for success. For visual clarity, result plots are smoothed.

Table 1. Problem Domains

Problem	Sizes			
	$|S|$	$|A|$	$|\Omega|$	Ref.
Mini-hall	13	3	9	[7]
Virtual Office	38	4	12	[3]
McCallum's maze	23	4	9	[8]
McCallum's maze extended	32	4	9	-

Table 2. Learning Settings

Parameter	Value
α	0.125
γ	0.9
ϵ	0.1
K-S test treshold	0.01
max. fringe depth for USM	4
ψ_{decay}	0.95
ξ_{decay}	0.99
$\psi_{treshold}$	0.01
$\xi_{treshold}$	0.01

4.2   Results and Discussion

In general, results show that USM can benefit from $EST_{MSR/USM}$ to increase the learning performance for the selected problems.

In the *Mini-hall* domain, $EST_{MSR/USM}$ mechanism boosts learning beginning with the very early steps of the experiments (Figure 2). Moreover, in the long term, learned abstractions can assist the agent to increase average reward obtained for both abstraction methods, since the refined abstract actions contain no observation ambiguity, and can by-pass the stochastic action decision semantics (i.e. ϵ-Greedy) of USM.

In *Virtual office* domain, USM with $EST_{MSR/USM}$ provides an initial boost of learning (Figure 3). When the transition dynamics of the problem is examined, it can be identified that each of the two goal states are reached through long observation-action sequences with ambiguous observations, which are better maintained and used by $EST_{MSR/USM}$ method in the long term.

USM with $EST_{MSR/USM}$ seem to perform slightly better for *McCallum's maze* (Figure 4). This maze is specially designed by its creator to demonstrate the power of USM algorithm. In other words, this problem is where USM shines by itself. Nevertheless, $EST_{MSR/USM}$ improves learning speed, although performance increase is not significant since USM can successfully overcome state ambiguities beginning at the very early steps of learning.

In *McCallum's maze extended*, on the other hand, more experience is required for USM alone to discriminate all observations, since every observation after the first one in an episode is ambiguous. At this point, $EST_{MSR/USM}$ support the USM algorithm very well, speeding it up significantly at the early stages of learning.

Metrics given in Table 3 shows that $EST_{MSR/USM}$ takes advantage of abstractions by constructing HA-EST trees of sizes varying according to the problem complexity (average number of HA-EST nodes). It also makes significant use of derived abstractions (average use of options, as the percentage of actions invoked within options over the entire episode).

Since HA-EST may be implemented in various different ways (in terms of internal data structures used and insertion/deletion algorithms invoked), average

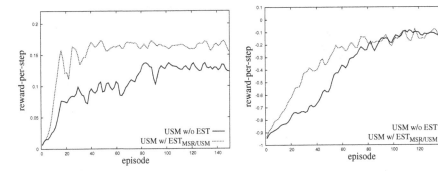

Fig. 2. Experiment results for *Mini-hall* domain

Fig. 3. Experiment results for *Virtual office* domain

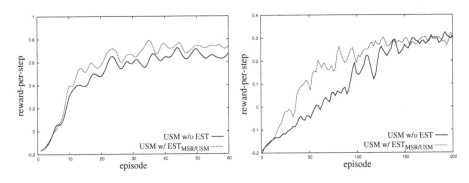

Fig. 4. Experiment results for *McCallum's maze* domain

Fig. 5. Experiment results for *McCallum's maze extended* domain

number of HA-EST nodes is provided instead of size in memory bytes, as an indication of memory usage.

Average total CPU times elapsed per experiment empirically shows that, in all cases, USM without abstraction takes more time than the cases with abstraction. In fact, these results mostly depend on the USM learning parameters and the nature of the selected problem domain. Cost of USM tree maintenance (statistical tests, fringe promotions, and history links etc.) seems to dominate the cost of maintaining HA-EST data structure, in such a way that gain achieved by $EST_{MSR/USM}$ (in terms of number of steps to goal) can reduce total time spent.

Obviously, these results could have been completely different if some other USM learning setting were used. For example, if fringe depth parameter of USM is set to 0 (zero), the $EST_{MSR/USM}$ mechanism reduces to EST_{MSR}, and it can not be possible to make use of history distinctions of USM anymore. Since the original USM algorithm can not decide the optimal value of this parameter for a given problem, $EST_{MSR/USM}$ depends on the representational power of USM.

Table 3. Comparison of some experiment metrics

Problem	average use of options (%)	average number of HA-EST nodes	average CPU usage (msec)	
			without abstr.	with abstr.
Mini-hall	68	65.80	2498	1917
Virtual office	38	515.49	46621	34146
McCallum's maze	51	33.18	997	755
McCallum's maze ext.	43	207.01	234434	106960

Nevertheless, the results show that, $EST_{MSR/USM}$ can provide some gain also in terms of CPU time, in addition to discrete time steps of the problems.

At this point, it is worth noting that time and space complexities of the abstraction mechanism are not easy to analyse, because they are directly affected by the problem semantics (i.e. state transition function and observation function of POMDP model), and the abstraction potential of the problem dynamics. For example, although *Mini-hall* is a smaller problem compared to *McCallum's maze* (in terms of $|S|$ and $|A|$), it makes more advantage of options, resulting in significantly larger HA-EST data structure.

5   Conclusion

This paper proposes a way to improve learning speed of a memory based model-free RL algorithm for hidden state problems (USM), by using a sequence based automatic temporal abstraction mechanism (EST). We show that, an existing EST variant, namely EST_{MSR}, can effectively be used to support USM. We propose a way to couple EST_{MSR} and USM to handle intermediate abstractions. The new abstraction strategy, $EST_{MSR/USM}$, makes use of USM state information, and thus performs well to leverage USM learning. Theoretically, with minor modifications, USM can be replaced with any other memory based model-free RL algorithm with hidden state.

An obvious future research direction would be the transfer of learned abstractions among the agents in a multi-agent learning setting. Besides, modification of $EST_{MSR/USM}$ via a distributed collective update mechanism would be a challenging alternative in a multi-agent scenario, since learning abstractions in cooperative reinforcement learning is an unexplored area of research.

One of the major drawbacks of $EST_{MSR/USM}$ is that, depending on problem characteristics, it may fail to catch redundant repetitions of observation-action sequences. An alternative solution can be using fringe leaf nodes instead of official leaf nodes in history generation. However, this solution may cause over-discrimination of estimated states, which may harm quality of options in the long term. Inherited from EST_{MSR}, $EST_{MSR/USM}$ also fails to handle non-determinism and a changing environment, which is another topic for future work. Although $EST_{MSR/USM}$ has no restrictions on scalability, an immediate next step would be experimentation of the method on larger problems, in terms of state and observation space sizes.

Acknowledgments. This work is partially supported by the Scientific and Technological Research Council of Turkey under Grant No. 113E239.

References

1. Chrisman, L.: Reinforcement learning with perceptual aliasing: the perceptual distinctions approach. In: Proceedings of the Tenth National Conference on Artificial Intelligence, pp. 183–188. AAAI Press (1992)
2. Çilden, E., Polat, F.: Generating memoryless policies faster using automatic temporal abstractions for reinforcement learning with hidden state. In: IEEE 25th International Conference on Tools with Artificial Intelligence, pp. 719–726 (2013)
3. Dung, L.T., Komeda, T., Takagi, M.: Reinforcement learning for POMDP using state classification. Applied Artificial Intelligence 22(7-8), 761–779 (2008)
4. Girgin, S., Polat, F., Alhajj, R.: Improving reinforcement learning by using sequence trees. Machine Learning 81(3), 283–331 (2010)
5. Hengst, B.: Discovering hierarchy in reinforcement learning with HEXQ. In: Proceedings of the Nineteenth International Conference on Machine Learning, pp. 243–250. Morgan Kaufmann Publishers Inc. (2002)
6. Hochreiter, S., Schmidhuber, J.: Long short-term memory. Neural Computation 9, 1735–1780 (1997)
7. Littman, M.L., Cassandra, A.R., Kaelbling, L.P.: Learning policies for partially observable environments: Scaling up. In: Huhns, M.N., Singh, M.P. (eds.) Readings in Agents, pp. 495–503. Morgan Kaufmann Publishers Inc. (1998)
8. McCallum, A.K.: Reinforcement Learning with Selective Perception and Hidden State. Ph.d. thesis, University of Rochester (1996)
9. McGovern, A.: acQuire-macros: An algorithm for automatically learning macroactions. In: The Neural Information Processing Systems Conference Workshop on Abstraction and Hierarchy in Reinforcement Learning (1998)
10. McGovern, A., Barto, A.G.: Automatic discovery of subgoals in reinforcement learning using diverse density. In: Proceedings of the Eighteenth International Conference on Machine Learning, pp. 361–368. Morgan Kaufmann Publishers Inc. (2001)
11. Peshkin, L., Meuleau, N., Kaelbling, L.P.: Learning policies with external memory. In: Proceedings of the Sixteenth International Conference on Machine Learning, pp. 307–314. Morgan Kaufmann Publishers Inc. (1999)
12. Sutton, R.S., Barto, A.G.: Reinforcement Learning: An Introduction. MIT Press (1998)
13. Sutton, R.S., Precup, D., Singh, S.: Between MDPs and semi-MDPs: a framework for temporal abstraction in reinforcement learning. Artificial Intelligence 112(1-2), 181–211 (1999)
14. Yoshikawa, T., Kurihara, M.: An acquiring method of macro-actions in reinforcement learning. In: IEEE International Conference on Systems, Man, and Cybernetics, vol. 6, pp. 4813–4817 (2006)

The Effects of Variation on Solving a Combinatorial Optimization Problem in Collaborative Multi-Agent Systems

Christian Hinrichs and Michael Sonnenschein

Department of Computing Science, University of Oldenburg, Germany
{christian.hinrichs,michael.sonnenschein}@uni-oldenburg.de

Abstract. In collaborative multi-agent systems, the participating agents have to join forces in order to solve a common goal. The necessary coordination is often realized by message exchange. While this might work perfectly in simulated environments, the implementation of such systems in a field application usually reveals some challenging properties: arbitrary communication networks, message delays due to specific communication technologies, or differing processing speeds of the agents. In this contribution we interpret these properties as sources of variation, and analyze four different multi-agent heuristics with respect to these aspects. In this regard, we distinguish synchronous from asynchronous approaches, and draw conclusions for either type. Our work is motivated by the use case of scheduling distributed energy resources within self-organized virtual power plants.

Keywords: Heuristics, Distributed Problem Solving, Self-Organization, Synchronous vs. Asynchronous Approaches, Virtual Power Plants.

1 Introduction

According to Ferber [1], interaction between agents is a main component of multi-agent systems (MAS). A special case is *collaboration* situations, in which the agents in a MAS pursue a common goal, and have to join forces in a co-ordinated manner in order to reach that goal. This paradigm does not exclude self-interested or untrustworthy agents per se, as the effects induced by those properties can be tackled by proper coalition formation and incentivization mechanisms, cf. [2–4].

For example, such collaboration situations may arise in energy systems with a significant share of distributed energy resources (DER) like small scale combined heat and power (CHP) plants. As of today, in many European countries, especially Germany, DER operate under financial security of guaranteed electrical feed-in tariffs. However, in order to follow the goals as defined by the European Commission, this subsidy dependence should be reduced. The formation of virtual power plants (VPPs) as an aggregation level for small scale DER, to overcome market barriers and to increase mutual reliability within a VPP by

J.P. Müller, M. Weyrich, and A.L.C. Bazzan (Eds.): MATES 2014, LNAI 8732, pp. 170–187, 2014.

redundant dimensioning and adaptive compensation techniques [5], forms a possible integration path for these DER. In [6], a concept of self-organized VPPs is proposed, which involves both coalition formation and scheduling tasks as distributed optimization problems. The coalition formation process allows self-interested agents to join forces towards the common goal of offering reliable energy products at the market. This includes admissibility checks regarding the underlying power grid as well as monetary incentivization for the agents, as described in e. g. [7]. Each of those VPPs then represents a collaborative MAS as described above, as the participating DER have to coordinate their actions (e. g. their generation of electrical power) cooperatively in order to reliably deliver energy products as an aggregate.

In this paper, we focus on the effects of variation in collaborative MAS. Based on the findings of Ashby [8], who identified variation and error as important properties for the control of complex technical systems, Campbell et al. [9] studied variation in the context of MAS solving a distributed task allocation problem. Subsequently, Anders et al. [10] extended this work by introducing uncertainty from the environment of the MAS, and demonstrated the effects of variation on multi-agent algorithms solving the frequency stabilization problem in the power grid (cf. [11]). There, variation was modeled as a randomized threshold parameter for the activation of agents, thus affecting the participation of agents in the optimization process stochastically. The objective of the contribution at hand is to continue this research by addressing further types of variation:

- environmental effects, e. g. communication delays or arbitrary communication topologies and
- technical aspects, e. g. differing processing speeds of the participating agents.

Our study is motivated by the scheduling of DER in self-organized VPPs as described above. Because this task targets a critical infrastructure, robustness against variation is crucial here. Therefore, we examine different approaches for solving this scheduling problem with regard to the variation sources above, which are likely to be faced in deployed field applications.

The contribution proceeds as follows: In Sect. 2, we give a formal description of the optimization problem and subsequently present different solution strategies for this task in Sect. 3. Following, Sect. 4 describes the considered types of variation in detail. Sect. 5 then describes our evaluation setup and discusses the results. There we show that some approaches suffer significantly from variation, whereas others are basically unaffected or even benefit from certain types of variation. Finally, Sect. 6 concludes the paper.

2   The Multiple-Choice Combinatorial Optimization Problem

The motivation for this paper is the task of scheduling DER within self-organized VPPs. More specifically, we are referring to the use case of active power products traded on a day-ahead power market like the European Power Exchange (EPEX

SPOT), cf. [12, 6]: Given an active power profile over a future planning horizon (e. g. the next 24 hours, discretized into 15 minute intervals) as scheduling target (in the following denoted as *active power product*), the task is to select a schedule for each participating DER for the planning horizon, such that the aggregation of all selected schedules within the VPP yields the active power product as close as possible. From a centralized point of view, this optimization problem can be expressed as *Multiple-Choice Combinatorial Optimization Problem* (MC-COP), an integer programming model that was already introduced in a similar form in [13]:

$$
\min \ \left\| \zeta - \sum_{i=1}^{|A|} \sum_{j=1}^{|S_i|} (\theta_{ij} \cdot x_{ij}) \right\|_1 \tag{1a}
$$

$$
\text{subject to} \ \sum_{j=1}^{|S_i|} x_{ij} = 1, \quad x_{ij} \in \{0,1\}, \quad i = 1 \ldots |A|. \tag{1b}
$$

Here, A denotes the set of agents in the considered MAS, i.e. the set of DER in a self-organized VPP. Each agent $a_i \in A$ has an associated set of schedules $S_i = \{\theta_{i1}, \theta_{i2}, \ldots\}$ for the considered planning horizon. The task, as depicted in (1a), is to find a selection of schedules for the agents, such that the distance of the aggregation of the selected schedules to the active power product ζ, cumulated over all planning intervals, is minimized. The constraints in (1b) make sure that for each agent exactly one schedule is selected.

3 Solution Strategies for MC-COP

The MC-COP in (1) refers to a global view on the MAS. A central optimizer, with full knowledge about every S_i, could find an optimal solution using standard solving techniques for integer programs. However, in the considered use case, each S_i is represented by a self-interested agent acting on its own behalf. While a cooperative attitude for the agents is incentivized throughout the coalition formation process of the self-organized VPP (cf. [7]), the transfer of all S_i to a central instance should be avoided due to privacy aspects as well as technical difficulties, as discussed in e.g. [13–15]. Moreover, due to the nonseparability of the considered optimization problem with respect to the occuring constraints between schedule selections, approaches from the domain of Distributed Constraint Optimization Problems (DCOP) cannot effectively be applied here either, cf. [16]. Therefore we present a number of feasible approaches for MAS (i.e. each DER is represented by an agent) in the following, classified by their underlying coordination mechanism.

One possible solution strategy for the MC-COP is realizing a virtual market. In such a coordination mechanism, agents place bids on fulfilling (parts of) the power product ζ in a virtual marketplace. A central auctioneer then performs a market matching by selecting and combining appropriate bids. This process can be repeated iteratively, in order to approximate an optimal solution. Examples for this strategy can be found in [17–19]. Common to such market-based approaches is a tree topology with a central auctioneer as root node. The agents generally keep their search spaces private, and publish only selective parts of it in the form of bid proposals.

Another strategy that relies on a tree topology is the *Energy Plan Overlay Service* (EPOS), as proposed in [20]. Similar to the market setting, the root node acts as a global controller of the system and announces the aspired power product ζ to all agents. After that, at first the leaf agents send their whole search spaces to their respective superordinate agents in the topology. Subsequently, each intermediate agent executes the following actions: Upon receiving the search spaces of all its subordinate agents (and possibly also schedule selections from lower levels, see below), the intermediate agent calculates the best schedule combination from these search spaces with respect to ζ. Then, on the one hand, the selected schedules are sent back to the corresponding subordinate agents, thus informing them about their obligations. On the other hand, the intermediate agent sends the calculated schedule combination together with its own search space to its superordinate agent, which then executes the very same actions. In summary, in this approach agents select schedules for their subordinates within a tree topology, thus realizing a bottom-um planning with a certain degree of parallelism. Similar to market-based approaches, this planning can iteratively be repeated, in order to approximate an optimal solution.

An alternative strategy is the *Stigspace* approach [21]: All agents have access to a central information repository called the *Stigspace*, hence this is an instance of the black board coordination mechanism. In principle, the agents perform an iterative improvement process by adapting their schedule selection according to updated information in the *Stigspace*. After such an adaptation, an agent is obliged to publish its schedule selection by placing it into the *Stigspace* again, thus triggering adaptation in other agents regarding this choice. The process terminates either if no agent can improve the current situation any more with respect to fulfilling ζ, or if an external termination criterion holds (e. g. a predefined timespan, as used by the authors in [21]).

Finally, a completely distributed and asynchronous approach is given with the *Combinatorial Optimization Heuristic for Distributed Agents* (COHDA), see [13]. The key concept of COHDA is an asynchronous iterative approximate best-response behavior, where each agent reacts to updated information from other agents by adapting its own selected schedule with respect to the power product ζ. The agents are placed in an artificial communication topology (e. g. a *small world* topology), such that each agent is connected to a non-empty subset of other agents. To compensate for the resulting non-global view on the system, each agent a_i collects two distinct sets of information: on the one hand the believed current configuration $\gamma_i = \{\theta_1, \ldots, \theta_{|A|}\}$ of the system (that is, the believed set of currently selected schedules of all agents), and on the other hand the best known combination γ_i^* of schedules with respect to the power product ζ it has encountered so far. All agents $a_i \in A$ initially only know their own respective set of schedules S_i, and the difficulty of the problem is given by the distributed nature of the system in contrast to the task of finding a common allocation of schedules. Thus, the agents coordinate via message exchange. Beginning with an arbitrarily chosen representative of the self-organized VPP, each agent a_i executes the following three steps, cf. [13]:

1. (update) When an agent a_i receives information from one of its neighbors (say, a_j), it imports this information (γ_j and γ_j^*) into its own knowledge base by updating γ_i and, if better, replacing γ_i^* with γ_j^*.
2. (choose) The agent now adapts its own schedule according to the newly received information. If it is not able to improve the believed current system configuration γ_i, the agent reverts its current schedule to the one stored in γ_i^* (note that γ_i^* contains a schedule for each agent in the system and a_i takes its own of course).
3. (publish) If γ_i or γ_i^* has been modified in one of the previous steps, the agent finally publishes its knowledge base (γ_i, including its own selected schedule, and γ_i^*) to its neighbors.

The heuristic terminates when for all agents γ and γ^* are identical. At this point, γ^* is the final solution of the heuristic and contains exactly one schedule for each agent.

4   Sources of Variation

For the evaluation of the influence of variation on collaborative MAS solving the MC-COP, we considered different types of variation. We specifically focused on the effects that occur when finally implementing such a MAS in the targeted field application:

Communication topologies. We consider this as a source of variation, because it is not known in which topology such a system would operate in the field. For example, in our use case of self-organized VPPs, the participating DER might be connected to a given restricted communication network like power line carrier (PLC) [22] or a wireless mesh network [23].

Message delays. Another important aspect arising from the underlying communication technology is message delays. While it is possible to implement communication networks with real-time properties, a more likely scenario would be to reuse already available technologies like PLC or mesh networks as described above, or alternatively utilizing general purpose commmunication networks like broadband internet connections. In these cases it is important to know how an algorithm that heavily depends on communication behaves.

Reaction delays. Besides the communication technology, the agents themselves are a source of variation. In our use case of scheduling DER, agents would be implemented on different hardware platforms, depending on the manufacturer and model of the appliance under control. This would lead to different processing speeds of the agents. Combined with a dynamically changing environment for the executed agent with respect to available information (e. g. dynamically updated knowledge in the EPOS, *Stigspace* and COHDA approaches), this results in dynamically changing delays while reacting to incoming messages. While these differences may be quite small, their effects are still interesting with regard to the performance of collaborative MAS.

Of course, there are more possible sources of variation one might want to consider. For example, regarding robustness, message losses and (temporary) node failures are such types. However, due to the *FLP impossibility proof* by Fischer et al. [24], we defer the task of handling these to the control layer of the communication protocol (e. g. as in [23]), and do not consider them in our study. Similarly, examining the adaptivity of an approach with respect to e. g. dynamically changing search spaces or optimization goals is an interesting aspect. For the former, we refer to the ongoing work in [6] and [25]. For the latter, a respective study is presented in [26, in press].

5 Evaluation

The objective of the paper at hand is to evaluate the effects of variation on collaborative MAS solving the MC-COP. For this, we will focus on the sources of variation introduced in Sect. 4 one by one, each with respect to the different solution strategies presented in Sect. 3. We do not study second order effects in this paper, hence the parameters are analyzed independently from each other. In general, we consider three different effect types: solution quality, run-time and communication expenses.

In cases where the arising effects are straightforward and easy to derive, we argue verbally about them. For the remaining cases, we present results from respective simulation experiments. These have been conducted using a system that is capable of simulating an asynchronous MAS with configurable parameters matching the considered sources of variation. But instead of restricting our study to the motivating use case, e. g. by simulating different types of DER, we use synthetic problem instances. This has the advantage that the inherent properties of the problem instances are known beforehand, so that simulation results can be interpreted independently from specific use cases. More specifically, we tailored the problem instance $P(m, n, q)_{h/s}$ from [27] for our problem. Originally, the problem instances in [27] were designed for the multiple-choice knapsack problem (MC-KP). But as the MC-COP defined in (1) is closely related to the MC-KP (more specifically, the MC-COP is a generalized multiple-choice subset sum problem, MC-SSP, which in turn corresponds to the MC-KP without profits), we can reuse the construction method easily by neglecting the profit values that are present in the MC-KP. To preserve consistency with the referred work, we use the very same parameter values for m, n and q for constructing our problem instances as in [27, Sect. 5]. Following, the considered instances then comprise $m = 10$ agents with each $n = 5$ available elements to choose from. Referring to the symbols defined in Sect. 2, this means that $\forall a_i : S_i = \{\theta_{i1}, \ldots, \theta_{i5}\}$. The parameter $q = 5$ defines the dimensionality of the elements, i. e. in our use case, the schedules of each agent would span a planning horizon of 5 intervals. Finally, the parameter h determines the position of the optimization target ζ in the solution space of the optimization problem, which is divided into S partitions. In our study, we set $S = 100$, and treat h as random variable that is uniformly distributed over $[1, S]$, such that the actual optimization goal varies with each executed simulation run. In summary, using fixed values for m, n and q, while applying varying values for h, yields problem instances that are directly comparable due to their identical basic structure, but nonetheless allow us to derive statistically sound conclusions. For more details on the construction of the problem instances, especially on how to define the concrete values of ζ and the elements θ_{ij}, please refer to [27, Sect. 4].

The considered sources of variation are each modeled as a stochastic process (which will be described in more detail in the respective sections below), thus we repeated each experiment for 100 times. An *experiment* is thereby defined as a specific parameter setting for the considered source of variation, i. e. the amount of variation that we impose on the system. For each variation type, the examined range of this amount is chosen such that the resulting effects could be clearly identified, respectively. Within each experiment, for each executed simulation, we recorded the number of simulation steps until the heuristic terminated and the total number of exchanged messages during the whole process. Additionally, the quality of the final solution is calculated according to (1a) for each simulation. This calculated value is then normalized regarding the theoretically best and worst solution possible (which in turn have been calculated using an exhaustive search method in advance). Thus, in the following, solution quality is expressed as remaining error in the range $[0, 1]$, i. e. as normalized distance between the final solution and the optimization target, so that lower values denote better solutions. Please note that a preliminary study using similar performance indicators has been published in [28]. However, that work focused on the CO-HDA heuristic only and is based on a simulation scenario specific for the use case of scheduling DER. Moreover, the interpretation of the results has been done there on a qualitative level only. In order to gain resilient knowledge about the effects of variation, we re-enacted the study using synthetic problem instances as described above. Further, we performed a regression analysis on the resulting data series to examine the effects quantitatively.

For each simulation experiment, we show a figure containing the results for the three performance indicators solution quality, run-time and communication expenses as boxplots, where the respective box spans from the upper to the lower quartile of the results. The median is shown as horizontal line within a box, whereas the whiskers span over $1.5 \times$ the interquartile range. Additionally, the average is denoted with a star marker and outliers are illustrated by plus markers.

Table 1. Transformations used in the linear regression tests

Method	Transformations	Regression equation	Predicted value
Logarithmic model	lin-log	$y = \beta_0 + \beta_1 \cdot \ln x$	$\hat{y} = \beta_0 + \beta_1 \cdot \ln x$
Power model	log-log	$\ln y = \beta_0 + \beta_1 \cdot \ln x$	$\hat{y} = e^{\beta_0} \cdot x^{\beta_1}$
Linear	lin-lin	$y = \beta_0 + \beta_1 \cdot x$	$\hat{y} = \beta_0 + \beta_1 \cdot x$
Quadratic model	sqrt-lin	$\sqrt{y} = \beta_0 + \beta_1 \cdot x$	$\hat{y} = (\beta_0 + \beta_1 \cdot x)^2$
Exponential model	log-lin	$\ln y = \beta_0 + \beta_1 \cdot x$	$\hat{y} = e^{\beta_0 + \beta_1 \cdot x}$

In the subsequent regression analysis, the goal was to identify the exact intercorrelation between the respective source of variation and each of the performance indicators. For that, we took the medians of each recorded data series, and applied different variable transformations to the resulting series of medians for each experiment, which are summarized in Tab. 1. For each transformed data series, we then performed a standard linear regression and calculated the according coefficients of determination $R^2 \in [0, 1]$ based on Pearson's correlation coefficient R. For a given data series, the transformation method that yields the highest R^2 for this data then describes the estimated intercorrelation model.

5.1 Communication Topologies

Depending on the considered solution strategy, varying communication topologies can have a more or less severe impact. For example, market based approaches as well as EPOS and the *Stigspace* approach all require a very specific communication topology to work properly (i. e. tree topologies in the former two cases and a star topology in the latter one). Hence, to be able to cope with arbitrary topologies in the field, techniques like overlay networks [29] have to be implemented in order to overcome the inherent restrictions of these approaches. Due to the thereby induced routing overhead, arbitrary communication topologies will result in possibly longer transmission times, but will have no *direct* effect on solution quality, run-time and communication expenses. Thus we refer to the examination of message delays in Sect. 5.2 for these approaches.

More interesting in this regard is the COHDA approach, as this heuristic is inherently able to cope with arbitrary topologies, as long as the topology forms a connected graph. A complete graph naturally yields the fastest spreading of information in the network. But as COHDA is an asynchronous heuristic where the agents become active upon receiving updated information from their neighborhood, and subsequently send messages back into their neighborhood, such a topology also leads to a maximal number of exchanged messages. On the other hand, if all agents are connected e. g. in a ring, the system will show the opposite behavior, as each agent is able to send messages to exactly two other agents. Hence, in such a topology, information spreads more slowly while exhibiting fewer messages.

In order to gain more detailed insight into the resulting effects, we studied this in terms of the *density* of the communication topology, i. e. different sizes of neighborhoods for the agents. For this, based on the ring topology and the fully connected graph as extreme cases, we simulated different increments of link densities ϕ. This parameter is based on the definition of small world networks in [30]: Starting with a ring topology, the density of the network is increased by adding up to $n \cdot \phi$ links to the topology. This is done by randomly choosing two agents in each of the $n \cdot \phi$ iterations of this construction process, and connecting these agents if they aren't already connected in the communication topology.

The results for a series of simulations with $\phi \in \{0, 0.1, 0.5, 1, 2, 4\}$ are summarized in Fig. 1. All results in this experiment generally show the same solution quality. Hence, the quality of the solutions produced by COHDA is almost independent from the density of the communication topology. Regarding the simulation length and the amount of communication, an opposing trend between those two is visible. Obviously, if more communication links are present, the simulation terminates faster while exhibiting a larger amount of messages, and vice versa. The regression analysis for these two effects is shown in Fig. 2. In either case, both the logarithmic and the power model yield very high coefficients of determination. A closer look at the estimated model parameters reveals that, in the power model, the elasticity coefficient in both cases is quite low ($\beta_1 = 0.14$ for the simulation steps data and $\beta_1 = 0.26$ for the messages data, not shown in the figure), yielding a very similar intercorrelation in comparison to the logarithmic model (cf. Tab. 1). Therefore, the sensitivity of the simulation steps and the messages to the communication topology, respectively, decreases with increasing link density.

In summary, the link density of the underlying communication topology acts as a trade-off parameter for COHDA, resulting in either less simulation steps or less messages sent in the process of the heuristic. However, this effect is less present in topologies with larger link densities. The effect on solution quality is minimal.

5.2   Message Delays

For the evaluation of the effects due to delayed messages in the communication layer, we have to distinguish synchronous from asynchronous approaches. In the context of our study, the former are characterized by the existence of synchronization points. These define algorithmic *phases*, such that all agent's actions within a specific phase have to be completed before the next phase can start. Moreover, the agent's actions do not depend on each other within a single phase. For example, in market-based approaches as described in Sect. 3, each *call for bids* forms such a phase. The central auctioneer waits and collects proposals (and refusals) until all agents have answered. Only then the answers are being evaluated. Hence, message delays have no influence on the structural process in such a situation, and there is no effect regarding solution quality or communication expenses. But it is easy to see that message delays indeed have a proportional influence on the run-time, as they directly affect phase durations. Besides market-based approaches, the EPOS approach is synchronous as well and thus shows the same effects.

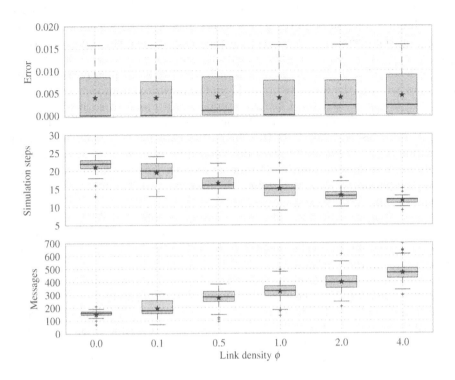

Fig. 1. Simulation results for different link densities in the COHDA approach

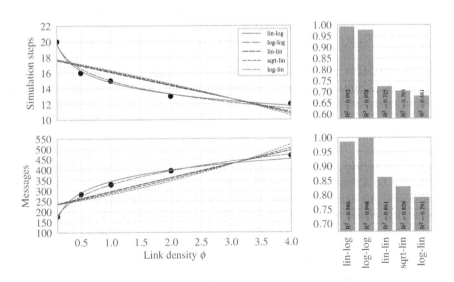

Fig. 2. Regression results for different link densities in the COHDA approach

On the other hand, asynchronous approaches are characterized by the absence of synchronization points. In these approaches, message delays can have a severe impact on the overall progress, because they may change the order of actions that exert influence on each other. In extreme cases, even the order of messages sent by a single agent can be disturbed, such that two subsequently transmitted messages arrive in the opposite order. From the presented approaches in Sect. 3, both the *Stigspace* and the COHDA approach are prone to such effects. For evaluating these, we set up our simulation environment as follows: The delivery of sent messages is delayed by the simulation core for a random number of simulation steps. The actual delay is determined for each message at runtime by calculating a uniformly distributed random number from the interval $[1, d_{max}]$. Hence, the parameter d_{max} determines the maximal possible message delay per simulation run. We studied $d_{max} \in \{1, 2, \ldots, 10\}$.

For the *Stigspace* approach, the results are quite sobering. With no message delays, the approach exhibits synchronous behavior: All agents first read the *Stigspace* in parallel and subsequently write their adapted solutions (i.e. schedule selections in the considered use case) back into the *Stigspace*. As there is no further coordination mechanism, the system shows no convergence in this case. Instead, in almost half of the simulation runs, the system started oscillating between some solutions. In the other half of the simulation runs no oscillations occured, but no trends towards superior solutions were visible either, such that no convergence was possible and the simulations had to be stopped manually. By introducing message delays as defined above, the access to the *Stigspace* is partially being desynchronized, which effectively prevents oscillations, but still shows no convergence. Only in the other extreme, i.e. configurations with very large message delays in the order of $d_{max} \approx m = 10$, a slight trend towards optimal solutions becomes visible. This indicates that the approach operates properly only with a *sequential* access paradigm for the *Stigspace*. Thus we conclude that the approach is not capable of handling variation in form of message delays at all.

For the COHDA approach, the results of the simulation study are summarized in Fig. 3. Similar to the experiment regarding varying link densities, all results in this experiment generally show the same solution quality with no noticeable trend. Hence, the quality of the solutions produced by COHDA is almost independent from possible message delays induced by the underlying communication technology. The run-time of the heuristic in terms of simulation steps rises constantly with increasing delays, while the amount of sent messages seems to converge to a fixed value. More information on this reveals the according regression analysis in Fig. 4. These results show a linear intercorrelation between message delays and simulation steps. Similar to the experiment regarding varying link densities, the most likely intercorrelation models regarding the effect of message delays on the amount of sent messages are both the logarithmic model and the power model. The power model here is estimated with a quite small elasticity coefficient $\beta_1 = 0.25$ and thus again rather describes a logarithmic intercorrelation.

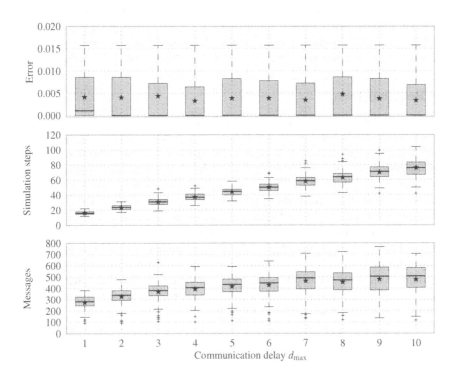

Fig. 3. Simulation results for different message delays in the COHDA approach

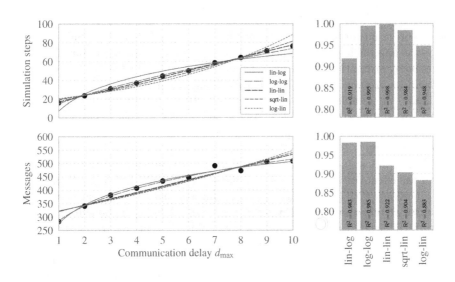

Fig. 4. Regression results for different message delays in the COHDA approach

In summary, the message delays induced by the underlying communication technology have a direct proportional influence of run-time of the COHDA approach in terms of simulation steps, while the amount of sent messages is less sensitive to this sort of variation. The effect on solution quality is minimal.

5.3   Reaction Delays

We define reaction delays as follows: In the progress of an approach, messages between agents are being delivered without delay, but instead the receiving agent will wait for a certain amount of time before processing the contents of the received message. As a side effect, an agent might receive multiple messages before it processes them all at once. Similar to message delays, we have to distinguish synchronous from asynchronous approaches in order to evaluate the effects of varying reaction delays. At first glance, reaction delays seem to have the same effects as message delays: For the synchronous approaches, there is no effect on the structural process, i.e. neither on solution quality nor on communication expenses, because the agent's actions within the same algorithmic phase are independent from each other (cf. Sect. 5.2). But again the run-time will increase proportionally with increasing reaction times due to the larger phase durations.

For the considered asynchronous approaches, we again have to look at the actual behavior of the approaches in simulation. Hence, in our simulation study, the actions of agents upon incoming messages are delayed by the simulation core for a random number of simulation steps. This is realized quite similar to the message delays above by calculating a uniformly distributed random number from the interval $[1, r_{max}]$ as reaction delay. Hence, the parameter r_{max} determines the maximal possible delay per simulation run. We studied $r_{max} \in \{1, 2, \ldots, 10\}$.

Simulations of the *Stigspace* approach show the very same behavior as with message delays. So indeed, for this approach, there is no difference between both sources of variation. Following the results from Sect. 5.2, we conclude that the *Stigspace* approach was designed with asynchronicity in mind, but lacks the necessary coordination mechanism to actually be able to handle the variation that will be present in a true asynchronous environment.

Finally, the simulation results for the COHDA approach regarding reaction delays are summarized in Fig. 5. Again, all results in this experiment generally show the same solution quality, and no specific correlation to the amount of reaction delays is visible. Hence, the quality of the solutions produced by COHDA is almost independent from differing reaction delays of the agents. Similar to the effects of varying message delays, the run-time in terms of simulation steps increases with larger reaction delays. Interestingly, the amount of messages *decreases* at the same time. Obviously, the COHDA heuristic benefits from variation by differing processing speeds in the deployed agents regarding the amount of coordination that is needed to converge to a joint solution in the collaborative MAS. The regression analysis for this experiment (see Fig. 6) again reveals a linear intercorrelation between reaction delays and simulation steps. Regarding the amount of sent messages, a logarithmic decrease is detected, indicating a less sensitivity here in comparison to the simulation steps.

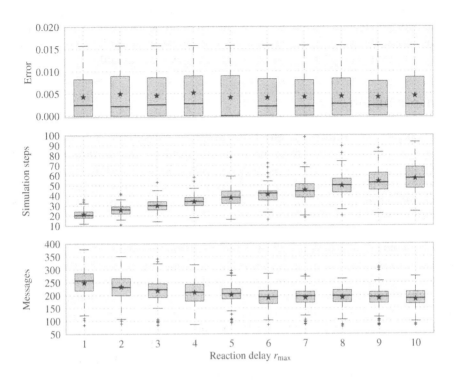

Fig. 5. Simulation results for different reaction delays in the COHDA approach

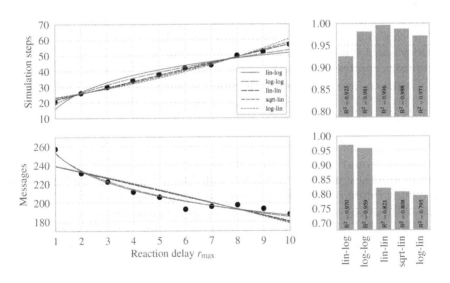

Fig. 6. Regression results for different reaction delays in the COHDA approach

In summary, the varying reaction delays induced by differing processing speeds in the deployed agents have a direct proportional influence on run-time in terms of simulation steps, while the amount of sent messages actually decreases with larger variation. The effect on solution quality again is minimal.

6   Conclusion

In this paper, we studied the effects of variation on collaborative multi-agent systems solving a combinatorial optimization problem. Our work is motivated by the use case of scheduling distributed energy resources within self-organized virtual power plants. For this, we presented the multiple-choice combinatorial optimization problem, MC-COP, and described four different solution strategies for such a task.

Our study is focused on the sources of variation that are likely to be faced in deployed field applications: arbitrary communication topologies, varying message delays, and differing reaction delays of the participating agents. In cases where the resulting effects were not obvious, we performed simulation experiments using a simulation system that is capable of simulating the considered variation types. We used synthetic problem instances that allowed us to interpret the simulation results independently from any specific use case. The simulation results were analyzed using descriptive statistics for determining qualitative properties regarding the general type of influence for each source of variation on the three performance indicators solution quality, run-time and amount of transferred messages, respectively. Further, regression analyses have been performed to detect the quantitative intercorrelations between those properties.

To interpret the results of our study, we categorized the presented solution strategies into synchronous and asynchronous approaches. Our findings indicate that synchronous and asynchronous approaches behave quite differently: Due to the existence of synchronization points, the structural process of the considered synchronous approaches is unaffected by both message delays and reaction delays. Therefore, those approaches only suffer in terms of run-time penalties from these types of variation. In contrast, the presented asynchronous approaches do not have inherent synchronization points, such that their structural process directly depends on the order of exchanged messages. The order is affected by both message delays and reaction delays. In the *Stigspace* approach, this effectively inhibits convergence and renders the approach infeasible in such situations. The COHDA approach, however, is able to handle these delays quite well: The solution quality exhibited by COHDA is almost independent from each considered source of variation, rendering the heuristic very robust in this regard. Both communication delays and reaction delays affect the run-time of the heuristic directly proportional, while the amount of messages is less sensitive to these delays. Interestingly, the amount of messages increases with larger communication delays, but decreases with larger reaction delays. This indicates that COHDA actually benefits from that source of variation regarding communication expenses. Moreover, from the considered approaches, COHDA is the only one that supports varying communication topologies. Here, the link density of the underlying communication network acts as a trade-off with respect to both simulation length and messages, where a higher density yields a faster convergence using more messages, and vice versa.

Our contribution intended to extend the research line of the influence of variation on multi-agent systems started by Campbell et al. [9], which was subsequently followed up by Anders et al. [10]. In summary, our study indicates that, depending on the type of the solution strategy, variation can have more or less severe impacts. Synchronous approaches tend to be robust against the considered sources of variation, but compensate this with increasing run-time. Asynchronous approaches, while having other advantages, are more prone to these factors. In this regard, the *Stigspace* approach suffers heavily from variation, whereas the COHDA approach was explicitly designed to overcome the difficulties induced by variation, and in one case actually benefits from it. But as we analyzed the effects from the considered sources of variation independently from each other, future work would be to study higher order effects as well.

We conclude that, in order to build reliable systems, the potential effects of variation should directly be accounted for when constructing collaborative MAS for field applications. Especially asynchronous approaches should be designed with care, as those can exert their possible benefits over synchronous approaches to the full extent only if the targeted environment is carefully considered in the design of the approach. Although we presented our work in the context of a specific use case, the general methodology of studying the considered sources of variation by conducting parameter variation experiments based on synthetic problem instances, followed by regression analyses, is applicable to a wide range of algorithms. We suggest adopting this methodology as a guideline for future developments that are targeted at field applications.

Acknowledgments. The simulations for this contribution were performed at the HPC Cluster HERO, located at the University of Oldenburg (Germany) and funded by the DFG through its Major Research Instrumentation Programme (INST 184/108-1 FUGG) and the Ministry of Science and Culture (MWK) of the Lower Saxony State.

We thank the anonymous reviewers and the program committee chairman for their detailed comments.

References

1. Ferber, J.: Multi-Agent Systems: Introduction to Distributed Artificial Intelligence. Addison-Wesley – An Imprint of Pearson Education (1999)
2. Shehory, O., Kraus, S.: Methods for task allocation via agent coalition formation. Artificial Intelligence 101(1-2), 165–200 (1998)
3. Shehory, O., Kraus, S.: Feasible formation of coalitions among autonomous agents in nonsuperadditive environments. Computational Intelligence 15(3), 218–251 (1999)

4. Griffiths, N., Luck, M.: Coalition formation through motivation and trust. In: Proc. of the 2nd Int. Joint Conf. on Autonomous Agents and Multiagent Systems, pp. 17–24. ACM (2003)

5. Tröschel, M., Appelrath, H.-J.: Towards reactive scheduling for large-scale virtual power plants. In: Braubach, L., van der Hoek, W., Petta, P., Pokahr, A. (eds.) MATES 2009. LNCS, vol. 5774, pp. 141–152. Springer, Heidelberg (2009)

6. Nieße, A., Lehnhoff, S., Tröschel, M., Uslar, M., Wissing, C., Appelrath, H.J., Sonnenschein, M.: Market-Based Self-Organized Provision of Active power and Ancillary services: An Agent-Based Approach for Smart Distribution Grids. In: Complexity in Engineering (COMPENG) (2012)

7. Beer, S., Sonnenschein, M., Appelrath, H.J.: Towards a Self-Organization Mechanism for Agent Associations in Electricity Spot Markets. In: Heiß, H.U., Pepper, P., Schlingloff, H., Schneider, J. (eds.) Informatik 2011 – Proceedings der 41. GI-Jahrestagung. GI-Edition – Lecture Notes in Informatics (LNI), pp. P-191. Bonner Köllen Verlag (2011)

8. Ashby, W.: Requisite variety and its implications for the control of complex systems. Cybernetica 1(2), 83–99 (1958)

9. Campbell, A., Riggs, C., Wu, A.S.: On the impact of variation on self-organizing systems. In: Fifth IEEE International Conference on Self-Adaptive and Self-Organizing Systems (SASO 2011), pp. 119–128. IEEE Computer Society (2011)

10. Anders, G., Hinrichs, C., Siefert, F., Behrmann, P., Reif, W., Sonnenschein, M.: On the Influence of Inter-Agent Variation on Multi-Agent Algorithms Solving a Dynamic Task Allocation Problem under Uncertainty. In: Sixth IEEE International Conference on Self-Adaptive and Self-Organizing Systems (SASO 2012), pp. 29–38. IEEE Computer Society (2012)

11. UCTE: UCTE Operation Handbook – Policy 1: Load-Frequency Control and Performance. Technical Report UCTE OH P1, Union for the Co-ordination of Transmission of Electricity (2009)

12. Abarrategui, O., Marti, J., Gonzalez, A.: Constructing the active european power grid. The Online Journal on Power and Energy Engineering (OJPEE) 1(4) (2010)

13. Hinrichs, C., Lehnhoff, S., Sonnenschein, M.: A Decentralized Heuristic for Multiple-Choice Combinatorial Optimization Problems. In: Operations Research Proceedings 2012, pp. 297–302. Springer (2014)

14. Lisovich, M.A., Mulligan, D.K., Wicker, S.B.: Inferring Personal Information from Demand-Response Systems. IEEE Security & Privacy Magazine 8(1), 11–20 (2010)

15. AlAbdulkarim, L., Lukszo, Z.: Integrating information security requirements in critical infrastructures: smart metering case. International Journal of Critical Infrastructures 6(2), 187–209 (2010)

16. Chapman, A.C., Rogers, A., Jennings, N.R., Leslie, D.S.: A unifying framework for iterative approximate best-response algorithms for distributed constraint optimization problems. The Knowledge Engineering Review 26(4), 411–444 (2011)

17. Kok, J.K., Warmer, C.J., Kamphuis, I.G.: Powermatcher: Multiagent control in the electricity infrastructure. In: Proceedings of the fourth international joint conference on Autonomous agents and multiagent systems (AAMAS 2005). ACM Press (2005)

18. Wedde, H.F., Lehnhoff, S., Rehtanz, C., Krause, O.: Bottom-Up Self-Organization of Unpredictable Demand and Supply under Decentralized Power Management. In: 2008 Second IEEE International Conference on Self-Adaptive and Self-Organizing Systems, pp. 74–83. IEEE (2008)

19. Anders, G., Siefert, F., Steghöfer, J.P., Seebach, H., Nafz, F., Reif, W.: Structuring and Controlling Distributed Power Sources by Autonomous Virtual Power Plants. In: IEEE Power and Energy Student Summit (PESS 2010). IEEE Power & Energy Society (2010)

20. Pournaras, E., Warnier, M., Brazier, F.M.: Local agent-based self-stabilisation in global resource utilisation. International Journal of Autonomic Computing 1(4) (2010)

21. Li, J., Poulton, G., James, G.: Coordination of Distributed Energy Resource Agents. Applied Artificial Intelligence 24(5), 351–380 (2010)

22. Horowitz, S.H., Phadke, A.G.: Power System Relaying, 3rd edn. John Wiley & Sons Ltd. (2008)

23. Geelen, D., van Kempen, G., van Hoogstraten, F., Liotta, A.: A wireless mesh communication protocol for smart-metering. In: 2012 International Conference on Computing, Networking and Communications (ICNC), pp. 343–349. IEEE (2012)

24. Fischer, M.J., Lynch, N.A., Paterson, M.S.: Impossibility of distributed consensus with one faulty process. Journal of the ACM 32(2), 374–382 (1985)

25. Nieße, A., Sonnenschein, M.: Using Grid Related Cluster Schedule Resemblance for Energy Rescheduling. In: Donnellan, B., Martins, J.A., Helfert, M., Krempels, K.H. (eds.) SMARTGREENS 2013 – 2nd International Conference on Smart Grids and Green IT Systems, pp. 22–31. INSTICC Press (2013)

26. Hinrichs, C., Lehnhoff, S., Sonnenschein, M.: Paving the Royal Road for Complex Systems: On the Influence of Memory on Adaptivity. In: Pelster, A., Wunner, G. (eds.) International Symposium Selforganization in Complex Systems: The Past, Present, and Future of Synergetics, Springer (in press)

27. Han, B., Leblet, J., Simon, G.: Hard Multidimensional Multiple Choice Knapsack Problems, an Empirical Study. Computers & Operations Research 37(1), 172–181 (2010)

28. Hinrichs, C., Sonnenschein, M., Lehnhoff, S.: Evaluation of a Self-Organizing Heuristic for Interdependent Distributed Search Spaces. In: Filipe, J., Fred, A. (eds.) International Conference on Agents and Artificial Intelligence (ICAART 2013), vol. 1, pp. 25–34. INSTICC Press (2013)

29. Doval, D., O'Mahony, D.: Overlay Networks: A Scalable Alternative for P2P. IEEE Internet Computing 7(4), 79–82 (2003)

30. Strogatz, S.: Exploring complex networks. Nature 410(6825), 268–276 (2001)

Complexity Measurement of Multi-Agent Systems

Toufik Marir[1], Farid Mokhati[1,2], Hassina Bouchelaghem-Seridi[3],
and Zouheyr Tamrabet[1]

[1] Department of Mathematics and Computer Science, University of Oum El Bouaghi, Algeria
{marir.toufik,mokhati,tamrabet.zouheyr}yahoo.fr
[2] LAMIS Laboratory, University of Tebessa, Algeria
[3] Department of Computer Science, LABGED Laboratory, University of Annaba, Algeria
seridi@labged.net

Abstract. Multi-Agent Systems (MAS) is a promising software paradigm. Considered as a natural metaphor to modeling complex systems, MAS are applied to develop a wide range of applications. However, the developed system's complexity is a hard obstacle to understand and maintain them. In this paper, some metrics are presented to measure the complexity of MAS. The proposition of these metrics is passed through the proposition of a complexity model for MAS. To validate our proposal, a tool has been developed to measure the JADE-based applications complexity. Furthermore, the collected metrics can also be used as a base to estimate the required effort to maintain *JADE*-based applications.

Keywords: Multi-Agent Systems, Complexity, Measurement, JADE.

1 Introduction

Multi-Agent Systems (MAS) is a promising software paradigm. It is applied nowadays to develop a wide range of applications from games to space shuttles. Specifically, we can consider it as an ideal paradigm to develop complex systems [1]. In fact, this paradigm provides several characteristics which allow modeling complex systems in natural way. The distribution of execution, the flexibility of agents and the richness of interaction's modes are examples of characteristics that motivate the use of such paradigm to develop complex systems.

The complexity notion is associated to the difficulty degree to understand a system [2]. This notion is a key factor in the development cost estimation and effort [3]. Moreover, it influences the understandability of developed software product. Consequently, the software product complexity has an impact on the maintenance effort and cost. Therefore, measuring the complexity of software product can be used as an indicator to estimate the required effort during the maintenance phase.

We think that the above characteristics of MAS (distribution, flexibility and richness of interaction's modes) can deepen the complexity effects. For example, the flexibility of agents makes their behaviors unpredictable and the understandability of developed system more difficult. Thus, the maintenance phase becomes more

J.P. Müller, M. Weyrich, and A.L.C. Bazzan (Eds.): MATES 2014, LNAI 8732, pp. 188–201, 2014.
© Springer International Publishing Switzerland 2014

complex. We address in this work the measurement of the complexity of MAS code. We propose a metrics that can be used as means to assess a developed MAS or as an indicator to estimate the required effort during the maintenance process. Before going ahead to the metrics presentation, we must first explain the proposed model for the complexity of MAS in order to identify the different facades affecting it. A tool has been developed to collect the proposed metrics for *JADE* platform.

The remainder of this paper is organized as follow: some related works are presented in section 2. Section 3 is devoted to present a model for the complexity of MAS followed by the presentation of proposed metrics to assess it (in section 4). In section 5 we present a tool we developed for collecting automatically the above metrics. Section 6 discusses our actual research, draws some conclusions and gives some future work directions.

2   Related Works

The complexity of software is a *critical question* during all the software development phases. Consequently, it has been studied quite a long time. McCabe [4] proposed one of the influential metrics to measure the complexity of software, called the *cyclomatic number*. This measure allows, among others, to estimate the required effort to understand the software code. *Although* it is old, this metric is still used in new works [5].

It seems evident that MAS, as a software paradigm, require their own development approaches [6]. Especially, we are in need to specific metrics to measure the different aspects of agent-based software. Several proposed metrics are presented by Dumke et al. [7].Measuring the complexity of agent-based software is our main purpose in this paper. We think that measuring the complexity can be used as an indicator to control the development of agent-based software and estimate the required effort to maintain it.

In the MAS field, the complexity has been studied across different points of view. Some studies targeted the computational complexity of MAS [8, 9]; others studied the complexity of MAS code [10, 11]. Our work shares the same goal with this second category of studies. The complexity of mobile agents implemented with *AspectJ* is studied by Dospisil [10]. The proposed metrics are based on the entropy measure. This work is mainly devoted to study the influence of implementing the interaction between mobile agents using *AspectJ* on the complexity of the developed software. Thus, we believe that the limited context of this study (the mobile agents implemented with *AspectJ*) affects negatively the proposed metrics applicability for general MAS.

In order to compare agent-based simulation to other simulation paradigms, Klügl [11] proposed metrics to measure the complexity of multi-agent simulations. These metrics can be classified into three categories: the overall system-level, the agent-level and the agent-system-level metrics. Many metrics are proposed for each level. The *Number of Agent Types*, the *Number of Resources Types* and the *Maximum Number of Agents* are examples of overall system-level metrics. The proposed metrics are closely related to simulation models (i.e., by considering the specificities of these models). Hence, relation between the model and the original system should be considered [11].

The author noted that the list of metrics is not complete. However, we believe that the lack of important metrics that affect significantly the complexity of MAS (like the interaction between agents) is a real drawback. Several missed metrics are more significant than the presented ones. Moreover, he emphasized that some metrics (like the *Size of Procedural Knowledge*) can be measured only for some kinds of MAS. In fact, MAS can be implemented using various software paradigms (such as the object-oriented programming or the knowledge-based systems). We think that it is important to consider the used software paradigm specificities in implementing MAS in order to propose metrics. Obviously, the software paradigm used to implement MAS can influence not only the metrics proposition but also the measurement method used to collect the metrics. The ISO/IEC 9126 quality standard [12] considered the measurement method as an essential part of metrics. Nonetheless, this aspect is omitted in the above work.

We think that the proposition of the three levels of complexity (overall system-level, agent-level and agent-system-level) is important to analyze and understand the complexity of MAS. Even if the existence of the three levels is justified for simulation models, it is not the case for general MAS. In fact, MAS are defined as a set of interacting agents in an environment. Consequently, we see that the agent-system-level is a natural part of overall system-level.

As conclusion, designed for agent-based simulations, the proposed metrics cannot be used for any other agent-based software. Consequently, it seems important to propose metrics to assess the complexity of MAS. As it is shown above, the complexity metrics can be used to evaluate a developed MAS. Therefore, the complexity metrics provide strong base to plan the maintenance phase. In order to propose the complexity metrics, firstly, we should specify the complexity notion of MAS. The next section is devoted to present a complexity model of MAS.

3   Complexity Model for Multi-Agent Systems

Before starting the measurement of the complexity of multi-agent systems, we should formulate the complexity concept. This concept should also be specified by considering the features of multi-agent systems.

One of the most accepted definition of the complexity is proposed by IEEE in the Standard Glossary of Software Engineering Terminology [2] as "*the degree to which a system or component has a design or implementation that is difficult to understand and verify*". Thus, the complexity is closely related to the required effort to understand, verify and maintain a software product. However, given a general statement, like the definition proposed by IEEE, is not enough. This definition did not give the possible causes that can influence the difficulty to understand software product. Therefore, we propose a model of the complexity concept in the MAS context. The proposed model simplifies the understanding and studying the MAS complexity.

MAS can be informally defined as a set of interacting agents in an environment. Naturally, the number of agents and interaction between them are the main factors that influence the MAS complexity. Furthermore, at the lower granularity level, the agent is not an atomic entity. Accordingly, the complexity of agents has a direct influence on the MAS complexity. To conclude, the MAS complexity may be viewed at two distinguished levels: agent-level and system-level (Fig. 1). By the agent-level complexity we intend to study, separately, the complexity of each agent (without taking its interaction with other agents into account). On the other side, the system-level specifies the complexity of the environment and the interaction between agents.

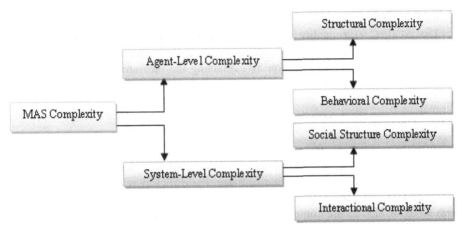

Fig. 1. A complexity model for multi-agent systems

The agent-level complexity can be analyzed using two orthogonal criteria: the complexity of the agent's structure and the complexity of agent's behaviors. The complexity of the agent's structure represents the internal elements composed the agent including the complexity of its knowledge. Obviously, the behavioral complexity is the complexity of the different behaviors implemented inner the agent in order to achieve its goal.

At the system-level, the complexity is composed of the social's structure complexity and the interactional complexity. The social structure indicates the global structure of the MAS. It encompasses all the agents composing the MAS and the objects that exist in its environment. The interactional complexity designates the collective behavior of the MAS. The collective behavior of this latter is ensured by the direct interaction between agents or the indirect interaction between them through the manipulation of the environment objects.

After specifying the complexity model of MAS, we should propose some metrics in order to measure each of the four components of our model: structural, behavioral, social structure and interactional complexities. The next section is devoted to this purpose.

4   Measuring the Complexity of Multi-Agent Systems

Modeling the complexity concept of MAS is the first step to assess it. This step should be followed by the proposition of metrics in order to measure, objectively, the complexity of the developed MAS. According to Alonso et *al.* [13], the measurement of metrics in MAS field is closely dependent on the implementation paradigm used to develop this system. Because the MAS can be implemented using various software paradigms (object-oriented paradigm, knowledge-base systems, etc), it seems hard difficult to propose adequate metrics for all these software paradigms. Consequently, we propose in this paper, only some metrics for MAS which are implemented using the object-oriented paradigm. As we will present bellow, the presented metrics will be applied to *JADE* platform.

The ISO/IEC 9126 quality standard [12] emphasized that the specification of the measurement method is essential in the proposition of metrics. According to this recommendation, we start this section by explaining the measurement method used in assessing the proposed metrics.

4.1   The Measurement Method

In software engineering, the metrics can be static or dynamic. The static metrics are assessed without executing the software. On the other side, the dynamic metrics are collected during the execution of the software. For difficulty reasons with assessment of dynamic metrics, the static ones are the most used [14]. However, we think that the two kinds of metrics are complementary. For instance, in dynamic system the static analysis of code cannot give the number of agent composed the MAS. Consequently, we opted in this paper, to both static and dynamic metrics.

The static metrics are collected by analyzing the code of the MAS. Based on the different language constructors of *JAVA* and specifically *JADE* platform, we can extract useful information about the complexity of the software.

The dynamic metrics are collected thanks to the aspect paradigm [15]. This software paradigm allows us to specify the metrics independently to the MAS as aspects. The implemented metrics are woven automatically in the adequate points of the MAS in order to pick up the execution trace of the software. Using the aspect paradigm we can measure the dynamic metrics without updating the code of the implemented MAS. Using *AspectJ* we can easily implement the metrics and use them with *JADE* applications.

4.2   The Proposed Metrics

This section presents the proposed metrics. Nevertheless, it is important to note that the proposition of a complete and exhaustive list of complexity metrics is beyond the scope of this paper. The proposed metrics to assess the complexity of MAS are:

1. **The structural complexity metrics:** we propose the following metrics to measure the structural complexity of agents:

   (a) *The Size of the Agent's Structure (SAS):* The agent's structure is presented using set of attributes. Generally, these attributes are used to specify the state of the agent. Consequently, increasing the number of attributes implies increasing the number of agent's states represented by the attributes combination. The variety of the agent's states influence the analysis of the agent. Thus, we use the *SAS* metric as an indicator to calculate the complexity of the agent's structure.

(b) **The Agent's Structure Granularity (ASG):** some attributes that composed the agent's structure can be objects which are composed also of attributes. Obviously, the structure of the agent will be more complex if it is composed of several composite attributes. We can represent the attributes of an agent in a tree known that its root is the agent, each node is an attribute and the leaves are the primitive attributes. Known that the height of the root is zero, this metric represents the average height of the nodes.

$$ASG = \frac{\sum_{i=1}^{k} N_i}{K-1} \qquad (1)$$

Where k is the number of the nodes in the tree, N_i is the height of the ith node. We used $(K-1)$ as the divider in this metric in order to exclude the root of the tree because it is not an attribute. If an agent has not attributes, its structure granularity becomes naturally zero.

(c) **The Dynamicity of the Agent's Structure (DAS):** in addition to the composed attributes, the ones of the agent can be of a container nature. By the container attributes we mean the attributes allowing adding and removing variables like the list. Known the number of variables encompassed in the container allows knowing exactly the size of the agent's structure. Moreover, the extensive dynamicity of the agent's structure designates instability in the agent's structure which means more complexity. Hence, the dynamicity of the agent's structure is measured by identifying the structure update between two moments.

$$DAS = \frac{SC_t - SC_{t'}}{t - t'} \qquad (2)$$

Where SC_t (respectively $SC_{t'}$) is the size of the container in the moment t (respectively t').

2. **The behavioral complexity metrics:** the behavioral complexity of the agent can be assessed using:

(a) **The Behavioral Size of the Agent (BSA):** is the number of behaviors ensured by agent. This metric gives an indicator to the degree of agent's specialization. Obviously, an agent that ensures various behaviors is more complex than the one which ensures fewer behaviors.

(b) **The Average Complexity of Behaviors:** the previous metric seems not sufficient because an agent who ensures several simple behaviors may be simpler than an agent that ensures only one complex behavior. The *JADE* platform, for example, gives the possibility to define composite behaviors. We can specify the composite behaviors by finite state machine. Hence, the complexity of a behavior can be calculated using the *cyclomatic number* proposed by McCabe [4]. Taking a composite behavior (*B*) presented by graph (*G*), its *cyclomatic complexity* (CC_B) is calculated by the equation:

$$CC_B = (E_G - N_G) + 2P_G \qquad (3)$$

Where E_G is the number of edges of the G; N_G is the number of node of G and P is the number of connected component of G. It is clear that the complexity of simple behaviors is 1. The complexity of an agent's behaviors is calculated as the average of all its behaviors.

(c) *The Average Number of Scheduled Behaviors (ANSB)*: an agent can launch several behaviors. Then, a started behavior is inserted into a scheduling list until its turn. The scheduling behaviors are those that are waiting for their execution. This mechanism is made for ensuring the concurrency in the agent's functionalities. However, this concurrency may be the cause of the difficulty to understand the functionalities of an agent which change frequently the executing behavior. Moreover, this concurrency requires managing the behaviors' priorities for ensuring coherent and validating results. In the complex systems, the management of the scheduling behaviors is a difficult task. Hence, we propose to calculate the average number of scheduling behaviors in each moment as an indicator of the concurrency intra-agent. As it is explained above, despite the advantages of the concurrency inner the agent, it represents a cause of the complexity.

3. **The social structure complexity metrics:** a MAS is composed of set of agents existing in an environment. The environment is composed of set of objects. Consequently, we can measure the complexity of the social structure of MAS by:

(a) *The Heterogeneity of Agents (HA)*: this metric indicates the number of classes of agents. We think that MAS composed of heterogeneity agents is more difficult to be understood than a homogeny MAS. Moreover, to maintain heterogeneous MAS we need to update several agents.

(b) *The Heterogeneity of the Environment's Objects (HEO)*: the environment of the MAS is composed of objects. Like the previous metric, we think that the existence of heterogeneous objects composed the environment can be considered as an indicator to the complexity of the MAS. The heterogeneity of the environment's objects metric corresponds to the number of classes of environment's objects.

(c) *The Size of the Agent's Population (SAP)*: in the MAS, the agents can be created and killed dynamically. Known that the agents operate in concurrence, increasing their number increases the complexity of the MAS. Moreover, increasing the number of agents introduces more interactions between them. Consequently, the complexity of the MAS increases.

4. **The interactional complexity metrics:** the interaction between agents is ensured directly by means of messages or indirectly by manipulating the object of the environment. We measure the interaction between agents by:

(a) *The Rate of Interaction's Code (RIC)*: this metric presents the rate of source code devoted to ensure the communication between agents. Consequently,

$$RIC = \frac{SC}{SB} \tag{4}$$

Where *SC (Size of Communication)* is the total number of line of code devoted to the communication between agents composed the MAS and *SB (Size of Behaviors)* is the size of all the behaviors of agents composed the MAS. Computing the size of communication includes all the operation related to the communication process like messages processing, sending and receiving. Despite that this metric does not give the rate of interactions because the interaction's code can be repeated several times; but it can be used as an indicator to estimate the required effort to maintain the MAS. Increasing the result of this metric means that the behaviors of agents are probably most coupled. Thus, updating the code of an agent may require updating the code of the others.

(b) *The Average of Exchanged Messages per Agent (AEMA):* as we indicate previously, the *Rate of Interaction's Code* metric gives only partial information about the collective behavior of agents because the possible repeat of the sent messages. Therefore, we propose the *Average of Exchanged Messages per Agent (AEMA)* metric to estimate the real number of exchanged messages. Obviously, this metric is of dynamic nature. Using this metric we can estimate the required effort to understand the collective behavior of the MAS. It seems evident that the higher exchanging of messages can influence the complexity, because it means the difficult to study each agent alone.

(c) *The Rate of the Environment's Accessibility (REA):* the agents can be interacting indirectly by manipulating the environment's objects. In order to apply this kind of interaction, the environment's objects should be accessible. Hence,

$$REA = \frac{NPOA}{NAOA} \tag{5}$$

Where *NPOA* is the *Number of Public Objects' Attributes* and *NAOA* is the *Number of All Objects' Attributes*. This static metric is an indicator to the complexity of the MAS because of the existing of public attributes increases the agents coupling. For that reason, it becomes difficult to understand and maintain the collective behaviors of multi-agent systems.

The above metrics are proposed to assess the complexity of MAS that are implemented using the object-oriented paradigm. A multi-agent system is firstly software. Consequently, the proposed metrics to assess the conventional software (like the size in *Line of Code* metric) can be combined with our metrics to provide more information about the complexity of agent-based software. Especially, the proposed metrics for object-oriented software (like the depth of inheritance) can be used to calculate the complexity of the environment's objects.

Naturally, the comprehensive complexity of MAS is obtained by computing the average of all the above metrics. As appropriate, we can associate to each metric a weight which reflects its importance. We think that it is difficult to propose unanimously these weights. They are left to the appreciation of the users of the proposed metrics.

5   A Tool to Assess JADE Complexity

In order to assess the complexity of *JADE*-based MAS, we developed a tool that calculates automatically the above metrics. Figure 2 illustrates the architecture of the tool
we developed.

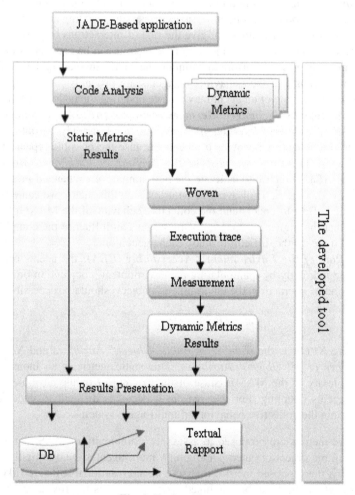

Fig. 2. Tool architecture

The measurement process passes through two phases. First, the MAS code should
be analyzed to calculate the static metrics. Calculating the static metrics is based on
the search of specific language construct of *JADE*. Second, *AspectJ* wove the developed dynamic metrics (as aspects) with the *JADE*-based software. As a result, we
obtain the execution trace of the MAS. This latter is used to measure the different
dynamic metrics. Both static and dynamic results will be presented in several forms

(textual rapport, graphical presentation and saved in data-base) for increasing the readability of the obtained results.

The following code is an example of aspect used to pick up an event during the execution of the MAS. This aspect is used in order to collect the information about the created agents. Thus, before creating an agent by the method *createNewAgent*, the aspect should be executed. In the same manner, the library of our dynamic metrics is composed of aspects to pick up the execution of the *main* method, the creation of objects, the updating of containers' size, the exchanging of messages and the scheduling of behaviors.

```
public aspect CreationOfNewAgent {
    pointcut CreationOfAgent():execution(*
            *createNewAgent(..));
    before() : CreationOfAgent(){
        // Saving information about the created agent
        }
}
```

The tool we developed has been validated using two case studies. We choose the *FSMAgent* and *ContractNet* interaction protocol examples available in [16]. The first example is to show the finite state-based behaviors. The agent executes a composite behavior which is composed of several simple behaviors. The composite behavior is presented using finite state machine. The following code presented the skeleton of the *FSMAgent*.

```
public class FSMAgent extends Agent {
  protected void setup() {
    FSMBehaviour fsm = new FSMBehaviour(this) {
      public int onEnd() {
          // the onEnd method
      }
    };
  // The composite behavior's description using the FSM
    addBehaviour(fsm);
  }
  private class NamePrinter extends OneShotBehaviour {
    //the code of the NamePrinter behavior
  }
  private class RandomGenerator extends NamePrinter {
    //the code of the RandomGenerator behavior
  }
}
```

The second example presents the implementation of the famous *Contract Net* interaction protocol. This example is composed of two classes of agents: the initiator and the participant. The *Initiator* starts its behavior by sending call for proposal to all the participants. Then, it processes the responses provided by the participants in order to select the best proposal. After the reception of a *CFP* message, a *participant* agent formulates and sends its proposition if it wants to participate in the interaction protocol, or sends a refuse message in the other case. Depending on the response of the *Initiator*, the *participant* terminates its execution if it received reject message or executes the adequate action in order to provide the results to the *Initiator*. The limited size of this paper prevents us to present the code of the *ContractNet* example. However, the complete codes of the both examples are available in [16].

Table 1 gives the results of the collected static metrics of the two examples. We omit the *Heterogeneity of the Environment's Objects (HEO)* and *the Rate of the Environment's Accessibility (REA)* metrics because their values are zero (there is no objects in the environment of the presented examples). For instance, three behaviors are specified inner the agent *FSMAgent* which is presented by the *Behavioral Size of the Agent (BSA)* metric. Because one of these behaviors is a composite behavior which is presented with finite-state machine (with eight edges and six nodes), the *Average Complexity of Behaviors* metric becomes two. This metric corresponds, as explained above, the average *cyclomatic* number of all the behaviors of the agent.

Against by the *ContractNet* example is composed of two agents with single simple behavior in each one. Consequently, its *Average Complexity of Behaviors* metric becomes one. However, we can easily remark that the *Rate of Interaction's Code (RIC)* metric of this example is 0.46. Thus, almost half of the behaviors' code of the agents composed, this example is devoted to the communication.

Table 1. The results of the static metrics

The Metrics	FSMAgent	ContractNet
The Size of the Agent's Structure (SAS)	06	0.5
The Agent's Structure Granularity (ASG)	01	0.5
The Behavioral Size of the Agent (BSA)	03	01
The Average Complexity of Behaviors	02	01
The Heterogeneity of Agents (HA)	01	02
The Rate of Interaction's Code (RIC)	00	0.46

Thanks to the aspect-oriented programming, we can capture the events execution of the *JADE*-based applications in order to calculate the dynamic metrics. Hence, we use the tool we developed to execute the two above examples. We note that the *ContractNet* example is executed with single *Initiator* and three *participants*.

Table 2 gives the execution trace of the two above examples with the corresponding dynamic metrics: *The Average of Exchanged Messages per Agent (AEMA), The Size of the Agent's Population (SAP)* and *The Average Number of Scheduled Behaviors (ANSB)*. The *Dynamicity of the Agent's Structure (DAS)* metric is omitted because it has the zero value and it does not changed during the examples execution. Obviously, this value is justified by the lack of container in the agents' structures.

For limited size reasons, we will present only the *Average of Exchanged Messages per Agent (AEMA)* metric of the *ContractNet* example. This metric starts with the zero value as is presented in Table 2. At the time 4672 ms the *Initiator* agent sent a *CFP* message to the three *participants* and the value of *AEMA* metric becomes 0.75. During the execution of the MAS this metric progresses until reaching the value 2.5 messages per agent at the time 4938 ms.

Table 2. The results of the dynamic metrics

	Time	Event	AEMA	SAP	ANSB
ContractNet	00	Starting the execution	00	00	00
	4297	Creation of the agents: *Participant_01*, *Participant_02* and *Participant_03*	00	03	00
	4375	Creation of the *Initiator* agent	00	04	00
	4422	Scheduling the behaviors of the agents: *Participant_01* and *Participant_02*	00	04	0.5
	4485	Scheduling the behavior of the agent *Participant_03*	00	04	0.75
	4672	The *Initiator* send *CFP* message to the three participants: *Participant_01*, *Participant_02* and *Participant_03*	0.75	04	0.75
	4719	Scheduling the behavior of the *Initiator*	0.75	04	1
	4766	The three participants (*Participant_01*, *Participant_02* and *Participant_03*) send their propositions	1.5	04	1
	4875	The *Initiator* agent send a response to the participants (*Participant_01*, *Participant_02* and *Participant_03*)	2.25	04	1
	4938	The agent *Participant_02* send *Inform* message to *Initiator* agent	2.5	04	1
FSMAgent	00	Starting the execution	00	00	00
	3407	Creation of the agent	00	01	00
	3422	Scheduling the behavior of the agent	00	01	01

We conclude after the above results analysis that the individual aspect is the complexity's source of the first example because it is composed of a single agent with a composite behavior. On the other side, the complexity of the second example is the result of its social aspect. The second example is composed of four agents that are instantiated from two different classes. Moreover, the interaction between these agents used most of the code. We can also remark that the results of the both kinds (static and dynamic) of metrics are not contradictory. In fact, both kinds of metrics associate the MAS complexity to the individual aspect in the first example and associate it to the social aspect in the second one. However, it will not strange to find inconsistency results between the static and dynamic metrics in some cases. Known that the two kinds of metrics are complementary, we think that a deeply analysis of all the results may conduct us to identify the real reason of the complexity.

For increasing the readability of the obtained results, our tool gives also the collected metrics using graphical presentation. Figure 3 gives the evolution of *Average of Exchanged Messages per Agent (AEMA)* metric of the *ContractNet* example explained above.

The Average of Exchanged Messages per Agent

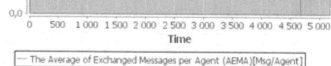

Fig. 3. The results of the *AEMA* metric of the *ContractNet* example

6   Conclusion

The software complexity is considered as an important indicator to estimate the required effort to understand and to maintain it. Recognizing its importance, this concept has been studied since the 1970s. However, the evolution of the software paradigms requires updating the complexity measurement according to the novelties provided by these paradigms. Nowadays, the multi-agent systems is one of the most applied software paradigms. Consequently, it seems very useful to measure the MAS complexity. This paper introduced a set of static and dynamic metrics in order to assess their complexity. These metrics are relative to a novel complexity model proposed for MAS. The proposed model allows simplifying and understanding the main characteristics that influence the complexity of MAS. The proposed metrics can be used, among others, as indicators to estimate the required effort to understand and maintain the implemented MAS. The proposed metrics can be calculated automatically for *JADE*-based applications using a tool we developed.

As future work directions, we plan to extend this work to support some specific kinds of multi-agent systems (e.g., mobile agent and adaptive agent). Moreover, we will target the complexity of multi-agent systems at early development stages (the specification and design of MAS).

References

1. Gutiérrez, T.N., Ciarletta, L., Chevrier, V.: Multi-Agent Simulation Based Control of Complex Systems. In: Lomuscio, A., Scerri, P., Bazzan, A., Huhns, M. (eds.) Proceedings of the 13th International Conference on Autonomous Agents and Multi-Agent Systems (AAMAS 2014), Paris, France, May 5-9 (2014)
2. IEEE: IEEE Standard Glossary of Software Engineering Terminology. IEEE Std 610.12-1990 (1990)
3. Tran-Cao, D., Abran, A., Lévesque, G.: Functional Complexity Measurement. In: International Workshop on Software Measurement (IWSM 2001), Montréal, Québec, Canada, August 28-29 (2001)
4. McCabe, T.J.: A Complexity Measure. IEEE Transactions on Software Engineering SE-2(4) (December 1976)
5. Tiwari, U., Kumar, S.: Cyclomatic Complexity Metric for Component Based Software. ACM SIGSOFT Software Engineering Notes 39(1), 1–6 (2014)
6. Gómez-Sanz, J.J., Gervais, M.P., Weiss, G.: A Survey on Agent-Oriented Oriented Soft-ware Engineering Research. In: Bergenti, F., Gervais, M.P., Zam-bonelli, F. (eds.) Methodologies and Software Engineering for Agent Systems - The Agent-Oriented Software Engineering Handbook, pp. 33–62. Springer US (2004)
7. Dumke, R., Mencke, S., Wille, C.: Quality Assurance of Agent-Based and self-Managed Systems. CRC Press (2010)
8. Dekhtyar, M., Dikovsky, A., Valiev, M.: Complexity of Multi-agent Systems Behavior. In: Flesca, S., Greco, S., Leone, N., Ianni, G. (eds.) JELIA 2002. LNCS (LNAI), vol. 2424, pp. 125–136. Springer, Heidelberg (2002)
9. Dziubiński, M., Verbrugge, R., Dunin-Kęplicz, B.: Complexity Issues in Multiagent Logics. Fundamenta Informaticae 75, 239–262 (2007)
10. Dospisil, J.: Code Complexity Metrics for Mobile Agents Implemented with Aspect/J^{TM}. In: Mařík, V., Müller, J.P., Pěchouček, M. (eds.) CEEMAS 2003. LNCS (LNAI), vol. 2691, pp. 647–657. Springer, Heidelberg (2003)
11. Klügl, F.: Measuring Complexity of Multi-Agent Simulations – An Attempt Using Metrics. In: Dastani, M., El Fallah Seghrouchni, A., Leite, J., Torroni, P. (eds.) LADS 2007. LNCS (LNAI), vol. 5118, pp. 123–138. Springer, Heidelberg (2008)
12. ISO: ISO/IEC 9126-1:2001 Software Engineering - Product Quality (2001)
13. Alonso, F., Fuertes, J.L., Martinez, L., Soza, H.: Towards a set of Measures for Evaluating Software Agent Autonomy. In: Proceedings of the Eighth Mexican International Conference on Artificial Intelligence (2009)
14. Tahir, A., Ahmad, R., Kasirun, K.M.: Maintainability Dynamic Metrics Data Collec-tion Based on Aspect-Oriented Technology. Malaysian Journal of Computer Science 23(3) (2010)
15. Kiczales, G., Lamping, J., Mendhekar, A., Maeda, C., Lopes, C.V., Loingtier, J.M., Irwin, J.: Aspect-Oriented Programming. In: Akşit, M., Matsuoka, S. (eds.) ECOOP 1997. LNCS, vol. 1241, pp. 220–242. Springer, Heidelberg (1997)
16. The Official JADE site web, http://jade.tilab.com/

Extensible Java EE-based Agent Framework in Clustered Environments

Dejan Mitrović[1], Mirjana Ivanović[1], Milan Vidaković[2], and Zoran Budimac[1]

[1] Department of Mathematics and Informatics
Faculty of Science, University of Novi Sad, Serbia
{dejan,mira,zjb}@dmi.uns.ac.rs
[2] Faculty of Technical Sciences
University of Novi Sad, Serbia
minja@uns.ac.rs

Abstract. Modern enterprise-scale applications are executed on computer clusters in order to achieve horizontal scaling, as well as uninterrupted delivery of services. However, the industry-based standards and technical solutions have rarely been utilized by agent developers. This paper presents recent research effort aimed at improving our existing *Java EE*-based agent framework in order to fully exploit the benefits of clustered computing. Among other benefits, the new architecture provides automatic agent load-balancing and fault-tolerance, without "reinventing the wheel."

1 Introduction

A computer cluster is a network of physical or virtual nodes that, from the external user's point of view, operate as a single coherent system. In the world of enterprise application development, clusters are of a special importance. They enable *high availability* of deployed applications, which is concerned with fault-tolerance, scalability, and constant, uninterrupted delivery of services, regardless of software or hardware failures [34].

Extensible Java EE-based Agent Framework (*XJAF*) is our multi-agent middleware built using the *Java Platform, Enterprise Edition* (*Java EE*) [22,30,31]. One of the driving forces behind the development of *XJAF* was to re-use existing, proven technologies of *Java EE*. While there exist many *Java*-based agent middlewares, almost all of them are based on the *Standard Edition* of Java (*Java SE*). On the other hand, *Java EE* provides many ready-made technical solutions that can be used to realize various functionalities of an agent platform [9]. The goal is, therefore, to avoid reinventing the wheel, and to embrace technologies that represent the standard for developing enterprise applications.

While previous versions of *XJAF* did successfully utilize many *Java EE* concepts and technologies, the support for clustered environments was lacking. The system was capable of operating in a distributed environment, by manually constructing a network of separate *XJAF* instances [22]. However, it did not provide high availability of agent-based applications. This paper presents recent efforts

J.P. Müller, M. Weyrich, and A.L.C. Bazzan (Eds.): MATES 2014, LNAI 8732, pp. 202–215, 2014.
© Springer International Publishing Switzerland 2014

aimed at redesigning the *XJAF* architecture in order to harness the benefits of clustered computing.

There are a number advantages that emerge from this new design approach, the two most important of which are agent load-balancing and fault-tolerance. Load-balancing is concerned with automatic distribution of *XJAF* agents across the cluster, in order to share the computational load. Fault-tolerance, on the other hand, replicates the agent state between different cluster nodes; in case of the node's failure, the agent can be restored to continue its execution elsewhere. Again, none of these features are directly implemented in *XJAF*. Rather, existing functionalities, in form of an *enterprise application server*, are used.

Although *Java EE* is mostly used to build web-based software solutions, this is not its only purpose. Enterprise applications are layered, with more front-oriented *web*, and more back-oriented *business* layers [12]. Almost all major functionalities of *XJAF* are realized in the business layer, which is completely independent of the web. It includes a range of technologies that fit into the agent-oriented programming paradigm. For example, *Java Message Service* [14] exists to provide peer-to-peer messaging, as well as the publish-subscribe communication pattern. Similarly, load-balancing and fault-tolerance of *Enterprise JavaBeans* [16], which represent agents in *XJAF*, work in the same way regardless of the nature of the caller – whether it's a remote web client, or another business-layer component.

XJAF is released as a free software, under the *Apache License, Version 2.0* [2]. The full source code of our solution, along with pre-compiled binaries, documentation, examples, etc. can be found at the *XJAF* homepage [35].

The rest of the paper is organized as follows. A comparison of *XJAF* and other, existing multi-agent solutions is given in Section 2. Section 3 describes a high-level overview of *XJAF*. A case-study and runtime evaluation of our framework are given in Section 4. Finally, overall conclusions and future research directions are outlined in Section 5.

2   Related Work

The importance of a multi-agent middleware in the wider adoption of the agent technology has been thoroughly discussed in [26]. Several key properties of a middleware have been identified, including interoperability through the adoption of well-established standards, as well as the availability of an open-source, free implementation. These are just some of the guidelines that have been taken into account during the development of *XJAF*.

As outlined in [5], a large number of multi-agent middlewares has been developed over the years; it appears that the "not-invented-here" philosophy has been especially influential among agent developers. In the end, however, only a handful of those systems are still being actively developed and/or used today. As the first step aimed at avoiding this faith for *XJAF*, and as noted earlier, the full source code of our system is freely available [35].

Agentis is one of the earliest multi-agent architectures [7, 18], built on top of the *BDI* reasoning engine *dMARS* [8]. It placed a great emphasis on agent interaction protocols, which were designed as reliable and efficient, supporting multiple concurrent executions. Agents were organized in a hierarchical fashion, and communicated using a strongly-typed language. Their capabilities were expressed in terms of *services*, complex activities initiated by external clients, an *tasks*, simpler activities used to realize services.

Cognitive Agent Architecture (*Cougaar*) is a *Java*-based distributed agent architecture specifically designed for operating in unstable settings [6]. It was developed over a number of years as a military research project, and later released as an open-source software. It is designed as a component-based architecture, with a wide-range of functionalities and a special focus on fault-tolerance. The *Persistence* component, for example, is in charge of storing agent's state to an external medium (e.g. a remote database) in order to protect it from failures. The persistence can be performed in two modes: *conservative* and *lazy*, with the latter being optimized for more stable environments. *Cougaar* consists of a number of *nodes* which act as agent hosts. A node is executed inside its own *Java VM*, and, being an agent itself, is resilient to failures through state persistence.

Cougaar offers a number of advanced features for building large-scale agent-based applications, some of which are superior to those offered by *XJAF*. However, the development of *Cougaar* has been supported by *far* more resources. One of our goals with *XJAF* is to demonstrate that many features found in *Cougaar* can now easily be implemented with much less effort, by re-using existing *Java EE* technologies.

Magentix is a multi-agent platform developed with execution performance as the primary focus [1]. It is implemented in *C* for the *Linux* operating system. Each agent is represented by a distinct *Linux* process, with 3 separate threads. The agent management sub-system can be distributed across multiple computers and can replicate information about running agents, again mainly for performance reasons. The runtime evaluation of *Magentix* has shown that it achieves a remarkable execution speed [1]. Although inevitably slower than *Magentix*, *XJAF* provides more advanced features that stem from it support for clustered environments.

JADE is probably the most stable and widely-used multi-agent framework [3]. The system is *FIPA*-compliant [11] and provides a wide range of functionalities to agent developers, either as built-in features, or through its extensive ecosystem of plug-ins. It can be used to deploy both reactive and reasoning agents. The system itself can be executed as a set of containers on top of a computer network. Fault-tolerance is achieved through both container and agent state replication processes.

There are many differences between inner workings of *JADE* and *XJAF*. By analyzing the source code of *XJAF*, for example, one can conclude that there is no messaging infrastructure implementation; instead, the underlying *Java Message Service* (*JMS*) [14] is used. The biggest difference is that *JADE* agents have to be manually distributed among the containers, whereas in *XJAF* this process is performed automatically. More concretely, an *XJAF* agent lives on top of the entire cluster, and not on a single computer. When it needs to process a message, for example, it can do so on any computer available. This design approach offers numerous benefits, as described in the next section.

The end-goal of *XJAF* is not to replace *JADE*, but to offer an alternative solution. The two systems are applicable to different scenarios. We argue that, due to its clustering features, *XJAF* represents a better solution for applications that need to launch large populations of agents (e.g. [13]), and/or need to provide high-level of fault-tolerance. For example, *JADE* consumes a single thread per agent and has a pre-fixed number of message processing threads. In *XJAF*, these numbers are increased or decreased automatically, depending on the current load. For other use-cases, using *JADE* might represent a better approach, since it consumes less resources and its usage is a bit simpler.

So far, only a few agent middlewares have been built using *Java EE*. *Agent Developing Framework* [25] employed a minimum set of *Java EE* technologies for some of its functionalities, but does not seem to be developed anymore. *Voyager* [32] is a commercial product, and more of an enterprise middleware with agent support, than a fully-featured multi-agent framework.

Whitestein LS/TS represents a comprehensive set of development tools, a *UML*-based modeling language, and a high-level *Java* library for writing and deploying agents [27]. It is offered in three different editions – *Personal, Business*, and *Enterprise*, with the first two running on *Java SE*, and the third one employing *Java EE* technologies. Due to the high-level library, an agent is written only once and can run on any of the editions. The *Enterprise* edition can be run on top of a computer cluster in order to provide fault-tolerance. However, since this edition is a commercial product, a deeper comparison with *XJAF* could not be provided.

3   XJAF Architecture

The new version of *XJAF* follows the same design philosophy of earlier implementations [22, 30, 31]. The framework is organized as a set of loosely-coupled components called *managers*. Each manager is dedicated to handling a distinct part of the overall functionality. A manager is represented and used only by its interface, and even multiple implementations of the same interface can be active simultaneously. This design approach offers the highest level of flexibility, and allows third-party re-implementations of individual components.

In this latest incarnation, *XJAF* includes *agent, message*, and *connection* managers. Their high-level functionalities are very similar to those found in the earlier versions: agent manager controls the agent life-cycle, message manager handles the inter-agent communication, while the connection manager is in charge of maintaining networks of distributed *XJAF*s [30, 31]. Internal workings of managers have, however, been significantly updated, in order to accommodate new clustered environments, and fully exploit the capabilities of the modern *JBoss* enterprise application server.

3.1 Agent Management

XJAF agents are developed and deployed as *Enterprise JavaBeans* (*EJBs*, or simply, *beans*) [16]. *EJBs* are server-side *Java EE* components that implement the business logic of an application. They can be categorized as *message-driven* or *session*. Message-driven beans are used as receivers in the *JMS*-based communication [14]. *Session* beans can further be categorized as *singleton*, *stateless*, and *stateful* [16].

An agent in *XJAF* is mapped to either a stateless or a stateful session bean. The choice of which category to use has an implication on the agent's runtime behavior, as described in the next sub-section. For a deeper discussion on stateless and stateful beans and their usage in agent development see e.g. [21, 24].

It has been argued that *EJBs*, as reactive components, might not be suitable for developing more complex agent architectures [19]. While, in their simpler form, our agents do operate by reacting to external messages, *XJAF* includes a service that can be used to implement more complex behavior. The idea is to register an internal timer, named *heartbeat*, to ping the agent at certain time intervals, allowing it to perform tasks when there is no external stimuli. This approach of having an external component calling pre-defined methods of the agent class is also found in other software systems for developing reasoning agents (e.g. [4]).

Each *XJAF* agent has its own thread of execution, but there is no thread-to-agent mapping. Instead, the *JBoss* server maintains a thread pool and automatically assigns threads to agents as needed. For example, when a message is received, the agent will be given a thread to process it. In the worst-case scenario, when all agents are actively executing tasks, there will be as many threads as there are agents. However, the server will try to reduce the resource consumption when possible, by, for example, deallocating threads that have not been used for a certain amount of time. Additionally, if an agent is inactive for a sufficient amount of time, it will be *passivated* [12]: removed from the runtime memory and stored on a secondary storage (e.g. the hard-disk). When needed, the agent will be re-activated to resume its execution.

The directory of agents [9] is implemented through *Java Naming and Directory Interface* (*JNDI*) [15], which also works in clustered environments. It enables any interested third-party to find details about available agents, with the support for pattern-based searches.

3.2 Clustering Capabilities of XJAF

The organization of an *XJAF* cluster is shown in Fig. 1. A single node within the cluster is described as *master*, while the others (zero or more) are described as *slaves*. Within a node, the *JBoss host controller* is used to manage the *XJAF* instance [33]. In addition, the master node can be used to remotely control the entire cluster, through the *JBoss domain controller* [33]. This is the only difference between the master and the slaves; all nodes in a cluster have the same execution priority, can directly communicate to each other, etc.

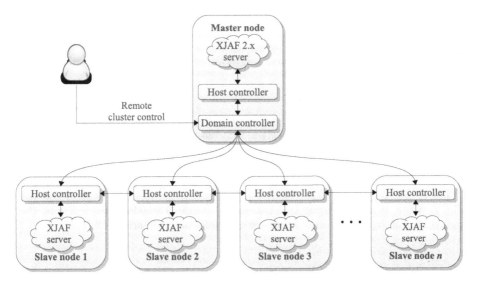

Fig. 1. *XJAF* operates in a symmetric cluster: each node is connected to every other node. A single node is recognized as the *master* and can be used to remotely control the cluster.

XJAF managers are designed to be completely independent of each other. The preferred approach of their mutual communication and information sharing is through the *Infinispan cache* system [20], as shown in Fig. 2. *Infinispan cache* is one of the core clustering technologies used by *JBoss*. It is a distributed, concurrent and highly-efficient $key \rightarrow value$ data structure. *Infinispan cache* represents the backbone of the state replication and failover process described later, but it can also store arbitrary user data. Whenever it runs a new agent, for example, the agent manager stores all the necessary information in the *Infinispan cache* (e.g. $agentIdentifier \rightarrow beanInstance$). This information can later be retrieved by the message manager to deliver a message to the agent. Since the cache is distributed across the cluster, the managers themselves can be hosted on any node. In fact, for maximum performance, they are implemented as clustered stateless beans by default.

The cluster has two main functionalities: *state replication and failover* and *load-balancing*. State replication and failover are applicable to stateful beans only. Whenever a stateful bean's internal state is changed, the replication process copies it across other nodes in the cluster. In case the bean's node becomes unavailable, the failover process fully restores the bean object on one of the remaining nodes. From the client's point of view, the entire process is executed transparently: all subsequent method invocation will end-up in the newly created object.

Two state replication modes are supported [29]: *replicated* and *distribution*. The replicated mode copies the state across all nodes in the cluster. It can withstand high failure rates, but works efficiently only in clusters that consists

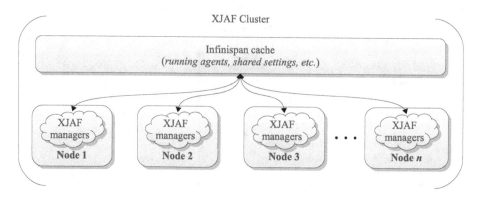

Fig. 2. *XJAF* managers, being loosely-coupled, clustered stateless beans, rely on the highly-efficient *Infinispan cache* for distributed information sharing

of up to 10 nodes [29]. The distribution mode, on the other hand, is more suitable for larger clusters, as it copies the state to a configurable number of nodes. It uses hashing algorithms and parallel execution to achieve linear scaling as more nodes are added to the cluster. The distribution mode includes other advanced features as well, such as *L1* caching [29].

Load-balancing is used to automatically distribute agents across different nodes in the cluster, and to speed up the overall runtime performance of *XJAF*. It works with both stateful and stateless beans, although the behavior is slightly different. When the client creates a new stateful bean instance, the server places it in one of the available nodes, and all subsequent invocations of the bean's methods end-up there. In case of stateless beans, the load-balancing works on a *per-method* basis. At any time, there can be many instances of the same stateless bean running in parallel across the cluster. Once the client invokes a method of the bean, one of the instances is selected to serve the request.

The described load-balancing process has a major implication on the development of agents. If an agent is based on a stateless bean, it becomes theoretically impossible to send it more than one message. Since there is no state sharing between distributed stateless beans, two consecutive messages sent to the agent might end-up in two unrelated bean instances. Even a seemingly simple operation, such as replying to the message sender, cannot be performed. Given these properties, as well as the lack of state replication and failover, stateless beans have only a limited application in *XJAF*; in the majority of cases, stateful beans should be used.

3.3 Message Management

XJAF agents communicate by exchanging messages based on the standard *FIPA Agent Communication Language* (*FIPA ACL*) [10]. The exchange is asynchronous, although a number of methods is provided to enable blocking behavior, in order to simplify agent development in certain scenarios.

Java EE includes a communication architecture named *Java Message Service* for asynchronous message exchange between loosely-coupled components. It supports two communication patterns [14]: *point-to-point*, and *publish-subscribe*. In the first pattern, a *producer* places messages in a *queue* to be processed by a single *consumer*. On the other hand, the publish-subscribe pattern is realized around a *topic*: the producer sends a message to the topic to be processed by all subscribed consumers. In *XJAF*, the communication is achieved via the point-to-point model, with the message manager acting as the producer. Messages are first consumed by message-driven beans, and then forwarded to the appropriate receiving agents.

Each agent has its own message queue, and the messages are processed in the order they are delivered. The principal message processing method, *onMessage*, is called once per each received message, in a thread-safe manner. There is no external message processing entity; the process of delivering and handling messages within the agent itself is designed in a way that enables automatic message extraction and processing.

Listing 1.1 shows two agents, named *Ping* and *Pong*, and outlines the core concepts of writing *XJAF* agents. When it receives a *request* message [10], the *Ping* agents first outputs the name of its host cluster node. Then, it makes a request to the *Pong* agent, and waits for the response in a blocking fashion. The *Pong* also outputs its physical location within the cluster, and replies to the sender.

As shown, the standard *Java EE* approach of using annotations is employed to describe the agents' properties and behavior. Therefore, both agents are implemented as *clustered* stateful beans, accessible via the remote *AgentI* interface. The *@Clustered* annotation indicates that agents will be deployed to the entire cluster, and not just a single node.

Listing 1.1. Example of stateful, clustered *Ping* and *Pong* agents

```
@Stateful
@Remote(AgentI.class)
@Clustered
public class Ping extends Agent {
  private static final long serialVersionUID = 1L;

  @Override
  protected void onMessage(ACLMessage msg) {
    if (msg.getPerformative() == Performative.REQUEST) {
      logger.info("Ping @ [" + getNodeName() + "]");
      // send a request to the Pong agent
      String pongName = msg.getContent().toString();
      AID pongAid = new AID("Pong", pongName);
      ACLMessage pongMsg=new ACLMessage(Performative.REQUEST);
      pongMsg.setSender(myAid);
      pongMsg.addReceiver(pongAid);
      msm.post(pongMsg); // msm -> message manager
      // wait for the reply in a blocking fashion
      ACLMessage reply = receiveWait(0);
      logger.info("Pong says: " + reply.getContent()); } } }
```

```
@Stateful
@Remote(AgentI.class)
@Clustered
public class Pong extends Agent {
  private static final long serialVersionUID = 1L;
  private int number = 0;

  @Override
  protected void onMessage(ACLMessage msg) {
    logger.info("Pong @ [" + getNodeName() + "]");
    // reply with an auto-increasing content
    ACLMessage reply = msg.makeReply(Performative.INFORM);
    reply.setContent(number++);
    msm.post(reply); } }
```

Obviously, the code for writing *XJAF* agents is more verbose than in some other *Java SE*-based multi-agent solutions, such as *JADE*. However, this is a small price to pay for advanced clustering features offered by our proposed system. An ongoing work aimed at alleviating this verbosity is briefly described in Section 5.

4 Evaluation

In addition to the advanced programming features described earlier, an important factor for the wider acceptance of *XJAF* is its runtime performance. Therefore, a case-study has been developed to assess this aspect of our system.

The case-study includes a pair of agents, named *Sender* and *Receiver*. The first agent issues a request to the second, which then performs a computationally expensive task, and replies with the result. The message *round-trip time (RTT)* is used as a measure; it expresses the time since the *Sender* issues the request and until it receives the reply. This relatively simple, but effective performance study is inspired by those described in [17,23,28]. More complex use-cases, e.g. implementation of an ant colony optimization algorithm for the *Traveling salesman* problem [13], can be found at the *XJAF* homepage [35].

Experimental setup was as follows:

- Hardware: *Intel Dual-Core CPU* at 3 *GHz*, with 2 *GB* of *RAM*. The *CPU* is capable of executing four threads simultaneously;
- 32-bit version of *Ubuntu 14.04*;
- *OpenJDK 7*. The maximum heap size for each *XJAF* node / *JADE* container was set to 512 *MB*;
- *JBoss EAP 6.1*;
- The *Receiver* agent used a brute-force algorithm for finding all prime numbers up to a certain limit;
- Each of the two messages exchanged between a *Sender* and the *Receiver* included a string of 65K random characters.

The utilized *JBoss* server has a specific feature. When one *EJB* (directly or indirectly) invokes a method of another *EJB*, the target will be executed on the same node as the source *EJB*. This is an optimization feature, applied in order to reduce expensive network communication: if two agents exchange a lot of messages, then they should reside in the same node. Although this default behavior can (and, in case of multi-agent systems, often should) be changed, it was left as-is for this case-study. This means that the *Sender* and its corresponding *Receiver* are always executed on the same node.

A set of analogous *JADE* agents was implemented and used as a reference point. By default, during the load-balancing process *JBoss* selects an available cluster node randomly. In order to achieve a similar distribution of agents in both *XJAF* and *JADE* implementations, and obtain more relevant results, we've setup the *JBoss* server to use a *round robin* node selector. The final organization of the case-study and the distribution of agents in both implementations is shown in Fig. 3.

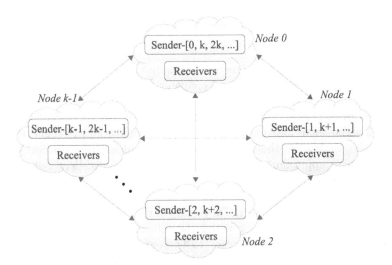

Fig. 3. Organization of the case-study and the round robin-based distribution of *Sender-Receiver* pairs in both the *XJAF* and the *JADE* implementation

Two evaluation scenarios were executed. First, we measured how many agents can each of the frameworks execute per machine, and how the average *RTT* changes as the number of agents increases. The results of this experiment are shown in Fig. 4. For lower numbers of agents, *JADE* offers better runtime performance. This is expected, since there is an overhead associated with remote *EJB* invocations. However, as the number of agents increases, *XJAF* scales better. Moreover, in our setup, once the number of pairs is set to 2048 (i.e. 4096 agents), *JADE* starts discarding messages and eventually crashes with the *out-of-memory* error. On the other hand, *XJAF* is perfectly capable of executing this many agents, due to built-in optimization features described earlier.

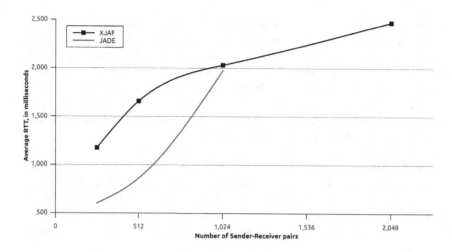

Fig. 4. Correlations between the number of agents and the average *RTT*s in *XJAF* and *JADE* implementations of the *Sender-Receiver* experiment (prime limit = 20000)

The second scenario was designed to measure the scaling factor of *XJAF* as more and more nodes are added to the cluster. The number of agent pairs was fixed to 2048 (i.e. 4096 agents), and the prime limit on the *Receiver*'s end was set to 60000. Four rounds of experiment were conducted: using 1, 2, 4, and 8 nodes, each having the same hardware and software configuration. It this evaluation, it was observed that, as the number of nodes doubles, the execution speed of *XJAF* increases approximately 3.5 times, which is an excellent outcome (the ideal would be 4 times).

These experimental results are very encouraging, and work in favor of the intended usage of our framework. They confirm the effectiveness of the inherent load-balancing capability. Along with other clustering features offered by the modern enterprise application server, *XJAF* represents an excellent framework for applications that require larger populations of agents.

5   Conclusions and Future Work

Java Platform, Enterprise Edition represents one of the leading industry standards for enterprise software development. It can bring many benefits to the agent-based software and should, therefore, be utilized more frequently by agent developers.

In this paper we have presented the latest version of our *Extensible Java EE-based Agent Framework*. During the development of *XJAF*, one of the main goals was to avoid reinventing the wheel, and instead rely on existing, tested technologies and technical solutions available in *Java EE*. The latest incarnation of our framework is focused on utilizing the advantages of clustered computing, namely:

- Load-balancing: *XJAF* agents are automatically distributed across the cluster in order to reduce to computational load of individual nodes;
- State replication and failover: the state of each agent is copied to other nodes, making it resilient to hardware and software failures.

The presented evaluation has shown that *XJAF* offers good runtime performance for applications that need to launch larger populations of agents. Moreover, it exhibits an excellent scaling factor as more and more nodes are added to the cluster.

There are several planned improvements of *XJAF*. Many of the standard agent functionalities, such as mobility and security, still need to be re-introduced to the new version [30]. The process of writing agents is inherently verbose – an agent needs to be described using several annotations. This issue can be alleviated through an agent-oriented programming language. We have already successfully developed such a language for an older version of *XJAF*, named *ALAS* [22,30]. Finally, the work is underway to implement a *Jason* infrastructure for *XJAF* [21]. This will enable development of more complex, reasoning agents in *Java EE* environments.

Acknowledgements. This work was partially supported by Ministry of Education, Science and Technological Development of the Republic of Serbia, through project no. OI174023: "Intelligent techniques and their integration into wide-spectrum decision support".

References

1. Alberola, J.M., Such, J.M., Botti, V., Espinosa, A., Garcia-Fornes, A.: A scalable multiagent platform for large systems. Computer Science and Information Systems 10(1), 51–77 (2013)
2. Apache license, version 2.0, http://www.apache.org/licenses/LICENSE-2.0.html (retrieved on April 22, 2014)
3. Bellifemine, F., Caire, G., Greenwood, D.: Developing Multi-Agent Systems with JADE. John Wiley & Sons (2007)
4. Bordini, R.H., Hübner, J.F.: BDI agent programming in AgentSpeak using Jason. In: Toni, F., Torroni, P. (eds.) CLIMA 2005. LNCS (LNAI), vol. 3900, pp. 143–164. Springer, Heidelberg (2006)
5. Bădică, C., Budimac, Z., Burkhard, H.D., Ivanović, M.: Software agents: languages, tools, platforms. Computer Science and Information Systems, ComSIS 8(2), 255–298 (2011)
6. Cougaar architecture document (2004), http://cougaar.org/doc/11_4/online/CAD_11_4.pdf (retrieved on April 22, 2014)
7. D'Inverno, M., Kinny, D., Luck, M.: Interaction protocols in Agentis. In: Proceedings of the Third International Conference on Multi-Agent Systems, pp. 112–119. IEEE Press (1998)
8. D'Inverno, M., Luck, M., Georgeff, M., Kinny, D., Wooldridge, M.: The dMARS architecture: A specification of the distributed multi-agent reasoning system. Autonomous Agents and Multi-Agent Systems 9(1-2), 5–53 (2004)

9. FIPA Abstract Architecture Specification (2002),
   http://www.fipa.org/specs/fipa00001/SC00001L.html
   (retrieved on April 22, 2014)
10. FIPA ACL message structure specification (2002),
   http://www.fipa.org/specs/fipa00061/SC00061G.pdf
   (retrieved on April 22, 2014)
11. FIPA homepage, http://www.fipa.org (retrieved on April 22, 2014)
12. Goncalves, A.: Beginning Java EE 6 platform with GlassFish 3, 2nd edn. Apress (2010)
13. Ilie, S., Bădică, A., Bădică, C.: Distributed agent-based ant colony optimization for solving traveling salesman problem on a partitioned map. In: Proceedings of the International Conference on Web Intelligence, Mining and Semantics, WIMS 2011, pp. 23:1–23:9. ACM, New York (2011),
   http://doi.acm.org/10.1145/1988688.1988716
14. Java Message Service homepage,
   http://www.oracle.com/technetwork/java/index-jsp-142945.html
   (retrieved on April 22, 2014)
15. JNDI homepage, http://www.oracle.com/technetwork/java/jndi/index.html
   (retrieved on April 22, 2014)
16. JSR 220: Enterprise JavaBeans, version 3.0,
   http://www.oracle.com/technetwork/java/docs-135218.html
   (retrieved on April 22, 2014)
17. Jurasovic, K., Jezic, G., Kusek, M.: A performance analysis of multi-agent systems. International Transactions on Systems Science and Applications 1(4), 335–342 (2006)
18. Kinny, D.: The Agentis agent interaction model. In: Papadimitriou, C., Singh, M.P., Müller, J.P. (eds.) ATAL 1998. LNCS (LNAI), vol. 1555, pp. 331–344. Springer, Heidelberg (1999)
19. Luck, M., Ashri, R., D'Inverno, M.: Agent-Based Software Development. Agent-Oriented Systems. Artech House Publishers (2004)
20. Marchioni, F., Surtani, M.: Infinispan data grid platform. Packt Publishing Ltd. (2012)
21. Mitrović, D., Ivanović, M., Bădică, C.: Jason agents in Java EE environments. In: Petre, E., Brezovan, M. (eds.) 3rd Workshop on Applications of Software Agents (WASA 2013), held within 17th International Conference on System Theory, Control and Computing (ICSTCC 2013), Sinaia, Romania, pp. 768–771 (2013)
22. Mitrović, D., Ivanović, M., Budimac, Z., Vidaković, M.: Supporting heterogeneous agent mobility with ALAS. Computer Science and Information Systems 9(3), 1203–1229 (2012)
23. Mitrović, D., Ivanović, M., Budimac, Z., Vidaković, M.: Radigost: Interoperable web-based multi-agent platform. Journal of Systems and Software 90, 167–178 (2014),
   http://www.sciencedirect.com/science/article/pii/S0164121214000028
24. Mitrović, D., Ivanović, M., Vidaković, M., Al-Dahoud, A.: Developing software agents using Enterprise JavaBeans. In: Local Proceedings of the Fifth Balkan Conference in Informatics (BCI 2012), pp. 147–149 (2012)
25. Nichifor, O., Buraga, S.: ADF – abstract framework for developing mobile agents. Tech. Rep. TR 04-01, Faculty of Computer Science, "A. I. Cuza" University of Iasi, Romania (2004)

26. Omicini, A., Rimassa, G.: Towards seamless agent middleware. In: Proceedings of the 13th IEEE International Workshops on Enabling Technologies: Infrastructure for Collaborative Enterprises, WETICE 2004, pp. 417–422. IEEE Computer Society, Washington, DC (2004), http://dx.doi.org/10.1109/ENABL.2004.73

27. Rimassa, G., Calisti, M., Kernland, M.E.: Living systems ®technology suite. In: Unland, R., Klusch, M., Calisti, M. (eds.) Software Agent-Based Applications, Platforms and Development Kits, pp. 73–93. Birkhauser Verlag (2005)

28. Such, J.M., Alberola, J.M., Mulet, L., Espinosa, A., Garcia Fornes, A., Botti, V.: Large-scale multiagent platform benchmarks. In: Proceedings of the MultiAgent Logics, Languages, and Organisations - Federated Workshops. Languages, Methodologies and Development Tools for Multi-Agent Systems (LADS 2007), pp. 192–204 (2007)

29. Surtani, M., Markus, M., Zamarreño, G., Muir, P.: Infinispan user guide, http://infinispan.org/docs/6.0.x/user_guide/user_guide.html (retrieved on April 22, 2014)

30. Vidaković, M., Ivanović, M., Mitrović, D., Budimac, Z.: Extensible Java EE-based agent framework – past, present, future. In: Ganzha, M., Jain, L.C. (eds.) Multiagent Systems and Applications. Intelligent Systems Reference Library, vol. 45, pp. 55–88. Springer, Heidelberg (2013)

31. Vidaković, M., Milosavljević, B., Konjović, Z., Sladić, G.: EXtensible Java EE-based agent framework and its application on distributed library catalogues. Computer Science and Information Systems, ComSIS 6(2), 1–16 (2009)

32. Voyager homepage, http://www.recursionsw.com/products/voyager/voyager-intro.html (retrieved on April 22, 2014)

33. WildFly 8 admin guide, https://docs.jboss.org/author/display/WFLY8/Admin+Guide (retrieved on April 22, 2014)

34. WildFly 8 high availability guide, https://docs.jboss.org/author/display/WFLY8/High+Availability+Guide (retrieved on April 22, 2014)

35. XJAF homepage, http://perun.pmf.uns.ac.rs/xjaf (retrieved on April 22, 2014)

Programming BDI Agents with Pure Java

Alexander Pokahr[1], Lars Braubach[1], Christopher Haubeck[1], and Jan Ladiges[2]

[1] Distributed Systems Group, University of Hamburg
[2] Automation Technology Institute, Helmut-Schmidt University Hamburg
{pokahr,braubach,haubeck}@informatik.uni-hamburg.de,
jan.ladiges@hsu-hh.de

Abstract. BDI represents a well-known agent architecture that has been successfully adopted for expressing agent behavior in terms of beliefs, desires and intentions. A core advantage of the architecture consists in its underlying philosophical model that relies on intuitive folk-psychological notions to describe rational human behavior. A key challenge consists in making the ideas of the BDI model easily accessible for software engineers. For this purpose many different BDI programming languages have been devised that differ considerably in their interpretation of the attitudes and the used programming paradigm. In many cases, novel agent languages such as AgentSpeak(L) have been developed which expose a new syntax and semantics to the user. On the one hand this is positive because it allows for introducing a compact and concise notation, but on the other hand the language is very different from well-known and adopted mainstream languages. To remedy this problem it will be shown that the BDI model can also be realized in a completely object oriented programming language by exploiting its metadata capabilities. We will show how the BDI attitudes can be mapped to slightly enhanced object oriented counterparts and how common BDI use cases can be realized using the novel approach. A key advantage of the approach is that BDI programming more closely resembles object orientation and the learning effort is reduced, because existing concepts and tool chains can be further employed. The usefulness of the approach will be illustrated with an example application from the area of production automation.

1 Introduction

The BDI (belief-desire-intention) model has been successfully used as agent architecture and led to the development of several BDI agent platforms and real world applications [17,4]. With PRS (procedural reasoning system) a hybrid architecture for BDI has been proposed [10] that allows for rational goal directed as well as fast and event driven agent behavior. The BDI agent platforms supporting this architecture differ considerably in the way the attitudes are represented as well as in the language that is offered to developers - ranging from custom agent languages to adapted mainstream languages. In this paper we will show how it is possible to completely embed PRS in a purely object oriented (OO) programming language (i.e., Java) by exploiting its metadata annotation

J.P. Müller, M. Weyrich, and A.L.C. Bazzan (Eds.): MATES 2014, LNAI 8732, pp. 216–233, 2014.

mechanism. The benefits of this approach are twofold: first, the learning effort is reduced and the barrier of using an agent approach is remedied and secondly, the existing object oriented development tool chain consisting of e.g. IDE, debugger and testing tools can be further used. The approach has been implemented as execution kernel for the Jadex agent platform [24] and is meant to replace the XML/Java driven BDI language used before.

In the next section related work is presented. Afterwards, in Section 3 a running example from the production automation area is introduced and in Section 4 the BDI core functionalities are explained. Implementation details are given in Section 5 before a summary of the main ideas concludes the paper in Section 6.

2   Related Work

BDI agent frameworks can be realized in a number of different ways regarding their relation to an existing OO language. *API-based approaches* like BDI4JADE [22] and PRACTIONIST [20] form one end of the spectrum and realize BDI agent concepts as a set of classes and methods. Using only the syntax and semantics of the host programming language, these API classes and methods can be subclassed or created and invoked to specify the desired BDI behavior. At the other end of the spectrum are approaches like Jason [5], which introduce *completely new languages* for specifying BDI behavior and proprietary means of interacting with the OO world. In between these extremes are *extensions of OO languages*, such as JACK [35]. These approaches introduce new keywords for agent specific behavior, but reuse existing language features where appropriate, e.g. for the code of plan bodies. Furthermore, the Jadex V2 BDI framework [24] is a *hybrid approach* that is API-based for programming plan bodies in Java, but introduces a new XML-based language for specifying the BDI structure of the agent.

From the perspective of an experienced OO programmer, sticking to the syntax and semantics of an existing language has a number of advantages, also for developing agent programs. One important point is the familiarity of the programmer with the language, but also with regard to her everyday workflow, an existing language is advantageous. Typical development tasks include *code editing*, *code documentation*, *testing*, and *debugging*. Furthermore, for larger projects, some kind of automated *build process* is needed. In addition to these common tasks also special purpose tasks exist, e.g., *profiling* an application to identify performance problems or memory leaks. In an existing language, a developer can always stick to her preferred suite of tools, such as an IDE for coding and debugging, a test framework for automated execution of unit tests, and a build process management tool. The reusability of support for common programming tasks is illustrated in Fig. 1. The API-based approaches (including Jadex) allow reusing existing IDEs, while JACK and Jason provide a custom IDE for the proprietary language (extension). Existing Java documentation tools such as Javadoc are only useful for PRACTIONIST and BDI4JADE. Existing Java test frameworks such as JUnit cannot be easily employed, therefore some approaches provide custom solutions. Java debugging is possible for all approaches, but does

	JACK	Jason	Jadex BDI V2	PRACTIONIST	BDI4JADE
Editing	custom IDE	custom IDE	any Java/XML IDE	any Java IDE	any Java IDE
Documentation	n/a	n/a	custom XML doc	Javadoc	Javadoc
Testing	n/a	n/a	custom	n/a	JADE testing
Debugging	any Java profiler on OO level, custom tools for BDI level				
Build process	preprocessor required	any Java build tool			
Profiling	any Java profiler, but only on OO level				

Fig. 1. Programming task support

not differentiate between user code and agent framework code, which is hard to understand for agent programmers. Supporting debugging on the level of beliefs, goals, and plans has been identified as important, thus all approaches provide additional custom tools for that task. Being Java-based, most approaches play well with any Java build tool. Only JACK requires a custom preprocessor that needs to be integrated in the build process. Similar to debugging, existing Java profiles only support the OO level, but here no additional BDI tools are available.

From the above discussion, the API-based approaches seem to be advantageous compared to the introduction of proprietary languages or language extensions. On the other hand, the realization of BDI concepts is often much more clean in languages, that are specifically developed for that purpose, because the meaning of the constructs is more closely related to the syntax. Furthermore in API-based approaches, the existing language compilers are unaware of the semantics of the API-constructs and thus cannot perform as many sanity checks for detecting programming errors as is possible with proprietary compilers. With annotations, Java provides a non-proprietary mechanism for extending the language with additional keywords. In the following, an approach is presented to combine the best of two worlds: a custom BDI language with an intuitive semantics that can be programmed in an existing OO language and thus allows reusing existing programming tools.

3 Running Example

The example application stems from the production automation domain which is increasingly using agents for controlling and monitoring production plants [19]. This trend includes the industrial-driven need for using standardized software technologies like high-level languages or Web Services already established in the company's business layers also for the industrial production systems itself [1]. The presented application monitors and controls the fulfillment of specified functional and non-functional requirements of a production plant, called "Pick and Place Unit" (henceforth "PPU"). This production plant serves as a case study to develop and benchmark approaches considering software and plant evolution, especially within the priority programme SPP 1593 of the Deutsche Forschungs-gemeinschaft (DFG) – Design for Future – Managed Software Evolution. In the SPP, the FYPA²C project aims at keeping plant documentation represented in

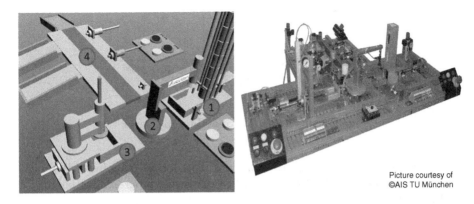

Picture courtesy of
©AIS TU München

Fig. 2. PPU plant overview

runtime behavior models up to date and ensuring the fulfillment of requirements during the evolution of production systems. BDI agents are used for controlling the actions of an evolution support software to ensure a goal-based operation. For further information, [34] gives more detailed information about the used benchmarking plant and [12] gives an overview of the FYPA²C project.

The PPU is depicted in Fig. 2 and consists of four subsystems. (1) An inlet stack providing the plant with workpieces. There are three different kinds of workpieces to be treated within the plant. Namely those are black and white plastic workpieces as well as metallic ones which can be distinguished by sensors in the plant. (2) A crane capable of transporting the workpieces between the other parts of the plant. The crane can move downwards and upwards as well as rotate around its axis. For transporting, the crane is able to suck in workpieces pneumatically. (3) A stamp stamping the workpieces with different kinds of pressure. It should be noted that just the white and metallic workpieces get stamped. Black ones will just be transported to the plant outlets. (4) A conveyor transporting the workpieces to three different outlet ramps by using pneumatic pushers.

4   BDI Functionalities

A BDI agent is constituted of attitudes as well as reasoning and interaction processes as depicted in Fig. 3. The agent is composed of the mental attitudes *beliefs*, *goals*, and *plans* [27]. It acts by realizing a practical reasoning process, which consists of two stages called *goal deliberation* and *means-end reasoning* [36]. In the former stage, a conflict-free subset of goals is chosen from the overall set of goals within the agent, whereas the latter phase deals with the accomplishment of an individual goal by executing suitable plans. Additionally, in multi-agent systems goal delegation is an interesting topic for realizing cooperative behavior among agents with different capabilities. This paper focuses on these common functional aspects of BDI and how a programmer can specify according BDI

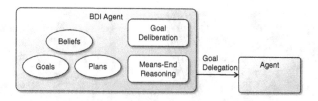

Fig. 3. Structure and processes of a BDI agent

agent code using only existing Java syntax. A more formal mapping of BDI concepts and OO concepts, that is independent of specific programming languages has been proposed in [7].

For pure Java BDI agents, an agent needs to be implemented as a Pojo[1] Java class or set of Java classes. For this purpose a normal Java class can be turned into an agent type and its fields and methods can be turned into beliefs and plans. Goals are currently always represented as inner or separate classes. We assume, that there is always one entry class that represents the agent as a whole and links to further classes, e.g. for representing specific goals or plans of the agent. In the following, important characteristics regarding the programming of attitudes and reasoning processes will be discussed by presenting the motivations, challenges and solutions for each aspect. Additionally, each solution will be illustrated with short example code snippets from the PPU use case.

4.1   Beliefs

Beliefs represent information that an agent has about itself and the world that it inhabits. Having accurate beliefs is important for the agent to make adequate choices about its courses of action. On the one hand, this means that an agent needs to be able to perceive the current state of its environment and also to quickly detect changes in that environment, e.g., to observe the effects of its actions. On the other hand, trying to process all available information and every single change can quickly lead to sensory overload, such that the agent actions cannot keep up with the state of the environment. Thus, mechanisms are required that balance processing effort against completeness and recency of beliefs.

For practical agent systems, beliefs allow connecting agents to external systems. A common solution is to use a traditional programming language such as Java to write concrete environment adapters for specific applications. These environment adapters would use the API of the BDI programming framework to feed information into the agents (e.g. *addPercept()* in Jason [5]). More advanced solutions provide explicit concepts and frameworks for modeling the environment [15,3]. In JaCaMo [3] the environment is composed of artifacts [28] and beliefs can be mapped to observable properties of these artifacts. In EnvSupport [15], the environment is modeled in terms of objects, tasks and processes. Interaction

---

[1] A Pojo (plain old java object) is a plain Java class that is not cluttered with framework dependencies.

```
@Agent
public class PPUAgentBDI {
  @Belief
  protected int stampedWps;

  @Belief(updaterate=1000)
  protected boolean hasStackWp = getSensorValue("stack.sliderSwitch");

  @Belief(dynamic=true)
  public boolean getStackWpMetal() {
    return getSensorValue("stack.capacitive")
  }
  ...
}
```

Fig. 4. Example beliefs of a PPU agent

between agents and the environment is described as actions and percepts. Using percept processors, the developer can specify individually for different agents, how the percept is reflected in the internal agent structure.

In pure Java BDI, belief contents can naturally be represented as domain-specific objects, stored as fields of the agent class or as bean properties represented by a getter/setter method pair. When a belief is just a passive data store, no special treatment of the field is necessary. When a field is annotated with *@Belief*, the field is monitored, such that the interpreter can also react to changes of the belief, regardless from where in the Java code the field is set. For connecting the belief to external stimuli, three automatic update modes are supported: push, pull, and polling. Push requires the stored Java-objects to provide the *add/removePropertyListener()* methods, such that external changes are pushed into the interpreter. When a belief is marked as *dynamic*, the field's initialization expression is re-evaluated (pulled) on every field access, which is e.g. useful for reading sensor values. With an optional *update rate*, time intervals can be specified, in which the belief is updated automatically (polling).

Within the production automation application, beliefs describe the observed state of the externally connected PPU system (cf. Fig. 4). As the listing shows, agents keep track of how many workpieces the system already has stamped (belief *stampedWps*). To react on changes for, e.g., issuing a message that the stamper needs a recalibration after 10000 workpieces, the corresponding instance variable is annotated by *@Belief*. Furthermore, the observed PPU agents are able to read and write sensor and actuator signals of the plant via an Ethernet connection as implemented in a *getSensorValue()* method (not shown). To ensure an up-to-date view in this context it is necessary to automatically re-evaluate a belief in a certain time interval. In terms of a workpiece that is ready to get picked up by the crane, the crane agent specifies an update rate to the belief, which checks the mechanical switch sensor of the stack (belief *hasStackWp*). To determine the type of a workpiece, a corresponding belief is annotated as a dynamic belief, which ensures that the belief is automatically re-evaluated whenever it is used (belief *getStackWpMetal*).

4.2 Goals

A goal represents an objective an agent should strive to achieve. According to [32] a goal has a motivational and an optative part. The optative part typically describes a world state, whereas the motivation characterizes the attitude towards that world state, i.e. if it should be achieved, avoided, etc. A major challenge consists in finding a comprehensible set of goal kinds (a.k.a. motivational types) that are sufficient for expressing many real world problems in a natural way and that additionally can be equipped with a clear operational semantics in order to be executed by a BDI agent.

BDI systems that are close to the original PRS such as Jason [5] and JACK [35] make use of a lightweight goal in terms of an event. For this reason, goals in those systems have only procedural character, i.e. the motivational and optative parts are not interpreted by the means-end reasoning process. As an extension of PRS an explicit representation of goals has been proposed [6] and support for procedural and declarative goals has been added. It has been found as consensus by several researchers [6,9,33] that perform, achieve, query and maintain represent a sensible set of complementary goal kinds for many real world scenarios. Their operational semantics has been defined by using a state based lifecycle model and corresponding transition rules.

The information related to a goal can be captured as a separate Java class for each goal. The most interesting aspect of pure Java goal programming is how the programmer can control state transitions in the goal lifecycle. To specify when a goal should be created, is achieved or failed etc., different goal conditions (*@GoalXYZCondition*) can be annotated to methods of the goal class. When the method returns true, the condition triggers and the state transition is performed. In Java, the goal class also can be declared as inner class of the agent class, such that the goal condition code can access agent beliefs. In this case, the goal conditions can be evaluated automatically, whenever corresponding belief changes are detected. Different goal kinds are supported by providing the required conditions, such as *@GoalTargetCondition* for an achieve goal and *@GoalMaintainCondition* for a maintain goal.

The PPU case study utilizes different kinds of goals (cf. Fig. 5). First, an achieve goal is shown that is automatically created whenever the stamp pressure is changed as specified by the *@GoalCreationCondition* annotated at the class constructor. The goal triggers plans to reduce the pressure plan until the target condition is reached (*isNotTooHigh()* method). Second, a maintain goal specifies a desired utilization of the stamp that should be obtained. When the condition (*checkUtilization()* method) evaluates to false the goal becomes active and triggers plans until the maintain condition is true again.

4.3 Plans

The plans of an agent contain the concrete steps towards coming closer to goal achievement. In BDI a plan consists of a declarative and a procedural part (called plan head and body respectively). The former contains information about the

```
@Goal(unique=true)
public class AchieveStampPreasureLimitGoal {
  @GoalCreationCondition(beliefs={"stampPressure"})
  public AchieveStampPreasureLimitGoal() {}

  @GoalTargetCondition(beliefs="stampPressure")
  public boolean isNotTooHigh() {
    return stampPressure<8000;
  }
}
@Goal
public class MaintainHighUtilisationGoal {
  @GoalMaintainCondition(beliefs="utilisationLast10Min")
  public boolean checkUtilization() {
    return stamp - utilisationLast10Min > 15;
  }
}
```

Fig. 5. Example goals of the stamper agent

usage context of a plan, inter alia the goals it is applicable for and a precondition, while the latter describes the actions that should be executed on plan execution. BDI systems use goal-plan hierarchies for a decomposition of the overall problem into more concrete sub problems at runtime. Therefore the abstractness of the goals and plans decreases from the top to the leaves. This leads to the conceptual question how different degrees of abstractness can be programmed within plans and which programming constructs help supporting this. In addition, from the agent's perspective plan execution is challenging, because multiple plans should run concurrently in order to make an agent multitasking capable. Moreover, plan execution depends on superordinated goals and in case a goal is e.g. dropped all plans below should be immediately terminated as well.

Defining plans has been addressed via visual as well as programmatic approaches. Visual approaches mostly rely on process descriptions similar to workflow languages like BPMN using events, gateways and activities and have been used e.g. in JACK [35] and Agentis [18]. Programmatic approaches are diverse and proposed novel languages e.g. in JAM [14] and Jason [5] as well as standard mainstream programming languages e.g. in JACK [35] and Jadex [24]. Although novel languages can provide concise and neat notations, typically the expressiveness of control flow and conditions is better in mainstream languages due to a rich set of programming constructs. To allow abstract as well as very concrete plans, a subgoaling concept is needed. In novel languages this is directly integrated as language feature while in mainstream languages a BDI API has to be provided. Concerning the execution of plans also different approaches have been pursued. In case of novel languages typically interpreters are used. These allow interrupting a plan after each executed command. In mainstream languages like Java this is far more difficult to achieve, because an executing thread cannot be interrupted while plan user code is executed. For this reason either a precompiler approach can be used to transform the code to a state machine as done in JACK [35] or asynchronous BDI API methods can be used as potential interruption and termination points as done in Jadex [24].

```
@Plan(trigger=@Trigger(goals=TransportRampGoal.class))
public class TransportRampPlan {
  @PlanBody
  public void transport(int rampno) {
    observingSensor("conveyor.PusherLightbarrier"+rampno, true).get();
    setActuator("conveyor.Pusher"+rampno);
  }
}
```

Fig. 6. Example plans of the conveyor agent

A natural Java mapping for plans is to describe the plan head using specific annotations and capture the execution logic as a simple method body. Most important part of the plan head is the *@Trigger*, which specifies the goals and/or belief changes that should lead to the execution of the plan. Similar to goals, also plans can define further conditions, such as pre- and context condition, using annotations for corresponding methods. For simplicity, plans should be specified in a synchronous sequential way. Nevertheless, interleaved plan execution should be supported, e.g. for executing subgoals. Therefore, interruption and termination points are identified by the asynchronous BDI API methods, which return future[2] objects. To continue execution with the result of an asynchronous operation, the programmer has to explicitly wait for the result by calling the get() method on the future. This ensures, that plans are not arbitrarily interleaved (unlike simple threads). Instead, the programmer has explicit control where possible interruptions of the plan are allowed to occur.

In the PPU case study, plans are used at different hierarchy levels (cf. Fig. 6). One example is the sorting process of the conveyor which ensures that each outlet ramp only contains one type of workpieces. A sorting plan (not shown) checks the type of the workpieces in the conveyor and triggers the goal for the corresponding ramp. In the *TransportRampPlan* the concrete transportation to a specific ramp is implemented by interrupting the plan execution until the sensor of a light barrier in front of the pneumatic pusher of the corresponding ramp is triggered. When this signal appears the workpiece is pushed into the outlet ramp. The ramp number is passed to the plan as method parameter from the goal. To make this work, goal fields and methods can be made to named parameters using *@GoalParameter*, which will automatically injected in the call.

4.4   Means-end Reasoning

Means-end reasoning is at the heart of PRS (procedural reasoning system) systems and represents the process how a goal is pursued. The underlying rationale of means-end reasoning is the conceptual separation of what is to be achieved (represented by a goal) and the way how a goal should be tackled (represented by a plan). This separation leads to advantages with respect to the flexibility and extensibility of behavior, because both sides can be changed independently of each other. E.g. changing the target condition of a goal does not necessarily

---

[2] A future is a place holder for a value that is not yet available [29].

affect the plans and adding a plan that is suitable for a new situation does not affect other plans or the goal. The key challenge is how the means-end reasoning can be made *effective* and *efficient*, whereby effectiveness ensures that a goal becomes eventually fulfilled and efficiency relates to optimal goal processing in terms of used resources such as time, costs etc.

The basic means-end reasoning process has been initially proposed in [10,27] with the abstract PRS deliberation cycle. Effective goal achievement is based on the idea of decoupling plan and goal failure/success. This important principle allows for tolerating plan failures and continuing goal processing by trying out other plans as long as options are available. Typically, an applicable plan list is built up at the beginning of the process, from which suitable candidates are selected and executed. Whenever a plan has finished, the means-end reasoning process is triggered again and decides whether goal processing is finished or which other plan is executed next. In order to achieve a goal it is typically helpful to exclude failed plans but there are also situations in which the same plan should be tried out more than once. To cope with such use case dependent differences it has been proposed to customize the process with behavior flags (cf. e.g. JACK [35]). The efficiency of plan execution is directly connected to the cleverness of the plan selection mechanism. Although also generic learning of plan preferences has been proposed [21], in many cases the concrete selection metrics are domain dependent. Meta-level reasoning, i.e. writing custom logic to choose among plans, has been proposed as a general mechanism for supporting plan selection with domain knowledge.

As a default, means-end reasoning is performed automatically by the agent interpreter. E.g., for a newly activated goal, it considers the triggers and pre- and context conditions of all plans, to build a list of applicable plans, which are then scheduled for execution. Besides specifying the plan heads accordingly, the programmer can exert additional control on the means-end reasoning process, by providing custom meta-level reasoning code. For this purpose, the *@GoalAPLBuild* annotation can be attached to a method of a goal class. It is invoked to produce the applicable plan list using any kind of required operations, e.g., also subgoals, if needed.

Regarding the PPU example, means-end reasoning can be seen in the controlling behavior of the crane agent. In the given example (cf. Fig. 7) a pickup goal, which holds the type as a parameter, is triggered in reaction to a present workpiece at the stack. At this point the crane has the possibility to turn clockwise or counterclockwise. Both actions are realized as plans. In any given situation, only one of these plans can succeed, because the crane can not perform a full 360 degree rotation. The default means-end reasoning process would try out the plans one after the other and eventually achieve the desired result. To improve the performance by avoiding unnecessary turns in the wrong direction, a custom specification of the means-end reasoning is provided with the *@GoalAPLBuild* annotation. Within the annotated method (*transportAPL()*) the crane position is checked and the agent chooses the most efficient plan relative to its current position.

```
@Goal
public class PickUpStackWpGoal {
  @GoalParameter
  protected String stackWpType;

  @GoalCreationCondition(beliefs={"hasStackWp", "stackWpType"})
  public PickUpStackWpGoal(String stackWpType) {
    this.stackWpType = stackWpType;
  }

  @GoalAPLBuild
  public List transportAPL() {
    List planList = new ArrayList();
    if(getCranePosition()>0 && getCranePosition()<180)
      planList.add(new TurnClockwisePlan());
    else
      planList.add(new TurnCounterClockwisePlan());
    return planList;
  }
}
@Plan(trigger=@Trigger(goals=PickUpStackWpGoal.class))
public class TurnClockwisePlan() {
  ...
}
@Plan(trigger=@Trigger(goals=PickUpStackWpGoal.class))
public class TurnCounterClockwisePlan() {
  ...
}
```

Fig. 7. Using domain knowledge for means-end reasoning in the crane agent

4.5   Goal Deliberation

Typically, agents should be able to pursue multiple goals at the same time. This raises the important question how an agent can *detect* and also *handle conflicts* between these goals. Conflicts can arise on the one hand from incompatible goals, e.g., requiring for a robot to be at two different places at once, and on the other hand from limited availability of resources, e.g., required for the plans to achieve the respective goals. Both types of conflict can be handled at the goal level, i.e., by delaying or dropping one of the incompatible goals. Resource conflicts can additionally be resolved on the plan level, by choosing alternative plans with different resource needs and thus allowing the agent to continue pursuing both goals.

Different goal deliberation strategies have been proposed to deal with the above challenges [31,30,26]. E.g., [31] describes how to derive minimal and maximal resource requirements for complex plans (i.e., plans with subgoals), when resource requirements of basic plans are known. The resource requirements can then be used to decide if two goals can be pursued in parallel in any case, only in case the plans are chosen properly, or not at all. In a slightly different approach, [30] uses information about preconditions of plans to check if a plan executed for one goal might prevent the execution of a plan required to achieve a different goal. A purely goal-level strategy is proposed in [26], that allows to specify inhibition links between goals and uses these links to derive an order for the sequential execution of conflicting goals. All of these strategies have different

```
@Goal(deliberation=@Deliberation(inhibits=MaintainHighUtilisationGoal.class))
public class MaintainHighThroughputGoal {
  @GoalMaintainCondition(beliefs="throughputLast10Min")
  public boolean checkThroughput() {
    return throughputLast10Min>20;
  }
}
```

Fig. 8. Goal deliberation example

strengths and weaknesses with respect to expressiveness, complexity and computational overhead. On the one hand, a more expressive strategy allows more detailed control over the agent execution to improve effectiveness and efficiency of the agent behavior. On the other hand, a more expressive strategy is more complex and error-prone in its specification and has a higher computational overhead with regard to memory and processing power required for the agent to execute the strategy at runtime.

In principle, all of the aforementioned deliberation strategies could be applied to pure Java BDI agents, given that appropriate annotations for goals and plans are provided and handled by the agent interpreter. In our approach, the goal-level strategy from [26] is already realized. Goal conflicts and priorities can be declared by specifying an *inhibits* relationship from one goal class to another in the *@Deliberation* annotation on a goal class. More fine-grained control over inhibits relationships is possible by using *@GoalInhibit* on a goal method. This annotation states, that one concrete goal instance inhibits another goal instance, if the method returns true for the given other goal instance. Furthermore, using the *cardinalityone* setting, the programmer can specify that only one instance of a goal class should be active at any given time.

Concurrent goals also exist in the PPU. For example a certain utilization of the stamp and a goal demanding a certain throughput rate of the plant should be reached. In order to achieve a high utilization, workpieces should be transported out of the stamp as soon as they are stamped. Secondly, workpieces to be stamped should preferably be transported to the stamp contrary to workpieces which do not need to be stamped. To reach a high throughput, in contrast, it is better to prefer workpieces which can be treated fast, e.g. those not to be stamped. Because throughput has, in the case study, a higher priority the *MaintainHighThroughputGoal* (cf. Fig. 8) inhibits the goal for high utilization (already shown in Fig. 5). This is done with the *@Deliberation* annotation leading to the intended behavior that stamped workpieces are left in the stamp while further workpieces (e.g. black ones) get transported between the stack and the conveyor.

4.6 Goal Delegation

In most non-trivial systems, agents are dependent on other agents or external systems to achieve their goals. Goal delegation is one promising approach for coordination in multi-agent systems, because it allows reusing the available internal attitudes. Furthermore, goal delegation represents a good trade-off between a low communication overhead and a moderate coupling imposed on the agents [23]. Important challenges exist with regard to the representation of a delegated goal. On the one hand, different BDI agents might want to represent the same goal differently and on the other hand, BDI agents should be enabled to coordinate their behavior with non-BDI agents and external non-agent systems.

Initial work in the area of goal delegation [2] considers the message level and proposes an interaction protocol between the initiator and the receiver of a goal delegation. The approach is independent of the internal agent architecture and thus allows coordinating arbitrary agents. However, it does not cover, how the message-level can be mapped to internal goals of a BDI agent. [23] proposes an OO / BDI integration by supporting to map goals to methods of provided or required services. Therefore it allows delegating goals to external non-BDI or even non-agent service providers and also to create internal goals in response to external service requests. When a goal is delegated between two BDI agents, each agent can have its own internal mapping of the goal, thus improving information hiding and loose coupling between implementations of different agents. A more tight coupling is provided by approaches such as joint intentions [8], which employs partial sharing of beliefs and goals, or joint responsibility [16], which in addition to beliefs and goals also introduces sharing on the plan-level. A more pragmatic approach to tight coupling is provided by Simple Teams [13], which introduces a separate team agent that coordinates team member agents by holding the team beliefs, team goals and team plans. As solution concept for goal delegation the service approach from [23] has been integrated also for pure Java agents because it allows for non-BDI agents contributing to goal achievement.

Goal delegation is very useful when a system with different actors exposing distinct capabilities exist. Assuming that in future the production environment becomes more dynamic and flexible in the sense of smart manufacturing infrastructures [11], it becomes interesting to consider single products (or workpieces) as agents. A main product's objective consists in being processed according to customer preferences, but it completely relies on machines and conveyors regarding all processing steps. When modeling this scenario with BDI, a product agent needs goal delegation to become refined in any respect. Regarding the PPU case the product agent may have the simple goal of becoming stamped with a specific text (e.g. production date). This goal can be achieved by automatically delegating it to the stamp agent which itself initializes the correct stamping action on the work piece. In case the product is not already positioned next to the stamp the stamp agent could - to achieve the stamp goal - first create a transportation subgoal.

In Figure 9 the corresponding example BDI code is shown. It consists of two agent types (stamp and workpiece), the goal type that is delegated (StampGoal) and the stamp service (IStampService) used to transfer the goal between the agents. The stamp agent uses the StampGoal and declares that it publishes this goal using the IStampService. This means that the stamp agent will automatically provide a service that creates for each incoming service call a new stamp goal. The stamp goal is handled by a stamp plan that prints out the workpiece

```java
// The stamp goal being delegated from workpiece to stamp agent
@Goal
public class StampGoal {
  @GoalParameter
  protected IComponentIdentifier wp;
  @GoalParameter
  protected String text;
  public StampGoal(IComponentIdentifier wp, String text) {
    this.wp = wp;
    this.text = text;
  }
}

// Stamp service internally used for delegation
@Service public interface IStampService {
  public IFuture<Void> stamp(IComponentIdentifier wp, String text);
}

// The stamp agent capable of stamping workpieces
@Agent
@Goals(@Goal(clazz=StampGoal.class, publish=@Publish(type=IStampService.class)))
public class StampBDI {
  @Plan(trigger=@Trigger(goals=StampGoal.class))
  public void stamp(IComponentIdentifier wp, String text) {
    // transport work piece to stamp and stamp with text
    System.out.println("Stamped workpiece: "+wp+" with text: "+text);
  }
}

// The workpiece agent dispatching a stamp goal
@Agent
@Goals(@Goal(clazz=StampGoal.class))
@RequiredServices(@RequiredService(name="stampser", type=IStampService.class,
  binding=@Binding(scope=RequiredServiceInfo.SCOPE_PLATFORM)))
@Plans(@Plan(trigger=@Trigger(goals=StampGoal.class),
  body=@Body(service=@ServicePlan(name="stampser"))))
public class WorkpieceBDI {
  @AgentBody
  public void body(BDIAgent agent) {
        agent.dispatchTopLevelGoal(new  StampGoal(agent.getComponentIdentifier(),  "date: "+Sys-
tem.currentTimeMillis())).get();
  }
}
```

Fig. 9. Goal delegation example

name and stamp date. The workpiece agent also uses the stamp goal and declares a plan that handles goals of that type by automatically delegating them via a service call (*@ServicePlan(name="stampser")*). The 'stampser' name references the required service declaration, in which it is stated what interface the service should have and in which scope it can be searched (here on the local platform using SCOPE_PLATFORM). When the agent is started it will create and dispatch a new stamp goal, which is forwarded as service call to a stamp agent. In the stamp agent a stamp goal will be recreated from the service call. After goal processing has finished at the stamp agent the service call returns and the workpiece agent is notified about the success of failure.

5   Implementation

The BDI annotations of an agent and associated goal and plan classes form the agent's implicit BDI model. As a first step, this indirect model needs to be made explicit by reading the annotations and generating an explicit BDI model. The resulting model contains all the declared belief, plan and goal declarations. Besides the model and the BDI agent class, further runtime elements are necessary to allow an execution. The general idea is that when a BDI agent is started, not only an instance of the Pojo agent class is created, but also a generic BDI interpreter object is created and linked to the agent object and its model. This interpreter has the purpose to realize the BDI reasoning processes according to the concrete BDI agent model. The underlying BDI interpreter architecture is close to the agenda based approach presented in [25]. It assumes that the interpreter has an action queue that contains BDI meta actions such as creategoal(X) or dropplan(Y). The interpreter removes actions one by one executes them, whereby executed meta actions as well as received messages can add new actions to the queue. After each step, an internal event-condition-action rule engine is used to check whether rules are activated. If this is the case the rules will be executed until quiescence and action execution continues. As part of action execution methods of the agent Pojo object can be invoked (e.g. executing a plan step). Finally, it has to be remarked that limitations of the Java programming language made it necessary to enhance the byte code of the Java class before it can be used. A core reason is that we want to automatically observe belief changes what is not directly possible using plain fields. Without bytecode enhancing, the programmer would explicitly have to throw change events whenever belief values change (e.g. in a set method). In addition, bytecode enhancement is automatically done at runtime when an agent model is loaded the first time, i.e. no special post-processing is necessary in the build process.

6   Conclusion

BDI programming is conceptually different from OO programming, because beliefs, goals and plans are introduced as first class entities and agent execution adheres to the practical reasoning process. Despite these fundamental differences, a mainstream language can be directly used for BDI programming, if the host language provides metadata mechanisms. Concretely, it has been shown how BDI can be embedded in Java by using annotations for transforming selected existing OO entities to BDI attitudes. The approach has been explained by illustrating core aspects of the attitude management as well by explaining how goal deliberation and means-end reasoning works. At runtime such a pure Java agent is executed using an interpreter that controls the adequate invocation of methods on the instantiated agent object. The approach has been implemented for the Jadex platform and has already been successfully used for application development in several projects. As part of future work it is especially planned to extend the set of provided goal types by considering also soft goals.

Acknowledgements. This work is funded in part by the Deutsche Forschungs-gemeinschaft DFG under the priority research programme *Design For Future - Managed Software Evolution (SPP 1593)* in the project *FYPA²C - Forever Young Production Automation with Active Components*.

References

1. Basanta-Val, P., Garcia-Valls, M.: A distributed real-time java-centric architecture for industrial systems. IEEE Transactions on Industrial Informatics 10(1), 27–34 (2014)
2. Bergenti, F., Botelho, L., Rimassa, G., Somacher, M.: A FIPA compliant Goal Delegation Protocol. In: Proc. Workshop on Agent Communication Languages and Conversation Policies (AAMAS 2002), Bologna, Italy (2002)
3. Boissier, O., Bordini, R., Hübner, J., Ricci, A., Santi, A.: Multi-agent oriented programming with jacamo. Science of Computer Programming 78(6), 747–761 (2013)
4. Bordini, R., Dastani, M., Dix, J., El Fallah Seghrouchni, A.: Multi-Agent Programming: Languages, Platforms and Applications. Springer (2005)
5. Bordini, R., Hübner, J.F., Vieira, R.: Jason and the Golden Fleece of Agent-Oriented Programming. In: Multi-Agent Programming: Languages, Platforms and Applications, pp. 3–37. Springer (2005)
6. Braubach, L., Pokahr, A., Moldt, D., Lamersdorf, W.: Goal Representation for BDI Agent Systems. In: Bordini, R.H., Dastani, M., Dix, J., El Fallah Seghrouchni, A. (eds.) PROMAS 2004. LNCS (LNAI), vol. 3346, pp. 44–65. Springer, Heidelberg (2005)
7. Braubach, L., Pokahr, A.: A generic mapping approach for the integration of bdi with object orientation. In: Proceedings of the 2014 IEEE/WIC/ACM International Conference on Intelligent Agent Technology (IAT 2014). IEEE Computer Society (2014)
8. Cohen, P.R., Levesque, H.J.: Teamwork. Technical Report Technote 504, SRI International, Menlo Park, CA (March 1991)
9. Dastani, M., van Riemsdijk, B., Meyer, J.-J.: Goal Types in Agent Programming. In: Brewka, G., Coradeschi, S., Perini, A., Traverso, P. (eds.) Proceedings of the 17th European Conference on Artificial Intelligence (ECAI 2006), pp. 220–224. IOS Press (2006)
10. Georgeff, M., Lansky, A.: Reactive Reasoning and Planning: An Experiment With a Mobile Robot. In: Proceedings of the 6th National Conference on Artificial Intelligence (AAAI 1987), pp. 677–682. AAAI (1987)
11. Ghonaim, W., Ghenniwa, H., Shen, W.: Towards an agent oriented smart manufacturing system. In: 2011 15th International Conference on Computer Supported Cooperative Work in Design (CSCWD), pp. 636–642 (June 2011)
12. Haubeck, C., Wior, I., Braubach, L., Pokahr, A., Ladiges, J., Fay, A., Lamersdorf, W.: Keeping pace with changes - towards supporting continuous improvements and extensive updates in production automation software. Electronic Communications of the EASST 56 (2013)
13. Hodgson, A., Rönnquist, R., Busetta, P.: Specification of Coordinated Agent Behavior (The SimpleTeam Approach). In: Proceedings of the Workshop on Team Behaviour and Plan Recognition at the 16th International Joint Conferences on Artificial Intelligence (IJCAI 1999), pp. 75–81 (1999)

14. Huber, M.: JAM: A BDI-Theoretic Mobile Agent Architecture. In: Proc. of the Conf. on Autonomous Agents (AGENTS 1999), pp. 236–243. ACM Press (1999)
15. Jander, K., Braubach, L., Pokahr, A.: Envsupport: A framework for developing virtual environments. In: Seventh International Workshop From Agent Theory to Agent Implementation (AT2AI-7). Austrian Society for Cybernetic Studies (2010)
16. Jennings, N., Mamdani, E.: Using Joint Responsibility to Coordinate Collaborative Problem Solving in Dynamic Environments. In: AAAI, pp. 269–275 (1992)
17. Jennings, N.R., Wooldridge, M.J.: Agent Technology - Foundations, Applications and Markets. Springer (1998)
18. Kinny, D.: The Agentis Agent Interaction Model. In: Papadimitriou, C., Singh, M.P., Müller, J.P. (eds.) ATAL 1998. LNCS (LNAI), vol. 1555, pp. 331–344. Springer, Heidelberg (1999)
19. Leitao, P., Marik, V., Vrba, P.: Past, present, and future of industrial agent applications. IEEE Transactions on Industrial Informatics 9(4), 2360–2372 (2013)
20. Morreale, V., Bonura, S., Francaviglia, G., Centineo, F., Cossentino, M., Gaglio, S.: Reasoning about goals in BDI agents: The PRACTIONIST framework. In: Proceedings of Joint Workshop "From Objects to Agents" (2006)
21. Norling, E.: Folk Psychology for Human Modelling: Extending the BDI Paradigm. In: Proceedings of the 3rd International Joint Conference on Autonomous Agents and Multiagent Systems (AAMAS 2004) (July 2004)
22. Nunes, I., Lucena, C., Luck, M.: BDI4JADE: A BDI layer on top of JADE. In: Proc. of the Workshop on Programming Multiagent Systems, pp. 88–103 (2011)
23. Pokahr, A., Braubach, L.: Goal delegation without goals - BDI agents in harmony with ocmas principles. In: Timm, I.J., Guttmann, C. (eds.) MATES 2012. LNCS, vol. 7598, pp. 116–125. Springer, Heidelberg (2012)
24. Pokahr, A., Braubach, L., Jander, K.: The jadex project: Programming model. In: Multiagent Systems and Applications, pp. 21–53. Springer (2012)
25. Pokahr, A., Braubach, L., Lamersdorf, W.: A Flexible BDI Architecture Supporting Extensibility. In: Proc. of the Int. Conf. on Intelligent Agent Technology, pp. 379–385. IEEE (2005)
26. Pokahr, A., Braubach, L., Lamersdorf, W.: A goal deliberation strategy for BDI agent systems. In: Eymann, T., Klügl, F., Lamersdorf, W., Klusch, M., Huhns, M.N. (eds.) MATES 2005. LNCS (LNAI), vol. 3550, pp. 82–93. Springer, Heidelberg (2005)
27. Rao, A., Georgeff, M.: BDI Agents: From Theory to Practice. In: Proc. of the Int. Conf. on Multi-Agent Systems, pp. 312–319. MIT Press (1995)
28. Ricci, A., Viroli, M., Omicini, A.: The A&A programming model and technology for developing agent environments in MAS. In: Dastani, M., El Fallah Seghrouchni, A., Ricci, A., Winikoff, M. (eds.) ProMAS 2007. LNCS (LNAI), vol. 4908, pp. 89–106. Springer, Heidelberg (2008)
29. Sutter, H., Larus, J.: Software and the concurrency revolution. ACM Queue 3(7), 54–62 (2005)
30. Thangarajah, J., Padgham, L., Winikoff, M.: Detecting and Avoiding Interference Between Goals in Intelligent Agents. In: Proc. of the 18th Int. Joint Conf. on Artificial Intelligence, pp. 721–726. Morgan Kaufmann (2003)
31. Thangarajah, J., Winikoff, M., Padgham, L., Fischer, K.: Avoiding resource conflicts in intelligent agents. In: Proc. of the Eur. Conf. on Artifical Intelligence, pp. 18–22. IOS Press (2002)
32. van Lamsweerde, A.: Goal-Oriented Requirements Engineering: A Guided Tour. In: Proceedings of the 9th International Joint Conference on Requirements Engineering (RE 2001), pp. 249–263. IEEE Press (2001)

33. van Riemsdijk, B., Dastani, M., Winikoff, M.: Goals in agent systems: a unifying framework. In: Proc. of the Int. Joint Conf. on Autonomous Agents and Multiagent Systems, pp. 713–720. IFAAMAS, Richland (2008)
34. Vogel-Heuser, B., Legat, C., Folmer, J., Feldmann, S.: Researching evolution in industrial plant automation: Scenarios and documentation of the pick and place unit: Technical report (2014)
35. Winikoff, M.: JACK Intelligent Agents: An Industrial Strength Platform. In: Bordini, R., Dastani, M., Dix, J., El Fallah Seghrouchni, A. (eds.) Multi-Agent Programming: Languages, Platforms and Applications, pp. 175–193. Springer (2005)
36. Wooldridge, M.: An Introduction to Multiagent Systems, 2nd edn. Wiley, Chichester (2009)

AGADE

How Individual Guidance Leads to Group Behaviour and How This Can Be Simulated

Thomas Farrenkopf[1], Michael Guckert[1],
Benjamin Hoffmann[1], and Neil Urquhart[2]

[1] KITE - Kompetenzzentrum für Informationstechnologie,
Technische Hochschule Mittelhessen, Germany
{thomas.farrenkopf,michael.guckert,benjamin.hoffmann}@mnd.thm.de
[2] School of Computing, Edinburgh Napier University, Scotland
n.urquhart@napier.ac.uk

Abstract. In this paper we will demonstrate how BDI agents can be used to model individuals as participants in social structures where they act as potential buyers in a simple mobile phone market simulation. The simulation presented here is run in AGADE (Agile Agent Development Environment) – a toolset that offers flexible simulation means for multi-agent scenarios. Classical BDI technology is enhanced by the use of semantic technologies (i.e. OWL (Web Ontology Language) ontologies and automatic reasoning) to describe beliefs and plans of individual agents. Proof of concept is given in a case study with a scenario where agents are part of a typical social structure (small world network). Necessary information about mobile phones is encoded in OWL ontologies. Mutual influence of agents is determined by underlying social structures of the community.

Keywords: Multi-Agent System, BDI, OWL Ontology, Market Simulation.

1 Introduction

Crowd behaviour is formed by individuals and depends on effects that can be attributed to the crowd itself and interactions between its members. Software simulations of these phenomena are common in the field of sociology and related disciplines. Simulations are an essential tool for understanding social structures in general and market mechanisms in particular.

Agents must be able to act according to what they know and should possess the ability to learn. With the rise of the so called semantic web ontologies became popular and we now have standardized formal languages to represent knowledge which can thus be made available to agents acting in simulations. With the use of these ontologies the refinement of agent-based simulation software can have a significant impact on the development of multi-agent software simulations. Every agent will maintain its knowledge in an ontology and can act according

J.P. Müller, M. Weyrich, and A.L.C. Bazzan (Eds.): MATES 2014, LNAI 8732, pp. 234–250, 2014.
© Springer International Publishing Switzerland 2014

to that individual knowledge. The combination of several established technologies promises innovation and the generic approach will allow the simulation of different scenarios.

The idea of supporting communities of agents with ontologies which describe the objects involved in the agents' interaction with other agents has originally been formulated by Gruber [13] and subsequently been discussed by various other authors e.g. [14]. Nevertheless, the combination of various agent-based systems with ontologies is still a challenge. Both concepts have been developed independently and the link has not yet been built completely.

Moreover, typical semantic technology gaps exist in the exploitation of current agent system frameworks: Frameworks mostly just perform a syntactic matching to detect analogies between data exchanged during the communication between agents [14, pp. 1–35]. The research presented here aims at building stronger connections between semantic technologies and multi-agent systems.

Together with the exploitation of network analysis algorithms the use of semantic technologies gives a powerful mechanism to simulate behaviour in communities.

In this paper we address this challenge through the development of a multi-agent simulation tool AGADE that incorporates semantic technologies and network analysis algorithms. It is a highly configurable tool that can run BDI (Belief Desire Intention) agent simulations (section 3) where agents can communicate with each other and have knowledge of their environment. Approved social structure algorithms like preferential attachment are used to build social networks (section 4). In AGADE the named technologies are integrated and we demonstrate how BDI agents and social network algorithms are connected to semantic technologies (section 5). Finally a scenario of a rudimentary mobile phone market verifies the architecture of AGADE (section 6).

2   Related Work

The review of software projects for multi-agent systems lists over 40 different multi-agent systems from one-man open source projects to commercial platforms [21]. This list can be extended continuously with new multi-agent systems year by year.

Some of the agent frameworks provide support for the implementation of agent internal structures for methodological behaviourism in which each agent is defined in terms of its goals, knowledge and social capability. Only a few of them support the use of ontologies, but OWL has gained wide acceptance in the agent community and it has already been used in agent frameworks like JADE [5]. The agent community agrees that flexibility requires a common language for cooperative tasks [7]. Frameworks, which already support ontologies, generally use them for describing facts that agents can use within the content of messages. For example, KQML (Knowledge Query and Manipulation Language) (a language and a protocol for communication among software agents and knowledge-based systems) allows a structured way for knowledge exchange [10]. As a result of this

KIF (Knowledge Information Format) was built for the representation of knowledge [12]. It is a computer-oriented language for the interchange of knowledge among disparate programs. It allows agents to express properties of objects of interest (e.g. the weight of the Samsung Galaxy S4 is 130g). But KQML was proposed without defined semantics.

Malucelli and colleagues introduced the ForEV platform which is implemented through a multi-agent system in which partners can negotiate upon common standards of which an ontology is part of [20]. Stuckenschmidt and Timm argue that ontologies play a key role in multi-agent communication and mentioned that there is a need for ontologies for interacting agents to understand the content of a message [30]. Ontologies have also been applied to help in solving the so called heterogeneity problem in e-commerce negotiations [19]. Furthermore, sharing terms are also important in robotic applications e.g. the RoboCup robot soccer domain to share knowledge and also to represent real world objects in software applications [23].

An agent-oriented programming language which is based on the BDI concept is AgentSpeak [22]. It was extended with semantic technologies by Mascardi et. al. and then called CooL-AgentSpeak. The main challenge of giving agents individual ontologies is that ontologies may differ in various ways. The difference can exist between the formulated atoms. Schiemann tackles the problem of merging OWL DL ontologies for multi-agent systems to allow communication between agents that use semantic contents for dynamic knowledge bases [29]. He published a semi-automatic method which uses the principle of minimal change of agent-based modeling theory [11, pp. 129–147].

Subercaze and Maret introduced SAM (Semantic Agent Model) which is a model that allows the programming of agents based on semantic rules [31]. SAM illustrates the opportunities of using semantic technologies in the area of multi-agent systems. However, the concept is a low level implementation of an agent programming language independent of the BDI concept.

Mousavi et. al. demonstrate an ontology driven approach for procedural reasoning systems like agent models [24]. They demonstrated an applicable simulation in mobile environments by using the BDI architecture and OWL ontologies. Mousavi et. al. underline that "semantic knowledge representation and reasoning techniques can be used as effective tools to empower agents which are situated in dynamic environment in performing their tasks, as well as in communicating with each other, in a robust and acceptable manner" [25].

The literature shows the breadth of approaches of agent-based simulation models and their use of semantic technologies. Agents must be able to act according to what they know and must be able to learn. The standardised agent communication language FIPA already allows the integration of ontologies, but currently agent frameworks have not yet made full use of this option. Description logics are the core of ontology languages, such as OWL [16]. These can be used to give agents access to a structured representation of what they know. The challenge is to minimise the described lack in integrating ontologies and agent frameworks.

3   The Tool

AGADE is a round based multi-agent simulation tool set designed to support the development and calibration of dynamic multi-agent simulations one of which will be discussed throughout this paper. Based on the Jadex BDI framework [27] it leverages semantic technologies to facilitate a precise yet comfortable modelling of the desired market context while empowering all actors to utilise their world knowledge for inferring implicit knowledge as well as deducing how to act in a specific situation. While doing so, AGADE fosters its agents to be active parts of a complex social structure, allowing them to not only communicate with but also permanently learn from each other.

Each simulation scenario requires the definition of agent types as well as the respective number participating in the simulated scenario. In the case study presented in this paper we distinguish between buyer and seller agents. Starting the actual simulation the first thing to be done is to define the social structure comprised of the mutual relations of all agents. Using a graphical adjacency matrix, the groundwork of the social structure is laid by defining who knows whom. On top of this groundwork an arbitrary number of additional relational aspects (each with its own adjacency matrix and influence matrix respectively) can be built, e. g. by defining the degree of technical understanding agent a attributes to agent b or simply the degree to which one agent is affected by another.

Each agent is equipped with its own reasoner and private ontology which is accessed using the OWL API [15]. Social aspects and information about the agent's current state are mapped to the ontology.

The simulation itself can be controlled using the GUI displayed in Fig. 1. On the top of the GUI the control buttons are located: Because of AGADE's round-based approach, between any two rounds a simulation can be halted so that further inspections of the current state of affairs are possible. Current simulation data is displayed continuously.

The right hand side of the screen is a graphical display of the social structure formed by all participating agents. The vertices of the graph represent the agents using different shapes for different agent types. Size and colour of the vertices can be used to display additional information on the respective agent (e.g. the personal state of the respective agent). The edges between the vertices depict the relations of the agents giving a precise description of each relation as they are labelled with the respective relation indices. However, the social graph can also be used to advance into the very mind of each agent, as it allows to take a look at the current ontology state belonging to an agent of interest as well as displaying every single message (i.e. communicative act) an agent has sent or received.

Fig. 2 provides an abstract overview of the AGADE architecture. Originating from the Jadex framework there are *participants* that actually take part in the simulation. These agents are conducted by a *director* agent who triggers the

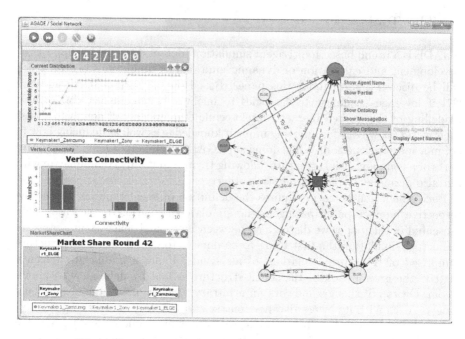

Fig. 1. The main GUI displayed during a simulation process

beginning of each new round. Each round is composed of six phases. In the first two phases of each round the *director* processes commands issued by the user during the simulation of the last round and arranges for the GUI components to be updated. At the beginning of the third phase, the *director* commands every single participant to make its necessary calculations (e.g. updating some status values). When all *participants* reported their respective calculation phases to be finished the socialisation phase, in which agents update their mutual relationships and probably build new relationships, is performed. After this phase the visualised social graph is to be updated. The last phase, called the acting phase, is where agents actually perform their domain specific actions.

As shown in Fig. 2, the *participants* are obliged to inform the *director* of any important event (e. g. the acquisition of a new phone) using the interface provided for this purpose. Being informed of any event of interest, the *director* becomes the omniscient entity feeding the GUI components with the required data. Apart from the *director* another entity storing huge amounts of information is the MessageCenter, where every message sent by any agent is stored.

Whenever the ontology of an agent is to be inspected, AGADE delegates the task of displaying the ontology to an external program specifically built for conveniently viewing and manipulating ontologies, thus making the analysis of agents' minds as easy and convenient as possible.

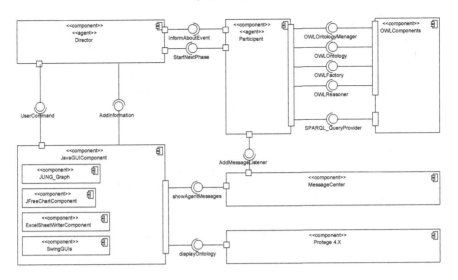

Fig. 2. Abstract view on the AGADE architecture

4   Small Worlds and Mutual Influence

Agents act as participants in social structures that can be visualised in a *sociogram* i.e. a graph with vertices representing the participants and edges their mutual relations. It is well known that social structures often are not as random as was long assumed. Rather than having arbitrarily connected nodes all being connected to a similar number of neighbours social networks frequently contain relatively few highly connected hubs and numerous nodes with only a limited number of neighbours [33].

In our approach we want to simulate the influence of members of such a community on the behaviour of others (in our case study the buying behaviour in particular). This influence is directed meaning that while agent a may ask b for advice b does not necessarily rely on a's opinion. Therefore we use a directed graph with directed edges where the head of the edge (i.e. starting vertex) can ask the tail (i.e. ending vertex) for advice and thus be influenced by him. Conforming to standard graph theory conventions we call the number of edges leaving a node its *outdegree* and the number of edges entering its *indegree* respectively. Obviously a node with a high indegree has a lot of influence and is consequently very important because it will be addressed frequently by many other members of the community. We will refer to this fact later when we discuss the weight of a node's influence. According to Katz who first coined the concept of opinion leadership, opinion leaders evolve because of their values, their competence or their social relations [17]. The latter is given for a node with a high indegree indicating its important role in the community. Therefore a node that lies above a given threshold is called a *hub* (sometimes referred to as a *rich node*) and is a potential opinion leader.

Classifying nodes by their degree leads to the graph's degree distribution. While the degree distribution of a random graph follows a binomial distribution a social network graph typically shows a power law distribution. This has been analysed and described by - among others - Barabási. Recent results show that virtual social networks (like Facebook) do not really follow that typical pattern. However, there exist hubs so that our considerations are still valid here [32].

Observing that communities rather evolve over time than being created in a single act Barabási's preferential attachment algorithm is an appropriate means for creating small world networks [1]. Nodes are added successively one at a time and each new node is linked to a given number of nodes already in the network. We adapted the algorithm so that it creates directed arcs whose tails are chosen randomly with a probability that depends on the number of nodes already linked to the node. Thus a hub is likely to get even more important ("the rich get richer" [4]). This models the fact that a newcomer will more likely get connected with someone popular. The algorithm is used to directly calculate the adjacency matrix with entries of 1 and 0. The entry 1 in cell i and j indicates that i and j are connected by an edge with head i and tail j. The entry 1 in all i,j indicates that an edge with head i and tail j exists.

Influence is not necessarily mutual and is therefore described in a non-symmetric *influence matrix*. Just like an adjacency matrix the influence matrix is indexed with the graphs nodes in row and column. The entry in cell i,j is zero if i and j are not connected and contains a measure for j's influence on i otherwise. As said before we assume that a hub's influence on others is higher because of the social status that is ascribed to such a position assuming that the influence of a person on another person depends on popularity. Instead of working with an influence matrix with predefined values we use structural aspects to compute a popularity factor for each node. Of course someone who is popular among other popular members of a community is more important than someone who is only popular in the eyes of the wallflowers. This line of argument leads directly to the famous page rank algorithm published by Page and Brin. The hyperlink matrix L is the transpose of the adjacency matrix where entries are divided by the sum of the entries in the corresponding column. This matrix obviously is a Markov matrix and Eigenvalues and Eigenvectors can be calculated iteratively. To guarantee convergence and to allow random effects we use the following iteration [2]:

$$p^{k+1} = \frac{1-\alpha}{n}e + \alpha L p^k$$

Starting with a vector that contains a valid probability distribution the limit of the sequence will yield a probability distribution over the set of agents whose values can be used to compute the influence matrix. In the formula α is a damping factor between 0 and 1 (0.85 is described to be a feasible value), e the vector with 1 in each component, and n the number of nodes. Nodes with outdegree 0 will get a value of $\frac{1}{n}$ in each corresponding cell in matrix L. Otherwise the matrix would not be a Markov matrix.

In its influence matrix AGADE assigns an *opinionInfluence* value between 0 and 1 to each consumer agent. For better readability the value is multiplied by 100 to lie between 0 and 100.

To calculate the influence matrix AGADE considers both the indegree and the page rank of a node. The ontologies of the consuming agents are architectured in a way that they can only be influenced by a peer agent if its respective opinion influence value is greater than a specific barrier denoted as β. To make sure that each hub possesses an opinion influence value in the range of $[\beta, 100]$ each hub is given β as a base value. Its pagerank is multiplied by $(1 - \beta)$ and added to the base value, leading to the following formula: Let A_C be the set of all consumer agents, ρ the page rank function that assigns the page rank to each agent $a \in A_C$ (according to its position in the associated sociogram), then the opinion influence ϑ of a is calculated as follows:

$$\vartheta(a) = \begin{cases} \beta + \rho(a) \cdot (1 - \beta) & \text{if } a \text{ is a hub} \\ 0 & \text{else} \end{cases}$$

Consequently agents can be ranked according to their influence value. While hubs are always ranked at the top, ordinary non-hub agents follow in the ranking. However both sets (hubs and non-hubs) are sorted. Agents have a numeric representation of their current state (their happiness so to say). In our case study this value is a representation of an agent's contentment related to his mobile phone (or the lack of one). This value may fluctuate randomly over time. Whenever it falls below a given threshold the agent gets active trying to improve his happiness (e.g. starts buying a new phone). One possible way to support the underlying decision process is looking for advice in the community. The agent will contact neighbouring hubs and will choose the one with the highest opinion influence value first. Because of this mechanism hubs that are only known by isolated nodes only influence those while real opinion leaders can also influence other hubs. This behaviour is coded in the agent's ontology which will be described in the next section. Thus, the opinion influence value is what really makes an opinion leader.

Our case study will demonstrate that following the response stimulus pattern setting the goal of an agent together with its plan to get advice from important participants of its social neighbourhood we can reproduce typical patterns of development.

5   Agents and Ontologies

An agent is an autonomous software entity which observes its environment, reacts to impulses and acts independently within a certain setting [34]. External stimuli and information gathered get processed and cause the agent to act. Agents focus their activities on achieving given goals while acting according to available plans. Such a goal is a desired state that can be reached by use of these plans. Literature also uses the term *intelligent agent*. An intelligent agent is capable of flexible autonomous action and can access existing knowledge and acquire new knowledge (i.e. learn) while pursuing goals.

Multi-agent systems contain numerous interacting agents that communicate using a formalised language. An appropriate paradigm for the development of intelligent agents is the so called BDI concept. It is characterised by the implementation of an agent's beliefs, desires and intentions which can be used to model aspects of human behaviour [26].

The agent belief base stores everything an agent knows (or believes to know) about the environment it lives and acts in. Ontologies now offer a standardised way to represent knowledge in general. This knowledge can be used for specifying the things that exist and how these things are related to each other (i.e. domain knowledge). Furthermore the ontology defines how conclusions can be drawn (i.e. inference knowledge) by using available reasoning instruments. Consequently ontologies are a promising tool to model agent belief bases.

Simply speaking an ontology $\mathcal{O}$ is a triple $(\mathcal{C}, \mathcal{R}, \mathcal{I})$ where $\mathcal{C}$ is a set of concepts, $\mathcal{R}$ a set of relations, and $\mathcal{I}$ a set of individuals. Concepts formally denote sets of individuals: a set of individuals is the extension of a concept while concepts are the intentional representation of sets of individuals. An individual that belongs to a concept is called an instance of that concept. The elements of $\mathcal{R}$ are relations (also called roles) that are defined with elements of $\mathcal{C}$ as domain and range. The extension of a role is a set of pairs $(c, d) \in \mathcal{I}$. Typically ontologies are formulated as description logics with differing levels of expressiveness [3].

We decided to use a three-layer ontology architecture for higher flexibility, reusability and to implement learning capabilities for agents (see Fig. 3). The abstract domain layer ontology (ADL) describes the general concepts and relations of the environment. The specific domain layer ontology (SDL) refines ADL by specializing abstract elements of ADL, thus every concept in SDL is a subconcept of concepts in ADL - possibly transitively. All agents share one common ADL and SDL and thus have a common basic understanding of the world they live in. Individuality is expressed in the next layer: the individual domain layer ontology (IDL) represents the individual beliefs and the definition of the individual behaviour of an agent (e.g. how an agent react to a certain stimulus). Each agent is initially equipped with a private individual layer ontology, which in turn imports the abstract domain layer and the specific domain layer.

In our case study ADL contains abstract information about market environments. Here we implemented concepts like *Person, Item, Product, Customer*, and *Institution* and relations like *owns* or *buys*. The specific domain ontology then specialises elements of ADL with mobile phone market specific terms (e.g it introduces *MobilePhone* as a subconcept of concept *Product* and *Samsung Galaxy S2* as an instance of concept *MobilePhone*). Finally the individual domain layer describes the individual factual knowledge of an agent (e.g. which phones is he familiar with) as well as the individual behaviour (e.g.: if you are unhappy, ask someone popular for help).

As mentioned before a BDI agent has a set of beliefs (i.e. knowledge), a set of desires (i.e. goals) and a set of intentions (i.e. plans of how they can reach

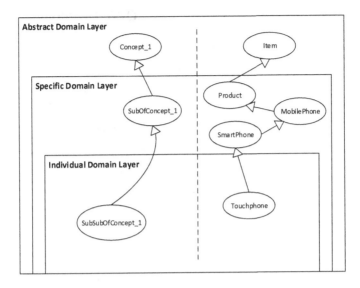

Fig. 3. Three-layer architecture

their goals). We define a mapping for each of these sets into our layered ontology by representing beliefs as relations, intentions and plans as OWL individuals of appropriate concepts (see Fig. 4). The mapper implemented in AGADE covers a prototypical implementation of a *belief change listener* which ensures that the beliefs of an agent are always up-to-date in its ontology.

Let $\mathcal{O}$ be an Ontology. Facts of the world of an agent are represented by individuals in the domain we are interested in. Properties allow the assertion of general facts about concepts and specific facts about individuals. It is possible to restrict a relation by specifying a domain and a range. We distinguish between data properties and object properties. Data properties are relations between individuals of concepts and RDF literals and XML Schema datatypes [6, 28]. Object properties are relations between individuals of two concepts.

In AGADE each agent a is described by an individual of the concept *Person* p (i.e. $a_1, a_2, ..., a_i \in \mathcal{I}$ and $a_i \in p$ are the representations of agents). Object properties such as *hasProduct* or *acquaintedWith* are elements of $\mathcal{R}$. For the first the range is the concept *Product* and for the second it is *Person*. The data properties *happinessValue* and *opinionInfluence* are elements of $\mathcal{R}$ with domain *Person* and range literal xsd:Integer. The instances of concept *AgentAction* represent all available plans and intentions an agent may have or use (e.g. *followOpinionLeadership*). An object property *nextAgentAction* (domain is set to *Person* and range is set to *AgentAction*) in connection with a rule expresses how the agent decides which plan to chose next:

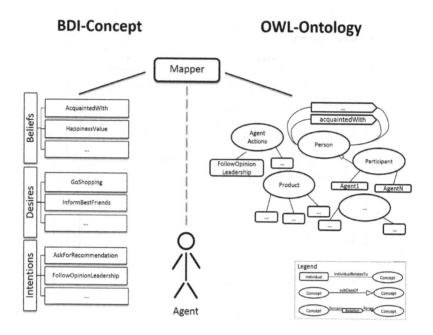

Fig. 4. OWL-BDI-Mapping

$$Person(myself), integer[< \gamma](?y), happinessValue(myself, ?y),$$
$$isAcquaintedWith(myself, ?a2), integer[> \beta](?z), opinionInfluence(?a2, ?z)$$
$$\rightarrow nextAgentAction(myself, followOpinionLeadership)$$

An agent $a1$ has a *happinessValue* ($h \in R$). If h is below a given threshold γ and if m is *acquaintedWith* ($aw \in R$) with another agent a_2 and a_2 has an *opinionInfluence* ($o \in R$) value higher than β (according to section 4) the next agent action will be set to *followOpinionLeadership* ($fol \in I$ and $fol \in AgentAction \in C$) by using ontology reasoning techniques.

Rule evaluation selects the *nextAgentAction* of an agent which will then be used as the next plan. Note that the ontology based belief base leads to a very flexible architecture, because important aspects of the agent do not have to be coded statically any more but may be expressed in the rules of the ontology.

OWL supports sharing and reuse of knowledge by importing ontologies or parts of ontologies into a given ontology. We use this to implement learning capabilities. On the one hand each agent is equipped with shared ontologies (common knowledge in ADL and SDL) on the other hand its IDL ontology is private. Therefore an agent's personal knowledge is limited by what is defined in its private ontology. Agents communicate with other agents (e.g. they exchange information about product details) and they possibly have to extend their knowledge base during a market simulation. Let o_1 and o_2 be individual ontologies.

The intersection of o_1 and o_2 ($o_1 \cap o_2$) is uncritical because it is obviously available to both agents. The intersection at least encompasses all elements defined in ADL and SDL (both are shared by definition). From the perspective of o_1 the set ($o_2 \setminus o_1$) is critical, because it contains elements of C, R or I which are relevant for the learning process. If an agent talks about such a critical element of o_2, an import process is started that gathers the definition of the element and adds it to the ontology o_1 .

For example: Each product u is represented as an instance of concept *Product* p ($u_1, u_2, ..., u_n \in I$ and $u_i \in p$, meaning u_i is an instance of *Product*). Facts about individuals are described by object properties (op_1, op_2,..., op_n and $op_i \in R$) as well as by data properties (dp_1 ,dp_2 , ...,dp_n and $dp_i \in R$). Let the IDL of an agent a_1 contain u_1 and that of agent a_2 contain u_2. If a_1 wants to show details of u_1 to a_2 and u_1 is totally new for a_2, the agent a_2 has to add u_1 into its IDL. Individuals and facts (properties) about individual can be added directly, if they are instances of a concept defined in ADL and SDL. But agents can also exchange definitions of concepts and information about individuals that are instances of concepts of an IDL. In this case the corresponding concept hierarchy will be added to the ontology of agent a_2. This learning capability has direct effects on the actions of agents (e.g. their buying behaviour).

The combination of BDI agents and ontologies with the use of reasoning techniques creates a new perspective for multi-agent simulation scenarios by describing agents with semantic technologies. The following case study shows a market scenario by using semantically advanced technologies.

6   Case Study

Opinion leadership is a well understood marketing mechanism that has gained new attention with the advent of social networks and their examination [18] in which opinion leaders strongly influence consumers' buying decisions. The process of passing information from person to person (e.g. about a product) is called word-of-mouth. "Opinion leaders are said to be the most influential and important in the word of mouth process" [18, p.6]. AGADE's mechanisms have been tested against an opinion leadership scenario in which opinion leaders pass information about their product to others.

The scenario models a rudimentary mobile phone market. Agents and their relations form a small world network of 100 nodes built with preferential attachment with parameters set according to Barabási's recommendations. Any node that is connected to more than 20 nodes is considered a hub. The weights of all edges connecting a node to one of these hubs is set to an opinion influence value of 80 to 100 making the hubs to opinion leaders (see section 4). These opinion leaders are equipped with new mobile phones. Agents have a happiness factor which they aim to maximise. This factor deteriorates continuously over time or by action of another agent. If the factor is below a given threshold the agents starts to act to make amends by starting the buying process. If agents without a phone are connected to an opinion leader, they will be directly influenced by him in their purchasing decision and follow the opinion leader's advice by buying the same phone. According to section 5 the behaviour is defined as an ontology rule. Agents that are not connected to an opinion leader look for a *friend* they are connected to. Currently, the value for the acquaintance value is according to section 4 either 1 or 0 multiplied by 100 which means that if two agents have a relationship it is concluded as a friend relationship. This behaviour can be modified by adding an appropriate value for the classification of the relationship. If they do not have a friend, they will not get a phone. If they have friends they will repeatedly ask one of them for a hint which phone to buy until they get the advice they need.

Agents can get information from their neighbourhood i.e. the set of all agents an agent is connected with. The addressed agent can answer such a request if he is able to. Alternatively he can delegate a request to one of his neighbours if he cannot create an answer by querying his ontology. For the time being we restrict the discussion to the mechanism of opinion leadership. Other influences such as advertising can also be investigated. Advertising for example can be modelled with a super hub that is extremely connected but has a rather low degree of opinion influence.

Experiments have shown that the structure of the graph scales up with a rising number of nodes. Fig. 5 shows a line graph with the number of phones sold after a simulation of 100 rounds. The x-axis describes the number of rounds and the y-axis describes the distribution of mobile phones. *Keymaker1_ELGE* increases rapidly at the beginning and runs into saturation. This demonstrates that innovation spreads from hubs through the network.

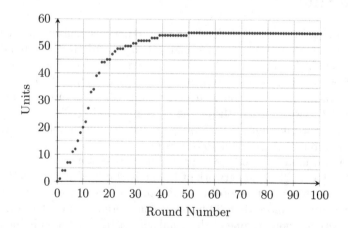

Fig. 5. Phone distribution after 100 rounds

The distribution of the product corresponds to data published by James S. Coleman, Katz and Menzel [8]. They studied the adoption rate of a new antibiotic (tetracycline – code-named Gammanym) by doctors in the field. They analysed prescription information and the spread of the use of that new drug and collected data about the mutual influence of the doctors' opinions. They detected that there were early adopters most of them well connected to other doctors (namely hubs) and that the use followed the social network structure.

Although one might argue that comparing medical drug distribution to the spreading of a specific phone type has some drawbacks. We argue that both scenarios can be compared when focussing on the decision processes (adoption of a new drug by doctors and mobile phone distribution as described here) that follow a pattern where personal influence plays a significant role.

Comparing Fig. 6 with the data created by the prototype shows significant similarity.

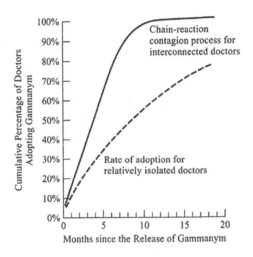

Fig. 6. The rate of adoption of Tetracycline by doctors [9, p. 147]

7   Conclusion and Future Work

The idea of supporting communities of agents with ontologies describing the objects involved in interactions is not new [13], but the idea of combining agent-based systems with ontologies for economic simulations has not yet been researched sufficiently because both concepts (web ontology languages and agent oriented programming languages) have been developed independently. AGADE shows a practical integration of a multi-agent based system and semantic technologies for a realistic modelling of individuals participating in a dynamic market environment, where plans are carefully written to use ontological descriptions.

The reference scenario *opinion leadership* was used to verify the architecture. AGADE has been tested with 5000 agents over 100 rounds on a quad core CPU and 16GB RAM. The prototype has the potential for further developments.

The generic approach will allow the simulation of different scenarios. Use of a distributed implementation allows to further scale up the simulations.

Future versions of AGADE will feature a domain specific language designed to both accelerate and facilitate the development of powerful AGADE components. This language will improve the readability allowing developers to focus on what is important and making development less error-prone. The modelling of scenarios with communities of a more inhomogeneous structure will be examined. Here agents will possess a broader variety of beliefs and follow different plans (they will use different ontologies). A generic approach of separating domain layer and inference layer will allow different problem solving strategies and the modelling of various set-ups.

References

1. Albert, R., Barabási, A.L.: Statistical mechanics of complex networks. Reviews of Modern Physics 74(1), 47–97 (2002)
2. Arasu, A., Novak, J., Tomlin, J.: Pagerank computation and the structure of the web: Experiments and algorithms (2002),
   http://citeseerx.ist.psu.edu/viewdoc/summary?doi=10.1.1.18.5264
3. Baader, F.: The description logic handbook: Theory, implementation, and applications. Cambridge University Press, Cambridge (2003)
4. Barabási, A.L., Albert, R.: Emergence of scaling in random networks. Science 286(5439), 509–512 (1999)
5. Bellifemine, F.L., Caire, G., Greenwood, D.: Developing multi-agent systems with JADE. Wiley series in agent technology. John Wiley, Chichester (2007)
6. Binstock, C.: The XML schema complete reference. Addison-Wesley, Boston (2003)
7. Boella, G., Damiano, R., Hulstijn, J., van der Torre, L.: A common ontology of agent communication languages: Modeling mental attitudes and social commitments using roles. Applied Ontology 2, 217–265 (2007),
   http://icr.uni.lu/leonvandertorre/papers/ao07b.pdf
8. Coleman, J.S., Katz, E., Menzel, H.: Columbia University. Bureau of Applied Social Research: Medical innovation: a diffusion study. Advanced Study in Sociology, Bobbs-Merrill Co (1966)
9. Cross, R., Parker, A., Sasson, L.: Networks in the Knowledge Economy. Oxford University Press, New York (2003)
10. Finin, T., Fritzson, R., McKay, D., McEntire, R.: Specification of the kqml agent-communication language (1993),
    http://www.csee.umbc.edu/csee/research/kqml/papers/kqmlspec.pdf
11. Fuhrmann, A., Rott, H.: Logic, Action, Information: Essays on Logic in Philosophy and Artificial Intelligence. De Gruyter (1996)
12. Genesereth, M., Fikes, R.E., Brachman, R., Gruber, T., Hayes, P., Letsinger, R., Lifschitz, V., Macgregor, R., McCarthy, J., Norvig, P., Patil, R.: Knowledge interchange format version 3.0 reference manual (1992),
    http://cs.auckland.ac.nz/courses/compsci367s2c/resources/kif.pdf
13. Gruber, T.: What is an ontology? (1992),
    http://www-ksl.stanford.edu/kst/what-is-an-ontology.html
14. Hadzic, M., Wongthongtham, P., Dillon, T., Chang, E.: Ontology-Based Multi-Agent Systems. SCI, vol. 219. Springer, Heidelberg (2009)

15. Horridge, M., Bechhofer, S.: The owl api: A java api for owl ontologies. Semantic Web 2(1), 11–21 (2011), http://dl.acm.org/citation.cfm?id=2019470.2019471

16. Horrocks, I.: Owl: a description logic based ontology language for the semantic web (2006),
http://www.dis.uniroma1.it/nardi/Didattica/RC/dispense/dlhb-14-2pp.pdf

17. Katz, E., Lazarsfeld, P.F.: Personal Influence, the Part Played by People in the Flow of Mass Communications. A Report of the bureau of applied social research Columbia university, Collier-Macmillan (1970)

18. Lerud, P., Molander-Hjorth, Söderstjerna, F.: Opinion leaders and word-of-mouth: A case study of Masai Barefoot Technology shoes. Ph.D. thesis, Lund University, Sweden (2007), http://lup.lub.lu.se/record/1345611/file/2434860.pdf

19. Malucelli, A., Palzer, D., Oliveira, E.: Combining ontologies and agents to help in solving the heterogeneity problem in e-commerce negotiations. In: IEEE Computer Society (ed.) International Workshop on Data Engineering Issues in E-Commerce, pp. 26–35. IEEE (2005)

20. Malucelli, A., Rocha, A.P., Oliveira, E.: B2B transactions enhanced with ontology-based services. In: Ascenso, J. (ed.) Proceedings of the First International Conference on E-Business and Telecommunication Networks, pp. 10–17. INSTICC, Setúbal (2004),
http://dblp.uni-trier.de/db/conf/icete/icete2004.html#MalucelliRO04

21. Mangina, E.: Review of software products for multi-agent systems (2002),
http://www.agentlink.org/admin/docs/2002/2002-47.pdf

22. Mascardi, V., Ancona, D., Bordini, R.H., Ricci, A.: Cool-agentspeak: Enhancing agentspeak-dl agents with plan exchange and ontology services. In: IEEE/WIC/ACM International Joint Conferences on Web Intelligence (WI) and Intelligent Agent Technologies (IAT), pp. 109–116 (2011)

23. Mendoza, R., Williams, M.A.: Ontology based object categorisation for robots. In: Meyer, T., Orgun, M.A. (eds.) Australasian Ontology Workshop (AOW 2005). CRPIT, vol. 58, pp. 61–67. ACS, Sydney (2005)

24. Mousavi, A., Nordin, M., Othman, Z.A., et al.: An ontology driven, procedural reasoning system-like agent model, for multi-agent based mobile workforce brokering systems. Journal of Computer Science 6(5) (2010)

25. Mousavi, A., Nordin, M., Othman, Z.: Ontology-driven coordination model for multiagent-based mobile workforce brokering systems. Applied Intelligence 36(4), 768–787 (2012), http://dx.doi.org/10.1007/s10489-011-0294-z

26. Norling, E.: Capturing the quake player. In: Rosenschein, J.S., Wooldridge, M., Sandholm, T., Yokoo, M. (eds.) Proceedings of the Second International Joint Conference on Autonomous Agents and Multiagent Systems, p. 1080. ACM, New York (2003)

27. Pokahr, A., Braubach, L., Jander, K.: The jadex project: Programming model. In: Ganzha, M., Jain, L.C. (eds.) Multiagent Systems and Applications, Intelligent Systems Reference Library, vol. 45, pp. 21–53. Springer, Heidelberg (2013),
http://dx.doi.org/10.1007/978-3-642-33323-1_2

28. Powers, S.: Practical RDF. O'Reilly, Beijing (2003)

29. Schiemann, B.: Vereinigung von OWL-DL-Ontologien für Multi-Agenten-Systeme. Ph.D. thesis, Universität Erlangen-Nürnberg, Universitätsstraße. 4 and 91054 Erlangen (2010),
http://www.opus.ub.uni-erlangen.de/opus/volltexte/2011/2352/pdf/BernhardSchiemannDissertation.pdf

30. Stuckenschmidt, H., Timm, I.J.: Adapting communication vocabularies using shared ontologies. In: Cranefield, S., et al. (eds.) Proceedings of the Second International Workshop on Ontologies in Agent Systems, Workshop at 1st International Conference on Autonomous Agents and Multi-Agent Systems, pp. 15–19 (2002), http://oas.otago.ac.nz/OAS2002/Papers/oas02-3.pdf
31. Subercaze, J., Maret, P.: Sam: semantic agent model for swrl rules based agents (2009), http://liris.cnrs.fr/Documents/Liris-4205.pdf
32. Ugander, J., Karrer, B., Backstrom, L., Marlow, C.: The anatomy of the facebook social graph. CoRR (2011), http://arxiv.org/pdf/1111.4503
33. Watts, D.J.: Small Worlds: The Dynamics of Networks Between Order and Randomness. Princeton studies in complexity. Princeton University Press (1999)
34. Weiss, G.: Multiagent systems: A modern approach to distributed artificial intelligence. MIT Press, Cambridge (1999)

A Tree-Based Context Model to Optimize Multiagent Simulation

Flavien Balbo[1], Mahdi Zargayouna[2], and Fabien Badeig[1]

[1] Institut Henri Fayol, ENS Mines Saint-Etienne,
158 Cours Fauriel, 42100 Saint-Etienne, France
{flavien.balbo,fabien.badeig}@mines-stetienne.fr
[2] Université Paris-Est, IFSTTAR, GRETTIA,
Champs sur Marne, France
hamza-mahdi.zargayouna@ifsttar.fr

Abstract. In most multiagent-based simulation (MABS) frameworks, a scheduler activates the agents who compute their context and decide the action to execute. This context computation by the agents is executed based on information about themselves, the other agents and the objects of the environment that are accessible to them. The issue here is the identification of the information subsets that are relevant for each agent. This process is time-consuming and is one of the barriers to increased use of MABS for large simulations. Moreover, this process is hidden in the agent behavior and no algorithm has been designed to decrease its cost. We propose a new context model where each subset of information identifying a context is formalized by a so called "filter" and where the filters are clustered in ordered trees. Based on this context model, we also propose an algorithm to find efficiently for each agent their filters following their perceptible information. The agents receive perceptible information, execute our algorithm to know their context and decide which action to execute. Our algorithm is compared to a "classic" one, where the context identification uses no special data structure. Promising results are presented and discussed.

Keywords: Multiagent simulation, Context, Agent models.

1 Introduction

One of the main functional objectives of the simulation domain is the controlled reproduction of complex systems. The simultaneity of actions, which means that several agents are activated at the same simulated time, is one of the properties that must be ensured. Therefore, the execution of a MABS model enforces a scheduling process (executed by a scheduler) that synchronizes the agents execution and simulates the simultaneity of their behaviors. Most of the MABS frameworks follows a cooperative model, where the activation of agents is controlled by a scheduler and their interruption is controlled by the agents themselves. When activated by the scheduler, the agent executes his current behavior and decides when to hand over to the scheduler.

When the agent is activated in a cooperative model, he is aware of the state of the simulation and his action will change that state. However, the agent takes simultaneously into account all the information accessible to him [5] and this could imply important computation times. The issue for the agent is to find the subsets of information

J.P. Müller, M. Weyrich, and A.L.C. Bazzan (Eds.): MATES 2014, LNAI 8732, pp. 251–265, 2014.
© Springer International Publishing Switzerland 2014

that are relevant for him. These subsets, that we call context, condition his behavior and belong to the his internal knowledge. In most MABS, the relevance criterion of a context is embedded in the agent implementation and is not separated from the actual action to execute. It is therefore difficult to customize the context computation without a modifying the agent's implementation. To decrease the context computation cost, designers often use nested contexts and/or behavioral automaton (NetLogo-like MABS). From our point of view, nested contexts make it hard to design agents and to customize context modeling. Behavioral automata on the other hand, by focusing on the internal state of the agent, neglect the other components of the agent context. Our proposal is the modeling of the contexts as "filters" to simplify the agent design without limiting the context computation possibilities. The activated agent receives his perceptible information from the scheduler and executes our algorithm to find the filters associated with his current context.

The remainder of the paper is organized as follows. Section 2 discusses the issues related to context computation. Section 3 presents an illustrative example that is followed all along this paper. Section 4 provides the formal definition of our proposal. Our context selection algorithm is provided in Section 5. Section 6 presents our experimentation and results. The paper concludes with a discussion and some perspectives to this work.

2 State of Art

When an agent is activated, he is aware that he is executing a new simulation time step. He can therefore compute his current context before to decide which action to execute. In this section, we discuss the options to compute the agent's context.

The first option, the most popular, is agent-oriented. The scheduler activates the agents either by calling a default method [3,13] or with a control message [11,14] and the activated agent computes his context. For instance in [3] the objects belonging to the perception field of the activated agent are given to him with a perception event. The logo-based multiagent platforms such as the TurtleKit simulation tool of MADKIT [7] or STARLOGO[1] have chosen this option. The agent is activated following the state of his behavioral automaton that has been computed at the previous activation.

The second option is scheduler-oriented. The scheduler computes for the agents which action to execute following their current context. To the best of our knowledge, the framework JEDI [9], the Repast Simphony simulation platform [4] and our own work [1,2] are the only proposals where the choice of the action that is executed by an agent is computed by the scheduler. In the JEDI framework [9], the choice of an action by the agent is based on an interaction matrix where a cell is a conditioned contextual interaction between two agents. For instance, an interaction is possible between two agents following their proximity. To each of these contexts, an action is associated and will be executed by the activated agent. This interaction matrix is defined by the designer and does not change during the simulation. Repast Simphony natively uses the first scheduling options (i.e. with a default method), but it also allows a sort of *contextual activation* based on "watchers". Watchers allow an agent to be notified of a state

---

[1] http://education.mit.edu/StarLogo/

change in another agent and schedule the resulting action. The designer specifies which agent to watch and a query condition that must be verified to trigger the resulting action. This activation process is limited by the expressiveness of the watcher queries language to express the activation context. The queries are boolean expressions that evaluate the watcher and the watchee using primitives such as *colocated, linked_to* [*network name*], *within X* [*network name*], etc. (a network is a graph of agents relationships) and the operators AND and OR. It is not possible to integrate complex conditions about other components (other than the watcher and the watchee).

In previous works [1,2], we have proposed a multiagent-based simulation process that belongs to this last option. We have modeled contexts with conditions about shared information on the MAS components. A subset of conditions defines a specific context and is called a filter. The multiagent environment is used as a scheduler and it activates the agents according to filters triggering based on perceptible information. In the proposal described in this paper, the environment activates the agents in turn with their accessible information and it is the activated agent who computes his context based on his own context model (his filters).

3   Illustrative Example

To illustrate our proposal, we present an example of context modeling for a driver entering a roundabout. This example illustrates the components of our proposal and our experiments are based on a theoretical example (Section 6). Figure 1 represents a roundabout with agents (vehicles, pedestrians and bicycles) and objects (traffic signs).

In our proposal, an agent context is a conditioned combination of the perceptible information that are relevant for him. The only perception of the information is not sufficient, their values have also to be taken into account. For instance, the pedestrian agent pa_1 is perceived by va_1 and va_2 (Figure 1) but the resulting context is not the

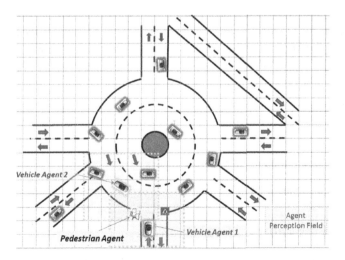

Fig. 1. Roundabout simulation example

same for each agent: 1) va_1 context could be *"my speed is excessive and there is a pa_1 crossing the street before me"*; 2) va_2 context could be *"I am about to cross entering traffic, which is blocked by the crossing pa_1"*. The information are indeed the same, but it is their combination that is relevant for the agents. After identifying their contexts, the agents have to decide which action to execute. The issue is that these combinations are multiple and their computation is time-consuming. The objective is to decrease the context computation time without limiting the expressiveness of the context definition. This definition is related to the domain expert, as well as their use in the decision process. Moreover, the design of the agents using context information remains free. For instance, va_1 could be a BDI agent who would have initiated a plan with this information and v_2 could be a reactive agent who would reacted with an acceleration. Our proposal is placed between the information acquisition and the decision process: we propose a data model and an algorithm to process information context.

4   Context Model Definition

Context computation assumes that agents have information about the MAS components (agents, objects, etc.) that are accessible to them. The accessibility conditions have to be specified for each simulation and, in our example, we associate to each agent a perception field where all simulation components are perceptible by him. In this section, we propose a context model. The first component of the model is called an entity and is a meta-information about a MAS component.

Definition 1 (Entity). *An entity $\omega \in \Omega$ is a $\langle r_\omega, d_\omega \rangle$ pair with :*

- *r_ω: reference to a real component of the the MAS, i.e. agent or object.*
- *d_ω: description of this component recorded in the environment. It is defined by a set of $\langle property, value \rangle$ pairs.*

r_ω gives access to the component (for the activation process if it is an agent); d_ω contains information to identify the context of the agents. An entity is the link between the MAS and the context model. In the following (except where noted), entity and description are used interchangeably. A property gives a specific information about a component of the MAS.

Definition 2 (Property). *A property $p_i \in \mathcal{P}$ is a function, which description domain $d_j \in \mathcal{D}$ is quantitative, qualitative or a finite set of data. A property is noted $p_i : \Omega \rightarrow d_j$, with Ω the set of descriptions.*

The properties are used to characterize subsets of entities.

Definition 3 (PDescription). *A PDescription is a subset of $\mathcal{P}$ and we note P_e the PDescription of the entity e.*

The extension of a *PDescription* is called a *Category*.

Definition 1 (Category). *A Category is a subset of semantically similar entities with the same PDescription : $\langle label, \{\omega \in \Omega | P_{\omega_i} = P_{\omega_j} \forall \omega_i, \omega_j \in C_x\} \rangle$ with label the name of the Category.*

In our example, vehicle agents (VA), pedestrian agents (PA) and traffic signs (*TS*) are category examples. At least, the list of the perceptible entities of an agent is given to him by environment at each time step. This list is called *PerceptibleCategories* and does not contain empty categories. For instance, the description of a vehicle agent could be (we note $\Omega_{\mathcal{A}} \subset \Omega$ the set of agents):

- *speed* $: \Omega_{\mathcal{A}} \rightarrow \mathbb{R}$: the speed of the agent;
- *location* $: \Omega_{\mathcal{A}} \rightarrow \mathbb{N}$: the distance from roundabout entry or a relative value for a roundabout lane;
- *street* $: \Omega_{\mathcal{A}} \rightarrow \{street\ name, lanelocation\}$: the name of the street or the location in the roundabout;
- *direction* $: \Omega_{\mathcal{A}} \rightarrow \{$ *to roundabout, from roundabout*$\}$;
- *turnSignal* $: \Omega_{\mathcal{A}} \rightarrow \{left, right, off\}$: the state of the turn signals;
- ...

Its *PDescription* is $\{speed, location, ...\}$ and its Category is $\langle vehicle, \{va_1, va_2, ...\}\rangle$. We propose to model a context as a filter, which tests the entity that the agent perceives. A filter generates processed information from raw information (description of the MAS components).

Definition 4 (Filter). *A filter* $F_j \in \mathcal{F}$ *is a tuple* $F_j = \langle f_a, f_C, n_f \rangle$ *with:*

- $f_a : \Omega_{\mathcal{A}} \rightarrow \{true, false\}$ *a mandatory assertion that expresses constraints on the agent who owns the filter;*
- $f_C : 2^{\Omega} \rightarrow \{true, false\}$ *an optional set of assertions expressing constraints on others components that complete the context;*
- n_f *the filter name.*

A filter identifies by unification the agent's description and the context (subset of entities) that matches the associated assertions. A filter is valid for tuples $\langle a \in \Omega_{\mathcal{A}}, context \subset \Omega \rangle$ such that $f_a(agent) \wedge f_C(context)$ is evaluated to true. When a filter is valid, the associated context, $\langle context, n_f \rangle$, is valid for the agent a. A context being formalized as assertions on the descriptions of the MAS components, the *context* and n_f information are complementary to characterize the MAS context. It means that the same description's subset can valid several contexts and a context can be validated by several description's subsets.

Let $\langle f_a, f_C, warning \rangle$ be a filter dealing with the detection of a warning related to the potential movement of vehicles. A filter belongs to an agent and is therefore built from his point of view. For the *warning* filter, the vehicle agent is on the central lane of the roundabout (fig 1) and a slower vehicle agent before him in the other lane turns on his left turn signal. The filter triggering depends on: i) the location of the agent (assertion f_a), ii) the perception of another agent with a perceptible property (assertion f_C). The filter *warning* has the following definition:

- $a \in \Omega_{\mathcal{A}}$: $f_a : [speed(a) = ?s_a] \wedge [street(a) = centralLane] \wedge [location(a) = ?l_a]$
- $b \in \Omega_{\mathcal{A}}$: $f_C(b) : [speed(b) < ?s_a] \wedge [location(b) < ?l_a + 2] \wedge [turnSignal(b) = left] \wedge [street(b) = externLane]$

The symbol "?" before an expression identifies a variable and the operator "=" is the comparison operator. With this filter, the agent a, when he is in the central lane, is aware of the b slower agents who are in the external lane and up to two units before him, with their left turn signal on. The scheduler has already filtered the perceptible entities based on the perception field of the agent a.

We assume that the number of entities by category (the categories' cardinality) is defined by the MABS designer, or that he is at least able to order categories following their cardinalities (without necessarily defining the exact number of entities per category). In our roundabout example, the designer does not know the exact number of entities but he is able to define the following order $\cdots < |TS| < |PA| < |VA| < \ldots$ if the simulation concerns rush hours with a great traffic activity, or $\cdots < |PA| < |VA| < |TS| < \ldots$ if the simulation concerns night time with low traffic. The rank of the filters will follow the chosen order.

Using this order, the context-knowledge of the agents is formalized as an ordered list of pairs, that we call *PotentialContext*. The first member of a pair is the label of a category, which is called *reference*, and the second member is an ordered tree of filters. This tree contains the filter with *reference* as the tested category with the minimal cardinality. For instance, Figure 2 describes the pair (TS, tree) for a vehicle agent. The category TS is associated to a tree containing the filters where the category TS is tested alone or with the categories PA and VA. We associate with the category PA (the second element of the list) the filters where the category PA is tested alone or along with the category VA. At least, we rank the *PotentialContext* list following the cardinality of the reference.

Each agent has his own customized instance of the proposed data structure and he processes our algorithm (described later in this paper) to browse it and find the filters

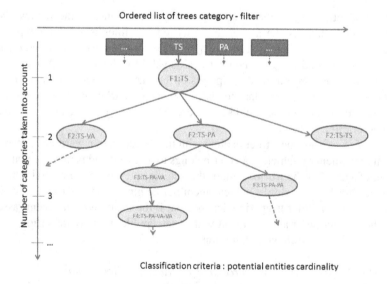

Fig. 2. Ordered list of filters

that match the accessible descriptions. The objective of this structure is to test the less filters given the number of categories that are perceived by the agent. The basic idea is the following: *The evaluation of a filter is conditioned by the existence of an entity for each category that it tests.*

The naming convention of the filters indicates the depth of the filters in the tree and the increasing cardinality-order of the categories to test. For instance *F2:TS-VA* (Figure 2) is a filter that is at the depth 2 and testing the categories *TS* then *VA*. The cardinality-order has two advantages. The first is algorithmic because it allows us to look efficiently for filters that can be evaluated (Section 5). The second advantage is practical since it insures the uniqueness of filters in the tree. For instance, the filter *F2:TS-VA* does not belong to the tree of the category *VA*. Nevertheless, for clarity's sake, when the position of the filter in the tree is not discussed, we use a more explicit naming, as for the *warning* filter defined earlier for the filter *F1:VAx*.

A node is a set of filters for which f_C validation concerns the same set of categories. To distinguish them, we append a letter to the end of the filters name. For instance, the node *F4:PA-TS-VA-VA* (Figure 2) contains all filters where f_C is validated with the description of a pedestrian agent, a traffic sign and two vehicle agents (in addition to the vehicle agent, owner of the list of filters' tree). The filter *warning* belongs to the node *F1:VA* since f_C is related to one vehicle agent.

An arc is an inclusion relation between subsets of filters: the deeper node (the child) contains the filters for which evaluation needs one more category to test than the shallower node (the parent). For instance, the children of the node *F1:TS* are *F1:TS-VA*, *F1:TS-PA* and *F1:TS-TS* with respectively the addition of the categories *VA, PA* and *TS*.

For a given depth, the filters are ranked in decreasing order of categories cardinality. For a given node, these children are explored if the additional category belongs to the perceptible categories (Section 5). Therefore, processing in priority the children that have potentially the more chances to have descriptions increases the possibility to have a valid context and to stop the search. For instance, there are potentially more vehicle agents than pedestrian agents that are perceived by a vehicle agent. In Figure 2, the filters belonging to the node *F3:TS-PA-VA* are tested before the filters belonging to the node *F3:TS-PA-PA* if the category *VA* belongs to *PerceptibleCategories*. However, if the objective is to retrieve all the possible contexts of the agents then the ordering of the nodes has no consequence.

If a child node has no parent, i.e. there exists no filter concerning only the parent's categories, then the parent node is created but is empty.

Starting from this structure of filters and the perceptible descriptions, we can design an algorithm that identifies efficiently the possible filters.

5   Context Computation Algorithm

The general principle is to test the only filters for which there exists descriptions that are accessible to the agent. For each reference, the agent has to test the filters contained in the root then in each of its children if the added category exists in *PerceptibleCategories*. It is noteworthy that a child node may have validated filters because accessible descriptions validate its conditions while its parent does not contain any valid filter. Our context model exploits the structure of the perceived information, the category, and not their value. The advantage is the independence of our proposal from the environment dynamics, avoiding costly updates of the agent knowledge.

In the scheduling Algorithm 1, the number of time ticks is fixed (T) and for each tick, the scheduler activates in turn the agents and provides a list *PerceptibleCategories* to each of them. This list is built by environment, which selects among perceptible entities the ones that are relevant for the activated agent (1-(5)). A category is relevant if it is related to at least one filter. The list *RelevantCategories* is defined for each agent as the list of the references of his relevant categories. This list is not sorted because our algorithm aims to provide all the possible contexts; it is then necessary to explore all the possible trees. The prefixed notation indicates the access to the members of the concerned element and we note $\mathcal{A}$ the set of agents.

When an agent is activated, he executes a *perception - decision - action* loop. A part of the perception step is already performed since the agent has the perceptible entities. The browsing of *PerceptibleCategories* (Algorithm 2) is already a selection of the filters, because if a category refers to a filter's tree ft but does not belong to *PerceptibleCategories*, ft is not explored. In Figure 3, only the list of filters' trees of the categories VA and TS are explored and not the filters' tree of the category PA following the selection labeled with the number 1.

In Algorithm 2, for each category belonging to *PerceptiblesCategories*, the agent explores the related filters' tree.

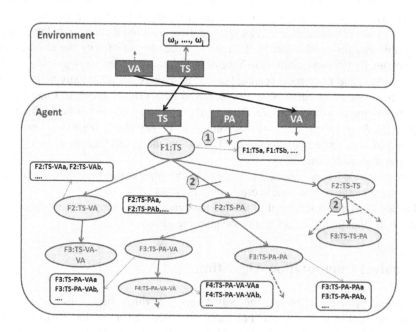

Fig. 3. Global overview of context model

Algorithm 1. Simulation scheduling algorithm

Require: $T > 0$
1: $t \leftarrow 0$
2: **while** $t < T$ **do**
3:     **for all** $a \in \Omega_{\mathcal{A}}$ **do**
4:        $PerceptibleCategories \leftarrow perception(a.position, a.RelevantCategories)$
5:        $a.activate(PerceptibleCategories)$
6:     **end for**
7:     $t \leftarrow t + 1$
8: **end while**

The filter's trees (*PotentialContext*) are recorded in an ordered dictionary with the category name as a key and the filters' trees as value. The algorithm explores the filter's tree in two steps:

1. It explores the filters of the current node (value 1 in Algorithm 2-(2)): it tests the f_a part of the filter (condition on the state of the agent) before to test f_C (the conditions on the concerned descriptions). This order avoids to browse the related categories if the current state of the agent makes the filter not adapted. For instance, for the filter *warning*, it is not useful to test all the perceptible vehicle agents if the activated vehicle agent is not in the central lane of the roundabout. If the agent uses a behavioral automaton, his current state can be used here to reproduce a logo-based simulation.
2. It explores the children saved in a sublist (value 2 in Algorithm 2-(9)): the exploration of the child is performed following a recursive process applying the same principles than for the root.

If the filter is valid given the state of the agent (Algorithm 2-(3)) and the necessary descriptions (Algorithm 2-(4)) then it is saved in the list of valid filters of the agent.

Algorithm 2. Activate: Agent activation algorithm

Require: *PerceptibleCategories*
1: **for all** $category \in PerceptibleCategories$ **do**
2:     **for all** $f \in self.PotentialContext[category][1]$ [2] **do**
3:        **if** $f.valid(self)$ **then**
4:           **if** $f.trigger(self, PerceptibleCategories)$ **then**
5:             $self.validFilter.add(f)$
6:           **end if**
7:        **end if**
8:     **end for**
9:     **for all** $t \in self.Filter[category][2]$ **do**
10:        $self.recursiveFilterTriggering(t, PerceptibleCategories)$
11:     **end for**
12: **end for**
13: $self.decision()$
14: $self.action()$

This list is made of sublists containing the name of the filter and the list of descriptions validating it. We choose not to compute all the combinations of perceptible descriptions of a given filter and to only select the first successful.

The input parameters of the recursive algorithm are the part of the filters' tree that is explored and the accessible descriptions. A partial filters' tree is a list of lists with, for each imbrication level, three information:

1. The name of the new category taken into account. For instance *VA* for the fist call following the filters tree given Figure 3.
2. The list of filters of the node. For instance the filters belonging to the node *F2:TS-VA* Figure 3
3. The list of children that reproduce this structure. For instance the structure related to the filters' tree with *F3:TS-VA-VA* as a root.

With these information, the algorithm tests the existence of the category (Algorithm 3-(1)) and if successful, it tests the nodes of the filter (Algorithm 3-(2)) then accesses the children nodes (Algorithm 3-(7)). If the category does not belong to perceptible categories then this part of the filters' tree is not explored. For instance, the filters' tree with the category *PA* (Figure 3-selection labeled with 2) are not explored because this category does not belong to perceptible categories.

6 Experimentation

To validate our proposal, we choose a theoretical framework in which we set categories and filters. Our environment is a 2D grid that contains 135,000 entities distributed in 6 Categories (C4 to C9) in addition of 100,000 agents (category C1). For each Category, we set a relative number of entities to have poorly represented categories (*C4*) or well represented categories (*C9*) (Table 1). For each description, random values between 0 and 20 for five properties are generated.

Algorithm 3. Recursive tree of filters exploration

Require: *partialTree*
Require: *PerceptibleCategories*
 1: **if** *partialTree*[1] ∈ *PerceptibleCategories* **then**
 2:     **for all** *f* ∈ *partialTree*[2] **do**
 3:         **if** *f.valid(self)* **then**
 4:             **if** *f.trigger(self, PerceptibleCategories)* **then**
 5:                 *self.validFilter.add(f)*
 6:             **end if**
 7:         **end if**
 8:     **end for**
 9:     **for all** *t* ∈ *partialTree*[3] **do**
10:         *self.recursiveFilterTriggering(t, PerceptibleCategories)*
11:     **end for**
12: **end if**

We simulate agents situated on a matrix with a size varying from 1000×1000 to 7000×7000. The agents must decide which action to perform following the MAS entities that are present in their perception field. The position of the entities is random.

Table 1. Cardinality of the Categories

nom	*cardinality*
C4	10000
C5	15000
C6	20000
C7	25000
C8	30000
C9	35000

The filters' tree for our tests is the one described in Figure 4. Filters are chosen to respect a homogeneous dispatching between categories in order not to introduce bias. An obvious bias is the overrepresentation of filters for an underrepresented category. Hence for each category, there exists 3 filters of first level (F1), 6 filters of second level (F2) and a filter of third level (F3) for a total of 41 filters. Each agent of the simulation has the same filters' tree there is therefore 4,100,000 filters to test at each simulation step.

We compare our proposal with a solution in which filters are not organized and are explored iteratively. The objective is to compare our proposal with an algorithm computing the context with conditional branching but that remains generic. We call this proposal a *classic* algorithm while ours is called *structured* algorithm. The computation cost of a filter is similar in the two algorithms only the search organization is different.

We perform 30 simulations of one time cycle and measure the time spent to generate the possible filters. To ensure a similar behavior of the two algorithms (same world state during evaluation), at each cycle the activated agent executes both algorithms and their computation time is measured before modifying the state of the world.

Our algorithm have been developed in Python 3.3 and processed on a PC with an Intel Core i5-2500 CPU@3.3GHz and 12 GB memory.

We present an algorithm to reduce the context computation time during the perception step. Nevertheless this step includes the browsing of the grid containing perceptible entities which is also a costly computation. Therefore we must assess the advantage of our proposal according to the global computation time of the perception step. We propose two parameters for the evaluation:

- The size of the perception field: the variation of this parameter enables to know when the decrease of the context computation runtime becomes negligible according to the time needed to explore the grid that contains the perceptible descriptions.
- The size of the grid: the variation of this parameter enables to modify the number of potential entities that are perceived by the agent with a constant grid exploration cost.

The first result is about the percentage that the context computation process represents within the global perception step for the classic algorithm. The results are given in Table 2. For instance, if the perception field value is 10 and the size of the 2D grid is 5000 × 5000 then 29.07% of the perception step execution time is related to the context computation and therefore 70.93% to the browsing of the 2D grid that is perceived by each agent. We observe that the context computation represents half the execution time of the perception process when the perception field is small and it decreases quickly (down to 17.53% for a 7000 × 7000 grid and a perception field of 20). If the perception field is greater than 20 then the runtime related to the context computation process becomes negligible. The increase of grid size causes a decrease of the context computation time because the time to explore the grid remains stable while the context computation time decreases (there are less entities to process).

The second result concerns a comparison between the structured algorithm and a classic algorithm w.r.t. the context computation time. Table 3 provides the improvement percentage when using our algorithm w.r.t the perception field and the size of the grid. It means that if the perception field value is 10 and the size of the 2D grid is 5000 × 5000 then the necessary time to compute the context is 48.1% less with the structured algorithm than with the classic algorithm.

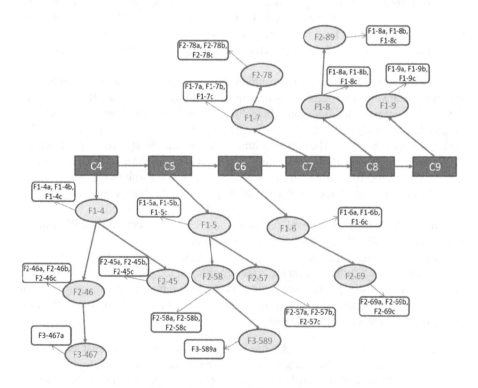

Fig. 4. List of trees of filters example

Table 2. Structured algoritm : Relative performance of context computation

matrix size	Perception field		
	5	10	20
1000 × 1000	49.03%	35.52%	20.23%
3000 × 3000	38.95%	35.31%	24.96%
5000 × 5000	37.97%	29.07%	21.51%
7000 × 7000	35.47%	25.75%	17.53%

Our algorithm is always better than the classic algorithm but this advantage decreases conversely to the increase of the perception field. The decrease in the improvement with the increase of perception field is coherent with the principle of the algorithm. Indeed, the more entities the agent perceives, the less there are empty categories. Nevertheless, we have seen with the first experiment that the perception field has to be limited to 20, because with a superior value, the context computation time becomes negligible according to the browsing of the grid that contains the perceptible entities.

Table 4 highlights the fact that our algorithm improves the simulation execution time whatever the perception field size. For instance if the perception field value is 10 and the size of the 2D grid is 5000 × 5000 then the time related to the perception step is 13.98% less with the structured algorithm than with the classic algorithm. For each simulation step and for all simulation configurations, the maximal gain is 1.82 second, the minimal gain is 0.52 second and the average gain is 1.15 second.

Our choice to separate the context modeling and the algorithm to determine current context allows to give to each agent his own list of filters trees. This customization of the context can be processed without modifying the implementation of the agents. We perform simulations where the size of the environment evolves from 500×500 to 3000×3000 with 120,000 agents with the same list of filters (Figure 4) that we compare with three agents' categories (C1,C2,C3) with 40,000 agents each. Theses categories have a subset of the list of trees of filters. Each of these subsets contains the categories given in Table 5.

The context computation time decreases for the two algorithms because agents take into account less information to compute their context. Nonetheless, our algorithm remains always better than the *classic* algorithm. With our algorithm, the average decrease of the time is 7.61 seconds by cycle in comparison with the execution without the customization of the agents' context.

Table 3. Structured algorithm vs classic algorithm : Relative performance of context computation

Matrix size	Perception field		
	5	10	20
1000 × 1000	8.11%	13.93%	8.46%
3000 × 3000	57.53%	20.85%	8.11%
5000 × 5000	82.35%	48.1%	10.66%
7000 × 7000	87.77%	69.04%	29.24%

Table 4. Structured algorithm vs classic algorithm : Relative performance of context computation

	Perception Field		
Matrix size	5	10	20
1000×1000	3.98%	4.95%	1.71%
3000×3000	22.41%	7.36%	2.02%
5000×5000	31.27%	13.98%	2.29%
7000×7000	31.13%	17.78%	5.13%

Table 5. Dispatching of relevant Categories by agent's Category

agent's Category	Relevant Category	Entities number
C1	C4, C5, C8, C9	90,000
C2	C6, C7, C8, C9	110,000
C3	C4, C5, C6, C7	70,000

7   Conclusion and Perspectives

In this paper, we proposed a solution to decrease processing time of a multiagent simulation without simplifying the context modeling. This issue is important because high execution times risk unfortunately to circumscribe the use of the multiagent paradigm to small-size simulations. Our proposal focused on the optimization of context computation. We propose to model a context as a filter, which allows us to propose a filters' structure as a tree and an algorithm for the agent to browse it efficiently. The proposed structure exploits the *a priori* cardinality of the different categories that an agent can take into account in the evaluation of his context. Our structure is simple and does not take into account the tests processed by the filters as an algorithm like RETE [8]. The advantages are a low memory cost and its independence against the environment dynamics. Our future work concerns the assessment of our proposal with distributed simulation like in [12] and the introduction of new data structures, such as lattices, in the organization of filters in order to take into account other filter's classification criteria. Our experimentation showed that our improvements became insignificant in comparison to the time to compute the set of perceptible data. Another perspective is to take into account the researches to optimize the environment data management like in [10,6]. In addition, we plan to enrich the evaluation of our proposal with several real world applications.

References

1. Badeig, F., Balbo, F.: Définition d'un cadre de conception et d'exécution pour la simulation multi-agent. Revue d'Intelligence Artificielle 26(3), 255–280 (2012)
2. Badeig, F., Balbo, F., Pinson, S.: Contextual activation for agent-based simulation. In: Proceedings of the 21st European Conference on Modelling and Simulation, ECMS (2007)
3. Béhé, F., Galland, S., Gaud, N., Nicolle, C., Koukam, A.: An ontology-based metamodel for multiagent-based simulations. Simulation Modelling Practice and Theory 40, 64–85 (2014)

4. Collier, N.: Repast: An extensible framework for agent simulation, vol. 36. The University of Chicago's Social Science Research (2003)
5. Abowd, G.D., Dey, A.K.: Towards a better understanding of context and context-awareness. In: Gellersen, H.-W. (ed.) HUC 1999. LNCS, vol. 1707, pp. 304–307. Springer, Heidelberg (1999)
6. Farenc, N., Boulic, R., Thalmann, D.: An informed environment dedicated to the simulation of virtual humans in urban context. In: Proceedings of EUROGRAPHICS 1999, pp. 309–318 (1999)
7. Ferber, J., Gutknecht, O.: Madkit: A generic multi-agent platform. In: 4th International Conference on Autonomous Agents, pp. 78–79 (2000)
8. Forgy, C.L.: Rete: A fast algorithm for the many pattern/many object pattern match problem. Artificial Intelligence 19, 17–37 (1982)
9. Kubera, Y., Mathieu, P., Picault, S.: Interaction-oriented agent simulations: From theory to implementation. In: Ghallab, M., Spyropoulos, C., Fakotakis, N., Avouris, N. (eds.) Proceedings of the 18th European Conference on Artificial Intelligence (ECAI 2008), pp. 383–387. IOS Press (2008)
10. Michel, F.: Translating agent perception computations into environmental processes in multi-agent-based simulations: A means for integrating graphics processing unit programming within usual agent-based simulation platforms. Systems Research and Behavioral Science 30(6), 703–715 (2013)
11. Sierhuis, M., Clancey, W.J., Van Hoof, R.J.: Brahms: a multi-agent modelling environment for simulating work processes and practices. International Journal of Simulation and Process Modelling 3(3), 134–152 (2007)
12. Šišlák, D., Rehák, M., Pěchouček, M., Rollo, M., Pavlíček, D.: A-globe: Agent development platform with inaccessibility and mobility support. In: Software Agent-Based Applications, Platforms and Development Kits, pp. 21–46. Springer (2005)
13. Wagner, G.: AOR modelling and simulation: Towards a general architecture for agent-based discrete event simulation. In: Giorgini, P., Henderson-Sellers, B., Winikoff, M. (eds.) AOIS 2003. LNCS (LNAI), vol. 3030, pp. 174–188. Springer, Heidelberg (2004)
14. Warden, T., Porzel, R., Gehrke, J.D., Herzog, O., Langer, H., Malaka, R.: Towards ontology-based multiagent simulations: The plasma approach. In: 24th European Conference on Modelling and Simulation (ECMS 2010). European Council for Modelling and Simulation, pp. 50–56 (2010)

Agent-Based Modeling and Simulation of the Emotional and Behavioral Dynamics of Human Civilians during Emergency Situations

Mouna Belhaj, Fahem Kebair, and Lamjed Ben Said

Higher Institute of Management of Tunis
Optimization Strategies and Intelligent Information Engineering Laboratory
Le Bardo, 2000, Tunisia
mouna.belhaj@hotmail.com, kebairf@gmail.com,
lamjed.bensaid@isg.rnu.tn

Abstract. Agent based social simulations are becoming prevailing tools in the context of human behavior studies. Researchers in psychology, cognitive science and neuroscience have proved the prominent role of emotion on cognition and behavior. Particularly, during emergency situations, human emotional dynamics have a major effect on behavior. In this context, we aim to study the role of emotions in reproducing human-like emotional civilian agents. The objective of the current research work is to model and to simulate human emotional dynamics and their effect on the behaviors of civilians in emergencies. In this article, we describe an emotional agent model that integrates a computational model of emotions. Agent perceptions are subject to a cognitive appraisal process to generate agent emotions. These have an effect on the generation of agent behavior.

Keywords: Emotional dynamics, Appraisal, Emergencies, Human behavior.

1   Introduction

Implementing human characteristics into artificial systems is a key and a multidisciplinary challenge. This implementation aims at building agents with believable and realistic behaviors. Different factors are modeled in human behaviors simulations. These include physical and physiological factors, cognition, emotions, personality traits, social relations among others. The interplay of emotion and cognition is particularly important in the study of human behaviors, particularly during emergency situations. In fact, emotions are important regulator factors of human behaviors, mainly to respond to highly emotive events such as those happening in emergency situations. Thus, humans that experience heightened emotional states can have unexpected behaviors [1]. Therefore, emotions are necessary to produce realistic social simulations in emergencies. These situations are characterized by their dynamicity and complexity. Hence, modeling human-like agents in such situations requires the integration of emotion modeling. In fact, emotions represent important adaptation mechanisms to changes that may occur in the agent environment.

J.P. Müller, M. Weyrich, and A.L.C. Bazzan (Eds.): MATES 2014, LNAI 8732, pp. 266–281, 2014.
© Springer International Publishing Switzerland 2014

The objective of the current research work is to study human emotional dynamics and their effects on civilian behaviors during emergencies via emotional artificial agents. We aim to construct an emotional agent based social simulation of human civilians in an emergency situation. In this paper, we describe the modeling and implementation of an emotional agent model of human civilians. The proposed model uses a crisis environment model and a computational model of emotions for the emergency situations context that were proposed in a previous work [2]. The first describes the different components of a crisis environment. This model is necessary to distinguish the entities that an agent may recognize in its encounter in order to model the agent perceptual mechanisms. However, the second is dedicated to the reproduction of human emotion mechanisms. It describes the process of emotions generation based on a psychological model of emotions named the OCC model [3]. It also gives details about the methods and the parameters (appraisal variables) used to compute emotions intensities. The proposed emotional agent model utilizes these models in order to perceive, appraise and respond emotionally and behaviorally to the facts that occur in an emergency situation.

In the reminder of this paper, we first outline related work from the literature. After that, we describe the emotional agent model we propose. Then, we give a description of the implementation and experimentations of the model in a multi-agent based simulation system of a crisis situation after a disaster (RoboCupRescue). Finally, we draw a conclusion and present perspectives of the current work.

2 Related Work

Approaches interested in human behavior modeling during emergencies may be classified into four categories. The first category includes researches based on mathematical equations estimated from data, obtained from real experiments [4]. The second class includes approaches based on physical phenomena (particles and fluids dynamics, forces) and are especially used to study the behavior of large crowds [5], [6]. The third category is based on cellular automata and represents mainly multi agent approaches. The environment is divided into a grid of cells and agent behaviors are simplified to the computation of a movement vector [7]. The complexity of the human behavior makes mathematical physical and cellular automata based approaches, that over simplify humans, unfeasible in the context of behavioral simulations [8].

More recent works, that are mainly multi-agent approaches, are based on social and psychological theories of human behavior. Researches based on social theories tend to reproduce social phenomena such as agent roles, social relations in groups and communication in agents [9]. However, approaches based on psychological theories tend to integrate emotions or personality in their modeling of human behavior. We are concerned with the last category of approaches. Particularly, we are interested in studies that integrate emotions into artificial agents in order to reproduce human-like behaviors in emergency situations. A work presented in [10] introduces a conceptual model of emotional agents based on rational BDI decision making processes: the EP-BDI (Emotion Personality- Belief Desire Intention) framework. It is based on the classical BDI architecture enriched by the role of emotions and personality on the selection of the suitable behaviors in emergency situations. In [11], the authors present an extension of the BDI architecture that considers physiology, emotion and personality (PEP→BDI). It was also used to simulate crisis situations.

These approaches are only concerned with the effect of emotions and personality on the decisional and behavioral processes. No or little indications are provided about the emotions eliciting conditions, intensity computation and decay. This is due to the complexity of representing emotions mechanisms though particular combinations of mental states (such as beliefs, desires, intentions and emotions). In other contexts, these conditions are formalized using logical relations between these mental states, such as in [12] and [13]. In these works, the authors tend to model the interplay of emotion and cognition in order to manifest the role of emotion in agent deliberation.

In [14], a different work is presented based on a naturalistic decision making theory named Recognition Primed Decision (RPD) making [15]. The latter is based on the fact that humans base their decisions on previous experiences when they are confronted with situations with acute stress. The objective of the work presented in [14] is to reproduce human-like behaviors in critical situations. This approach explains the role of the emotional process on an RPD-based agent model. However, it focuses on the influence of emotions on the decision making process, disregarding the emotion generation process. This model was enhanced in the work presented in [1], where the authors describe the emotion engine and its integration to the original model.

Emotion mechanisms are represented in more details in different approaches that propose computational models of emotions based on psychological theories. Some of these approaches are based on the theory of Scherer [16], such as the work presented in [1] used for crowd simulation in protest scenarios. We can also site EMA (Emotion and Adaptation) presented in [17] as an example of the works based on Lazarus theory of emotions [18]. EMA was employed in a military application. We are particularly interested in researchers that base their computational models of emotions on the OCC model [3]. Examples include the works presented in [19], [20] and [21] that were used in different contexts. A fast review of psychological and computational models of emotions can be found in [22].

In our work, we aim to provide a comprehensive agent model that integrates an emotion generation process. We use our proposed computational model of emotions for the emergency situations context presented in [2]. The agent model we propose is based on the appraisal process of the OCC model. The final goal is to allow, through simulations, the study of the effect of the resulting emotions on the selection of the appropriate behavior using a BDI-based [23] action selection mechanism.

3   Emotional Agent Model

The emotional agent model involves three main components: Perception module, Appraisal module and Behavior module (Figure 1). An agent perceives its environment in order to detect changes in the aspects of the environment. New significant information about the agent context are processed and categorized into five types of perceptual data. Each category is appraised by the corresponding appraiser using specific dimensions to generate emotions. The latter are used to update the emotional state of the agent. The resulting emotional state influences the importance of the agent goals and orients its BDI-based action selection process. Details about the processes of the emotional agent model are provided in the following subsections.

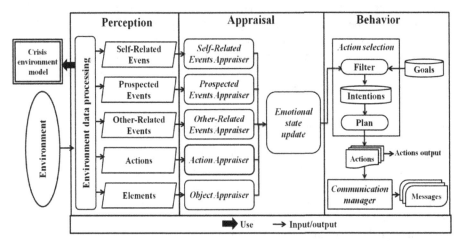

Fig. 1. The emotional civilian agent model

3.1   Crisis Environment Model

The proposed agent model uses a crisis environment model detailed in a previous work [2]. It was based on the conceptual model of the disaster space for emergency situation management presented in [24]. The model provided in [24] defines a generic taxonomy that describes the different elements of an environment during a disaster. This model was used to capture the different facts in the environment used as a basis for a Decision Support System for risk detection and management. The hierarchy of the conceptualized classes of the environment elements proposed in the model is representative of a crisis environment. However, we extended the existing model so that it represents all aspects of the environment that may influence the emotions of a civilian in the disaster space. Therefore, we take a civilian's perspective in modeling this environment. We defined new classes and reified the specification of the characteristics and methods of different classes. Details about these changes could be found in [2]. The resulting model distinguishes the different entities of the disaster space in order to identify the different objects that an agent may recognize in its environment. These objects cover the different elements in the environment (buildings and roads), other agents (civilians or actors: rescue personals), agent (self or other) actions and messages. An agent may also detect events organized into three categories. The first one includes events that affect directly the state of a civilian, and named Self-Related Events (SRE). The second class encloses events that a civilian may expect given its current state; Prospected Events (PE). Finally, the events related to other civilians are called Other-Related Events (ORE).

3.2   Perception

The emotional agent perceives its environment in order to detect changes in its encounter. Significant data, coming from the environment, are detected by the "Environment data processing" component. The latter has as role to filter perceptual information in order to detect significant changes (for the agent) in the environment. These changes are categorized according to the crisis environment model into five perceptual data categories. Each type of filtered environment data is used, in the appraisal phase, by a specific appraiser in order to elicit particular emotions that belong to one of the emotion categories of the OCC model of emotions [3].

3.3   Appraisal: The Emotion Generation Process

Agent perceptions are appraised in order to produce civilian emotions. The Appraisal module is composed of five Appraisers: the Self-Related Events Appraiser, the Prospected Events Appraiser, the Other-Related Events Appraiser, the Action Appraiser and the Object Appraiser. Each appraiser evaluates a particular category of perceptual data and generates specific emotions. The latter are then combined in order to generate the emotional state of the agent. The appraisal process is based on the OCC model of emotions. The OCC model considers emotions as the evaluation outcome of the relationship of a person with its environment. Emotion is then a valenced reaction that results from the detection and evaluation (appraisal) of a significant event for the person, according to some specific dimensions called appraisal variables. The OCC model defines three aspects of the environment that could be appraised: events, actions and aspects of objects. Different appraisal variables are defined to be relevant to each of these aspects and are used to deduce the intensity of the corresponding emotion. Therefore, combinations of particular values of these variables elicit specific emotions. We have identified five appraisers necessary to evaluate the different perceptions categories produced by the perception module.

Appraisers. The global structures of the five appraisers are relatively analogous. In fact, each appraiser receives a category of the processed environment data. The data in input is evaluated in order to generate a particular emotion that belongs to one of the emotion categories of the OCC model. The output of each appraiser is an emotion. The intensity of the emotion results from the combination of the values of the appraisal variables (defined in the OCC model) that are relevant to each of the five appraisers. Figure 3 presents the general process of each of the appraisers. The valence and nature of the resulting emotions depend on the valence and category of the perceptual data to be appraised (event, action or aspect of object). Each elicited emotion has as information its category, its label (name), its valence (positive or negative), its intensity, which is computed using the relative appraisal variables, its target (self, other, object) and its cause (event, action, object).

The computations of emotion intensities are performed using the computational model of emotions for the emergency management context, that we have proposed in [2]. The latter contains an extensive description of the theoretical foundation of the proposed model. It also includes detailed definitions of the appraisal variables of the OCC model we use, and an explanation of the methods and formula we employ to calculate their values and to compute emotion intensities. In this paper, we are rather concerned with the description of the emotional agent model and its implementation.

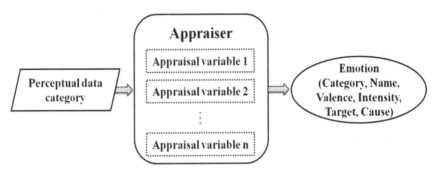

Fig. 2. General process of agent appraisers

In Table 1, we give a summary of the categories of perceptual data used by each Appraiser, and the emotion(s) of the OCC model that an appraiser may generate.

Table 1. Perceptual data in input of each appraiser and potential resulting emotions

Appraiser	Perceptual data category	Perceptual data	Elicited emotion(s)
Self-Related Events Appraiser.	Self-Related Events	Safe (self)	Joy
		InRefuge (self)	
		Injury (self)	Distress
		InDanger (self)	
		HealthStateDown (self)	
Prospected Events Appraiser	Prospected Events	ProspectRescue (self)	Hope, Satisfaction, Disappointment,
		Prospect Injury (self)	Fear, Relief
		ProspectDeath (self)	Fear-confirmed
Other-Related Events Appraiser	Other-Related Events	Safe (other)	HappyFor
		InRefuge (other)	
		Injury (other)	SorryFor
		InDanger (other)	
		HealthStateDown (other)	
		Death (other)	
Action Appraiser	Agent action	Self action	Pride/Shame
		Other action	Admiration/Reproach
Object Appraiser	Elements of the environment	Refuge	Like
		Blockade, collapsed Building	Dislike

Emotional State Update. During the evolution of the emergency situation, new events, actions or changes in object aspects may take place. Consequently, new emotions may appear and others may be updated. The different appraisers are only concerned with the generation of the new emotions, triggered by the appraisal of the altered aspects of the disaster environment. An *Emotional State Update* module is used to update existing emotions and to add new ones in order to generate the final emotional state of the agent.

The emotional state of a civilian at a time step of the simulation is a set of n vectors. Each vector corresponds to an emotion in the emotions space. The latter is composed of the set of emotions that could be felt by the agent in response to the cognitive appraisal of the perceptual data in input. A summary of these emotions is presented in Table 2. The latter includes the categories of the emotions considered for the proposed agent model, their causes and their labels in the OCC model. It also contains a description of the elicitation conditions of each emotion.

Table 2. Emotion categories of the OCC model, their cause and explanation

Emotion Category	Caused by	OCC Emotion	Elicitation condition
Wellbeing emotions	Certain event	Joy	Occurrence of a desirable event for self
		Distress	Occurrence an undesirable event for self
Prospect-based emotions	Prospected event	Hope	Prospect of a desirable event
		Fear	Prospect of an undesirable event
	Confirmed prospected event	Satisfaction	Occurrence of a prospected desirable event
		Fear-confirmed	Occurrence of a prospected undesirable event
	Disconfirmed prospected event	Disappointment	Non-occurrence of a prospected desirable event
		Relief	Non-occurrence of a prospected undesirable event
Empathetic Fortune-of-Other emotions	A desirable event for other	Happy-for	Occurrence of a desirable event for someone else
	An undesirable event for other	Sorry-for (Pity)	Occurrence of an undesirable event for someone else
Standard-based emotions	Agent action	Pride	Approving of one's own praiseworthy action
		Shame	Disapproving of one's own blameworthy action
	Other agent's action	Admiration	Approving of someone else's praiseworthy action
		Reproach	Disapproving of someone else's blameworthy action
Attitude-based emotions	An object	Like	Perceiving an appealing object
		Dislike	Perceiving an unattractive object

3.4   Behavior

Emotions that result from the appraisal process may affect the cognitive, behavioral (action selection processes), physical (facial expressions or motion) or emotive response (expressed emotions are different from felt emotions). The present work addresses the effect of emotions on behavior.

Action Selection Mechanism. The action selection mechanism relies on the BDI (Belief-Desire-Intention) model [23]. The decision about the actions to perform is taken in the light of the active goal (Intention) and the emotional state of the agent. Agent beliefs (processed perceptual data) include information about the agent itself (Self-Related Events), its expectations given its current situation (Prospected Events), other agents (Other-Related Events), and the objects and actions that appear in the disaster space. These information (Beliefs) are appraised in order to generate the emotional state of the agent. Intentions (selected goals) are induced by the current emotional state and agent goals (Desires). Given the active goal (Intention), the suitable sequence of actions is selected to be executed.

Civilian agents may perform some actions as behavioral responses to their current state such as Move (environment), Wait (person) and Find (person). They may also have empathetic behaviors as a response to the state of other people in need: Help (person). The action to perform may also be sending a message. In this case, it is processed using the communication manager, which is responsible for sending and processing messages.

Communication Manager. In a crisis situation, civilian agents can communicate with each other through the exchange of messages. These can be information messages that inform about an event or an injured person. Messages can also be sent to ask for help. These messages may induce emotional reactions in the receiver. An emotion-based communication process is therefore handled in a separate module.

4   Implementation and Experimentations

A part of the proposed civilian agent model was implemented into the civilian agents of the RoboCupRescue (RCR) simulation system [25]. In the following subsections, we first present the RCR simulator. Then, we describe the results obtained from the experimentations of four appraisers among the five ones defined in the model, in order to generate agent emotions that result from the evaluation of events and objects in the crisis environment.

The action appraiser takes as input agent actions to evaluate them. Therefore, it will be evaluated with the behavior module.

4.1   RoboCupRescue Simulator

RCR simulator is an agent-based urban disaster simulator of an emergency situation after an earthquake. The aim of the RCR project is to promote research works on the context of emergency management and to provide a virtual tool to test different communication, coordination and planning methods. It aims at exploring new procedures for emergency management [25].

We have chosen to test our implementation of the agent model in the RoboCupRescue (RCR) simulation project for two reasons. On the one hand, we take advantage of the completeness of this system that provides a realistic simulation of a disaster environment. Moreover, in RCR, information about changes in agent encounter could be collected and processed by the agent. On the other hand, the current civilian agents in RCR have simple behaviors and are not sufficiently involved in the study of the emergency situation [26]. Furthermore, RCR civilian agents are not endowed with emotions that have been proved to be necessary to reproduce human-like agent behaviors in emergencies. Therefore, we aim to improve the simulation of RCR civilians by implementing and integrating the proposed emotional civilian agents into the RCR simulation system.

The RCR simulation system is composed of a Kernel and a set of simulators and two categories of human actors (civilians and rescuers: police forces, ambulance teams and firefighters). In our work, we focus on the civilian agents of RCR in which we implemented the emotional agent model we proposed. Each simulator of RCR is responsible for the simulation of a particular aspect of the emergency situation. We can find a simulator of injuries, a simulator of buildings collapse, a simulator of fire, etc. During the simulation, civilians could be in different states. Some civilians may remain safe; others may be injured during the simulation. The health state of a civilian may decrease until his death or until being rescued by rescuer agents.

4.2   Perceptual Data Acquisition and Processing

At each time step of the simulation, the civilian agent receives perceptual information from the Kernel of the RCR simulation system. Agent perceptions include visual information that involve all the entities of the environment in the vision specter of the agent. An agent may perceive buildings, rescuer agents, other civilians and their properties. The second category of perceptions includes auditory information. The latter enclose messages that the agent can hear.

The perceptual data sent by the RCR Kernel are represented by changes in the elements properties of the crisis environment that are in the encounter of the agent. These precepts are processed to detect changes in the agent's context. The detection of a change involves the detection of a new event, an action or an object. Each perception is categorized and affected to the convenient appraiser.

4.3   Appraisal of Self-related Events and Generation of Wellbeing Emotions

The emotional agents are able to detect Self-Related Events (SRE) that can be positive events: *Safe (self)* and *InRefuge (self)* or negative events: *Injury (self)*, *InDanger (self)* and *HealtStateDown (self)*. The evaluation of positive SRE results on the *Joy* emotion. However, the appraisal of negative SRE elicits the negative emotion

Distress. The death of the agent itself is marked with the event "*Death*" that makes the emotion of the agent undefined (Figure 3).

The first plot (Plot 1) in Figure 3 illustrates the evolution of the intensities of Well-being emotions of a civilian agent. However, the second plot (Plot 2) shows the evolution of the *desirability* (appraisal variable) of the causing SRE.

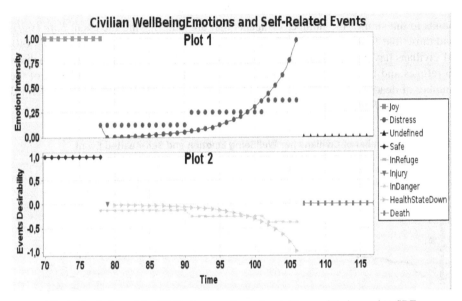

Fig. 3. Evolution of the Wellbeing emotions of a civilian and their causing SRE

In the illustrative example, the agent is safe (*Safe (self)* event) until instant 77 of the simulation. Therefore, it has the emotion *Joy*. At time step 78, the agent detects the *InDanger (self)* event that is associated to "being in a fiery building" in RCR. At instant 79, the civilian is injured (Plot 2). This is a negative undesirable event with a negative desirability degree (-0.1) and corresponds to a first decrease of the health state of the agent. This causes the appearing of the *HealthStateDown (self)* event (Plot 2). These negative self related events give rise to the emotion *Distress*. Each event is evaluated separately. Therefore, we find two corresponding *Distress* values at each time step in Plot 1. The intensities of this emotion, which corresponds to the absolute value of the desirability of the causing events, will be combined in the Emotional state update phase. More details about emotion intensity and event desirability computation are described in the computational model of emotions we have proposed in [2]. The intensity of the *Distress* emotion and the desirability of the causing events are recomputed at each time step of the simulation. In fact, the intensity of emotions may increase or decrease depending on the evolution of the causing events. These events could become more desirable or more undesirable depending on their valence (positive or negative). At instant 107, the civilian is dead: (Death event in Plot 2) and his emotion becomes undefined (Plot 1).

Figure 4 illustrates the evolution of the number of civilians detecting each type of self related events (Plot 2) and feeling the corresponding Wellbeing emotion (Plot 1) over time. We can notice that the curves of the evolution of *Distress* (respectively *Joy*) emotion and of the causing negative (respectively positive) SRE have similar shapes. In fact, the number of agents having the negative emotion *Distress* corresponds to the number of those facing the negative events defined above. Similarly, at each time step of the simulation, the number of agents having *Joy* emotion corresponds to the sum of the number of agents that are safe (having the event *Safe (self)*) and those that found a refuge (*InRefuge (self)*). For example, we have at time $t = 140$, 41 civilians having *Joy* emotion. This value corresponds to the sum of the 13 civilians in refuges and the 28 civilians that are safe (at $t = 140$). Finally, the evolution of the number of dead civilians (Death in Plot 2) corresponds to those having the undefined emotion (*Undefined* in Plot 1).

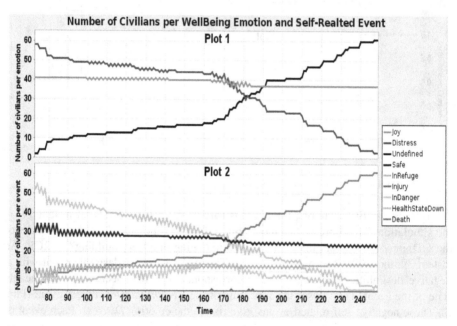

Fig. 4. Evolution of the number of civilians having a Joy or a Distress emotion and the corresponding SRE

4.4   Appraisal of Prospected Events and Generation of Prospect-Based Emotions

An agent may prospect negative events such as to be injured or to die and positive events like expecting to be rescued. Prospected Events (PE) arise when the agent is in a stressful situation such as being in a fiery building (*InDanger(self)*) or loosing health points (*HealtStateDown(self)*). Therefore, the number of civilians having a prospect-based emotion in Figure 5 corresponds to the number of those having the

Distress emotion in Figure 4. For example, we find that, at time $t = 100$, the number of civilians having a *Hope* or a *Fear* emotion is 10 and 38 respectively. The result of the addition of these values corresponds to the number of civilians having a distress emotion at $t = 100$ that is 48 (Figure 4). The prospect of a negative or a positive event is currently random. However, we aim to relate it to the civilian personality in the following step of this work. In fact, personality shapes human tendencies to expect positive or negative events when they face difficult situations.

Figure 5 demonstrates that the evolution of the number of emotional civilian agents having a *Hope* emotion (Plot 1) corresponds to those prospecting to be rescued (Plot 2). It also shows that the sum of the numbers of civilians prospecting negative events (Prospect Death or Injury) is equal to the number of civilians feeling a *Fear* emotion.

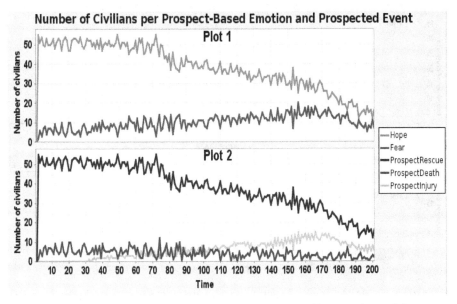

Fig. 5. Evolution of the number of civilians having a Hope or a Fear emotion and the corresponding PE

The number of civilians having prospect-based emotions at the beginning of the simulation (58 civilians at $t = 1$) decreases over time and is close to zero by the end of the simulation. This is due to the fact that almost injured civilians finish by dying inside collapsed buildings.

4.5   Appraisal of Other-Related Events and Generation of Empathetic Emotions

Agents are able to perceive Other-Related Events (ORE) of nearby agents. A *Happy-For* emotion arises from the appraisal of the events *Safe (other)* and *InRefuge (other)*. However, a *SorryFor* emotion is elicited when the agent detects that a negative event happens to another agent: *Injury (other)*, *InDanger (other)*, *HealthStateDown (other)* and *Death (other)*. In order to have an empathetic emotion (*HappyFor* or *SorryFor*), the target agent must be visible to the agent feeling the empathetic emotion.

In Figure 6, we notice that the number of agents having a *HappyFor* emotion is greater than the number of agents having a *SorryFor* emotion. This is due to the fact that agents must be actually visible to each other in order to generate empathetic emotions. However this number increases when communication will be implemented, since hearing ask for help messages may induce the *SorryFor* emotion towards invisible agents inside buildings. Obviously, the number of civilians having a *HappyFor* (respectively *SorryFor*) emotion corresponds to those perceiving *positive* ORE (respectively *negative* ORE) (Figure 6).

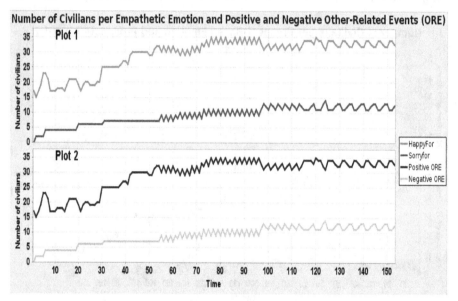

Fig. 6. Evolution of the number of civilians having a HappyFor or SorryFor emotions and the corresponding positive and negative ORE

4.6   Object Appraisal and Generation of Attitude-Based Emotions

RCR crisis environment contains different objects such as buildings (of civilian, Police offices, etc.), refuges, roads and blockades. We have associated, for civilian agents, the *Like* emotion to the perception of a *Refuge* and the *Dislike* emotion to the perception of a *Blockade* or a collapsed *Building* (Figure 7). We consider refuges, blockades and collapsed buildings as the most attractive objects for a civilian in the crisis environment. Civilians, perceiving the different elements of the crisis environment, are safe civilians and are able to move in the disaster space.

Blockades result from buildings collapses. This explains the equality of the numbers of civilians perceiving blockades and of those perceiving collapsed buildings (Figure 7, Plot 2). Consequently, the curves representing the number of civilians seeing blockades or collapsed building are too similar. Note that a civilian may perceive simultaneously several collapsed buildings and blockades. In that case, we suppose that the most negatively attractive building is the one that has the biggest damage. Similarly, we consider that the biggest blockade is the one appraised to generate the *Dislike* attraction emotion. The number of civilians having a *Like* (respectively *Dislike*) emotion (Figure 7, Plot 1) corresponds to those perceiving a *Refuge* (respectively a *Blockade* or a collapsed *Building*) in the disaster space (Figure 7, Plot 2).

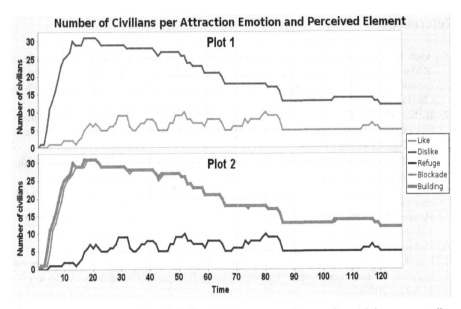

Fig. 7. Evolution of the number of civilians having an attraction emotion and the corresponding perceived element

Some of the blockades may disappear by the action of RCR police force agents whose mission is to clear blocked roads. Moreover, civilians may find and enter inside refuges. Therefore, they don't perceive blockades and collapsed buildings. This explains the decrease of the number of civilians perceiving negatively attractive elements of the environment over time.

5   Conclusion and Future Work

In this paper, we presented an emotional agent model for the simulation of human emotional and behavioral dynamics during emergency situations. The model emphasizes the role of emotions on producing realistic behaviors social simulations during emergencies. It relies on a process of cognitive appraisal of perceptual data that enables the production of the emotional reaction to events, actions or changes in object aspects. The implemented part of the model includes agent perceptions processing and emotions generation. Performed experimentations proved that the evolution of emotions is quite representative of the happening events and may affect considerably agent behaviors. Indeed, the next step of this work will deal with the development of the behavior module that aims to prove the effect of the emotional state of the agent on its behavior. We also intend to integrate the personality notion in the proposed model. This will enrich the proposed emotion generation process by creating more diversified and human-like emotional responses. In fact, human personalities define tendencies to feel particular emotions and behavioral predispositions.

References

1. Aydt, H., Lees, M., Luo, L., Cai, W., Low, M.Y.H., Kadirvelen, S.K.: A Computational Model of Emotions for Agent-Based Crowds in Serious Games. In: IEEE/WIC/ACM International Conferences on Web Intelligence and Intelligent Agent Technology, pp. 72–80 (2011)
2. Belhaj, M., Kebair, F., Ben Said, L.: A Computational Model of Emotions for the Simulation of Human Emotional Dynamics in Emergency Situations. J. Comput. Theory Eng. 6, 227–233 (2014)
3. Ortony, A., Clore, G.L., Collins, A.: The Cognitive Structure of Emotions. Cambridge University Press (1988)
4. Galea, E.R., Owen, M., Lawrence, P.J.: Computer Modelling of Human Behaviour in Aircraft Fire Accidents. Toxicology 115, 63–78 (1996)
5. Helbing, D.: A Fluid Dynamic Model for the Movement of Pedestrians. Complex Syst. 6, 391–415 (1992)
6. Helbing, D., Molnar, P.: Social Force Model for Pedestrian Dynamics (1998)
7. Pan, X., Han, C.S., Dauber, K., Law, K.H.: A Multi-Agent Based Framework For the Simulation of Human and Social Behaviors During Emergency Evacuations. Ai Society 22, 113–132 (2007)
8. Zaharia, M.H., Leon, F., Pal, C., Pagu, G., Baykara, N., Mastorakis, N.: Agent-Based Simulation of Crowd Evacuation Behavior. In: WSEAS International Conference on Mathematics and Computers in Science and Engineering, pp. 529–533 (2009)
9. Pelechano, N., Brien, K.O., Silverman, B., Badler, N.: Crowd Simulation Incorporating Agent Psychological Models, Roles and Communication. In: International Workshop on Crowd Simulion, pp. 21–30 (2005)
10. Zoumpoulaki, A., Avradinis, N., Vosinakis, S.: A Multi-agent Simulation Framework for Emergency Evacuations Incorporating Personality and Emotions. In: Konstantopoulos, S., Perantonis, S., Karkaletsis, V., Spyropoulos, C.D., Vouros, G. (eds.) SETN 2010. LNCS, vol. 6040, pp. 423–428. Springer, Heidelberg (2010)
11. Jones, H., Saunier, J., Lourdeaux, D.: Personality, Emotions and Physiology in a BDI Agent Architecture: The PEP PEP - ≫ BDI Model. In: IEEE/WIC/ACM International Joint Conference on Web Intelligence and Intelligent Agent Technology, pp. 263–266 (2009)
12. Steunebrink, B.R., Dastani, M., Meyer, J.J.C.: Emotions to control agent deliberation. In: AAMAS International Conference on Autonomous Agents and Multi-Agent Systems, pp. 973–980 (2010)
13. Adam, C., Gaudou, B., Herzig, A., Longin, D.: OCC's Emotions: A Formalization in a BDI Logic. In: Euzenat, J., Domingue, J. (eds.) AIMSA 2006. LNCS (LNAI), vol. 4183, pp. 24–32. Springer, Heidelberg (2006)

14. Luo, L., Zhou, S., Cai, W., Lees, M., Low, M.Y.H., Sornum, K.: HumDPM: A Decision Process Model for Modeling Human-Like Behaviors in Time-Critical and Uncertain Situations. In: Gavrilova, M.L., Tan, C.J.K., Sourin, A., Sourina, O. (eds.) Transactions on Computational Science XII. LNCS, vol. 6670, pp. 206–230. Springer, Heidelberg (2011)
15. Klein, G.: Sources of Power: How People Make Decisions, p. 330. MIT Press (1999)
16. Scherer, K.R.: Appraisal considered as a process of multilevel sequential checking. In: Scherer, K.R., Schorr, A., Johnstone, T. (eds.) Appraisal Processes in Emotion Theory Methods Research, vol. 92, pp. 92–120. Oxford University Press (2001)
17. Gratch, J., Marsella, S., Petta, P.: EMA: A process model of appraisal dynamics. Cogn. Syst. Res. 10, 70–90 (2009)
18. Lazarus, R.S., Smith, C.A.: Emotion and adaptation. In: Handbook of Personality: Theory and Research, pp. 609–637. Guilford, New York (1990)
19. El-Nasr, M.S., Yen, J., Ioerger, T.R.: FLAME—Fuzzy Logic Adaptive Model of Emotions. In: AAMAS Autonomous Agents and Multi-Agent Systems, pp. 219–257 (2000)
20. Dias, J., Paiva, A.: Feeling and Reasoning: A Computational Model for Emotional Characters. In: Bento, C., Cardoso, A., Dias, G. (eds.) EPIA 2005. LNCS (LNAI), vol. 3808, pp. 127–140. Springer, Heidelberg (2005)
21. Kazemifard, M., Ghasem-Aghaee, N., Ören, T.I.: Design and implementation of GEmA: A generic emotional agent. Expert Syst. Appl. 38, 2640–2652 (2011)
22. Gratch, J., Marsella, S., Petta, P.: Modeling the cognitive antecedents and consequences of emotion. Cogn. Syst. Res. 10, 1–5 (2009)
23. Rao, A.S., Georgeff, M.P.: Modeling Rational Agents within a BDI-Architecture. In: Allen, J., Fikes, R., Sandewall, E. (eds.) Proceedings of the 2nd International Conference on Principles of Knowledge Representation and Reasoning, pp. 473–484. Morgan Kaufmann, San Mateo (1991)
24. Kebair, F., Serin, F.: Towards a Multiagent Decision Support System for Crisis Management. J. of Intell. Syst. 20, 47–60 (2011)
25. RoboCup Rescue, http://www.robocup.org/robocup-rescue/
26. Khorsandian, A., Abdolmaleki, A.: RoboCupRescue 2009 – Rescue Simulation League (Infrastructure Competition) Team Description MRL 2009 - brave circles (Iran) (2009)

Author Index